antennae

earthly mattering

2023

antennae

THE JOURNAL OF NATURE IN VISUAL CULTURE
edited by Giovanni Aloi

Antennae (founded in 2006) is an independent, hybrid, peer reviewed journal. We are free to the public, non-funded by institutions, and not supported by grants or philanthropists. The Journal's format and contents are informed by the concepts of 'knowledge transfer' and 'widening participation'. Independent publications share histories of originality, irreverence, and innovation and *Antennae* has certainly been an important contributor to what will be remembered as the non-human turn in the humanities. The first issue of *Antennae* coincided with the rise of human-animal studies; a field of academic inquiry now become mainstream. Our independent status has allowed us to give a voice to scholars and artists who were initially not taken seriously by mainstream presses. Through our creative approach, we have supported the careers of experimental practitioners and researchers across the world providing a unique space in which new academic fields like the environmental humanities and critical plant studies could also flourish. In January 2009, the establishment of *Antennae*'s Senior Academic Board, Advisory Board, and Network of Global Contributors has affirmed the journal as an indispensable research tool for the subject of environmental studies and visual culture. Still today, no other journal provides artists and scholars with an opportunity to publish full color portfolios of their work or richly illustrated essays at no cost to them or to readers. A markedly transdisciplinary publication, *Antennae* encourages communication and crossover of knowledge among artists, scientists, scholars, activists, curators, and students. Contact Giovanni Aloi, the Editor in Chief at: antennaeproject@gmail.com Visit our website for more info and past issues: www.antennae.org.uk

Front cover: Andrea Conte (Andreco Studio), *Bituminose Geology*, bitumen and acrylic on paper, 2017

Back cover: Andrea Conte, *Deep Geology*, 2018, acrilic on paper, 2018 © Andrea Conte - Andreco.org

Antennae: The Journal of Nature in Visual Culture (ISSN 1756-9575) is published triannually by AntennaeProject, Chicago.

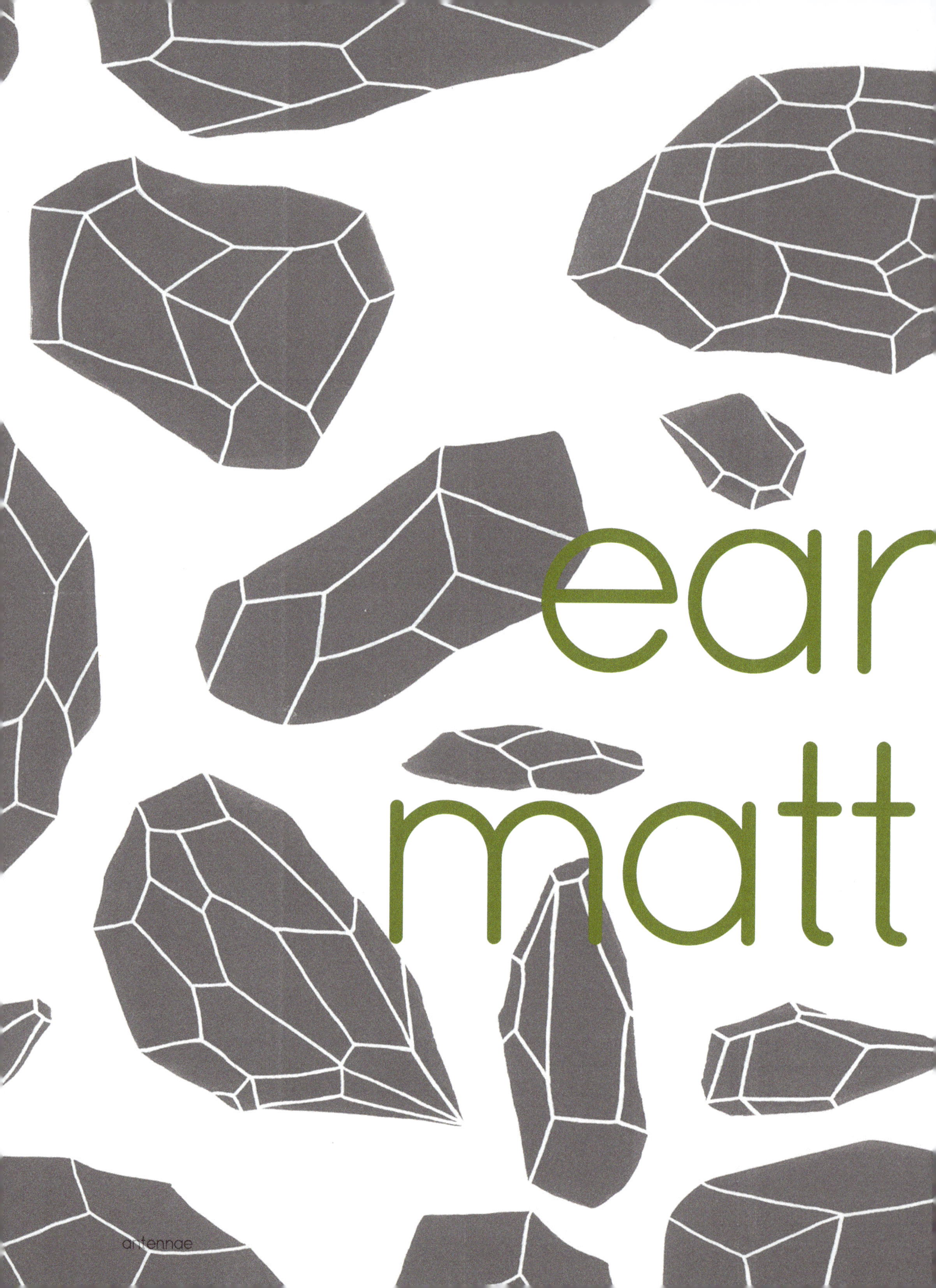
ear
matt
antennae

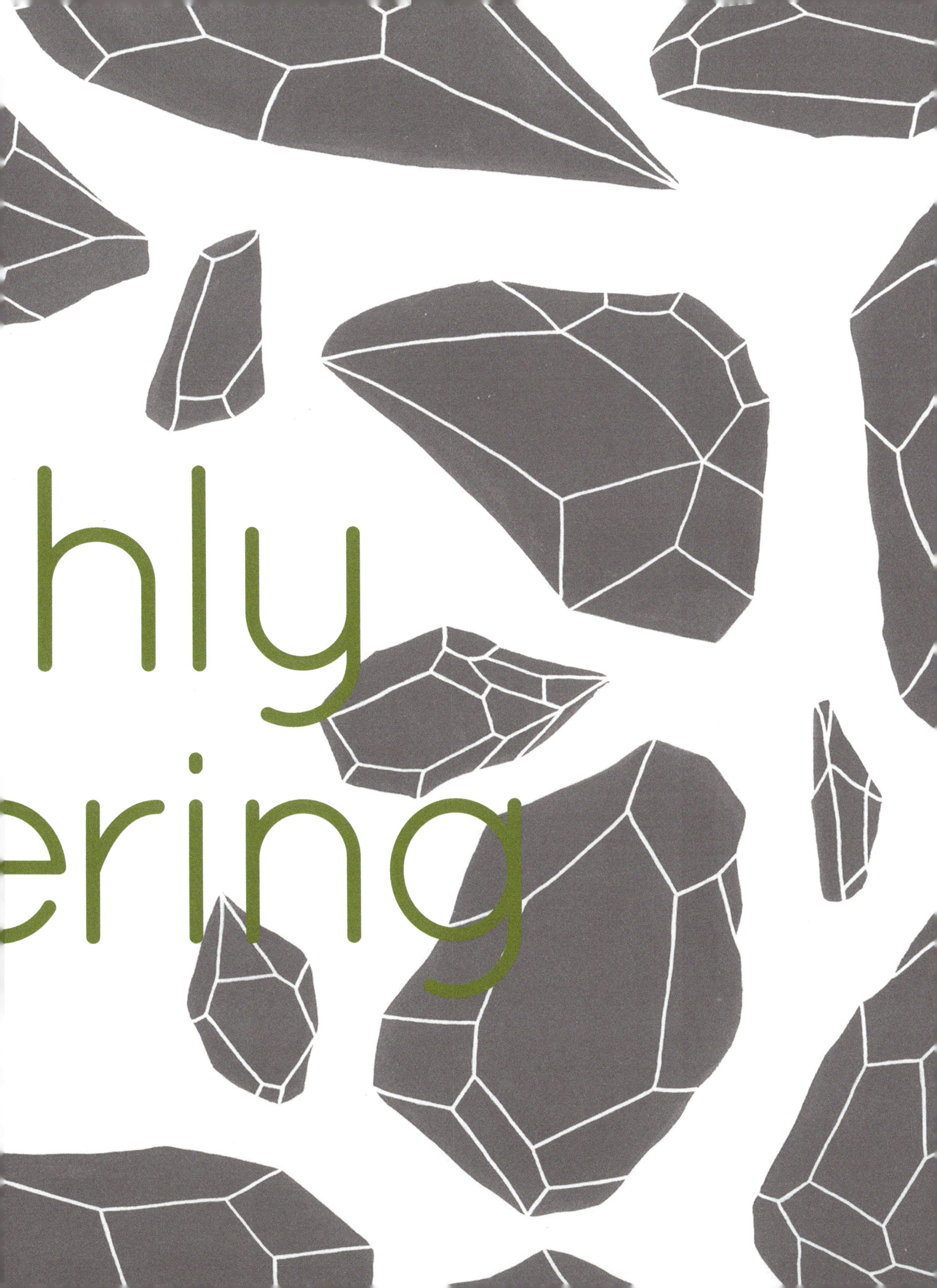
hly
ering

contents

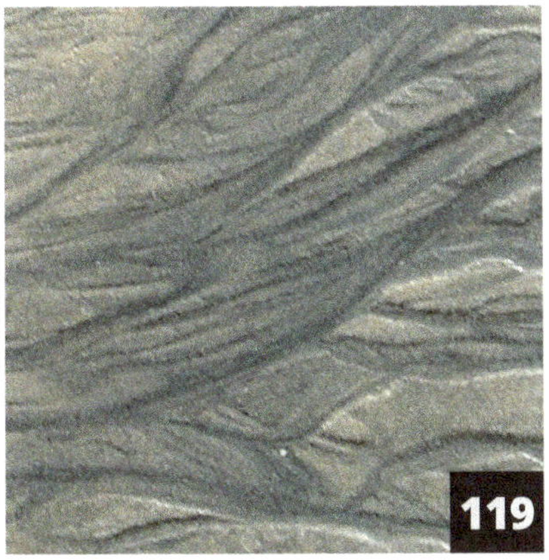

Will there be rooted belonging if home was a colony built on reclaimed land fill? If connecting with the earth is seeking support for healing, are nature-based therapies "resourcing" the earth just like the colonists?

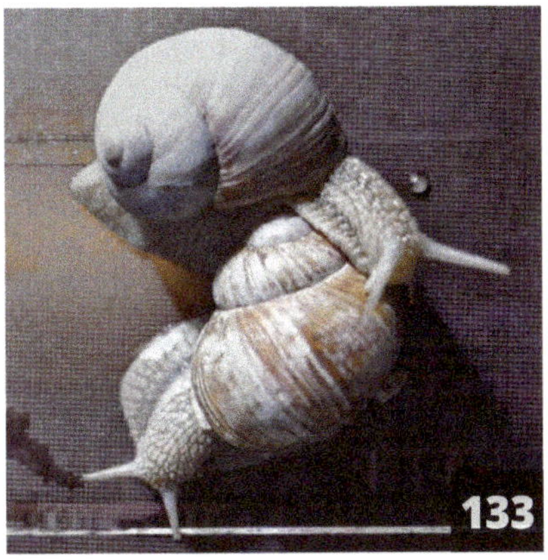

The landscape, environmental and aesthetic, is constituted in and by transformative alliances, where witnessing becomes wit(h)nessing. The reparative potential of environmental justice to attend to world-wounds, evokes a shared horizon staked in the process of destabilizing a singular gaze.

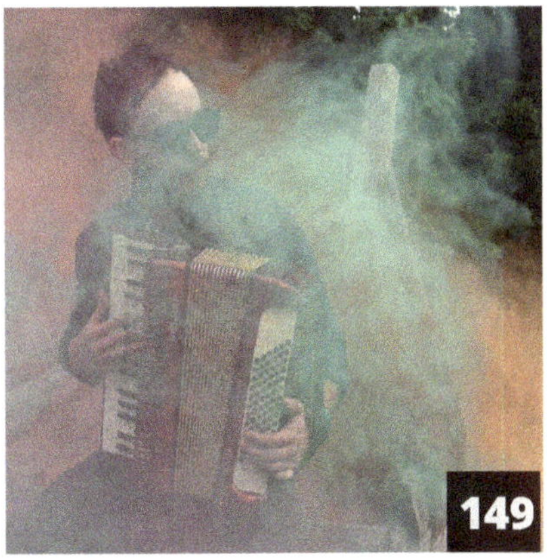

Being-in-the-Breathable, a collaborative artwork by Robert Bean and Barbara Lounder, was introduced in 2017 for the Contexts International Festival of Ephemeral Art in Sokolowsko Poland. *Being-in-the-Breathable: An Annotated Walk* responded to the earth's atmosphere as the last Commons shared by human and non-human entities. visual essay is about the first two works in the series.

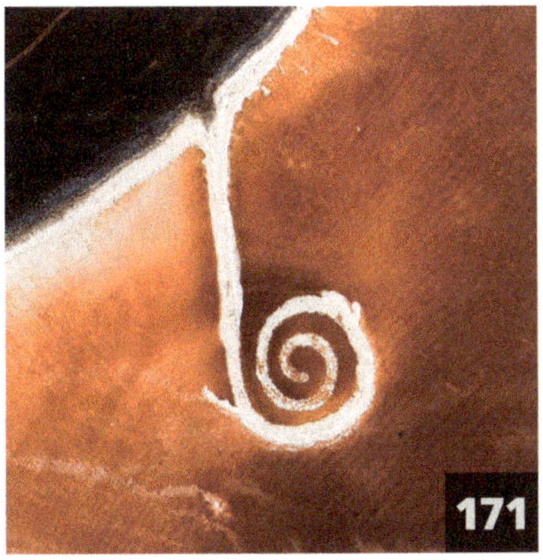

Robert Smithson envisioned art as a "catastrophe of mind and matter," a physical metaphor that moves one beyond the abstract grids of intelligibility into an abyssal materiality.

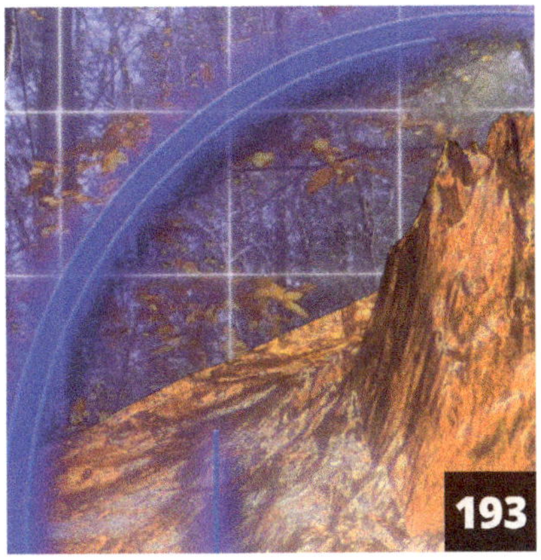

Integrating gaming and surveillance aesthetics with both animations and footage of the Rocky Mountain region, Mark Dorf's *A New Nature* collapses the barriers of what's real in a way that echoes our digital consumption of the world.

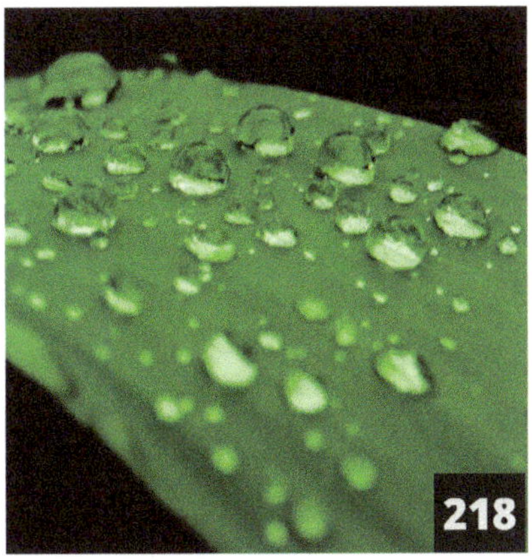

Self-described as an artist stuck in the body of a science writer, the writer, theorist, and independent scholar, Dorion Sagan is author or coauthor of twenty-five books translated into fifteen languages, including several with biologist Lynn Margulis on planetary biology and evolution by symbiosis.

contents

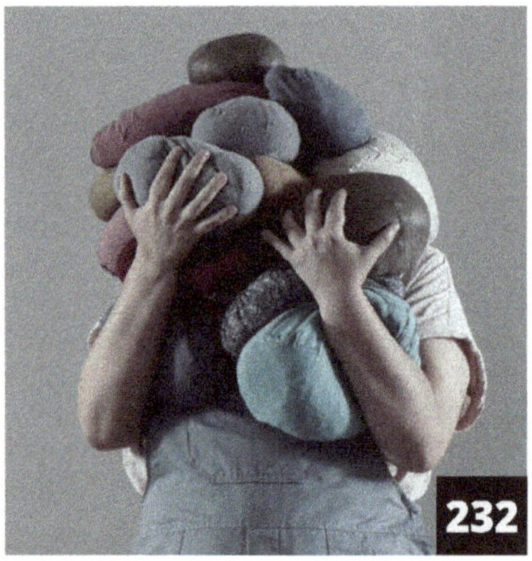

Manuela Infante
Como Convertirse en Piedra, performance, 2021 © Manuela Infante

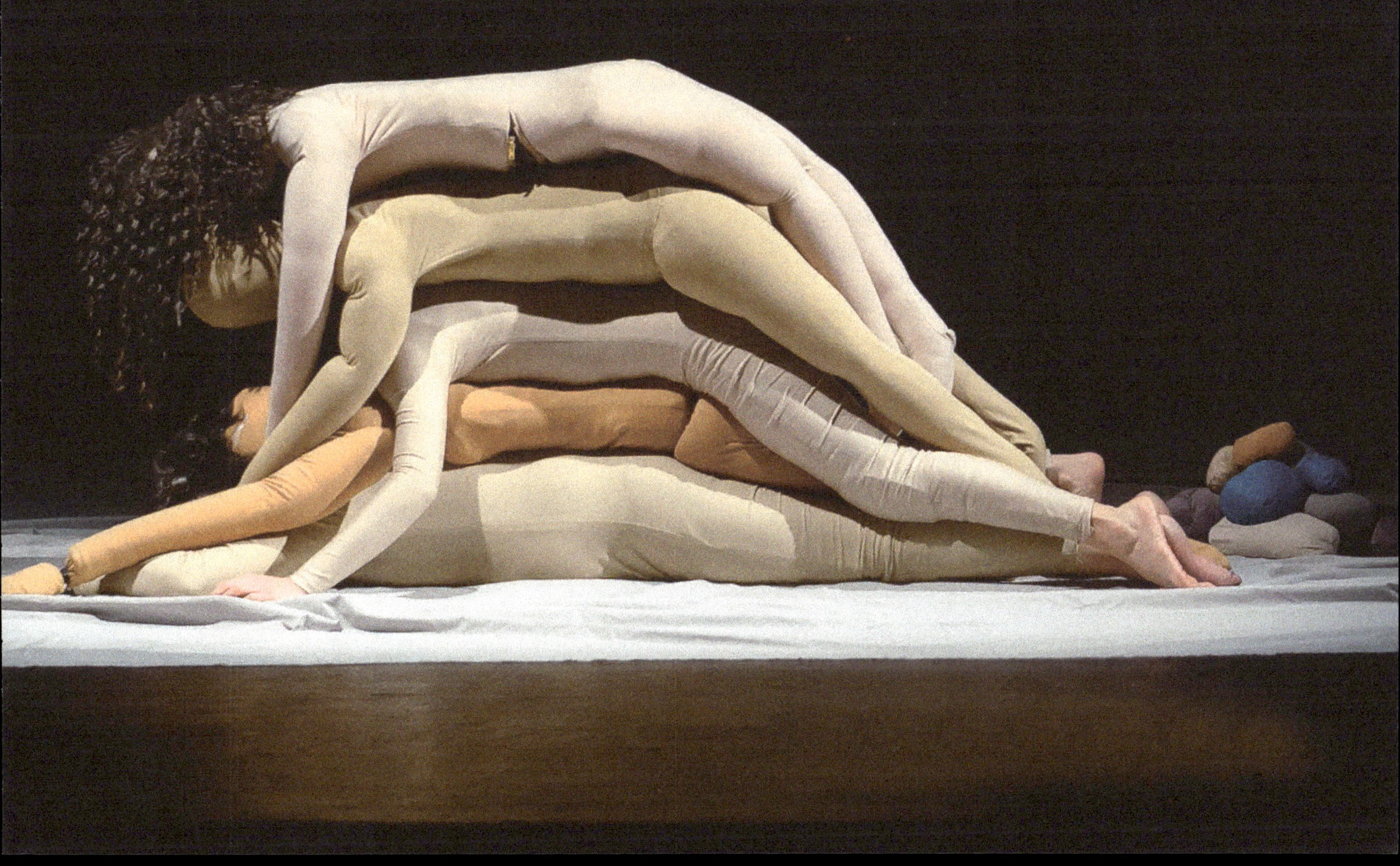

editorial

Giovanni Aloi

"To turn to stone". Across mythological and folk tales, this transmutation has often implied punishment of an irreversible kind. Turning to stone was an epitaph. According to myth, at Yunwitsule-nunyi (Standing Indian Mountain in North Carolina), are the petrified remains of a Cherokee warrior who was turned into stone by the Great Spirit for fleeing his sentinel post in fear. Stone, the antithesis of the human. The hardness and coldness of stone, radically opposed to the tender warmth of human flesh. The other end of the spectrum. The inferior. Less than human, but also less than animal, and even plant. Devoid of life, unworthy of it.

Those who dared to return the Medusa's stare would be turned into stone—instantly. Poseidon transformed the Phaeacians' ship into stone just as it approached land—the price to pay for helping Odysseus, his foe. In the Indonesian story of Malin Kundang, it was an infuriated mother who turned her ungrateful son into stone. The petrification of shame is a recurring motif. An endless reminder that one must live with the consequences of their actions.

At times, turning into stone could also take the form of voluntary sacrifice—a way out, as it was for the Vietnamese Trung Sisters who led a rebellion against China. When defeat appeared inevitable, they threw themselves into the Hat Giang River and transformed into statues. For centuries they have been worshipped in Hanoi's Hai Ba Trung. Sometimes, turning to stone has also entailed remembrance and compassion. According to legend, a group of Apache warriors rode their horses off the Yoo' Ligai mountain, in today's Arizona, when faced with defeat. The tears that wives and family members cried upon hearing the news turned to stone as they hit the ground. Today, the small black obsidian stones found only in the American Southwest, which go by the name of Apache Tears, tell stories of strength and remembrance. They bind communities and protect from evil forces. Emblems of resilience—the hardness of these stones embodying the heaviness of loss and the immobilizing power of deep grief. But it is their ability to humbly ground that ultimately elevates them into emblems of sheer courage.

Time, stillness, hardness, remembrance—rocks are solidifications. Igneous, sedimentary, or metamorphic—they are aggregations of minerals that regardless of their genesis contain infinite compressed landscapes that have formed over billions of years. Layers and strata—each embedded in the other, pushing against and resisting at once, for eternity. Some much force ingrained in perfect stillness.

Oftentimes, gaining any insights into this petrified universe entails destruction. Geology, petrology, mineralogy—we have devised different ways to crack open their mysteries and read the codes. Stony mineral essence is key to form and colors. What we can see is down to scale, the myopia of our anthropocentric gaze, and our willingness. How far, how close, and through which lenses should we look? How close is too close is only dictated by the episteme and what it allows us to see and say.

Roger Caillois and Andre Breton fell out on this archetypal scientific idea—opening something to understand its workings. Breaking the rock into its mineral components or preserving the magic of the whole. Breton felt that Caillois's approach was too closely aligned with the positivist philosophies of the Enlightenment. He thought that the poetic mystery contained within should not be mercilessly extracted, pinned down, and explained in the crude jargon of science. To Caillois, scientific methods and poetic engagements were indissolubly enmeshed. In 1934, he told Breton that newly discovered atomic theories would radically change our conception of nature by opening up a "new form of the marvellous". Caillois's material mysticism eventually led him to the publication of *The Writing of Stones* (1970): a sophisticated illustrated book merging poetry, philosophy, anthropology, and mysticism in the attempt to craft a new, composite, lens through which the pictographic nature of stones could be encountered anew. What do we see, what do we remain blind to, how do we engage, and what words do we hope the encounter might extract from the existentialist depths that are otherwise denied to us? At stake is the very constitution, structure, and fabric of meaning pushing against the ineluctable persistence of nothingness. At stake is the shape of the future.

This and more is explored in the current issue of *Antennae: Earthly Matters* which, following the previous installment *(Earthly Surfacing)* continues our journey deeper into the strata of knowledge and matter that define our existence as earthlings. Among all the extremely valuable contributions to this issue, those by playwright Manuela Infante and artist Jenny Kendler perfectly bookend the content. From altering scales and leading inquiries into deep time as an embodied dimension, they both pose radical questions about our relationships with memory and meaning. Kendler's *Underground Library* comprises a collection of discarded, neglected, or overlooked books on climate change published across the past five decades—some of these books are technical manuals containing information that could have avoided ecological crises but that went unread, or forgotten best-sellers written at a time when reversing the detrimental effects of climate change was still a possibility. As the artist notes: "Unread, these books became graves for the words they held. Left alone, fallen trees, uprooted plants and even our own bodies eventually return their borrowed carbon to the atmosphere—unless it is removed from the carbon cycle via sequestration. Creating biochar is one way to reduce CO2 in the atmosphere by making the normally carbon-neutral process of natural decay carbon-negative". At the end of each exhibition these petrified books are buried—their cultural silence now, at least, positively impacting the biochemical sphere in which they exist as mineral resources for other animals and plants.

Manuela Infante's performance *Como Convertirse en Piedra* furthers the playwright's speculative exploration begun several years ago in works like *Realismo* (2016) and *Estado Vegetal* (2017). The performance is an example of non-anthropocentric, nonhumanist theatre. It counters the modern notion of humanness as the measure of all things. Infante brings pieces of eroded stories together. The fragments become landscapes stacked one upon the other as geological rock layers through different mediatic approaches that entail sound loops and narrative circularities. This creates a 'mineral' representation telling us something, as the playwright explains "about what is written in stones, and what stones have written in us".

Both works, together with the others presented and addressed in this issue, outline important trajectories, materializations of opportunities to rethink our positioning on this planet and our relationship with its multiple and interlinked processes of mattering.

As always, I am indebted to all contributors, Antennae's Academic board, and everyone else who has tirelessly lent their skills and time to the making of this issue.

Giovanni Aloi
Editor in Chief of *Antennae*

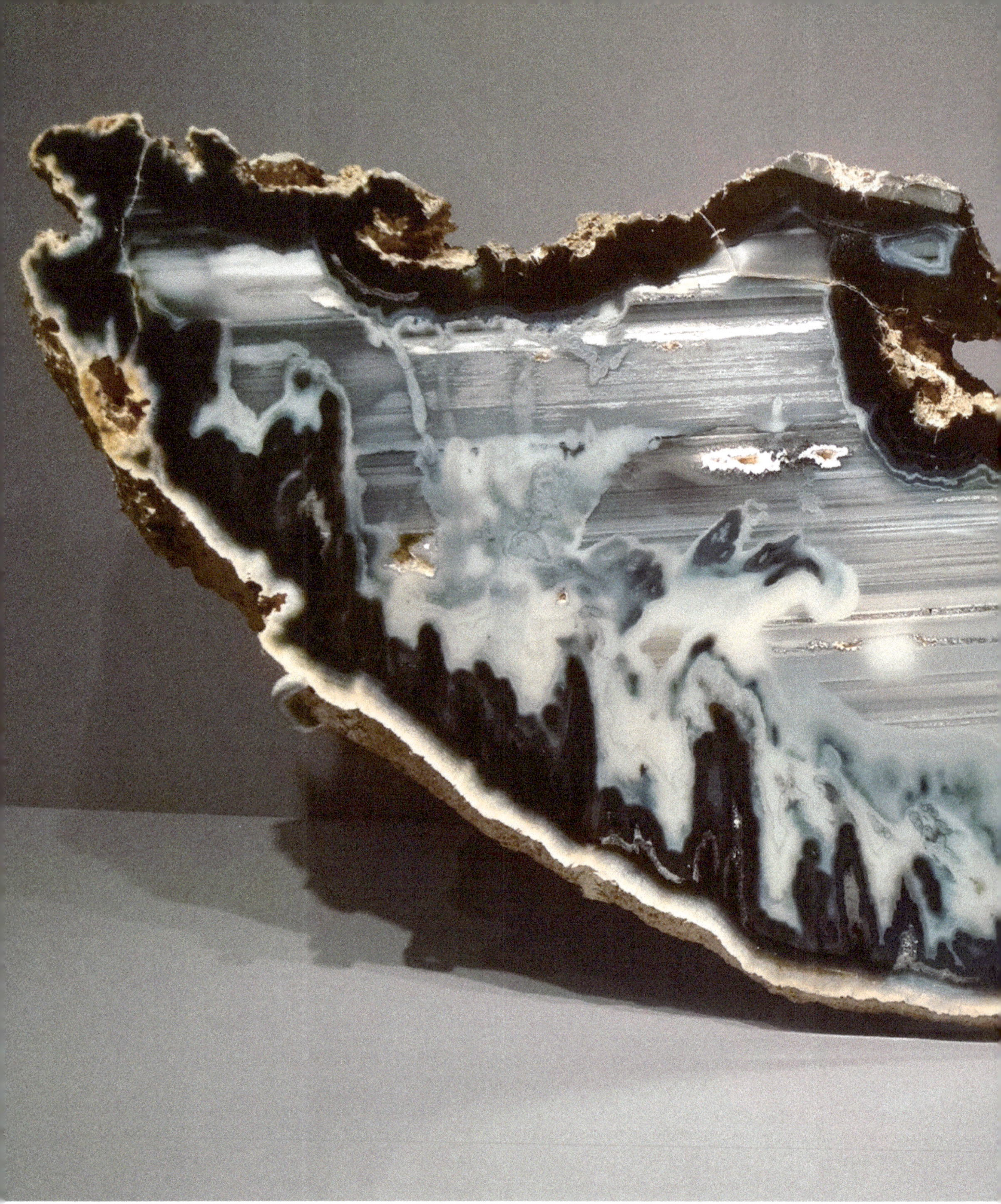

Roger Caillois
Le Vaisseau, agate, 37 x 14.5 x 2cm. Courtedy of the Roger Caillois Mineral Collection

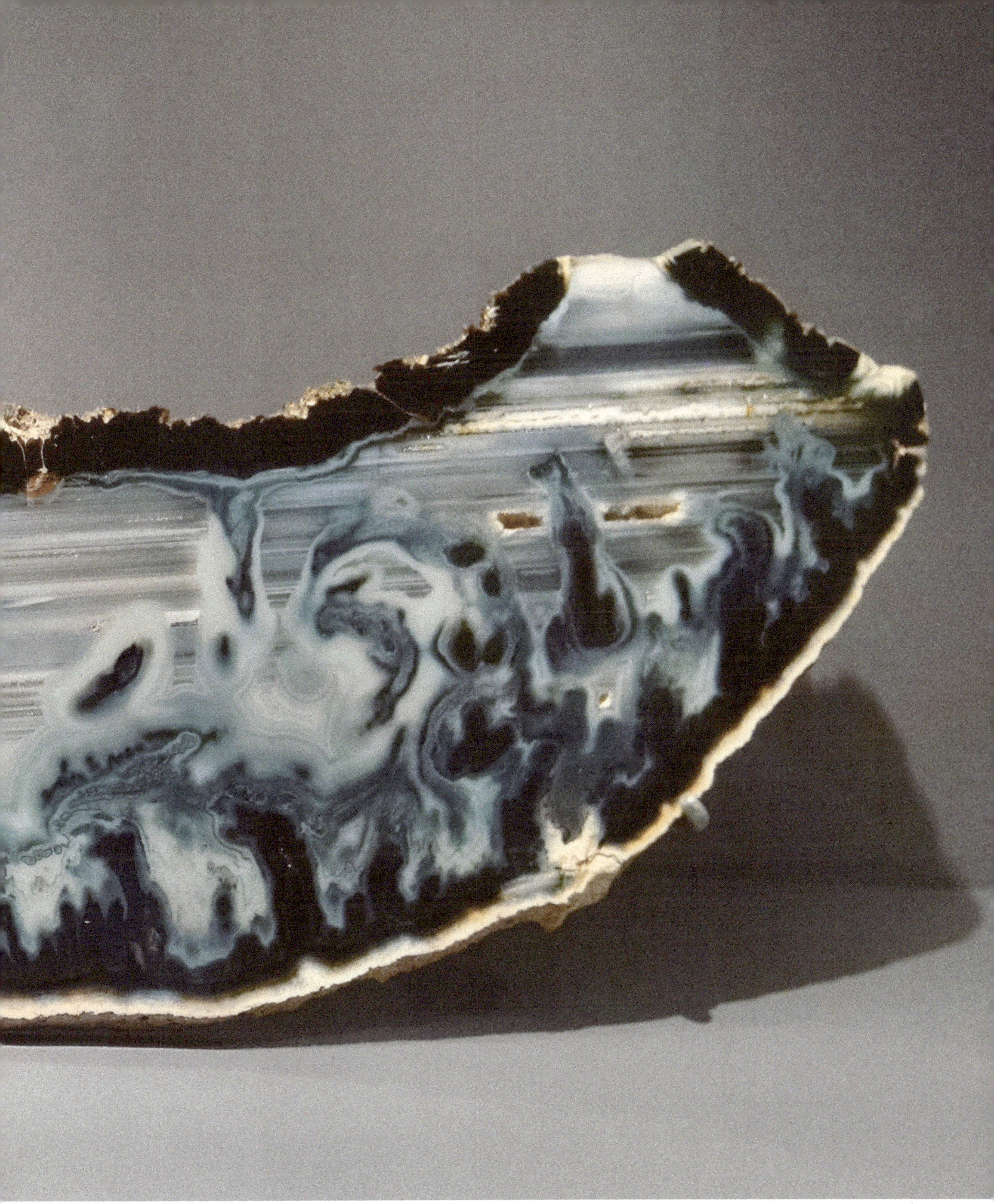

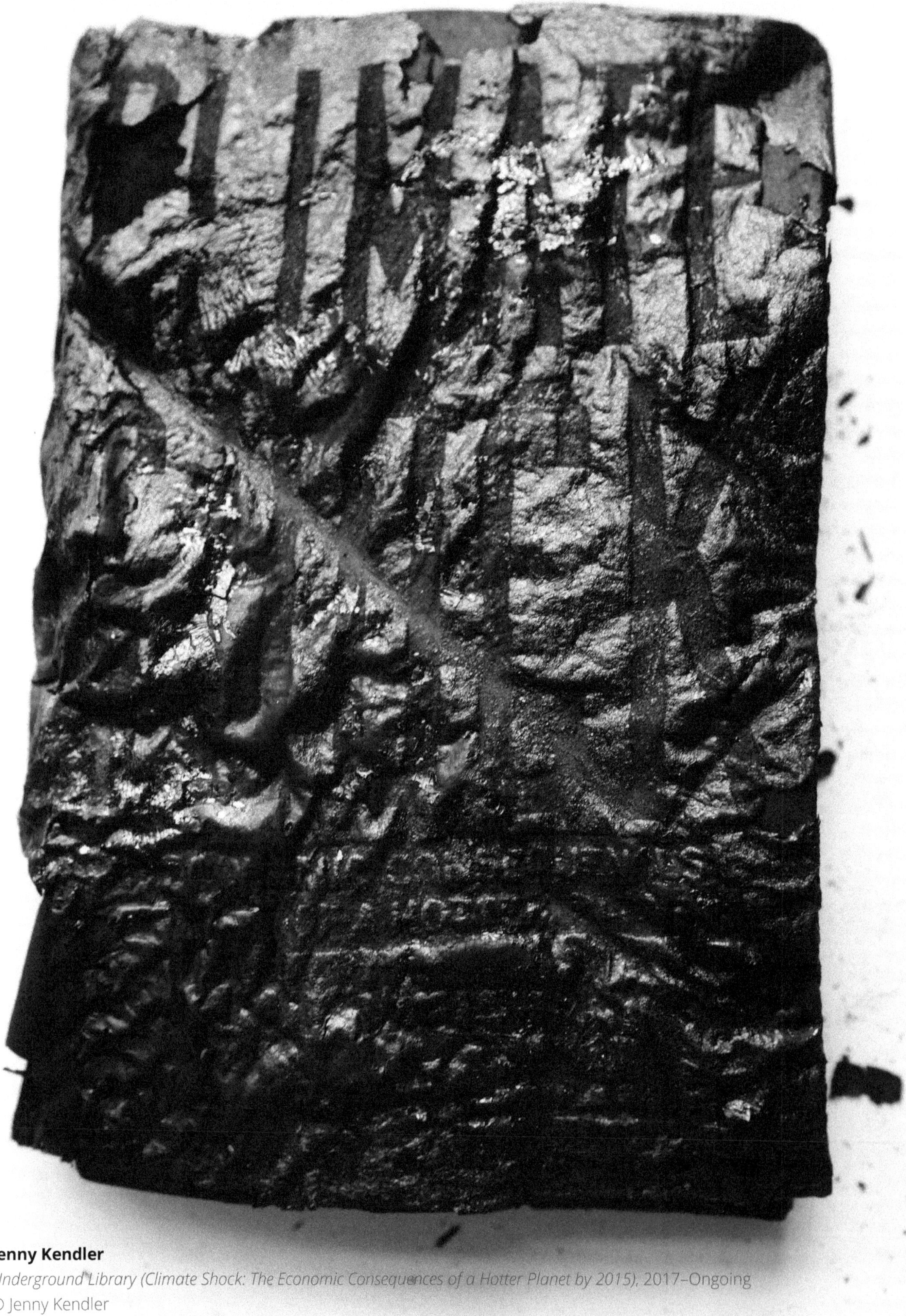

Jenny Kendler
Underground Library (Climate Shock: The Economic Consequences of a Hotter Planet by 2015), 2017–Ongoing

Underground library

Burned books are typically associated with censorship, and here, Kendler equates the inaction of global leadership against climate change with the censorship of the scientific community. With their warnings gone unheeded, these books are no different from other unwanted consumer products. However, by using the process of biocharring, Kendler makes these objects useful again by converting them into vessels for carbon sequestration.

text and images: **Jenny Kendler**

Underground Library is a project by environmental artist and activist Jenny Kendler, based around a collection of five decades of discarded, neglected, or overlooked books on climate change—from unread technical manuals to forgotten best-sellers of decades past. These literary artifacts hold a printed history of urgent pleas for action, largely ignored in a world consumed by an economic death cult.

With several family members who run used bookstores or collect rare books, Kendler has bibliophilia in her blood. Sourced by her from thrift stores, free book boxes, used book stores, and eBay, this library represents a printed history of individuals' and groups' unheeded calls to urgent action. The books also bear traces of their few readers, documented in the artist's photos: scrawls rebutting carbon calculations, airline tickets used as bookmarks, heartfelt margin notes—and notably, library cards marked with hardly a stamp, save the library's "withdrawn"— showing their removal from circulation. Unread, these books became graves for the words they held. Left alone, fallen trees, uprooted plants and even our own bodies eventually return their borrowed carbon to the atmosphere—unless it is removed from the carbon cycle via sequestration. Creating biochar is one way to reduce $CO2$ in the atmosphere by making the normally carbon-neutral process of natural decay carbon-negative.

Traditionally created by burning wood using a low-oxygen process called pyrolization, biocharring transmutes the carbon in organic matter into a highly stable form, able to be sequestered underground. When buried, biochar also provides several other benefits for plants and microorganisms, including increased water retention and bioremediation of pollutants.

For *Underground Library*, Kendler chose to carbonize wood in another form—books. At the conclusion of each exhibition, the books are permanently buried at an appropriate chosen site. This unusual book-burning and burying creates a literal underground library, restoring use value to these unread volumes by sequestering their carbon for millennia to come.

The charred books also evoke memories of other, more dystopian book burnings throughout history, which fostered underground libraries of forbidden knowledge passed clandestinely from hand to hand. While Exxon and other fossil fuel companies may not have physically burned books on climate change, they circulated doubt through deliberate and planned campaigns of disinformation—a subtler means to keep these crucial texts from the hands of the public.

These authors, represented in Kendler's library, worked to combat that doubt: to provide facts, to empower citizen action, and to hold economic, governmental, and corporate powers accountable.

In the embrace of the earth, these volumes become memorials to the tragedy of an unheeded call to action—a material legacy honoring those who, for decades, put pen to paper, even though no one was listening.

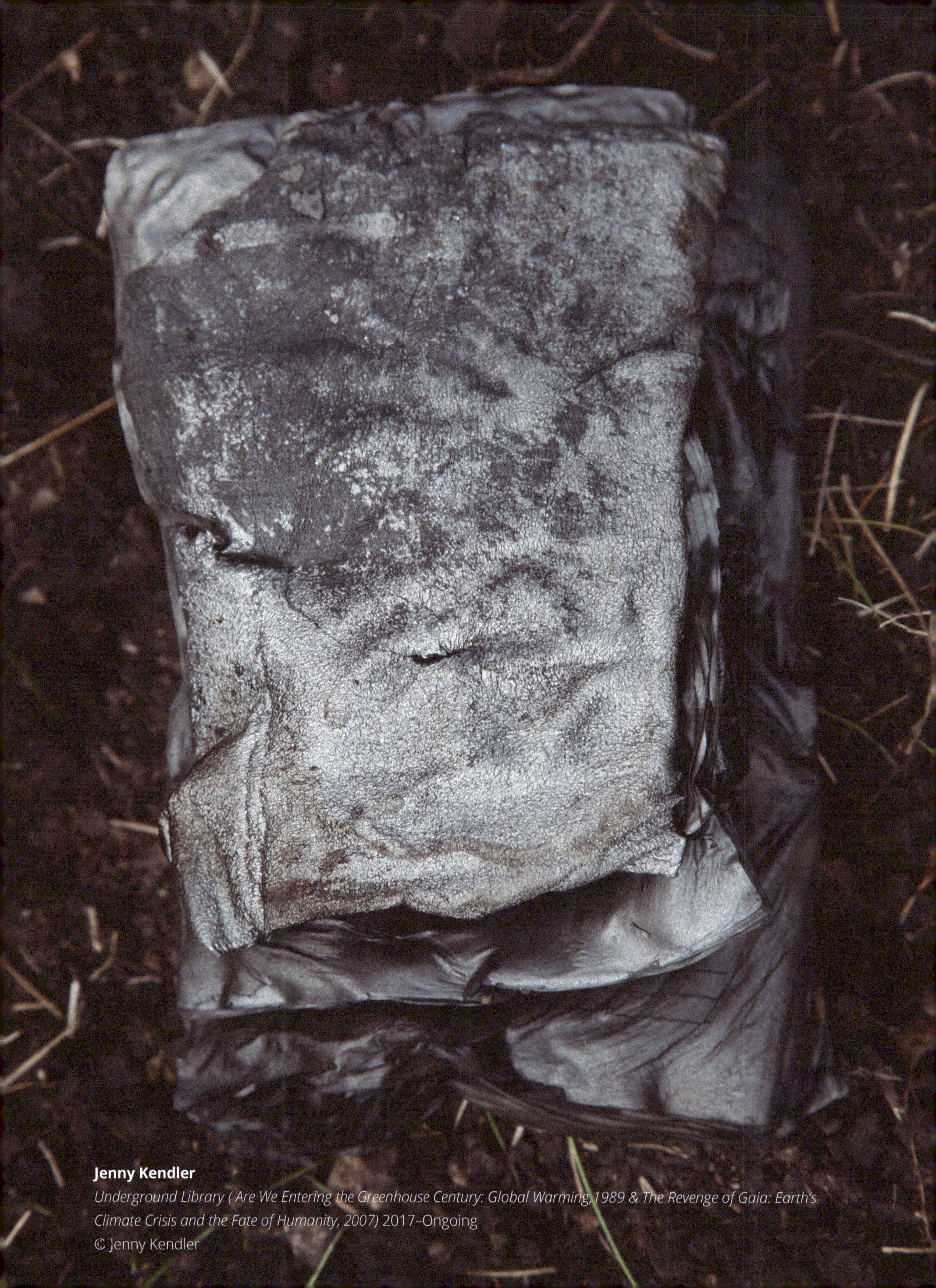

Jenny Kendler

Underground Library (Are We Entering the Greenhouse Century: Global Warming,1989 & The Revenge of Gaia: Earth's Climate Crisis and the Fate of Humanity, 2007) 2017–Ongoing

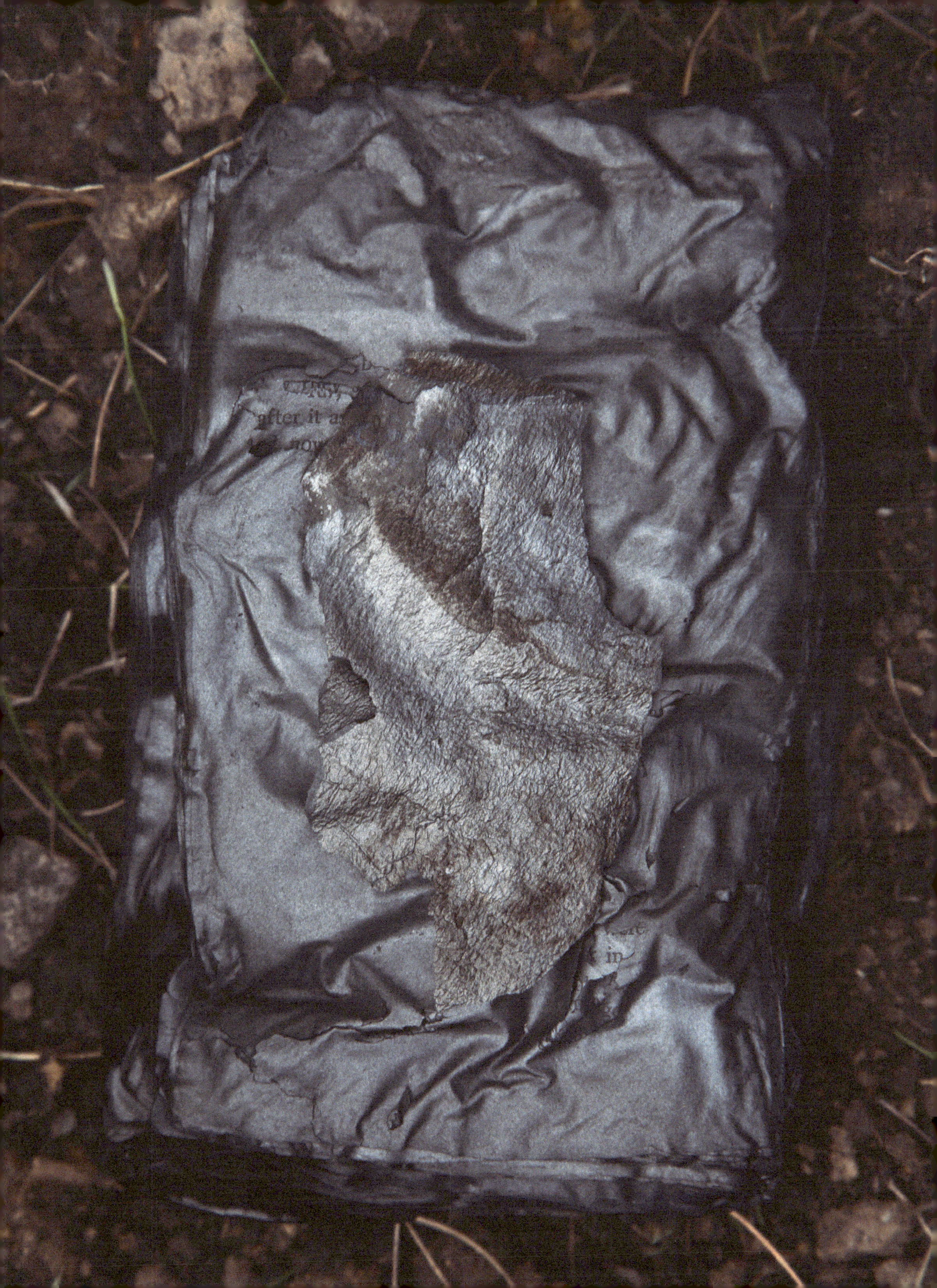

Jenny Kendler

Underground Library

(Soil Not Oil: Environmental Justice in an Age of Climate Crisis, 2015) 2017–Ongoing

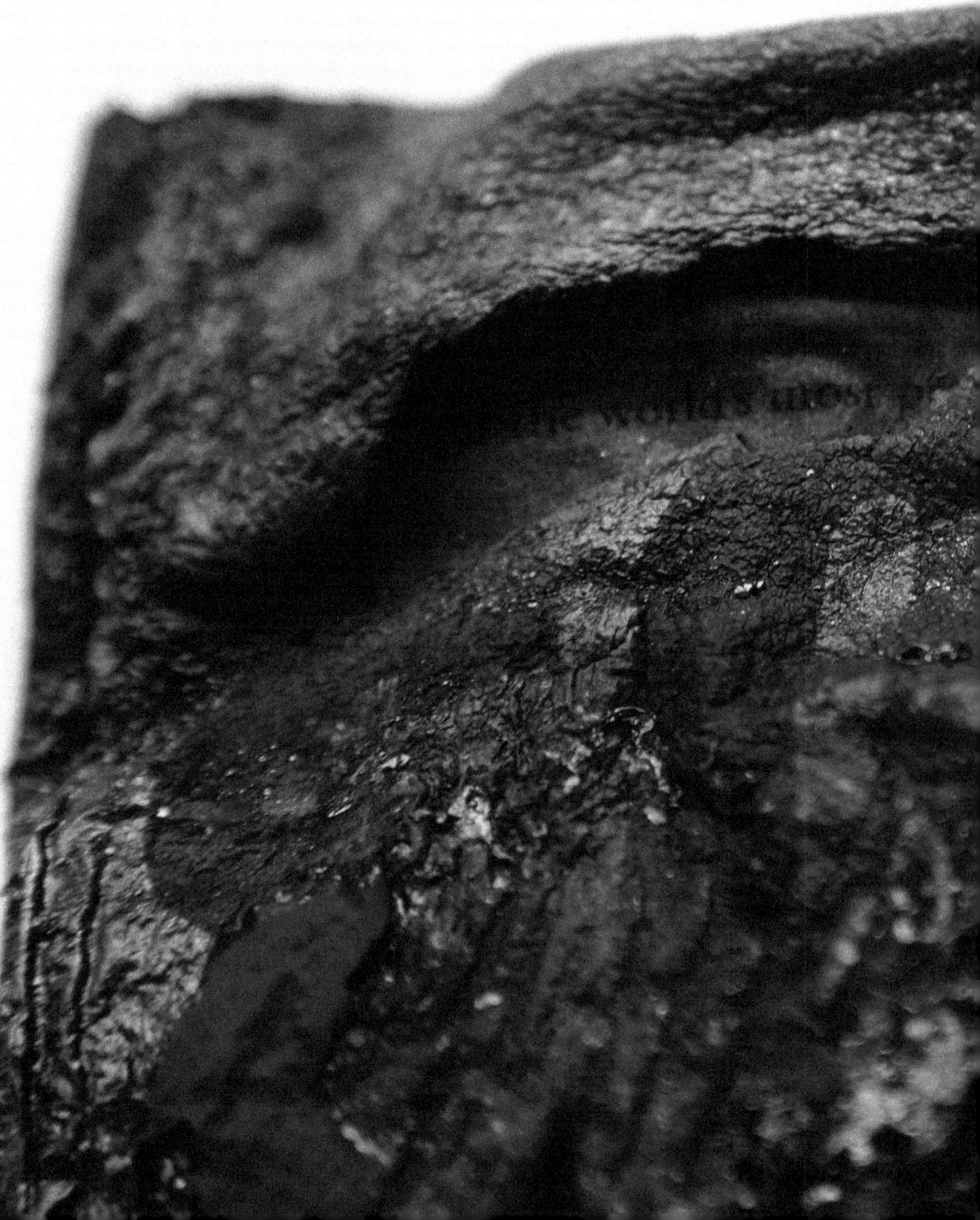

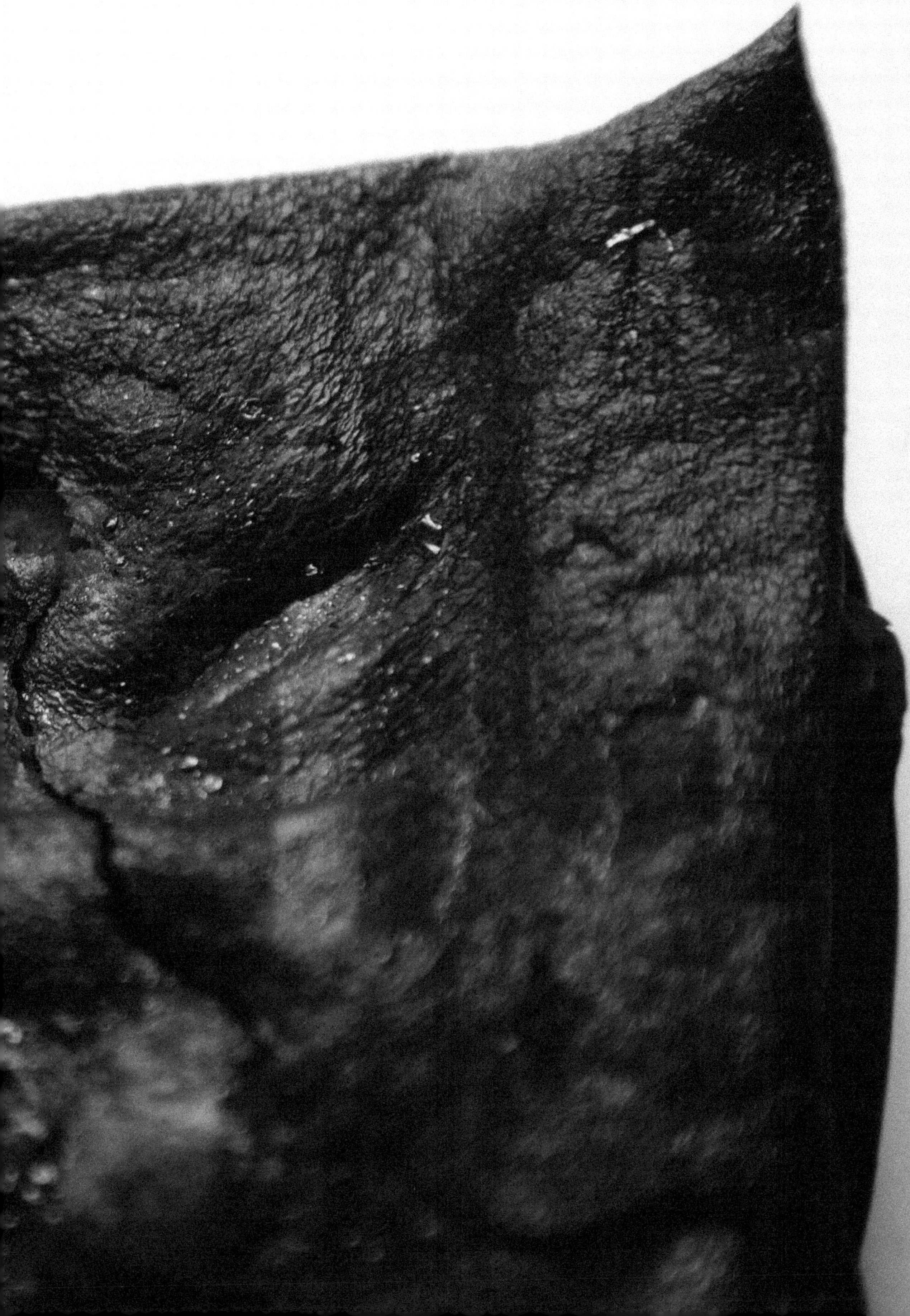

Jenny Kendler

Underground Library (Who Owns the Sky? Our Common Assets And The Future Of Capitalism, 2001)

2017–Ongoing

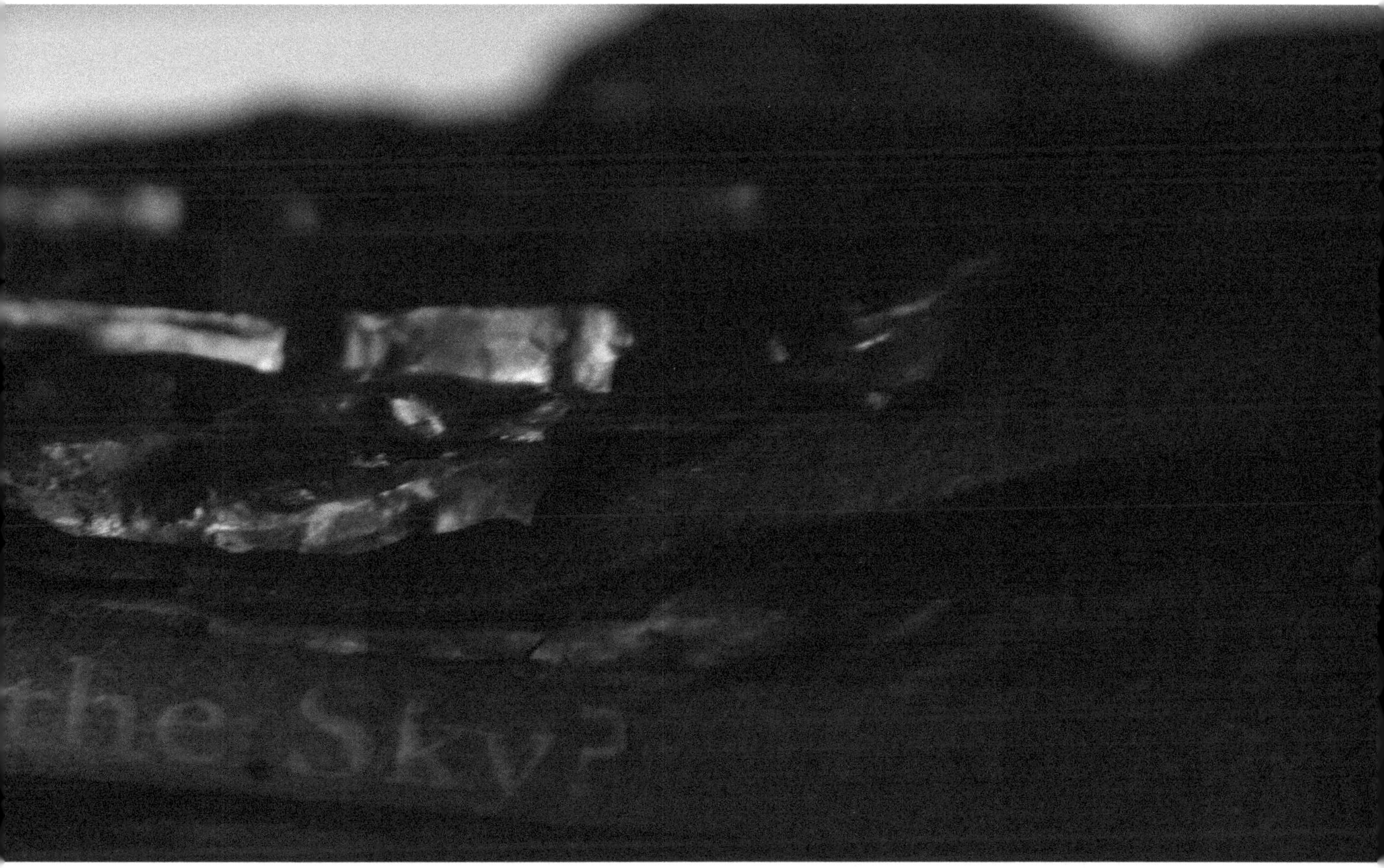
the Sky?

Jenny Kendler

Documentation of *Underground Library* as part of Storm King's 2018 exhibition, *Indicators: Artists on Climate Change*

At the conclusion of the exhibition, the books were permanently buried on site.

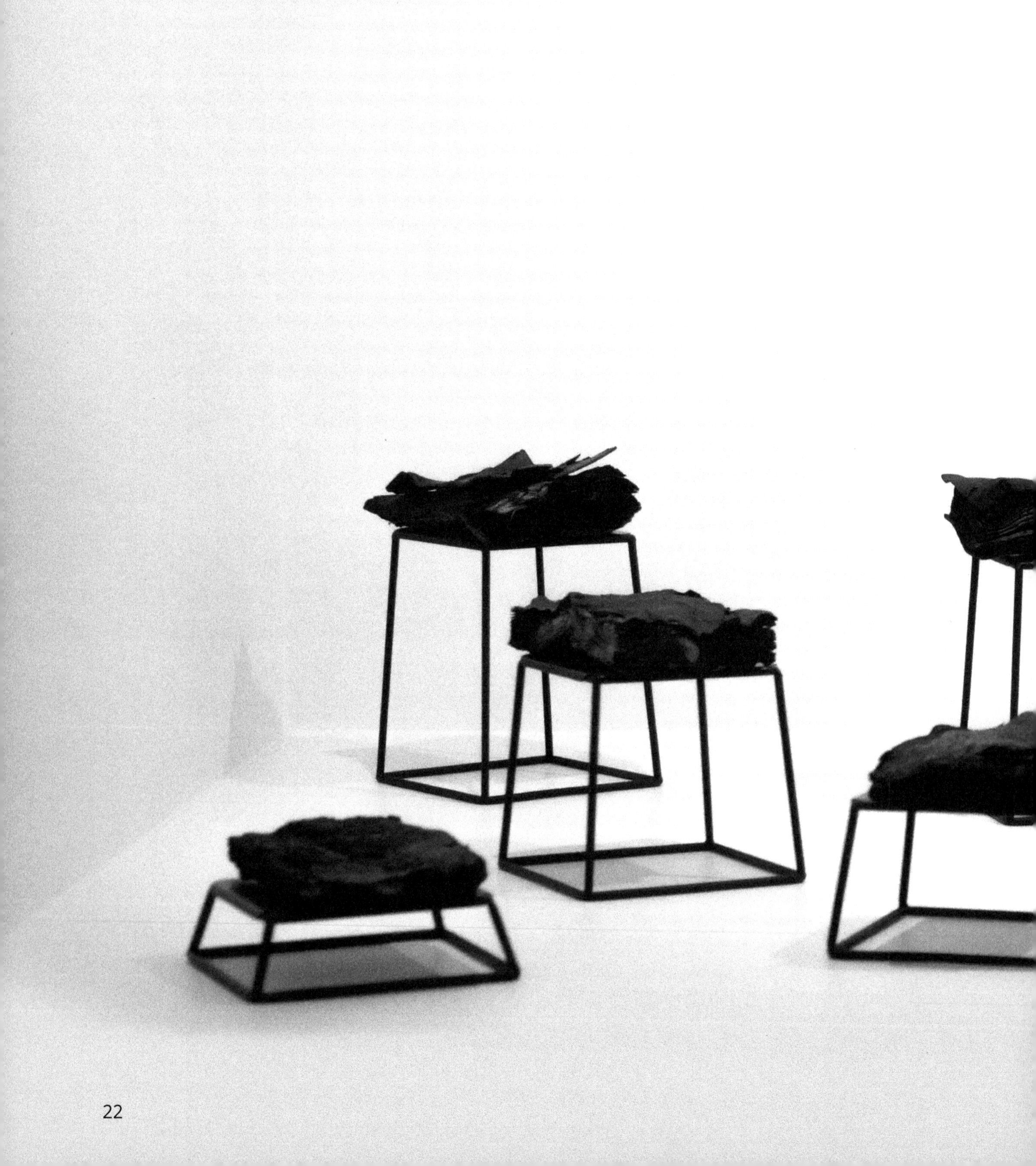

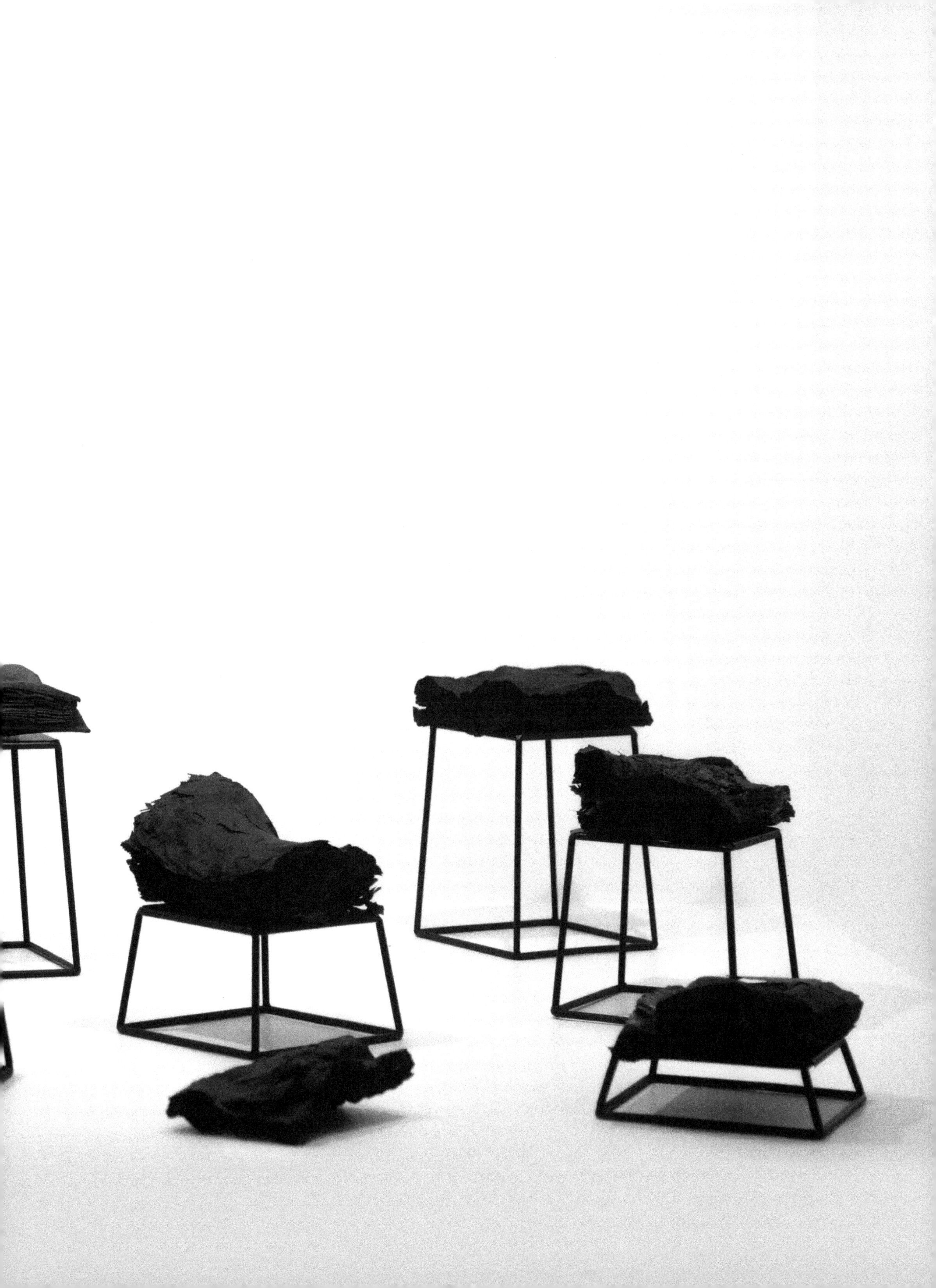

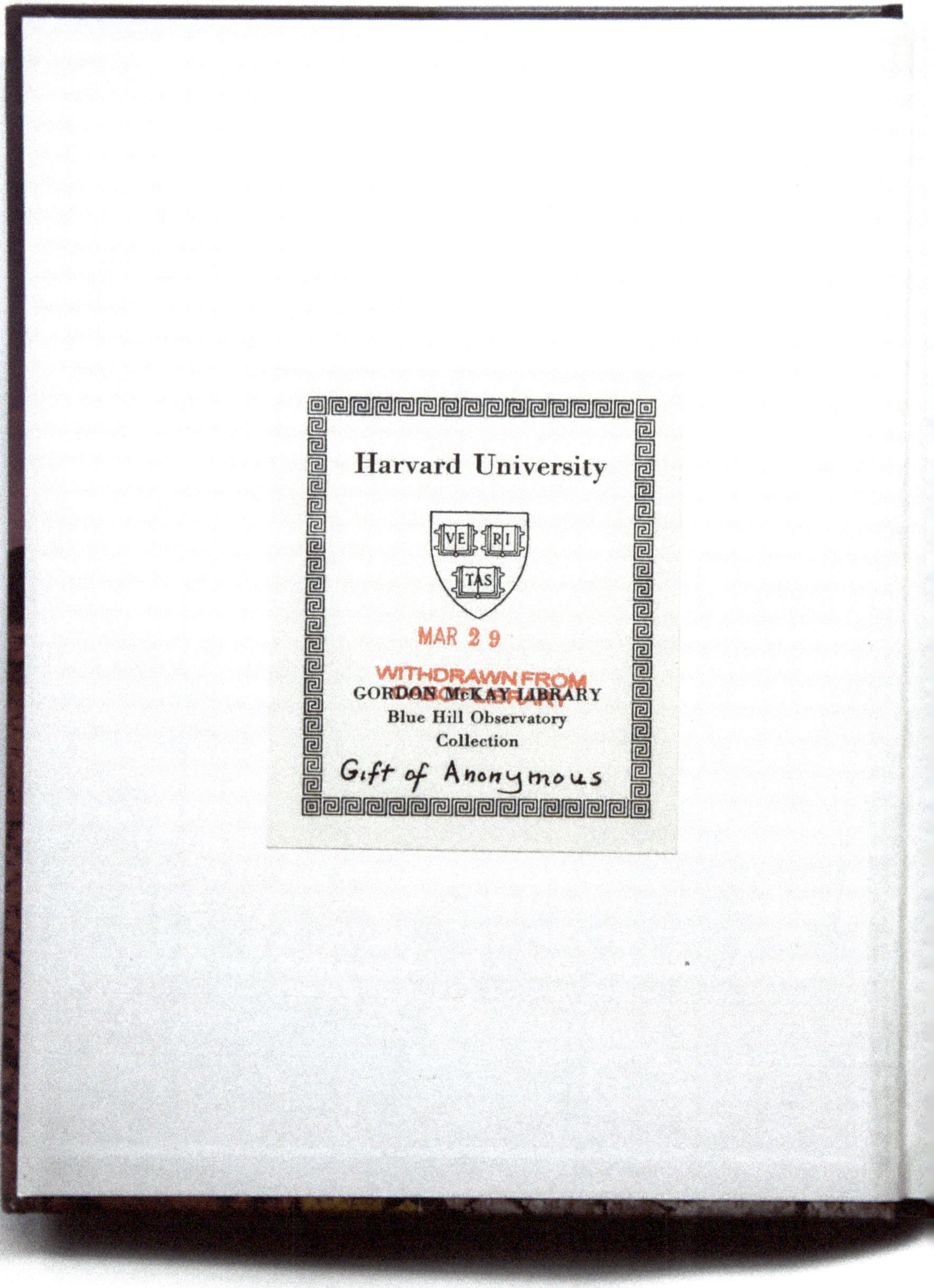

Jenny Kendler
Documentation from *Underground Library (Facing Climate Change Together, 2008)* 2017–Ongoing

DATE DUE

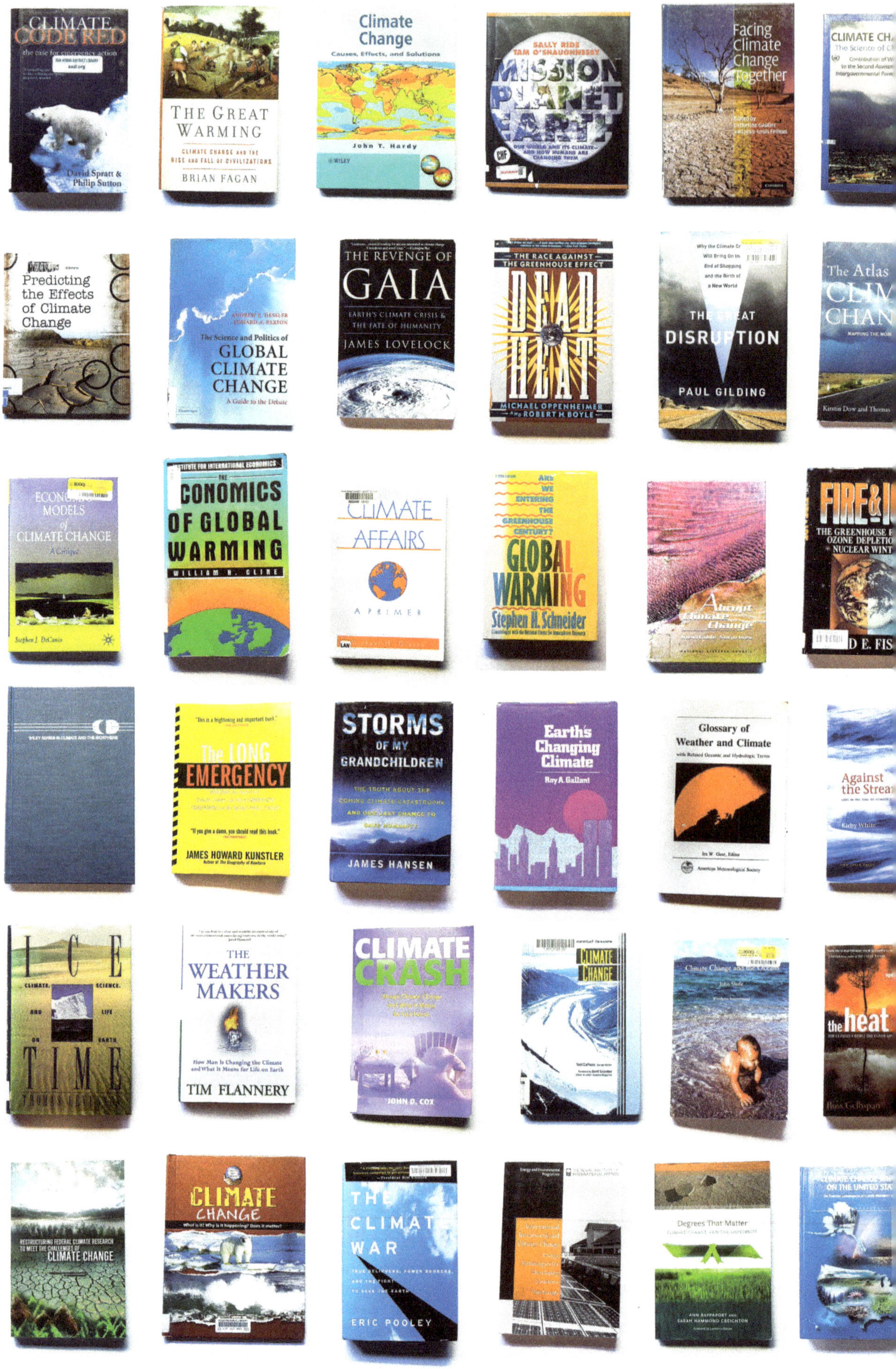

CLIMATE CODE RED
the case for emergency action
David Spratt & Philip Sutton
THE GREAT WARMING
CLIMATE CHANGE AND THE RISE AND FALL OF CIVILIZATIONS
BRIAN FAGAN
Climate Change
Causes, Effects, and Solutions
John T. Hardy
WILEY
SALLY RIDE
TAM O'SHAUGHNESSY
MISSION PLANET EARTH
Facing Climate Change Together
Predicting the Effects of Climate Change
The Science and Politics of GLOBAL CLIMATE CHANGE
A Guide to the Debate
THE REVENGE OF GAIA
EARTH'S CLIMATE CRISIS & THE FATE OF HUMANITY
JAMES LOVELOCK
THE RACE AGAINST THE GREENHOUSE EFFECT
DEAD HEAT
MICHAEL OPPENHEIMER
AND ROBERT H BOYLE
THE GREAT DISRUPTION
PAUL GILDING
The Atlas
ECONOMIC MODELS of CLIMATE CHANGE
A Critique
ECONOMICS OF GLOBAL WARMING
WILLIAM R. CLINE
CLIMATE AFFAIRS
A PRIMER
ARE WE ENTERING THE GREENHOUSE CENTURY?
GLOBAL WARMING
Stephen H. Schneider
About Climate Change
FIRE & ICE
THE GREENHOUSE
STORMS OF MY GRANDCHILDREN
THE TRUTH ABOUT THE COMING CLIMATE CATASTROPHE AND OUR LAST CHANCE TO SAVE HUMANITY
JAMES HANSEN
The LONG EMERGENCY
JAMES HOWARD KUNSTLER
Earth's Changing Climate
Roy A. Gallant
Glossary of Weather and Climate
With Related Oceanic and Hydrologic Terms
American Meteorological Society
Against the Stream
ICE TIME
CLIMATE, SCIENCE, AND LIFE ON EARTH
THE WEATHER MAKERS
How Man Is Changing the Climate and What It Means for Life on Earth
TIM FLANNERY
CLIMATE CRASH
JOHN D. COX
CLIMATE CHANGE
Climate Change and the Oceans
the heat
RESTRUCTURING FEDERAL CLIMATE RESEARCH TO MEET THE CHALLENGES OF CLIMATE CHANGE
CLIMATE CHANGE
What is it? Why is it happening? Does it matter?
THE CLIMATE WAR
ERIC POOLEY
Degrees That Matter

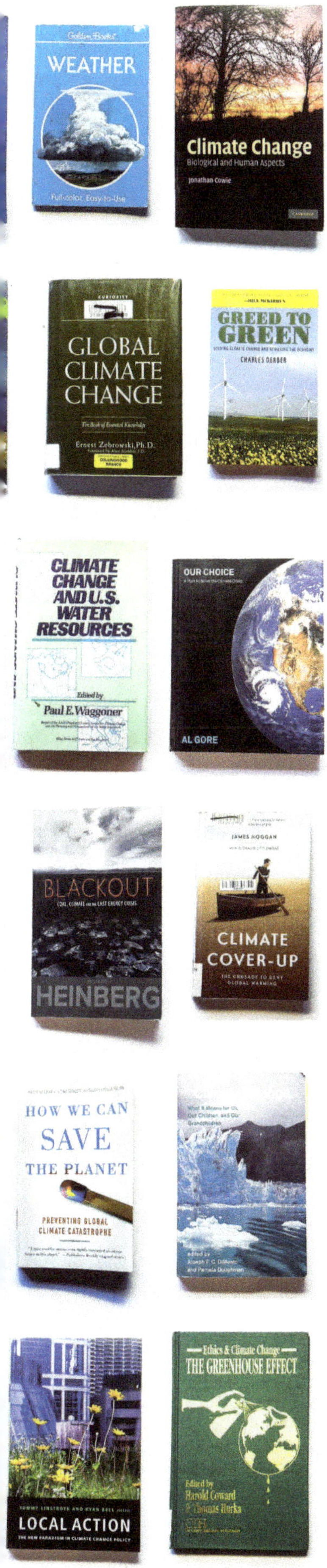

Jenny Kendler

Documentation from *Underground Library,* 2017–Ongoing

© Jenny Kendler

Jenny Kendler is an interdisciplinary ecological artist, environmental activist, naturalist & wild forager whose work has been exhibited nationally and internationally at museums, biennials, public spaces & natural areas. For the past two decades her work has focused on climate change and biodiversity loss. Her practice seeks to de-center the human in order to make space for the radical, transformative otherness of the more-than-human world. Her work is also informed by her identities as queer, Jewish and a single parent.

Since 2014, she has been the first Artist-in-Residence with Natural Resources Defense Council (NRDC). Kendler is also a founding member of Artists Commit—an initiative to raise climate consciousness in the art world and sits on the Board Fundraising Committee for international climate change organization 350.org and the Board of artist residency ACRE. She is a member of artist collective Deep Time Chicago and a local organizer for climate and environmental justice.

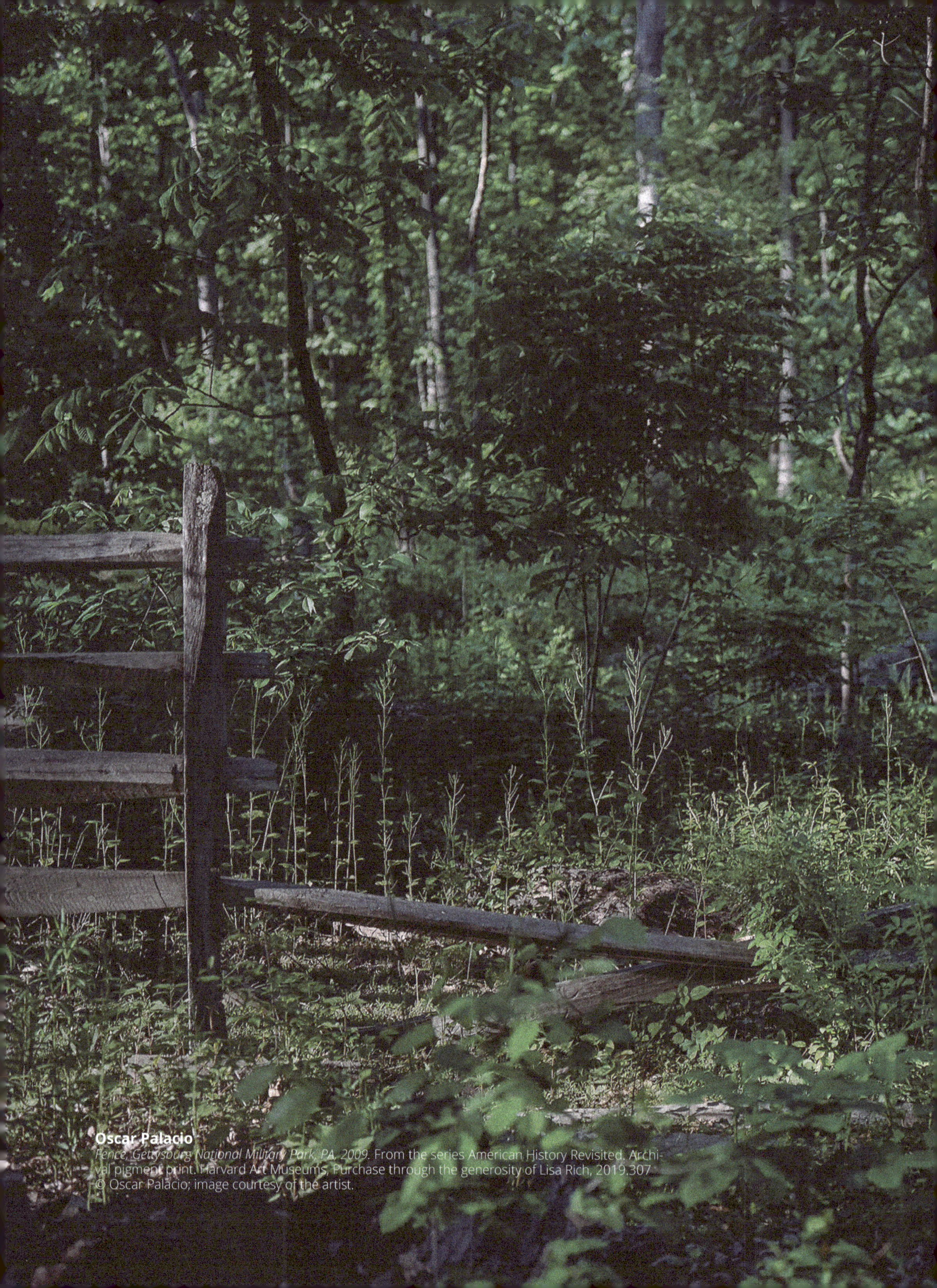

Oscar Palacio
Fence, Gettysburg National Military Park, PA, 2009. From the series American History Revisited. Archival pigment print. Harvard Art Museums, Purchase through the generosity of Lisa Rich, 2019.307
© Oscar Palacio; image courtesy of the artist.

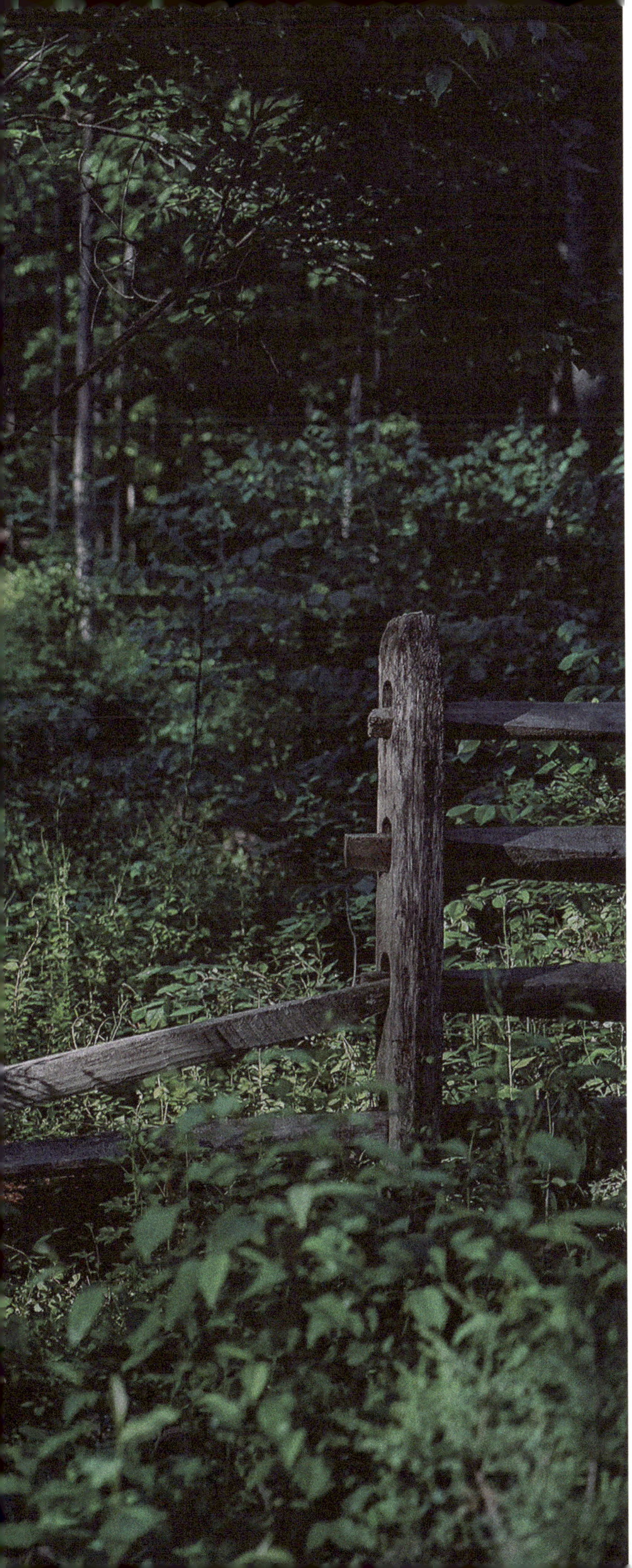

Devour the land

Featuring approximately 160 photographs from 60 artists, the exhibition Devour the Land: War and the American *Landscape Photography Since 1970* held at Harvard Art Museum between September 2021 and January 2022, invited visitors to explore the impacts of military activity on the American landscape—and how photography supports activism in response to these effects. In this interview, curator Makeda Best talks about the challenges involved in curating the exhibition.

in conversation: **Makeda Best and Giovanni Aloi**

Devour the Land shines a light on the unexpected and often hidden consequences of militarism on habitats and well-being in the United States. Featuring approximately 160 photographs across 6 thematic groupings, the exhibition reveals the nationwide footprint of the U.S. military, the wide network of industries that support and supply its work, and the impacts of—and responses to—this activity.

How do photographs portray environmental damage that can be difficult to see, much less identify and measure? By posing such questions, the exhibition provides visitors a space to consider our current challenges and shared future. At the same time, the works on view also suggest how preparations for war and the aftermath can sometimes lead to surprising instances of ecological regeneration and change.

Following a trajectory that originates in the Civil War era, *Devour the Land* begins with the 1970s, a dynamic period for both environmental activism and photography. From there, the focus expands to our contemporary moment. The 60 artists showcased in the exhibition bring a variety of practices and approaches to their work. They range from professional photographic artists and photojournalists to lesser known and emerging photographers; they include Robert Adams, Federica Armstrong, Sheila Pree Bright, Robert Del Tredici, Terry Evans, Lucas Foglia, Sharon Gilbert, Ashley Gilbertson, Peter Goin, Joshua Dudley Greer, David T. Hanson, Zig Jackson, Stacy Kranitz, Dorothy Marder, Susan Meiselas, Richard Misrach, Barbara Norfleet, Mark Power, Jeff Rich, Sim Chi Yin, Sharon Stewart, Robert Toedter, Phil Underdown, and Will Wilson.

The majority of works on display are drawn from the Harvard Art Museums collections, including many recent acquisitions. Additional works are on loan from other Harvard repositories, North American public institutions, and private collections.

An illustrated catalogue, presenting a lively range of voices at the intersection of art, environmentalism, militarism, photography, and politics, accompanied the exhibition. Besides critical essays, nearly a hundred plates, and poems by Ed Roberson, the catalogue includes interviews with nine of the artists featured in the exhibition. The publication won Photography Catalogue of the Year at the 2022 Paris Photo–Aperture PhotoBook Awards.

Organized by the Harvard Art Museums. Curated by Makeda Best, Richard L. Menschel Curator of Photography, Harvard Art Museums.

This exhibition was made possible in part by the generosity of the Terra Foundation for American Art and The Andy Warhol Foundation for the Visual Arts. Additional support for the project is provided by the Andrew W. Mellon Publication Fund and the Rosenblatt Fund for Postwar American Art. Related programming is supported by the M. Victor Leventritt Lecture Series Endowment Fund. Modern and contemporary art programs at the Harvard Art Museums are made possible in part by generous support from the Emily Rauh Pulitzer and Joseph Pulitzer, Jr., Fund for Modern and Contemporary Art.

Alex Webb
Mine shaft on northside of Treece (Kansas) filled with water and garbage, 2012. Archival pigment print. Harvard Art Museums, Fund for the Acquisition of Photographs, 2020.165. © Alex Webb; image courtesy of Robert Klein Gallery.

Giovanni Aloi: *Devour the Land: War and American Landscape Photography since 1970*, the exhibition you curated Harvard Art Museum in 2021, shed light on one of the most important and yet often overlooked historical and ecological realities that have shaped the American present: the US military apparatus. As I walked through the first two rooms of the exhibition it soon appeared clear to me that *Devour the Land* belongs to that category of rare exhibitions that radically challenge and ultimately change someone's pre-existing conceptions of history and social reality. From a personal standpoint, as an educator specializing in the representation of the non-human and the environment in art, the exhibition proposed an extremely important opportunity to visualize and assess the many ethical, ecological, architectural, humanitarian, material, and representational ramifications that, among other things, perpetuate social injustice in the US. It seemed to me that in the exhibition "the land" worked simultaneously as a very real, tangible and corruptible material entity as well as a broader metaphor of the histories and identities that become embedded in cultural stratifications. Can you tell us more

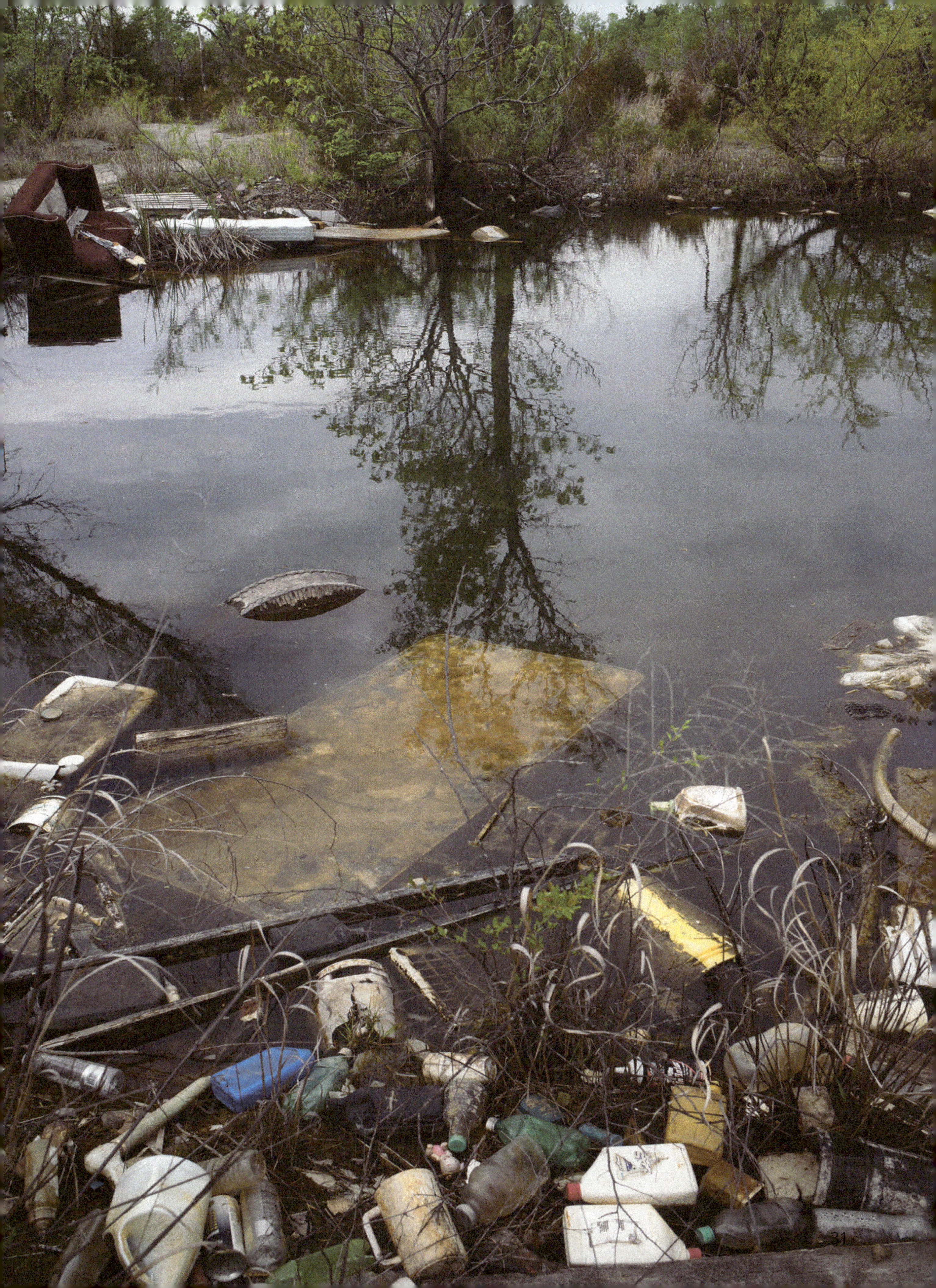

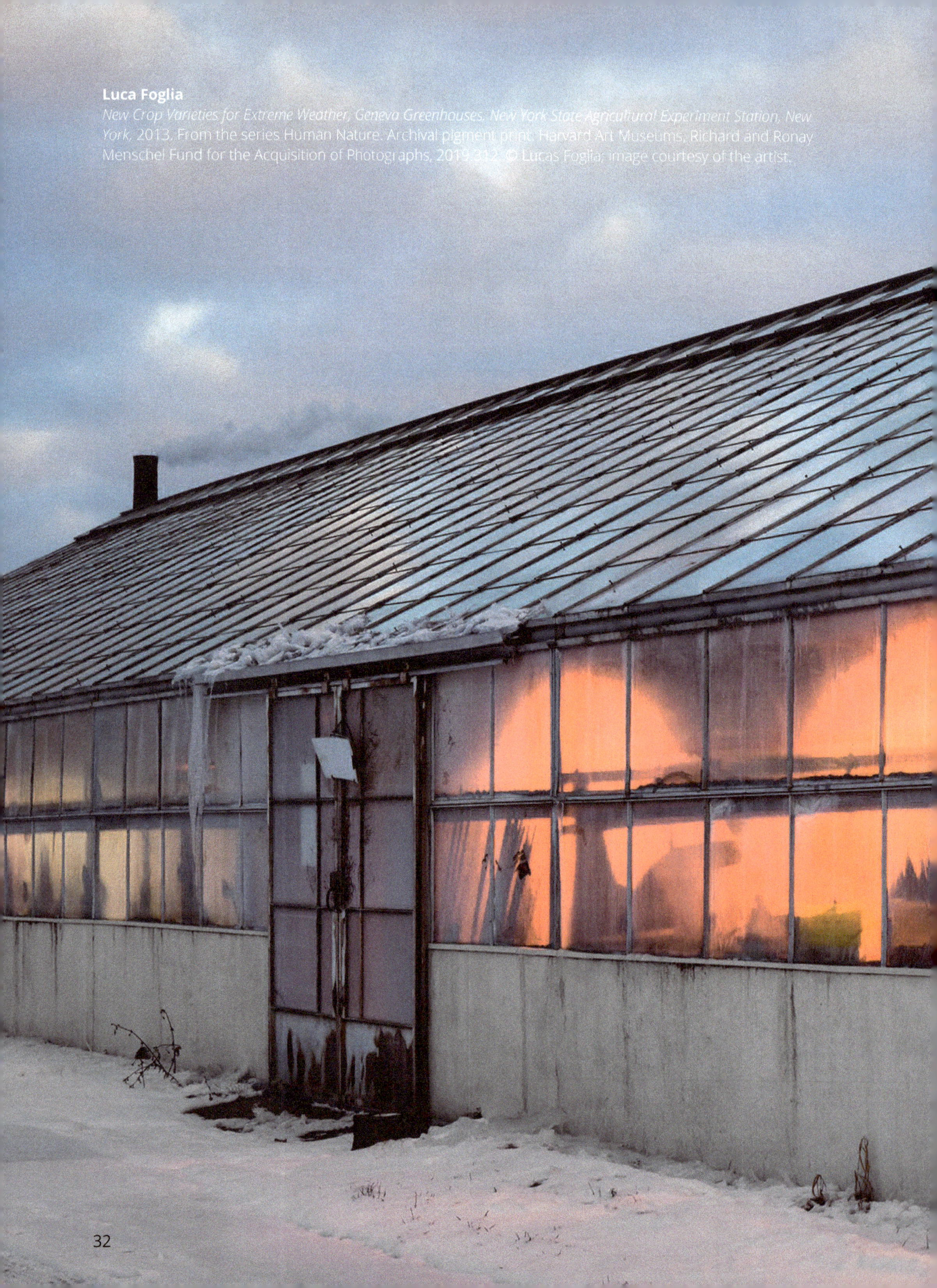

Luca Foglia
New Crop Varieties for Extreme Weather, Geneva Greenhouses, New York State Agricultural Experiment Station, New York, 2013. From the series Human Nature. Archival pigment print. Harvard Art Museums, Richard and Ronay Menschel Fund for the Acquisition of Photographs, 2019.312. © Lucas Foglia; image courtesy of the artist.

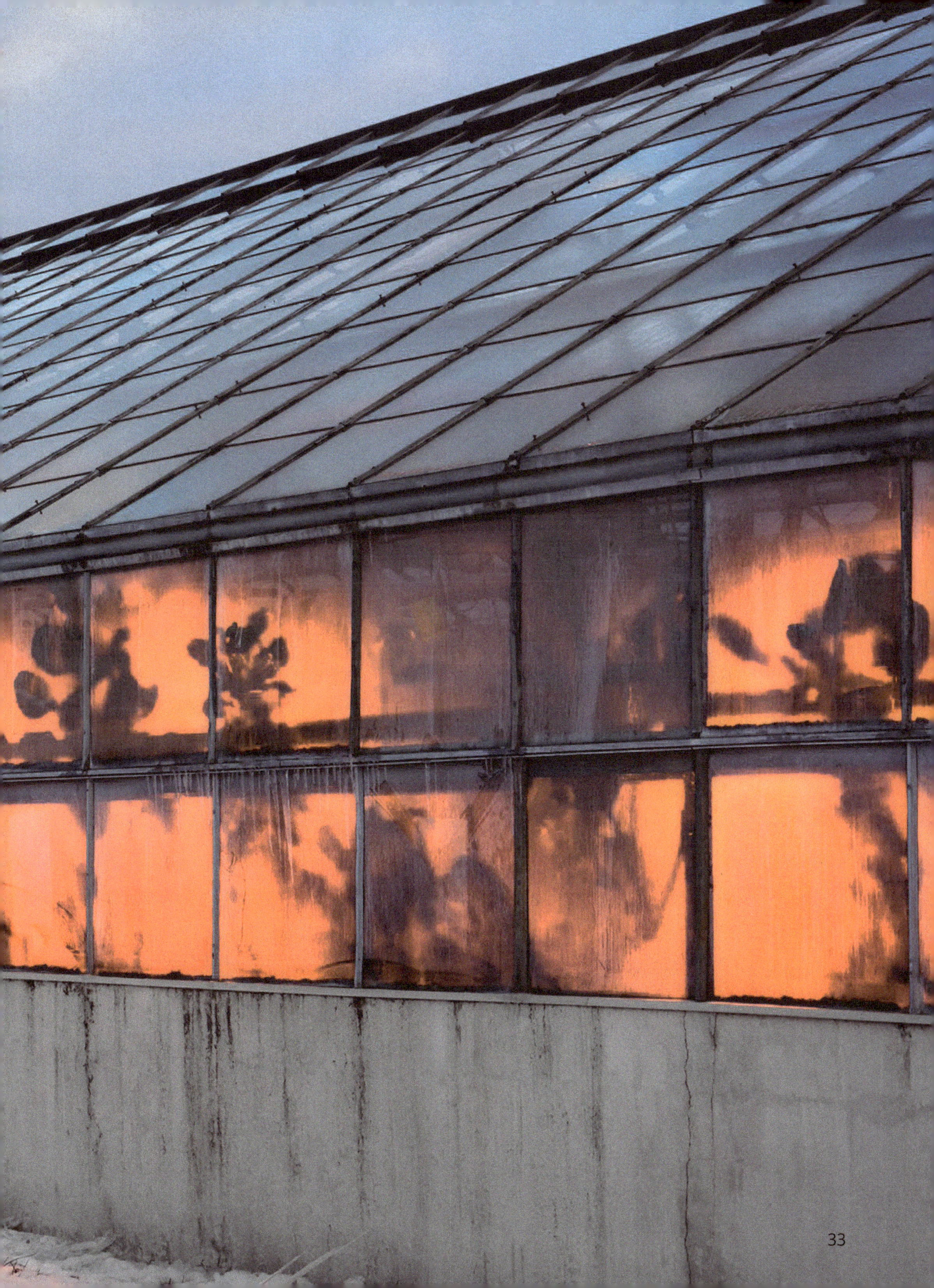

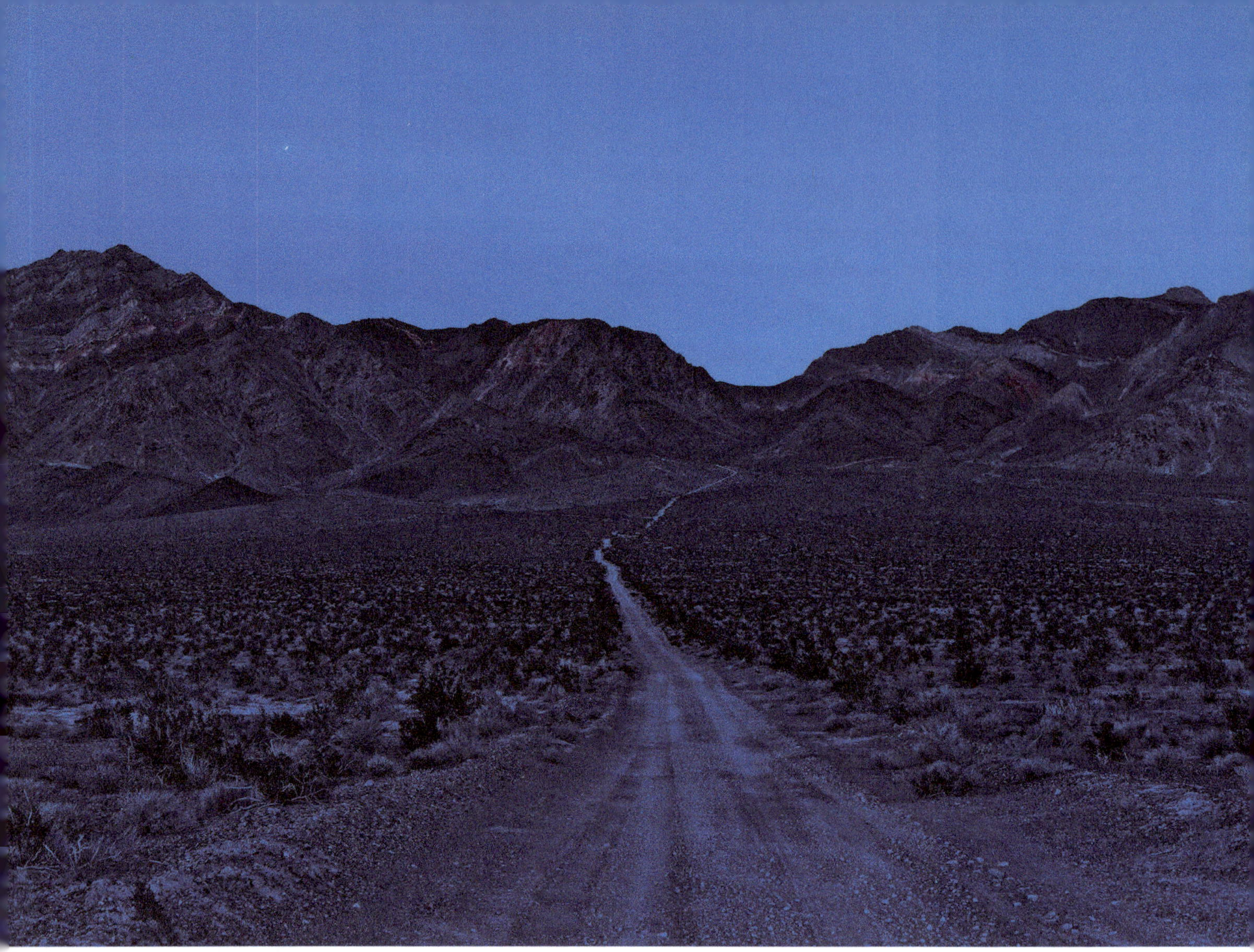

Sim Chin Yin
Mountain Range Surrounding the NevadaTest Site, November 2017. From the series MOst People Were Silent. Archival Pigment Print. Harvard Art Museums, Richard and Ronay Menschel Fund for the Acquisition of Photographs,
2020.181. © Sim Chi Yin; image courtesy of the artist.

about how the idea for the exhibition came about and how it developed?

GA: The exhibition was organized around 6 themes— Silent Spring, Arming America, Slow Violence, Regeneration, Other Battlefields, and Resistance—which illustrate the often otherwise invisible ways the US military has impacted, at times irreversibly, the land. How did you come to this organization and what stories did it allow you to tell?

MB: In the research phase, I thought the focus of the exhibition would be a nationwide survey of sites, with a kind of prologue. The formation of the sections was guided by the research into the images, and then the sections on the impacts into BIPOC communities (Slow Violence), Regeneration (the ways the land has been repurposed or renewed), Other Battlefields (a broader interpretation of the ways contemporary "wars" impact our environment) and Resistance (the work of people to come together and to fight against what is happening in their communities) were further extensions of the story that I wanted to pull out.

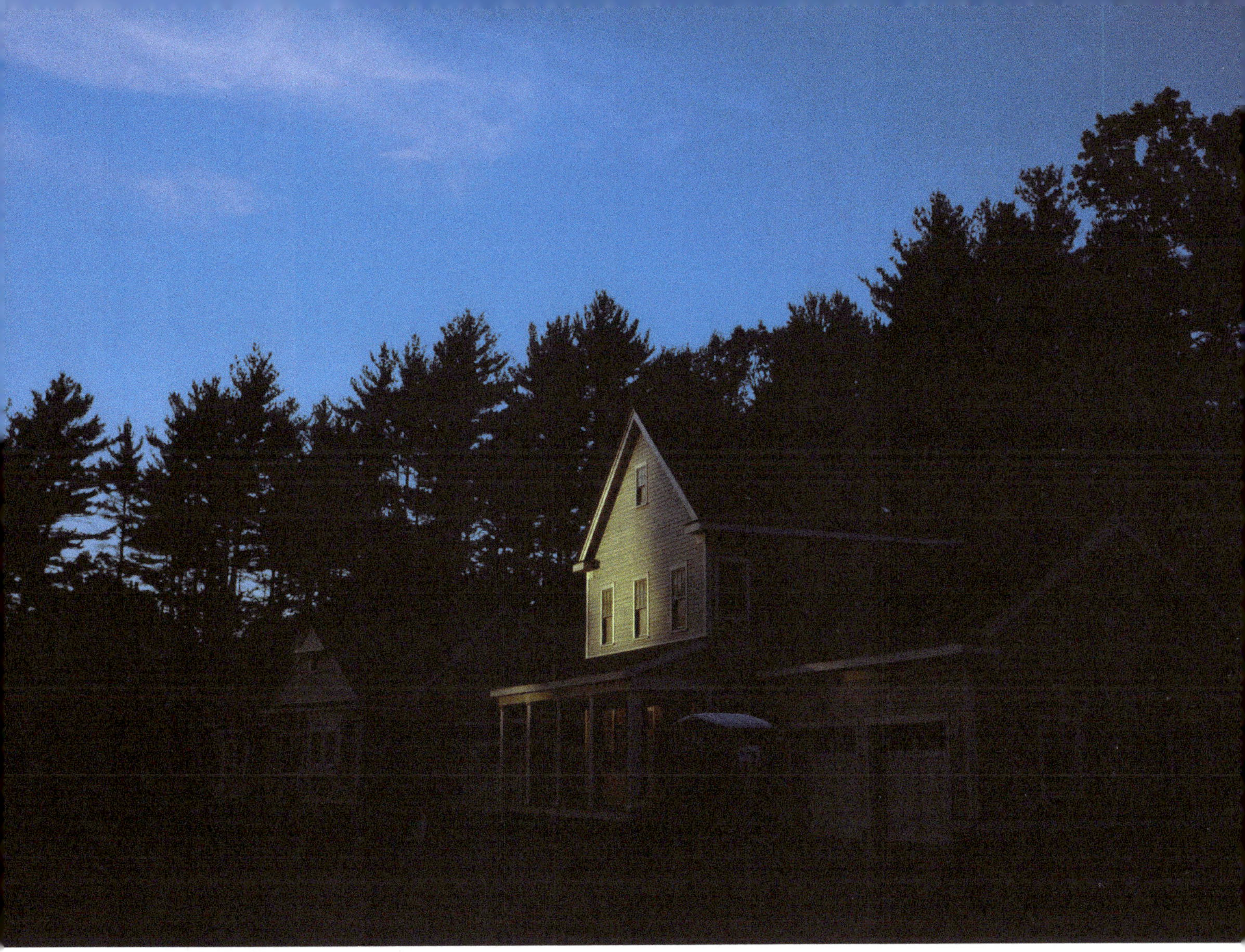

Nina Berman
A housing development bordering the Starmet Superfund site, Concord, Massachusetts, USA, July 3, 2016. From the series Acknowledgment of Danger. Pigment print. Collection of the artist, TL42305. © Nina Berman; image courtesy of the artist.

GA: *Devour the Land* featured 160 photographs by a very broad range of artists/practitioners. What curatorial principles guided the selection for the exhibition?

MB: An interest in an expanded interpretation of photography in the 1970s beyond New Topographics, representing the work of BIPOC and women land-based photographers, and portraying the specific impacts of pollution on BIPOC communities.

GA: In my review of the exhibition published in *Esse* magazine, I said that "a kind of seemingly inescapable apocalyptic sublime flickers across the curatorial selection". I am particularly interested in contemporary discussion about aesthetics and the apocalyptic—how we can make visible without sensationalizing or expose without objectifying. Or how can we avoid "ruin-porn" aesthetic paradigms?

How did you negotiate different aesthetic approaches and photographic practices in order to strike the right balance?

MB: The focus for me was always the land itself.

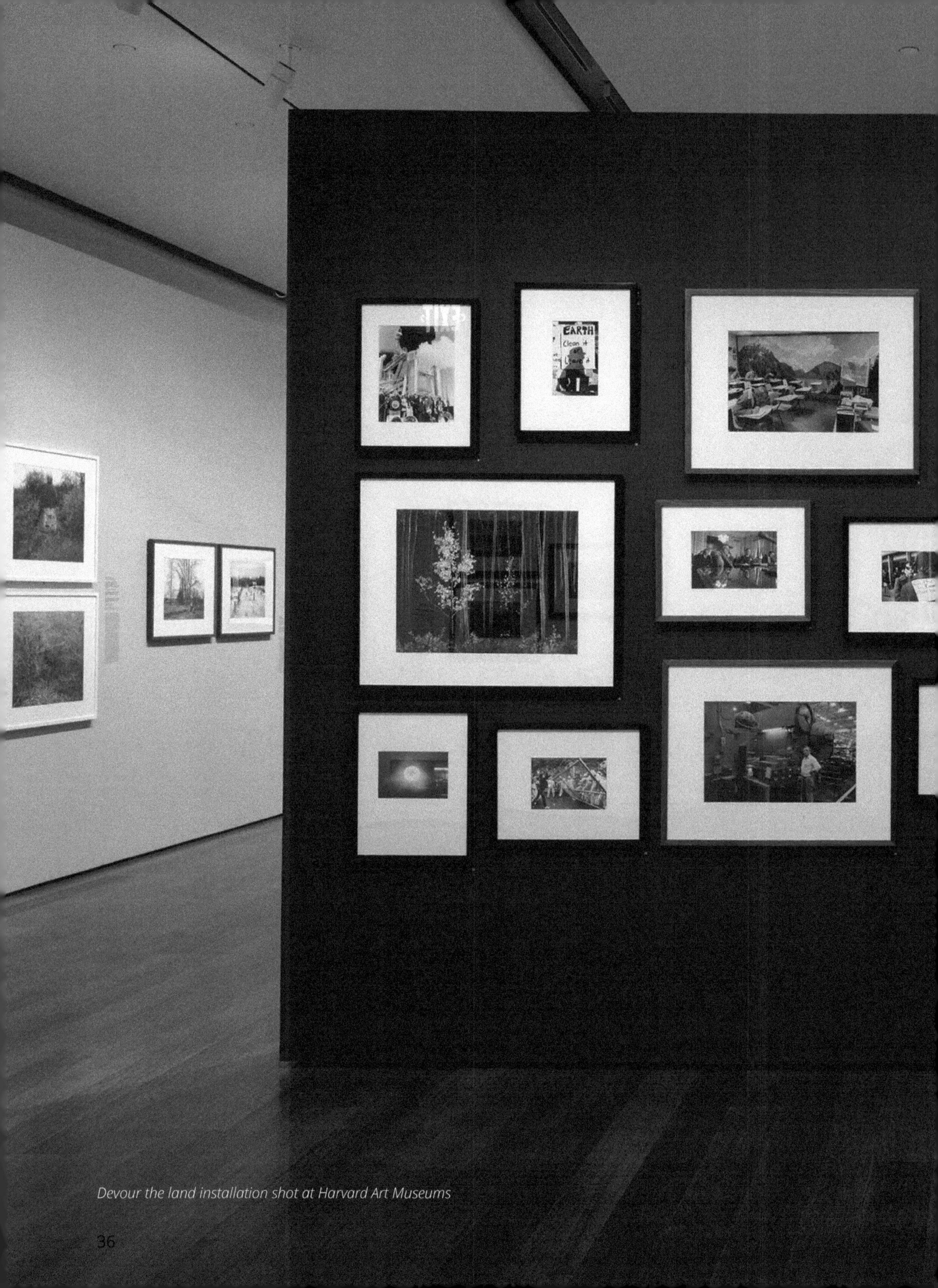

Devour the land installation shot at Harvard Art Museums

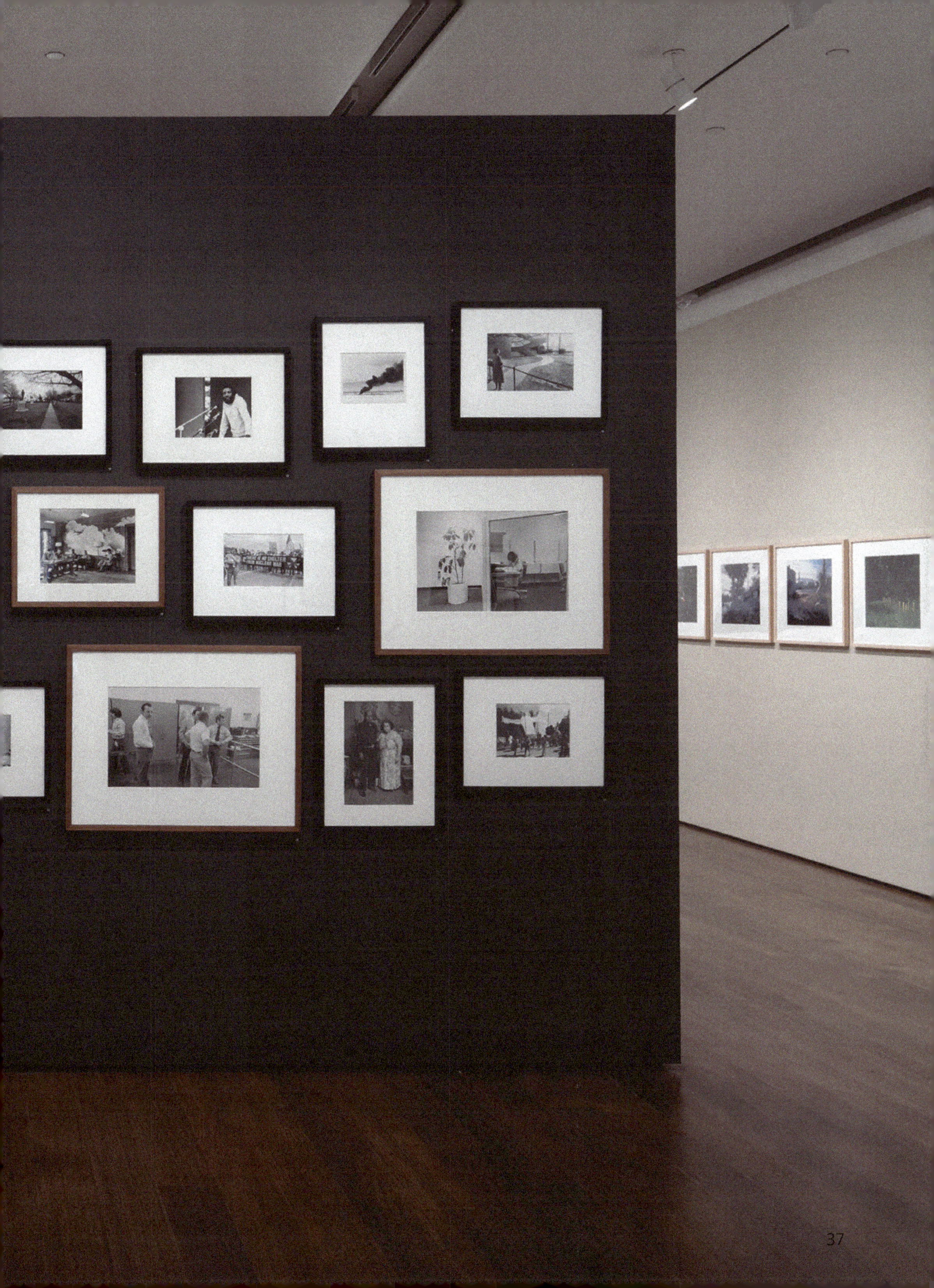

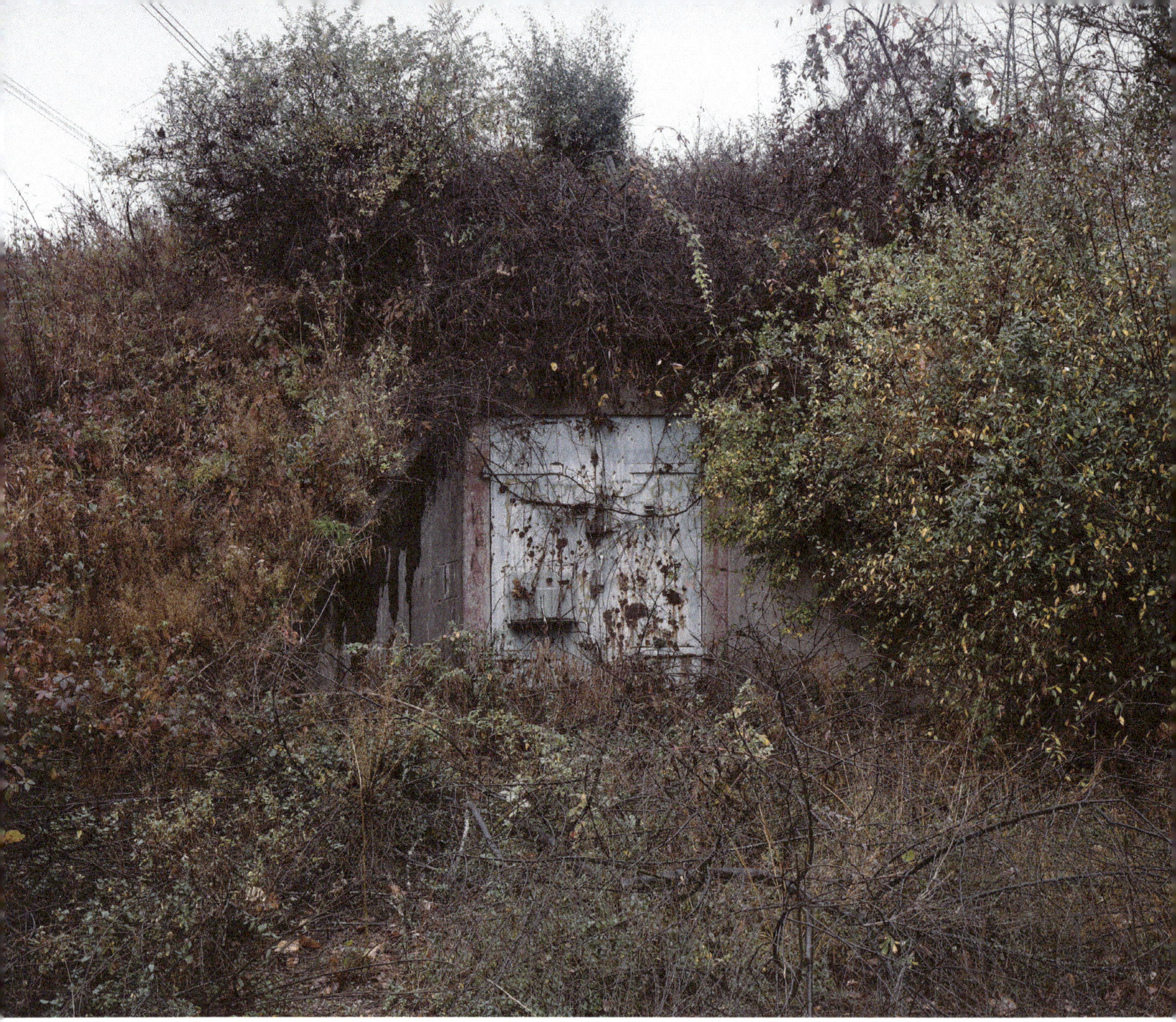

Joshua Dudly Greer
TNT Storage Igloo N6-B, Point Pleasant, West Virginia, 2012, 2012. From the series Point Pleasant. Archival pigment print. Harvard Art Museums, Richard and Ronay Menschel Fund for the Acquisition of Photographs, 2019.345. © Joshua Dudley Greer; image courtesy of the artist.

GA: You are a Lecturer at Harvard University. Did you use the exhibition as a didactic resource with your students or other groups at the University? What activities took place in the exhibiting space and what was the general response?

MB: Yes, For years I've taught the course 'Photography and Ecology' in the Department of Art Film and Visual Studies. It is an unusual course that brings together history, theory, and artistic production, and it draws on my own background in studio art. Before pursuing a PhD, I completed an MFA in Photography at the California Institute of the Arts). The format of the course is using photography as research. In terms of supporting my own research for the exhibition, the projects the students pursue were helpful for me to see. Over the course of the term, students create a project, and seeing how they grapple with the beauty in the landscape, the challenge of "seeing" and "representing" toxicity and history, was incredibly useful as a I conceptualized the exhibition.

The exhibition was presented mostly in fall 2021, and due to COVID protocols, it wasn't used as robustly in teaching, but we are a teaching institution, so the photographs are used in teaching. I should also add that about 90% of the exhibition were works that I acquired or that we already held. There were only a few loans.

GA: While not being the sole focus of the exhibition, the ecological theme is central to the themes of social injustice and systemic racism. Can you tell us more about your philosophical/cultural reference points in matters of environmental/ecological concern? Any book you'd recommend?

MB: My exhibition catalogue included a list of "further reading" - Dr. Robert Bullard's work is essential reading, as is the work by Dorceta Taylor.

GA: How does *Devour the Land* relate to other exhibitions that you have curated, like *Crossing Lines, Constructing Home: Displacement and Belonging in Contemporary Art*, for instance?

MB: My contributions to *Crossing Lines* also worked to address the domestic impacts and histories of migration and displacement.

GA: I know that you are currently working on a book on landscape photography. How did you become interested in the land as a political site? Can you tell us more about your next book?

MB: In the 1980s before people were talking about environmental racism, my mother founded one of the first prison horticulture programs in the country. She went on to create other environmentally based programs to address high rates of recidivism. So I grew up immersed in these conversations. And then in my own practice as a photographer, I was interested in how landscapes can speak about history.

GA: What does curating mean to you?

MB: For me, it is a way of thinking and problem solving.

Makeda Best is a curator, writer, and historian of American photography. Since 2016, she has served as the Richard L. Menschel Curator of Photography at the Harvard Art Museums. She holds a Ph.D. from Harvard University and a MFA in studio photography from CalArts.

Andrea Conte: art, sustainibility, and the climate emergency

Andrea Conte is an Italian artist, activist and environmental engineer specializing in sustainability. Active since the end of the 90s, the artist combines his scientific training, doctorate in Environmental Engineering, post-doctoral collaborations with the University of Bologna and Columbia University of New York on the sustainable management of resources in different climatic conditions, with the personal artistic path. His research focuses on the relationship between the built environment and the natural landscape. His conceptual imagery is characterized by the presence of natural elements, such as rocks and minerals. Through these symbols, Conte intertwines ecology, urban planning and environmental sustainability, with the idea of teaching and promoting sustainable and eco-centric development.

text & images: **Andrea Conte (Andreco Studio)**

One of my main projects is called *Climate Art Project (CAP)*, started in Paris, 2015, during the Climate Change conference COP21 as a transdisciplinary initiative that overlaps scientific and artistic research to raise awareness on social and ecological urgency as Climate Change. *CAP* uses the language of visual art to underline open questions in the contemporary debate and envision climate actions and possible scenarios for the future. Started as one of my artist practices, *CAP* became also a cultural association based in Rome, that coordinated all the initiatives. It is an itinerant and multimedia project that uses: installations, sculptures, paintings, wall paintings and performances as political ecology and nature-culture agency. *CAP* builds a network of partners and relations to develop complex projects on vulnerable territories. In every chapter of the project a network is built between scientific research centers, cultural institutions, museums, theaters, galleries, festivals, independent art organization, art foundations, environmental associations, schools, universities, grass roots organizations and civil society. In Venice the focus was on sea level rise, in Portugal, drought and wildfires, in Puglia, the desertification process in the Mediterranean south, in Delhi, air pollution, in Rome green spaces conservation and river pollution, in the Alps the glaciers melting and the rivers flooding and drought.

Nomad Landscape is an installation made of plants, soil, metal sculpture and tapestries, realized for the exhibition *Future Landscapes*. The plants are a different variety of ferns and hemps, chosen for their ability to treat the soil from metal pollutants. It's not only about moving the plants in the white cubes, as many artists did it before me. I have other motivations, I want to address the latest scientific research on Climate Chance, political ecology and on nature-based solution (NBS). I study the ecosystem process able to self-regenerate and transform the pollutants generated by the industrialized societies. I am interested in the relation between human / plants / geology / ecosystems. In my installations I am not showing the plants themselves but the invisible chemical-physical transformations that happen between the plants and the rest of the ecosystem.

NBS promotes ecological process to mitigate impacts due by human beings, are effective for the Climate Change adaptation and mitigation. It's been more than fifteen years that I've been doing this kind of installation with the plants that sometimes are combined with metal sculptures, textiles, paintings, photos or other artworks. In this case, tapestries that represent plant leaves and knives are hung on the walls.

Leaves are "imaginary weapons" considering the regenerative role that plants have in the ecosystem.

plants : ecosystems = revolutionaries : society

Plants in the ecosystems, with their capacity to rebalance and regenerate it, are like the revolutionaries in society when they become oppressive, authoritarian and liberticidal. This equation theoretically connects environmental science with critical thinking and political ecology.

The exhibition Future Landscapes was connected to a public program with outdoor activities such as workshops, citizen science activities, experiments, walks and performances. The initiative was realized with the help of Sara Alberani and with a vast group of partners, collaborators and friends as Anna Cestelli Guidi, Maurizia di Nata, Laura Passatore and many others.

At the end of the exhibition the plants from the installation were used for a pilot experimental project of Phytoremediation, measuring their ability to absorb metal pollutants from the soil. We analyzed the soil before and after the plantation for understanding how much the plants can treat the pollutants. Analyzing the plants before and after the vegetation period it is possible to discover the result of the deprivation.

The goal of this project is to speak about artistic practices also in the scientific fields. The title of the paper is 'Nature-Based Solution on the River Environment', an example of cross-disciplinary sustainable management with local community active participation and visual art as a science transfer tool.

Breaking the boundaries between disciplines and speaking about science in art and art in science it's one of CAP's main goals. It's a way to be "undisciplined", quoting Marco Armiero. The same plants before the installation and the experiment have been utilized for one of the first action-performances realized by the activist group Extinction Rebellion in Italy. A symbol of the extinction was realized with the plants at the center of the auditorium in Rome the day before the opening of the *Future Landscape* exhibition.

Another practice that lasts for more than fifteen years is related to the creation of visionary flags and tapestries dedicated to the landscape. In the Andreco Studio archive we count more than three-hundred flags. Imaginary Flags that have no need for identitarian representation as a Nations, a political parties or football teams, but instead are flags for the nonhumans, for the landscapes, rivers, green spaces, mountains, plants, clouds, rockslides, cliffs and so on.

Of course, it's a provocation, but it's needed to move the view from the humans to the landscape, to the nonhuman. I used these flags for small actions and performances as workshops, like the one that we do during the water sampling by the rivers or the one for the creation of the first *Aula Verde*, (in English Green Room or "Green Classroom").

Aula Verde is an open access circular space made by trees, a place for meeting and making kin, a place for environmental education and Forest

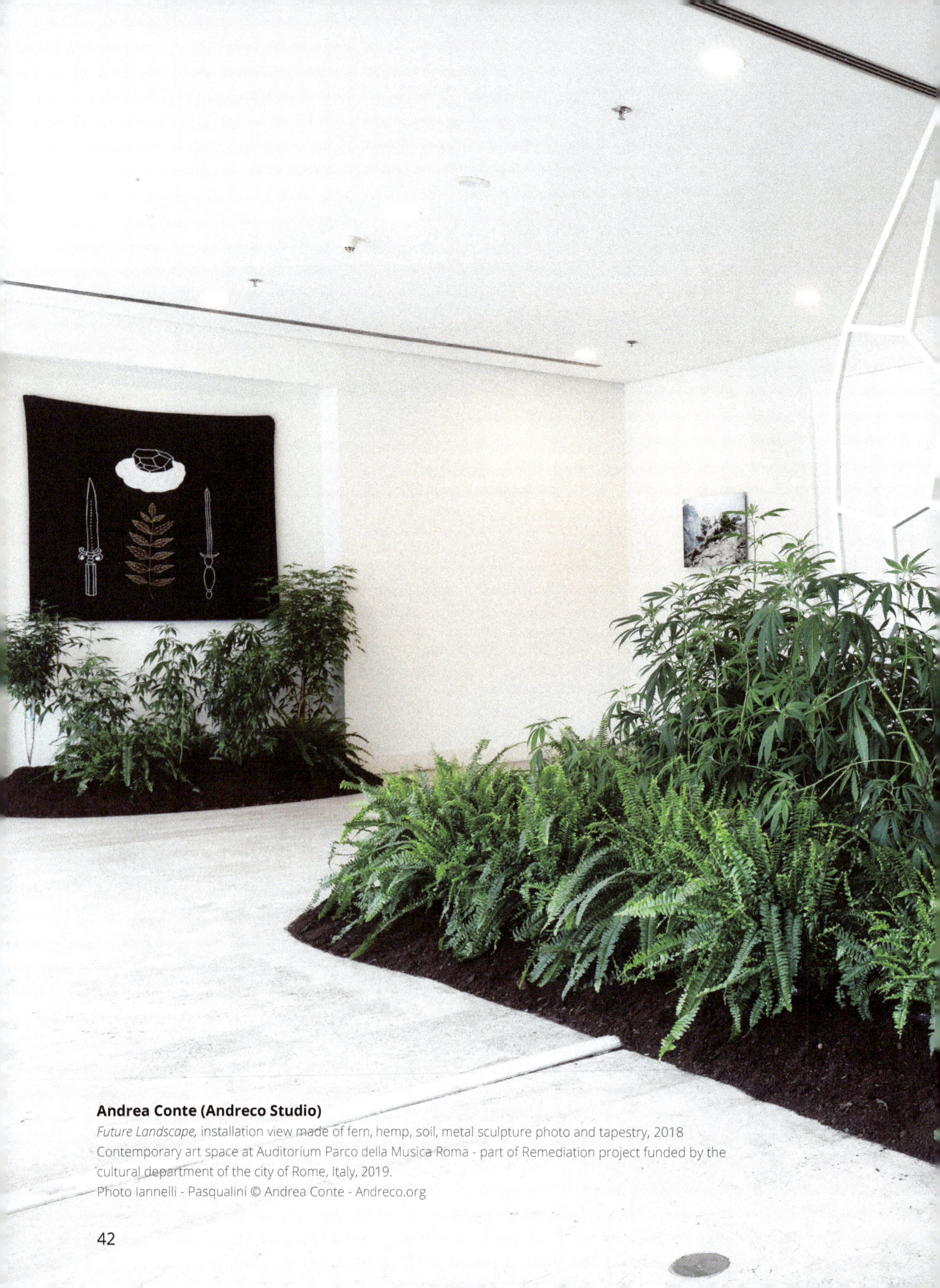

Andrea Conte (Andreco Studio)
Future Landscape, installation view made of fern, hemp, soil, metal sculpture photo and tapestry, 2018
Contemporary art space at Auditorium Parco della Musica Roma - part of Remediation project funded by the cultural department of the city of Rome, Italy, 2019.
Photo Iannelli - Pasqualini © Andrea Conte - Andreco.org

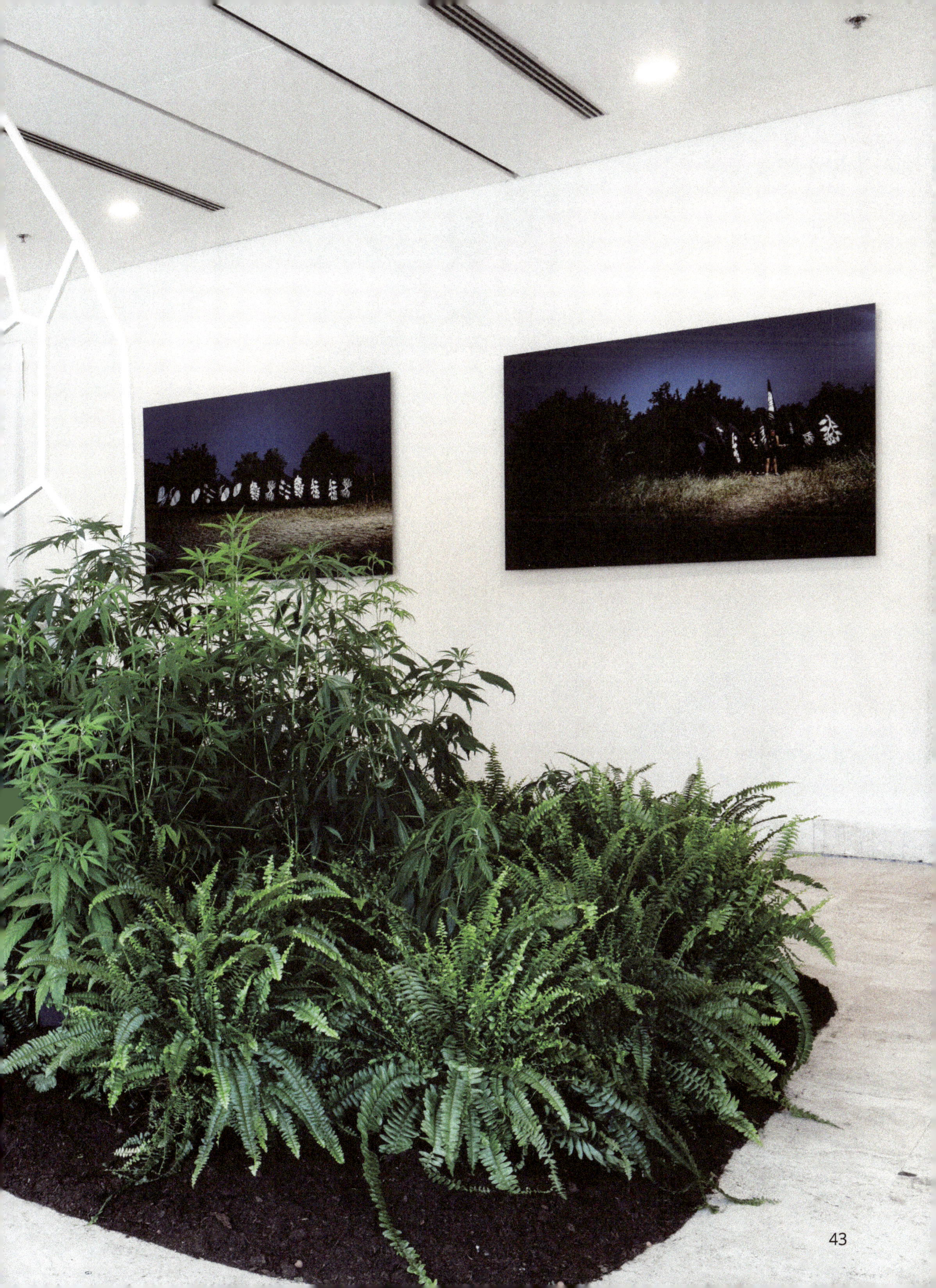

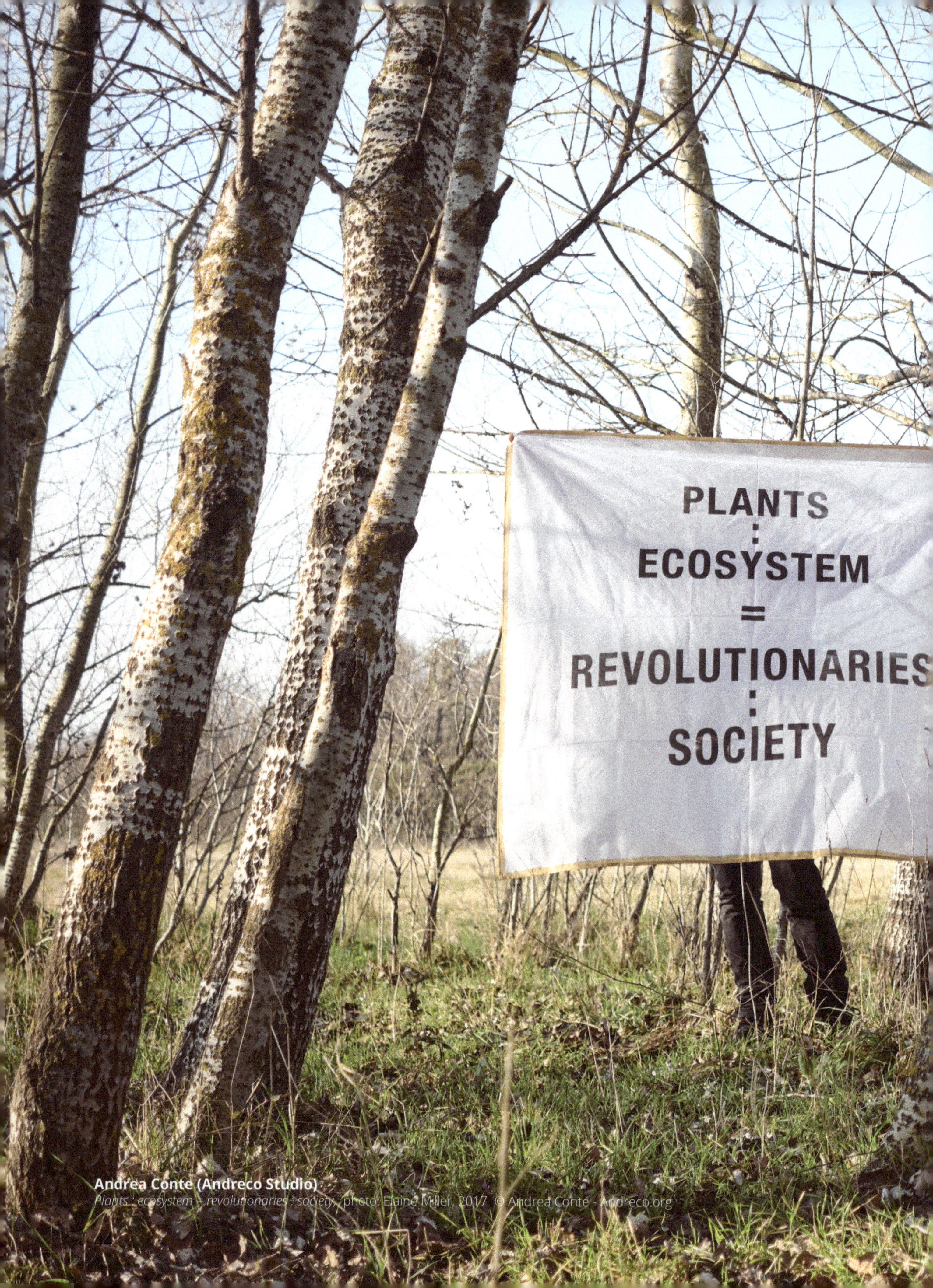

Andrea Conte (Andreco Studio)
Plants : ecosystem = revolutionaries : society, photo: Elaine Miller, 2017 © Andrea Conte - Andreco.org

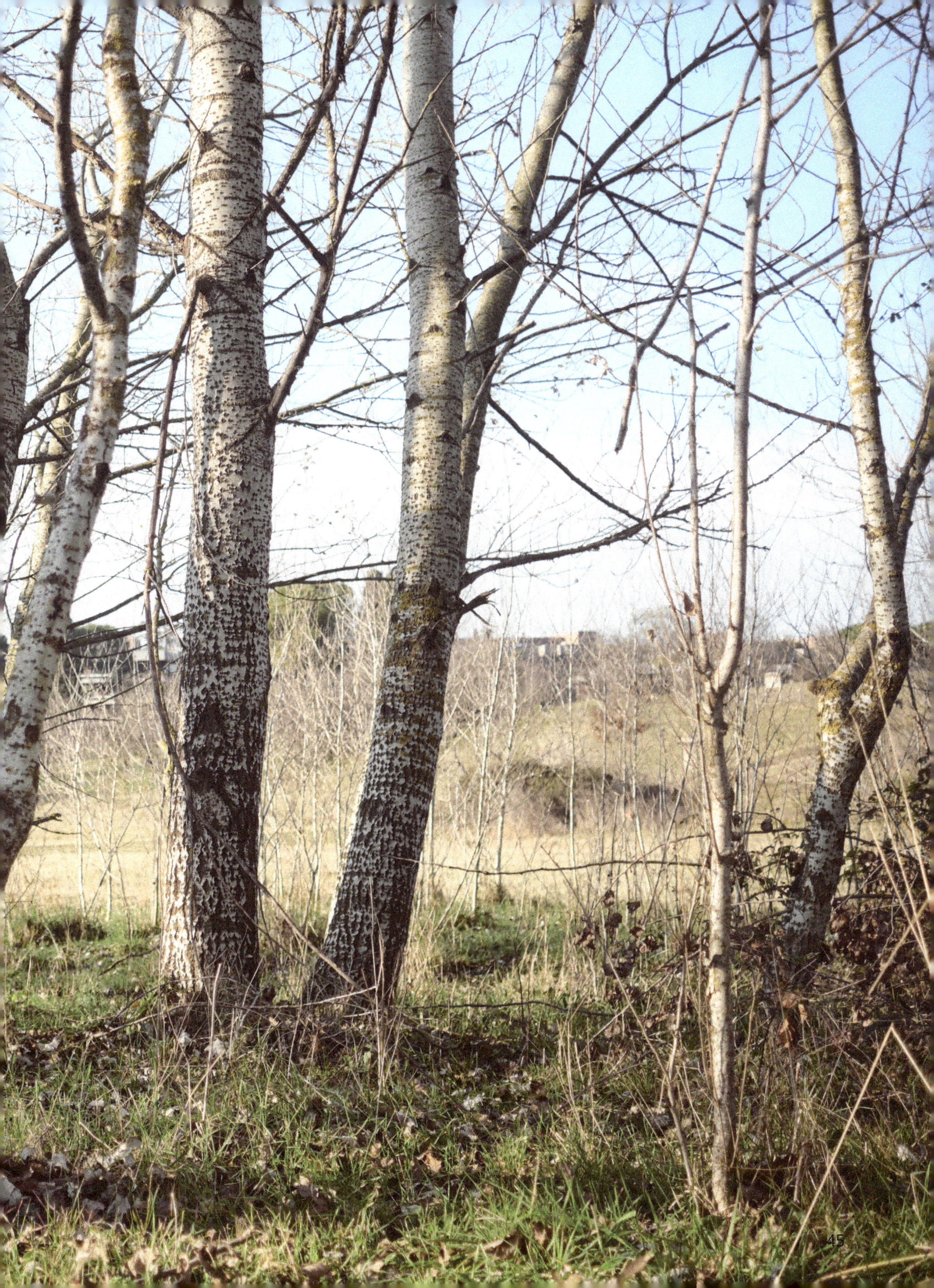

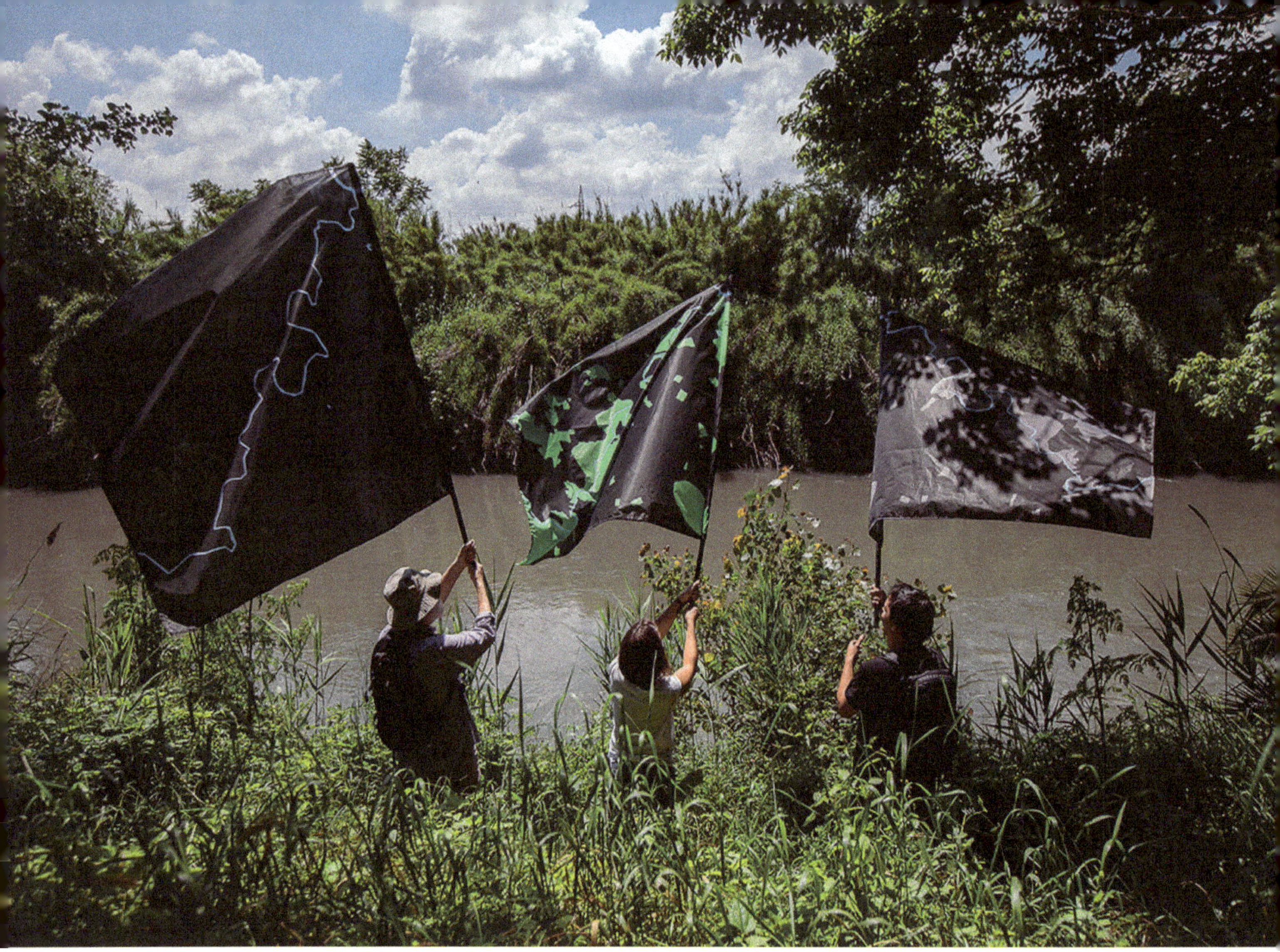

Andrea Conte (Andreco Studio)

Tribute to the rivers and green spaces, action performance with flags, PLANTAE, Climate Art Project, Valle dell'Aniene Natural Reserva, Rome, Photo: Blindeye Factory 2018 © Andrea Conte - Andreco.org

Medicine, a Land Artwork, a green infrastructure, a climate action, a Nature-Based Solution for Climate Change adaptation and mitigation.

Aula Verde is a new concept of urban forestation integrated with social and artistic aspects. The *Aula Verde* is made with a collective performance where the participant, non-professional performers, holds the new trees and the flags of the landscape. The flags are used also in more structured performances, choreography in the public space.

For example, *Parata Tiberina,* the parade for the river Tiber. When the city of Rome commissioned me to perform for the New Year Eves I decided to celebrate the river Tiber. The performance *Tiberina* was produced by the Romaeuropa Foundation, the Opera Theatre of Rome and the National Academy of Music Santa Cecila.

More than hundred people were involved in this project to celebrate the river Tiber. In the past the Tiber was venerated, Tiberino was the god to venerate for the protection of the river and the life of the city and the health of the citizens. The river is very polluted, since ancient times it was the drain of the romans, cloaca maxima, and after the industrial revolution also the manufactory production discharge causing several environmental problems. Nowadays the river is still polluted, even if there is more attention in terms of discharges in the superficial water basins. We need to do more for water preservation. The performance *Tiberina* was

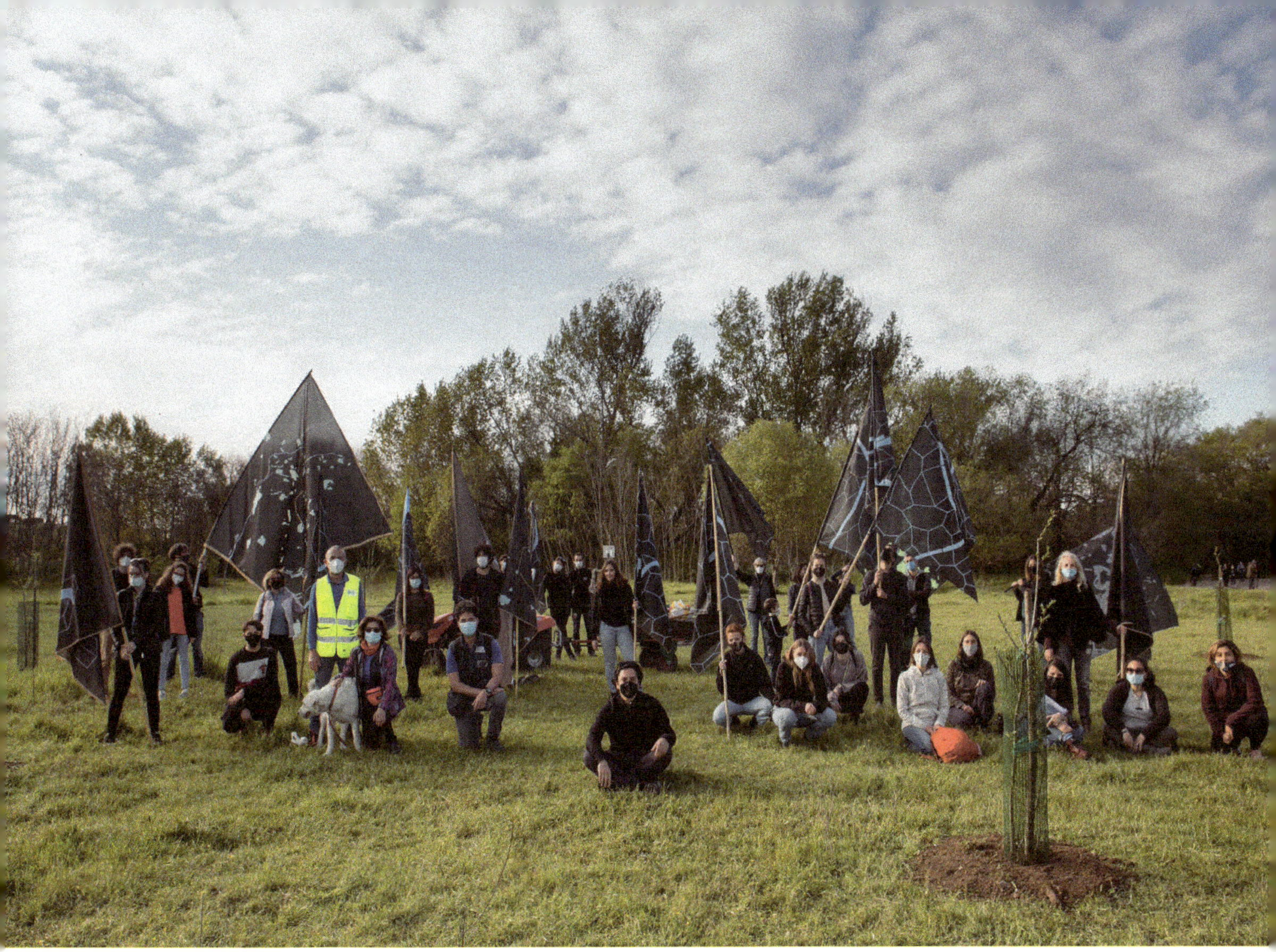

Andrea Conte (Andreco Studio)

Aula Verde, green room, collective performance + green infrastructure + land art + social space, FLUMEN, Climate Art Project, Rome, Photo: Futura Tittaferrante, 2021 © Andrea Conte - Andreco.org

made to contribute to create a river culture and to create environmental advocacy for the river. The performers were impersonating the river itself, an angry river that was flooding the city. They are the Tiber that took back the city.

> Like a river in flood, like water when, with an always equal distribution, it occupies the spaces it encounters, taking its shape. Mutability and adaptation, changes of state, water hammer, sudden, unstoppable peaks. We are the Tiber cry out for justice.

With the performance we demand a clean river, a healthy environment, a river park for all species. After the Ganges and the Yamuna in India, the Gesso and the Stura in Piedmont, it is the turn of the Aniene and the Tiber. Let's stop polluting this branch of the drainage basin that crosses the city of Rome, let's venerate Tiberino, the Tiber's patron deity, let's build a vector for sustainability, a green corridor, a space for socializing.

Rivers are the veins that nourish the territory, the sap that flows through the vegetation, not the bodies that receive anthropogenic waste. Cities were created along rivers because they are an indispensable source for the survival of us humans and other animal species. Humans used river water for agriculture and

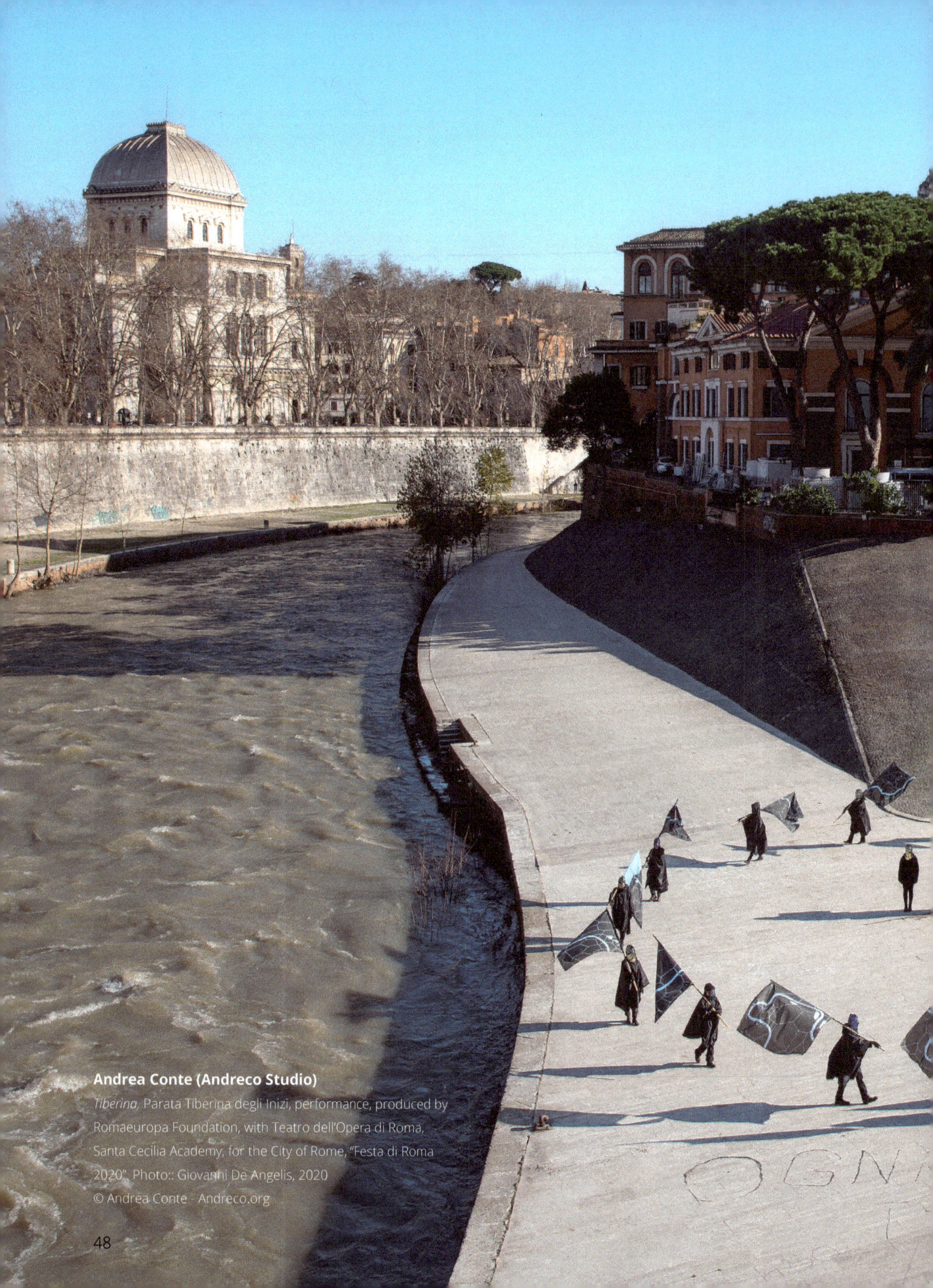

Andrea Conte (Andreco Studio)
Tiberina, Parata Tiberina degli Inizi, performance, produced by Romaeuropa Foundation, with Teatro dell'Opera di Roma, Santa Cecilia Academy, for the City of Rome, "Festa di Roma 2020". Photo:: Giovanni De Angelis, 2020
© Andrea Conte - Andreco.org

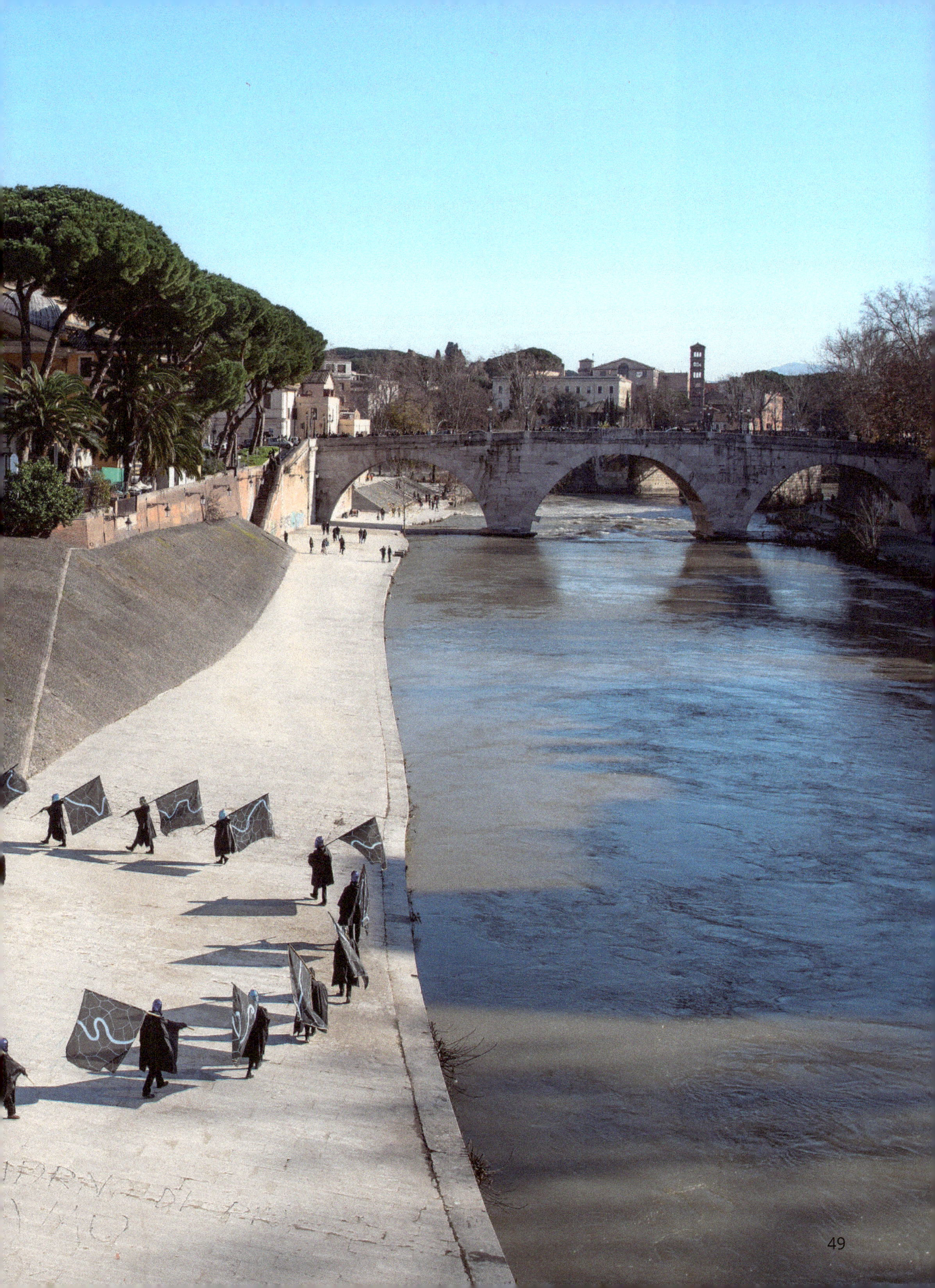

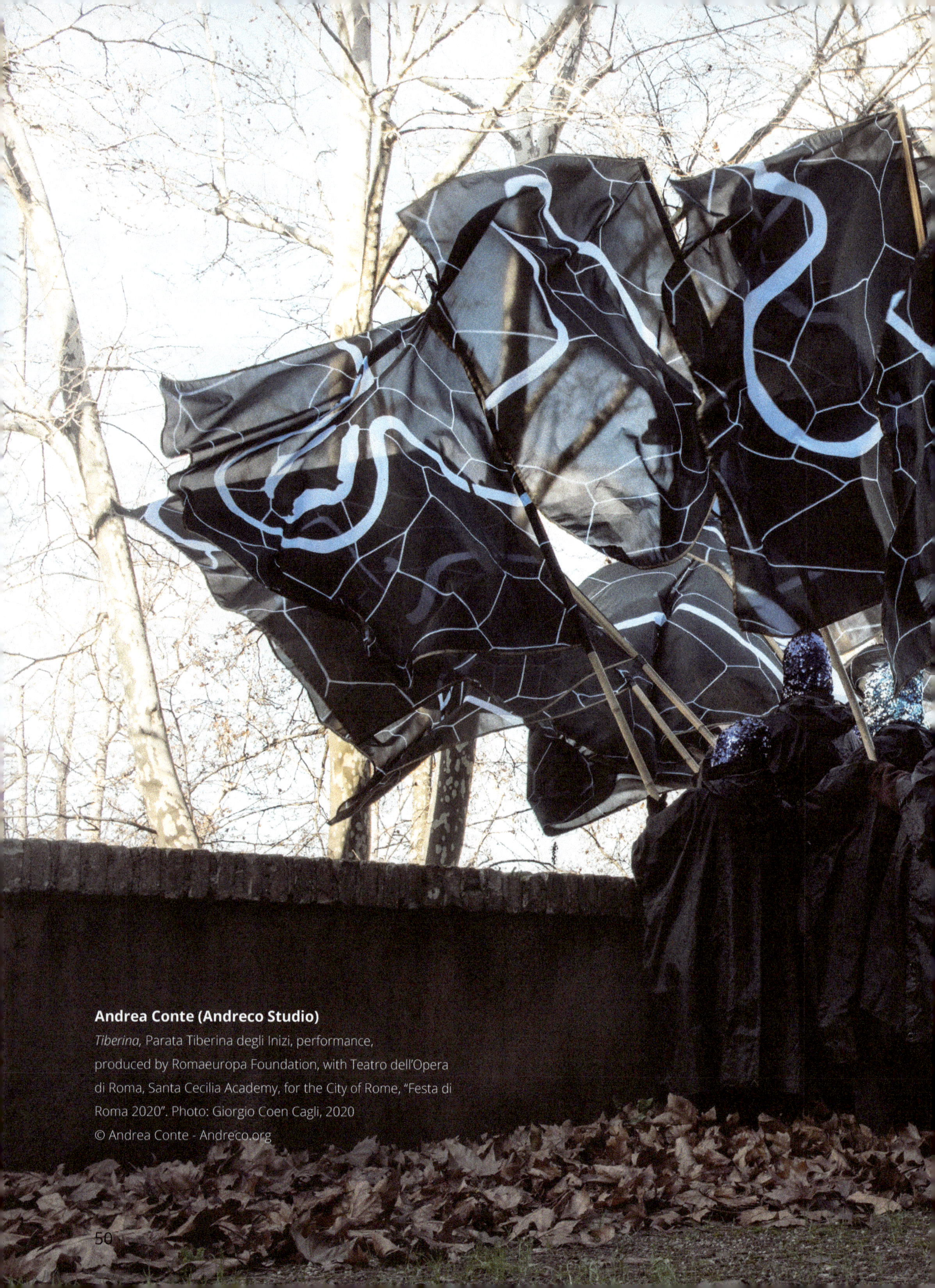

Andrea Conte (Andreco Studio)
Tiberina, Parata Tiberina degli Inizi, performance, produced by Romaeuropa Foundation, with Teatro dell'Opera di Roma, Santa Cecilia Academy, for the City of Rome, "Festa di Roma 2020". Photo: Giorgio Coen Cagli, 2020

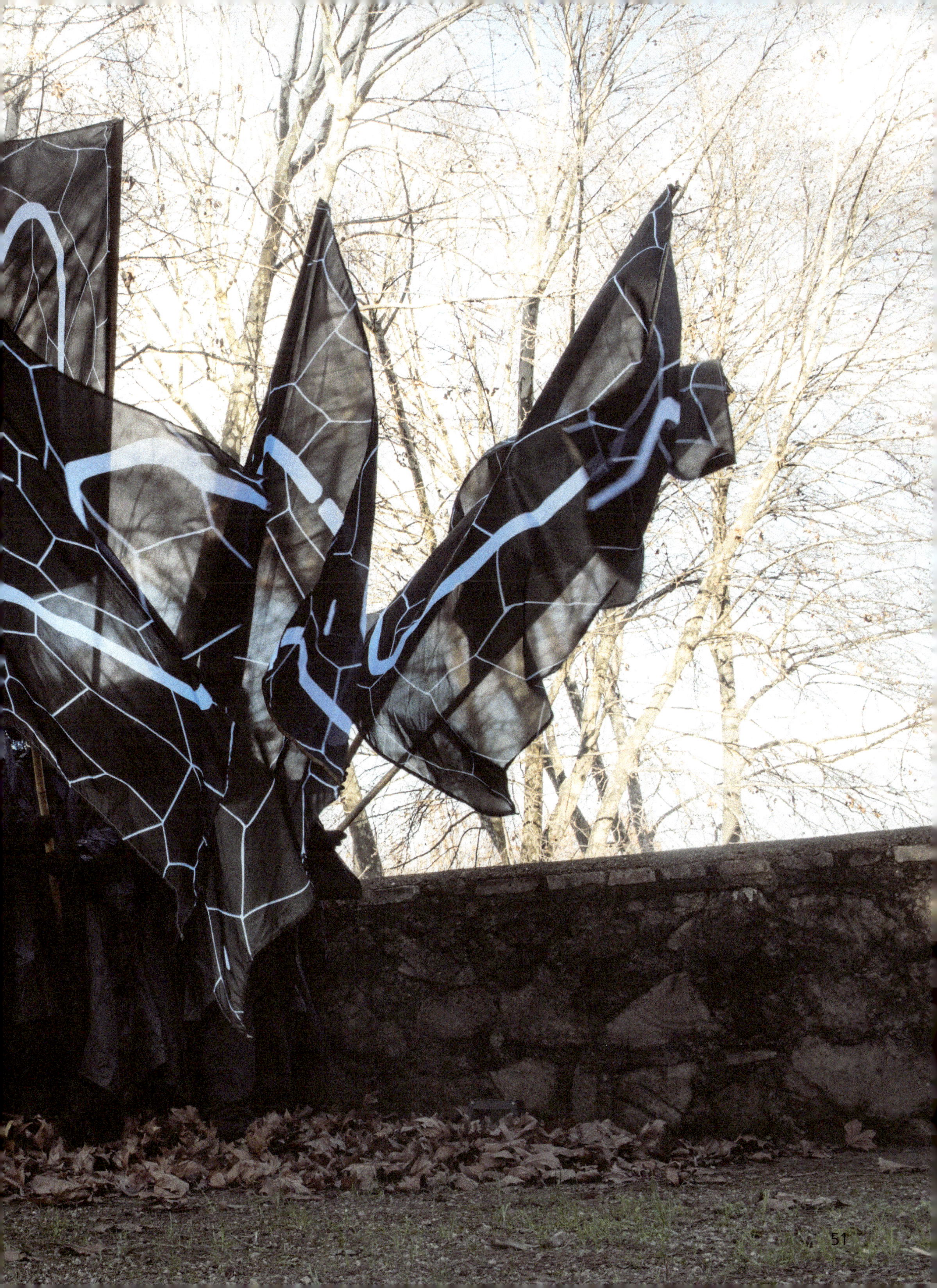

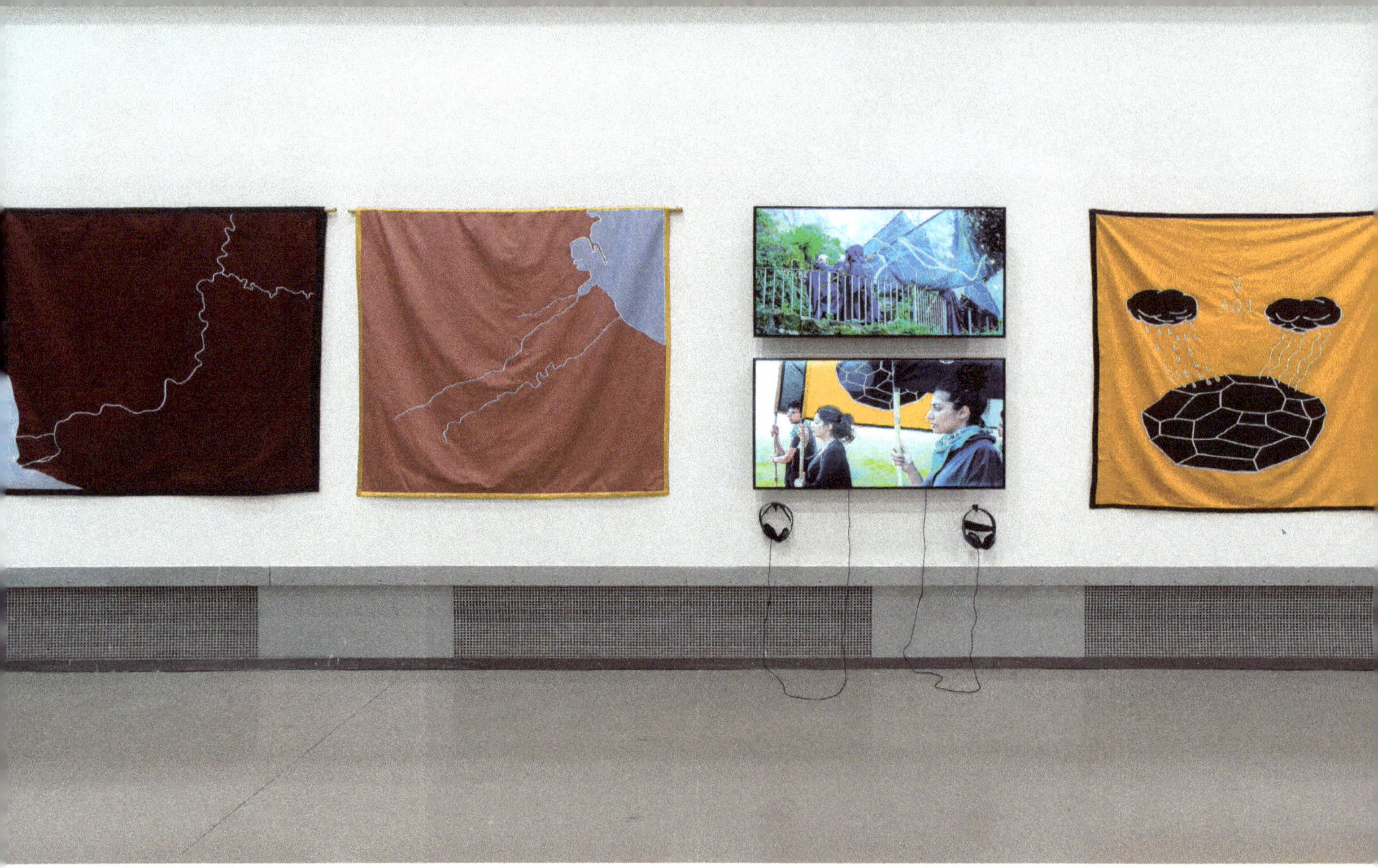

Andrea Conte (Andreco Studio)

Installation view, *Ordo Naturalis Ordo Artificialis*, exhibition view, Fondazione Merz, ZAC, Palermo, 2022.

production activities, and then poured pesticides, industrial chemical pollutants and plastics into it. In the cities the developers forced rivers into concrete channels by building on the banks. The capitalistic society is the cause of global warming that makes glaciers that feed rivers disappear and generates extreme rainfall that turns rivers into destructive floods.

Gone are the times when most of the humans worshiped rivers, because they knew that they depended on them in all respects. Tiberino,* divinity of the Tiber has been forgotten. In the era of the Capitalocene in which ignorance and anthropocentrism are at the highest levels, rivers scream revenge.

The *Tiberina Performance* wasn't made for entertainment but to address ecological issues, the condition of the river in Rome. From every performance, we produced a video, The *Tiberina* video was presented with the *Flumen Project* and screened at the MAXXI Museum in March. I directed fifteen performances in the last fifteen years, almost one a year. And what remains on this performance are videos and the flags. Of course. *The Parata Tiberina* video was been shown in Palermo for the collective show Ordo Naturalis Ordo Artificialis, curated by Beatrice Merz and Agata Polizzi. At the show also presented other three videos, *Parade for the Landscape*, S.M. Leuca 2013, *The state of Matter,* Rome 2020, *Reclaim Air and Water* the video of the performance in Delhi 2019. Delhi in 2018 was addressed as the most polluted city for air pollution in the world, the performance reclaiming air and water in the city thereafter. Near the videos on the same wall are also three tapestries for the Non-human. One shows an imaginary water cycle, the other two, rivers. On the Tapestries the rivers are embroidered, on the red one again the Tiber and the Aniene, and on the pink one there are three rivers of Palermo, which only one is visible now, *The Oreto* and the others two, Papireto and Kemonia are invisible because they were buried, during the evolution of the city, they decide to cover these rivers, so they run in the underground. I decided to make it visible. On the side façade of the building, there are the flags that I use for the *Parade Tiberina.*

Another chapter of the *Climate Art Project* is *Climate 04 -Sea Level Rise*, realized in 2017 in Venice, one of the most affected cities by it. A wall painting shows the recent studies and forecasts related to sea level rise and extreme waves. The wall painting is a data-driven artwork. Considering the bottom of the wall as the average sea level in 2017, measured data, going up it is possible to see the data forecast for 2040, 2080, and 2100 on the base of the IPCC (Intergovernmental Panel for Climate Change), the most relevant institutional agency that releases reports related to climate change.

Considering the study of prof. Stephan Rahmstorf, who considered mostly the contributes of the melting of the polar ice, in 2100 the height is more than 100 cm and in 2200 there will be more than 200 cm.

On the top part of the wall lines trace address the problem related to extreme wave events due to climate change. Variables, parameters, constants and formulas used for evaluating those phenomena are also in the wall painting. Scientific papers addressed the relationship between sea level rise and temperature rise and between temperature rise and CO_2 emissions, so reducing the CO_2 emissions, we can change those sea level rise forecasts.

What to do when there is a huge amount of data and studies? With the help and collaboration of scientists and research centers I decide what to trace on the wall. I prepare a raw sketch and I start to trace. In Venice I decided to not use the maximum value of the sea level prevision, but the average, because it is already scary enough. In the top part of the wall, it is possible to observe data related to the extreme waves. The classical shape that the scientists analyze to find the top of the wave, the highest part, delta H, is also represented on the wall.

The wall painting is hundred meters long by six high and it's the first wall painting ever authorized on the Grand Canal in Venice and is by the Santa Lucia train station. More than six months of meetings were needed to obtain the authorizations in 2017. After five years of the realization, in 2022, the city and the heritage office decided to keep it permanently because of the importance of the artwork themes and the echo that had on the media worldwide. It was completely restored thanks to an initiative of the University Ca' Foscari.

Climate 04 – sea level rise - is a "pointing operation", an artwork that underlines the climatic and social issue, it is a form of agency and environmental advocacy. *The Climate Art Project* wants to reflect also on possible futures, possible alternative scenarios and Best Practices that, for me, are mostly related to plants. From an ecological point of view, the most important things in Venice are the wetlands. The lagoon is fundamental for biodiversity, for water quality and also for protecting Venice and the cost from the sea and the sea level rise. I designed a seven meters high sculpture in iron painted gold with a small garden of lagoon plants underneath. This is another artwork dedicated to the ecosystem, the nature-based solutions, to the importance of the plant.

A similar sculpture I made in Bologna involved climbers. The plants slowly covered the sculpture completely every year. And after in the wintertime, they make it visible again and again, this process makes this sculpture in continuous transformation. This process is something that is part of the concept related to the sculpture, is a way to move the attention from an egoic and anthropocentric point of view to a larger frame, an ecosystem vision. The work of the artist disappears with his ego and the plants replace the structure. For me, actually, the plants become the sculpture. It's a moving sculpture, the plants are part of the sculpture itself. The plants became sculptures.

The tension between Nature – Culture – Society is central in my research. I

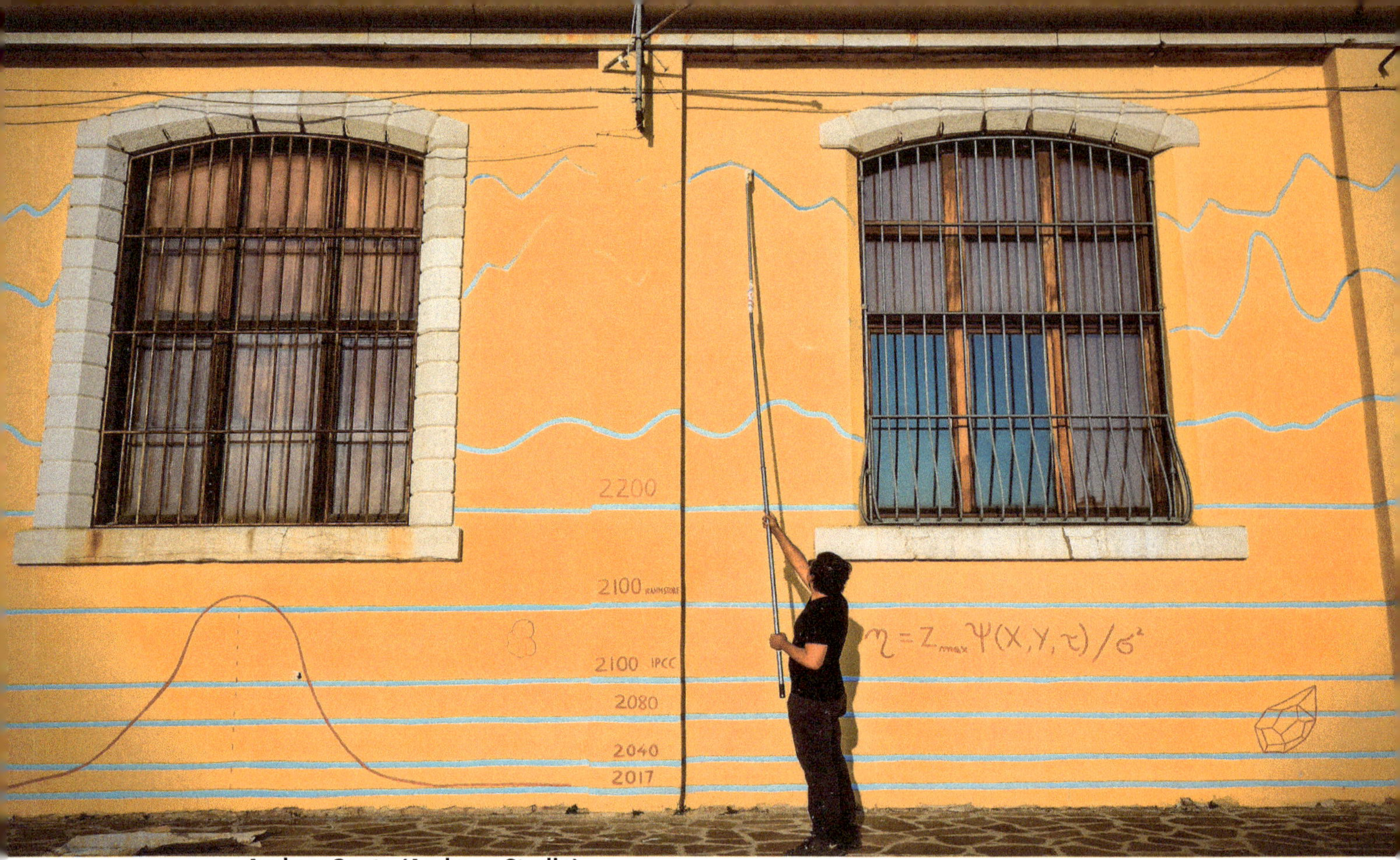

Andrea Conte (Andreco Studio)

Climate 04 - Sea Level Rise, wall painting on sea level rise data forecast - Venice, Photo: Like Agency, 2017

was particularly interested in Bruno Latour and in some reflections from Elisée Reclus, a Geographer that was on these themes at the end of the nineteenth century. Recently a selection of his best essays was published in Italy by Eleuthera, in the book *Nature and Society,* text about subversive geography, I wrote the postscript to the book.

Another fundamental contribution from the debate comes from Donna Haraway's book [insert title]. I really appreciate her "radical imagination" practices that positively affected my work. I was very happy when the Derive Approdi editors asked me to choose one of my paintings for the cover of the Italian version of Donna Haraway *Making Kin not Population*. I want to close it here, I will make it short, so we can have time for more questions to discuss and go deeper on what you find more interesting. Thank you.

Giovanni Aloi: Andrea, wonderful presentation. So many interesting works. It's really exciting to have the opportunity to hear you talk about them because I can sense the enthusiasm that I imagined to be behind them. I have been looking at your work now for some time and there is a sense that you really care about the subject and that you waste no opportunity to experiment with different media in order to convey the message to different audiences. One of the questions I have is with regard to your aesthetics because your work strikes me as iconic. I'm thinking about the paintings and the mural works, the black surfaces that appear to be faceted and fragmented. I was wondering if you could tell us a little bit more about what the aesthetics of your images entails.

Andrea Conte: I used to paint humans and animals a long time ago, with an existentialist approach, and at one point I shifted my interest to other elements. There is an image that represent the Aristotelian interpretation of the "natural hierarchy", the *Scala Naturae* engraving by Charles Bonnet, dated 1781, where

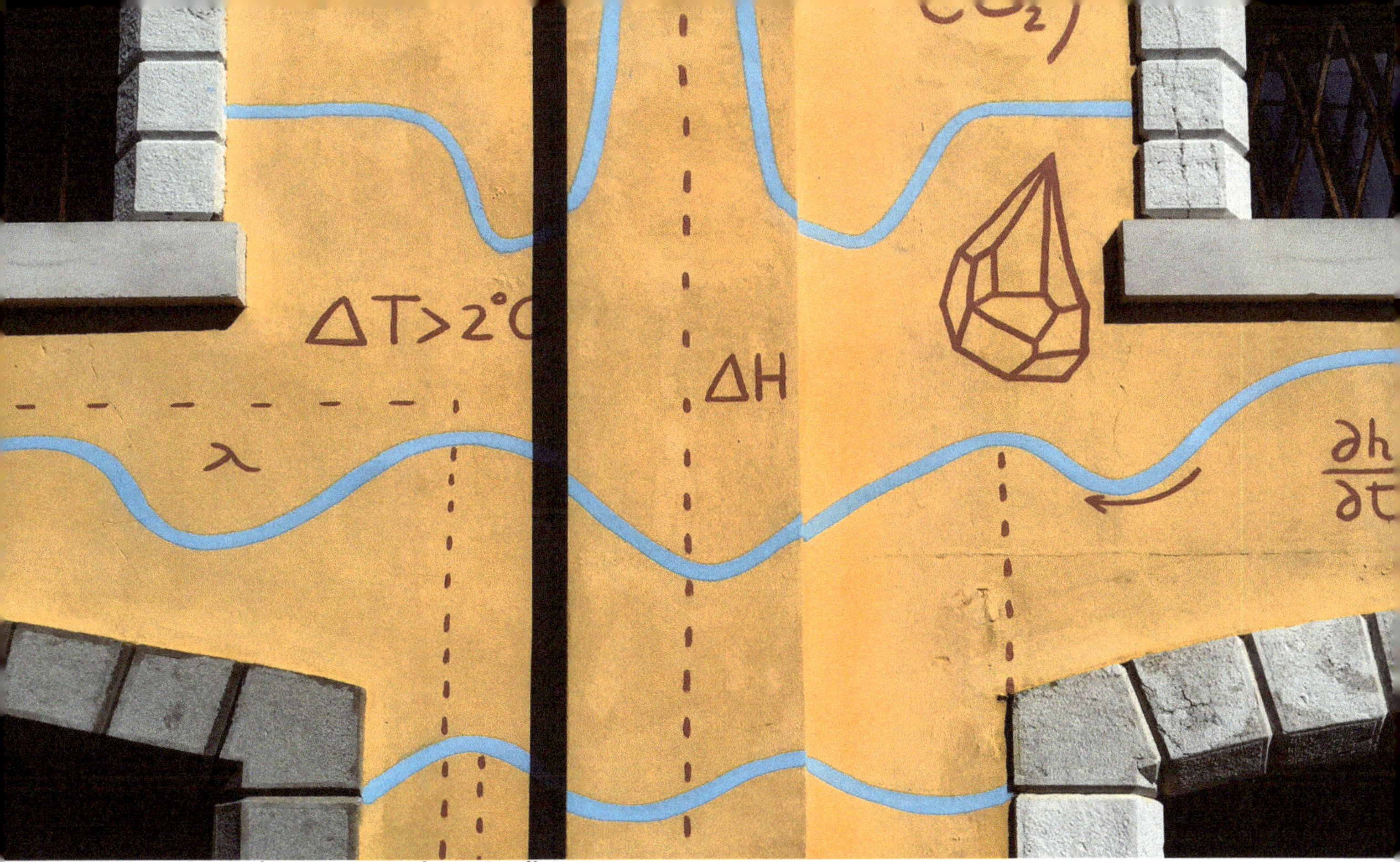

Andrea Conte (Andreco Studio)

Climate 04 - Sea Level Rise, data by l'IPCC and CNR-ISMAR, Venice, Photo: Like Agency. 2017

man is at the top and below the animals, the plants and at the last the minerals and the geology. This represent exactly the anthropocentric point of view that caused most of the environmental crisis and I want to subvert with my art. I am bored with the Renaissance rhetoric of the humans, even worst, Man, at the center of the world at the point that humans are already extinct in my artwork.

I am not representing humans and animals in my works, I wanted to invert the Scala Nature, subverting the anthropocentric hierarchy and giving value to the less considered. Plants, minerals, geology, big rocks, rivers, mountains and the microorganisms in the soil and water, fungi, bacteria's, viruses, biochemical elements. It is a provocation but is also a tentative way to move the anthropocentric perspective in a more ecocentric perspective.

Talking about forms and aesthetics, I try to make images simple, minimal and with strong intrinsic meanings hidden. Someone saw an influence from African Art and from Byzantine icons in my art. Probably the time I have spent traveling and living in different countries has affected my imagination. I am interested in creating a visual set of icons to support contemporary research and innovation related to sustainability, political ecology, climate and social justice. The flags and tapestries are elements of this visual set of iconic images to envision other possible desirable futures.

GA: Yeah, this comes across I think something is interesting about the accessibility of your images which is something that I find complicated in terms of the range of artists that I have encountered working with the environment. One of the things that I've noticed is that some artists tend to reinterpret or follow a personal dimension that's very much driven by an emotional reconnection with nature, which is also very interesting. And there are artists who are more engaged with the scien-

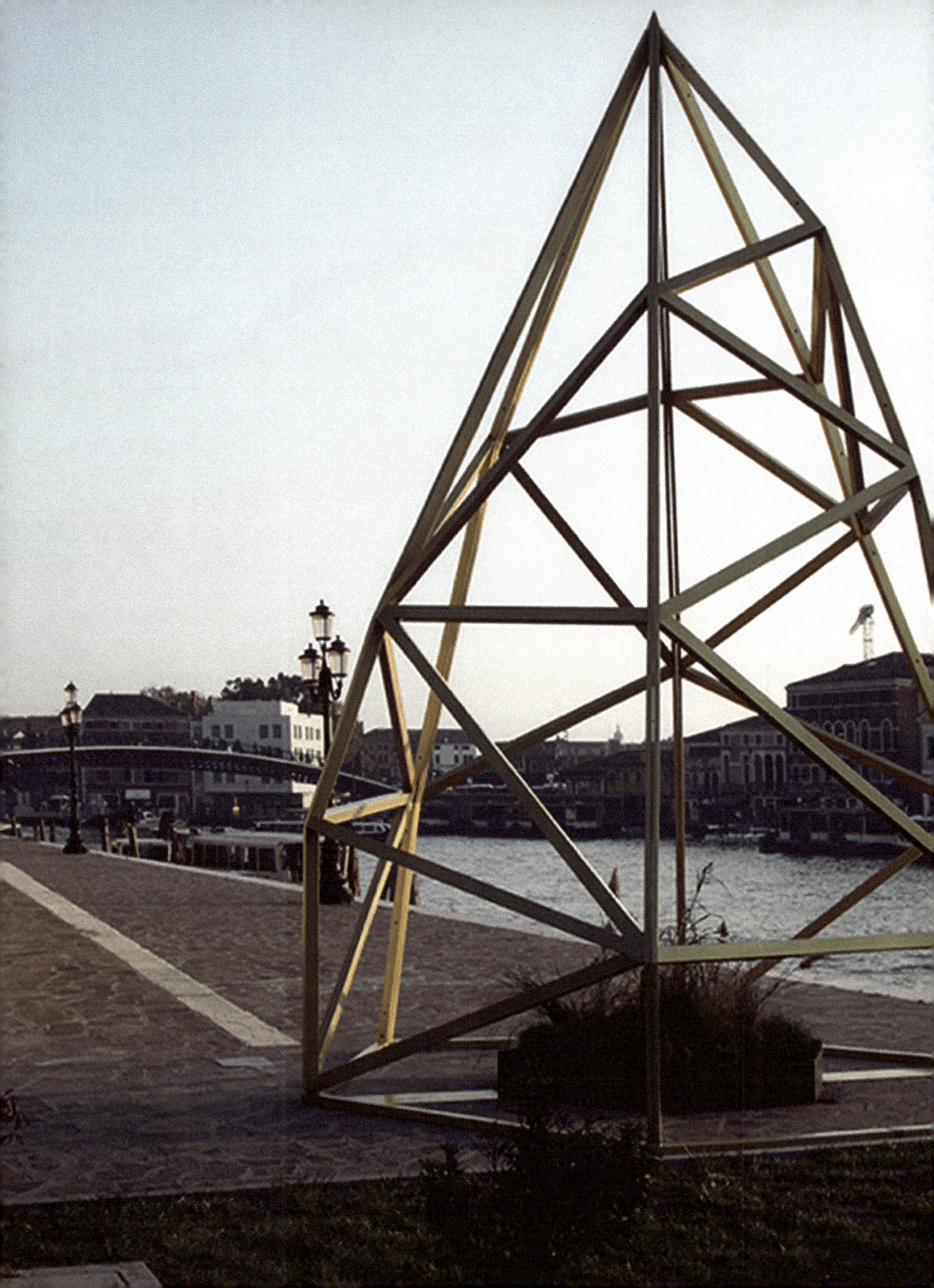

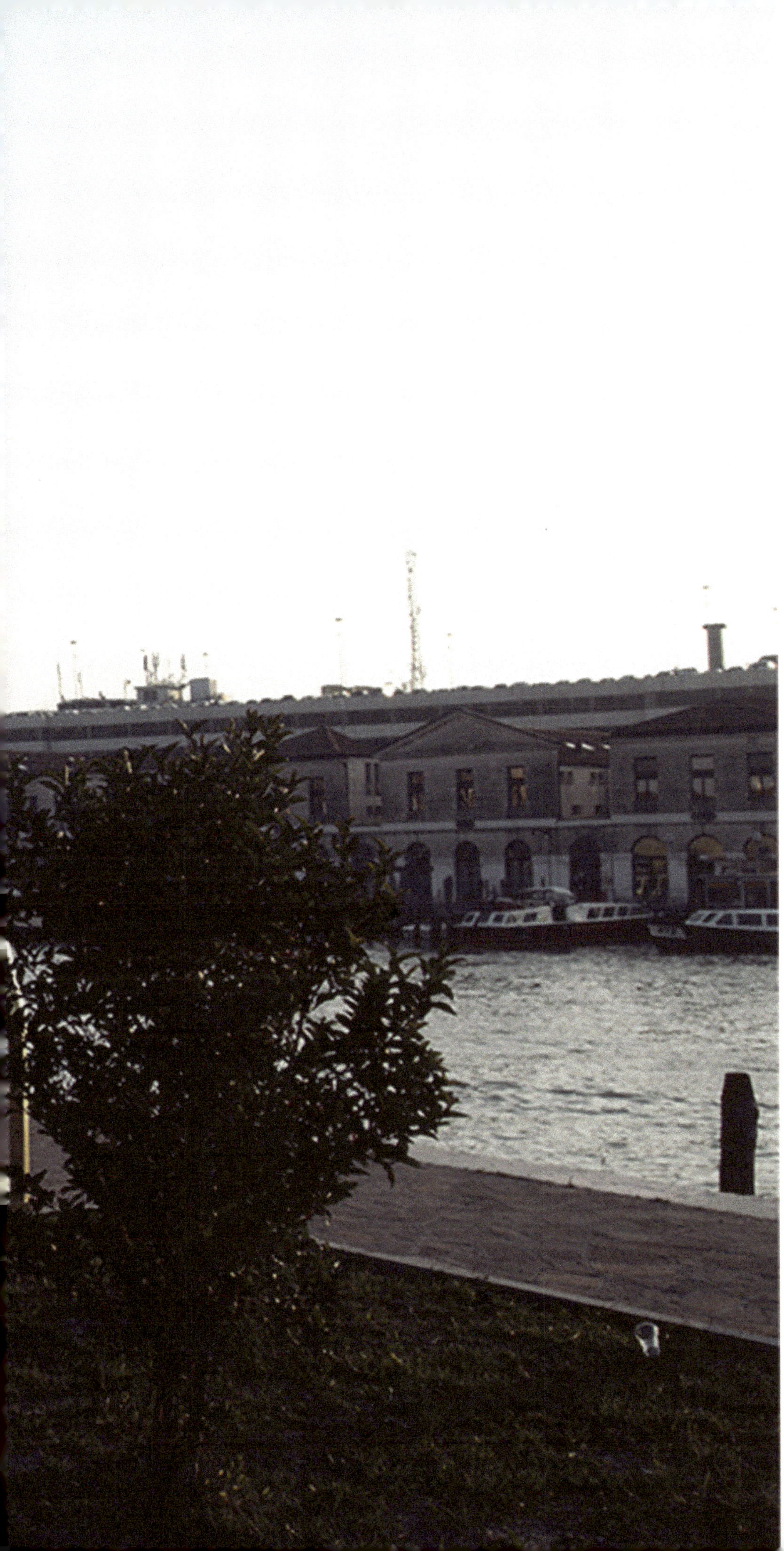

Andrea Conte (Andreco Studio)
Landmark 02, Climate 04 - Sea Level Rise, Venice, Metal sculpture and wetland plants garden,
Photo: Giovanni Fimminghi, 2017
© Andrea Conte - Andreco.org

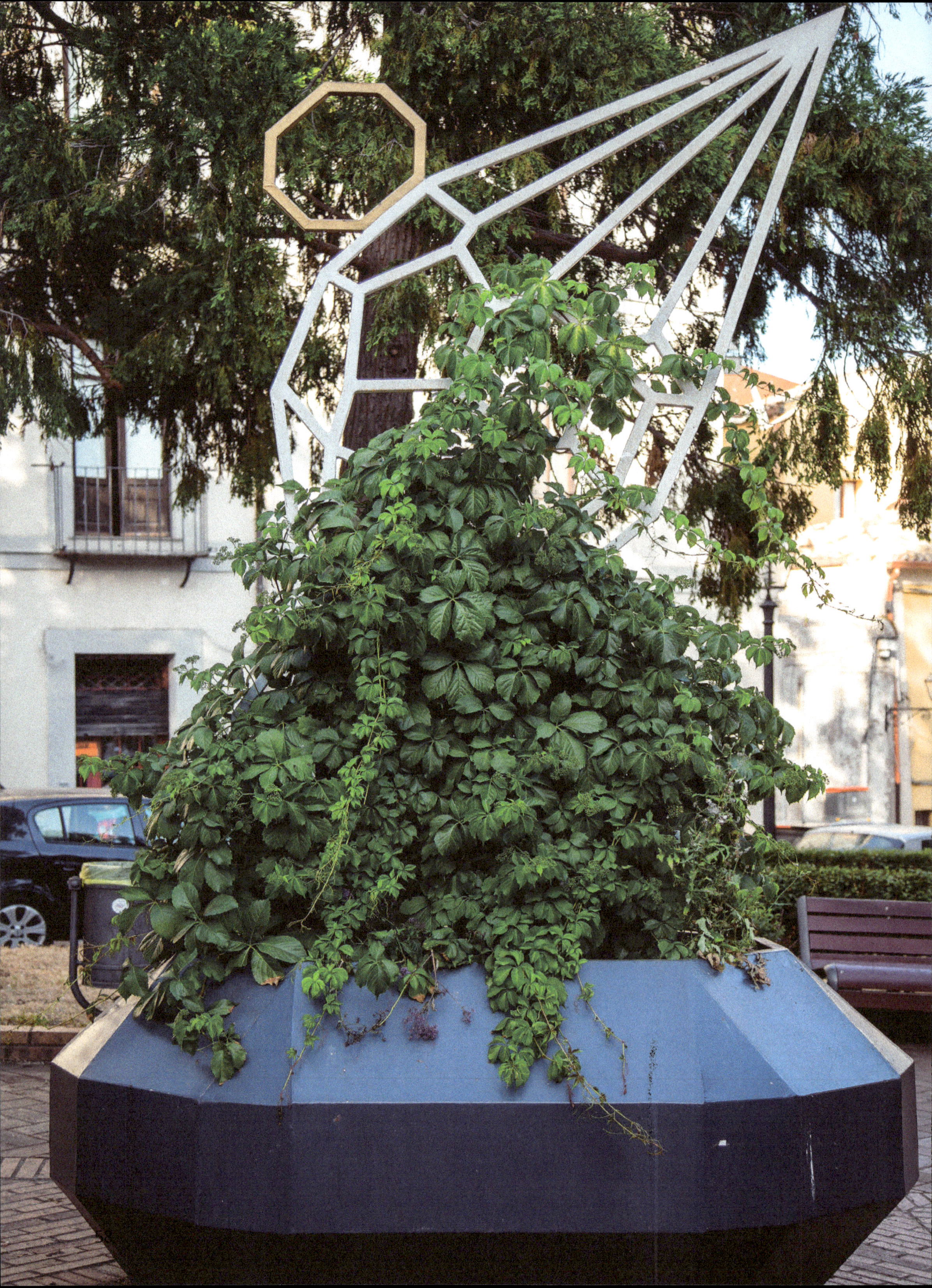

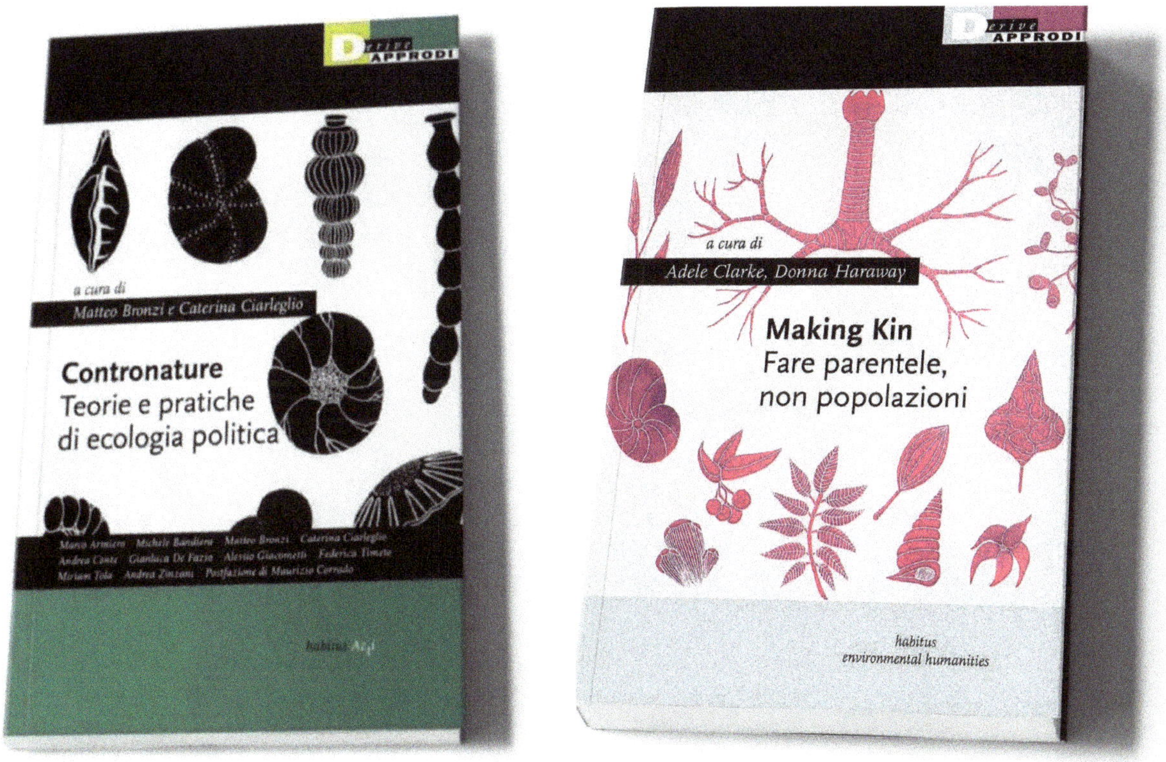

Andrea Conte (Andreco Studio)

Left: *Contronature, Theories and Practices of Political Ecologies,* book, curated by MAtteo Bronzi and Caterina Ciarlegio, text by: Marco Armiero, Michele Bandiera, Andrea Conte, Gianluca De Fazio, Alessio Giacometti, Federica Timeto, Miriam Tola, Andrea Zinzani, Maurizio Corrado. Book cover and drawings by Andrea Conte (Andreco Studio), 2022 © Deriveapprodi

Right: Donna Haraway, A. Clark, *Making Kin*, book, Deriveapprodi, - book cover by Andreco 2022 © Deriveapprodi

tific data and with the question of how to translate this data so that it becomes accessible to people. Of course, you're a scientist by training, so I'm assuming that data is not that mysterious to you. Can you tell us how you negotiate these two dimensions? And how do you elaborate data into visuals so that it produces a message that goes beyond just illustrating data? It seems to me that your work does a lot more than that, so it becomes art.

AC: You're right. It's very difficult to keep together the scientific part with the more emotional part. The scientific data with the tribal and ritualistic part of my work. But since I like to bring the complexity in my work, I try to put together different visions. A multidisciplinary approach It's needed for analyze complex topic such as climate change, or city making, or urban planning, or public administration. The ecosystem we are part of is complex and all connected. A multi-view, a lateral and critical view is fundamental when we try to approach complexity. I want to quote Andrew Revkin, who I met at the Earth Institute of Columbia University in New York. He said "how to convey urgency and complexity at the same time?" I think this is the point: it's important to speak about scientific data and the relations between causes and effects, keeping the emotional part and the complexity of the work. I don't want to simplify the concept too much and become Naive and superficial, just because it is needed to communicate to all.

Another important fact in my work is that "the images are open". I like to think the images I realize, open to the interpretation of the public. The art language is more ambiguous compared with other languages, such as the scientific

Andrea Conte (Andreco Studio)

Melancolia, metal sculpture with climbers plant, Altrove, Catanzaro, 2017 © Andrea Conte - Andreco.org

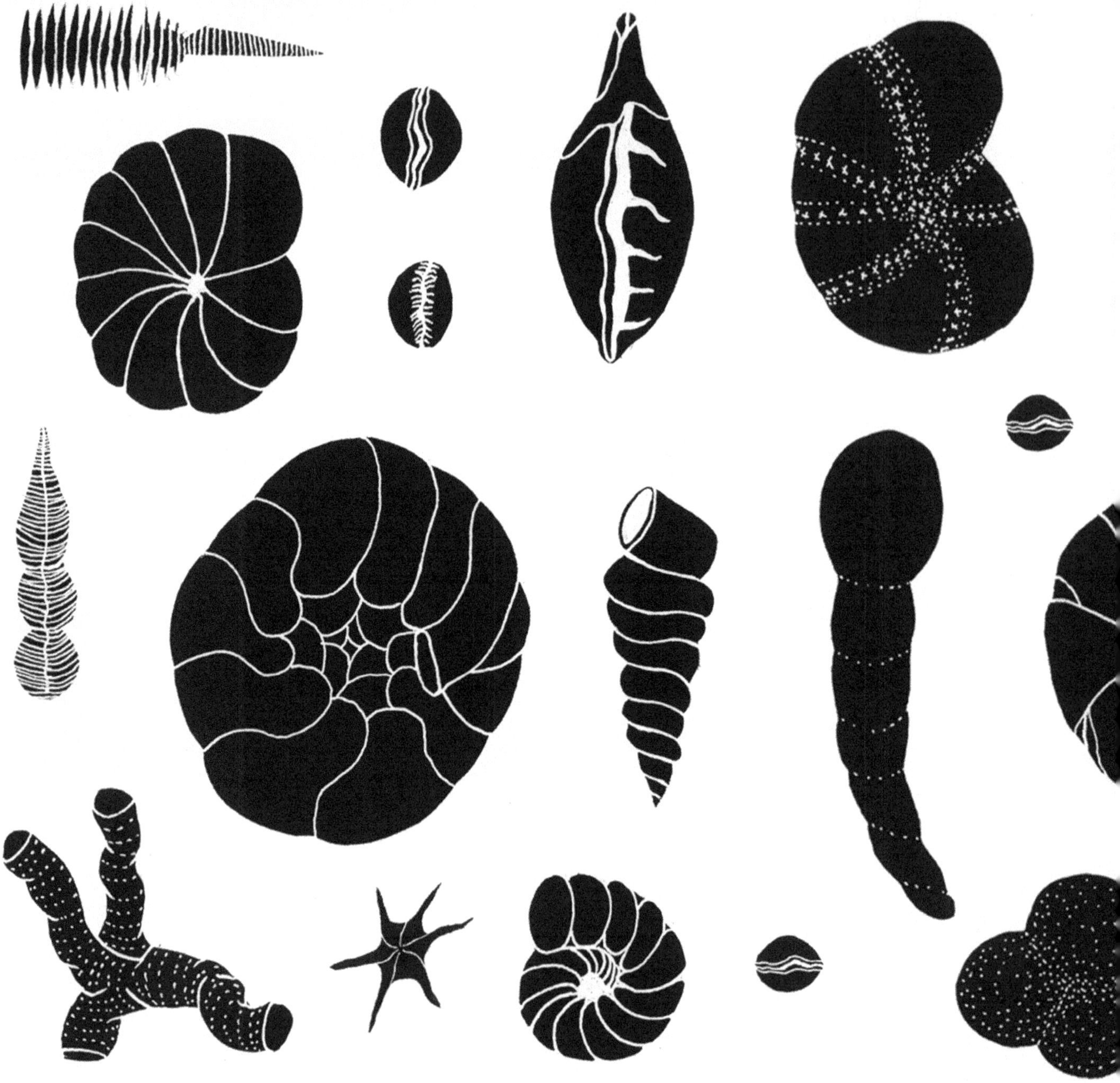

Andrea Conte (Andreco Studio)

Many Bioindicators, acrylic on paper, 2018 © Andrea Conte - Andreco.org

one. The message of the image is completed by who is observing it. It depends on his cultural background and his experience in life. This is why art can touch the sensibility of the persons, better than other languages, they can make it for themselves, they can feel it and connect to personal memories and feelings. It's about the perception of the symbolic images. The artworks maintain always a secret part that can't be explained, that is in the sphere of mystery. It is difficult but I'm trying to keep the complexity and urgency at the same time.

GA: Who are your artistic references. You've also talked about philosophy, you mentioned Donna Haraway. You also quoted Timothy Morton, who's another very important voice in the discussion on the Anthropocene. It sounds like you're also not just negotiating the scientific and the artistic lens, but you're also engaging with philosophical

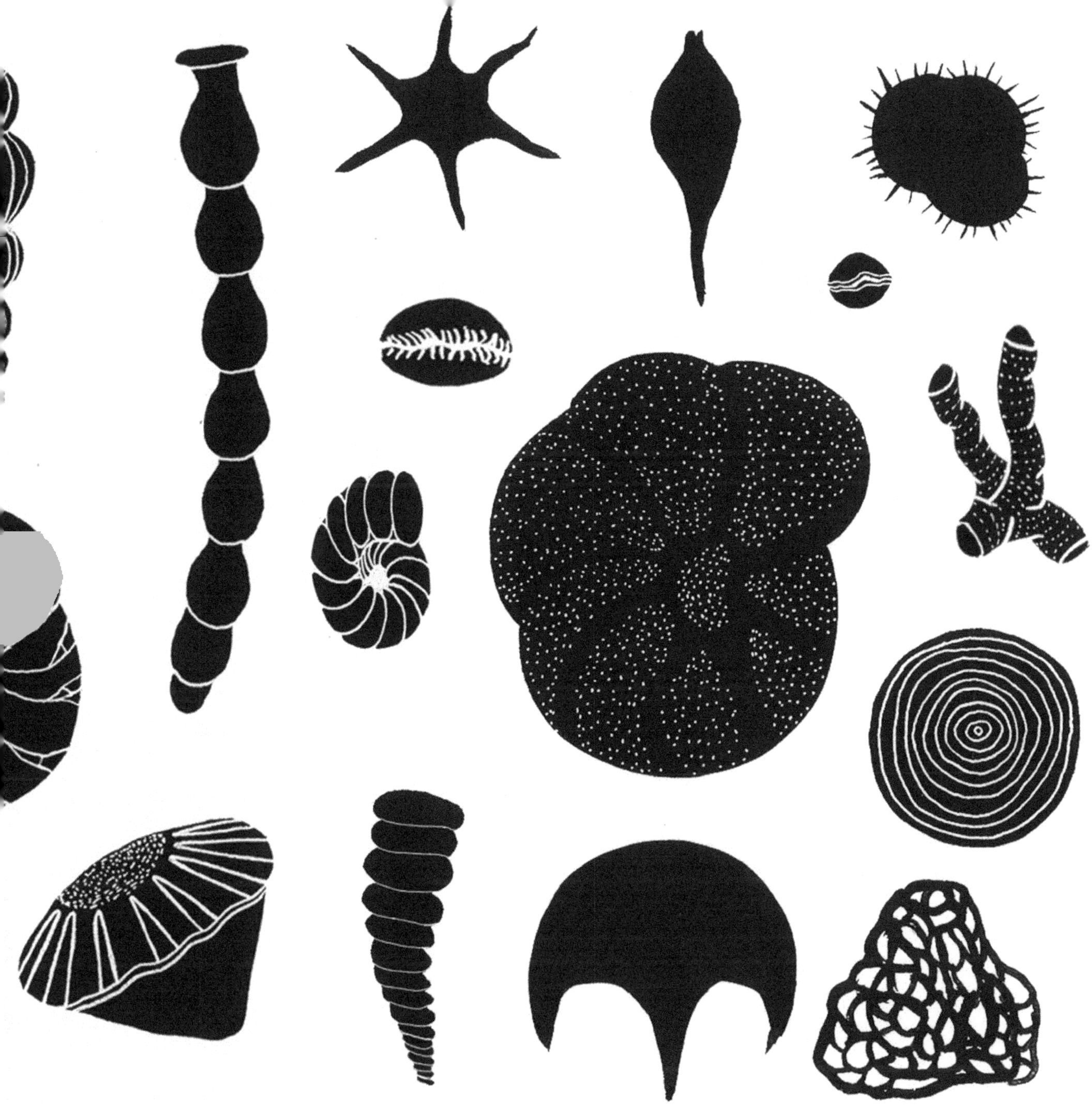

discourse, which is important, so important, I think, to actually negotiating the two.

AC: Yes, it's true I am very influenced by philosophers and Intellectuals especially the one that questioned the role of the humans on the planet in relation with the ecosystem: Descola, Deleuze, Latour, Reclus, Thoreau, Kropotkin, Haraway, Mancuso, Coccia. Regarding artists, usually, when someone speaks about my work, mention as reference the Land Art and the Arte Povera movements and of course Joseph Beuys and his Social Sculpture idea. I had the opportunity and the honor to participate in collective shows with artworks of Oppenheimer, Mario Merz, Giuseppe Penone, Ana Mendieta, Sol Lewit and J. Beuys. All artists that I appreciate deeply.

I always felt connected to an Italian artist in Rome that is Gianfranco Baruchello, (sadly he passed the way during the time of the transcription of this text)

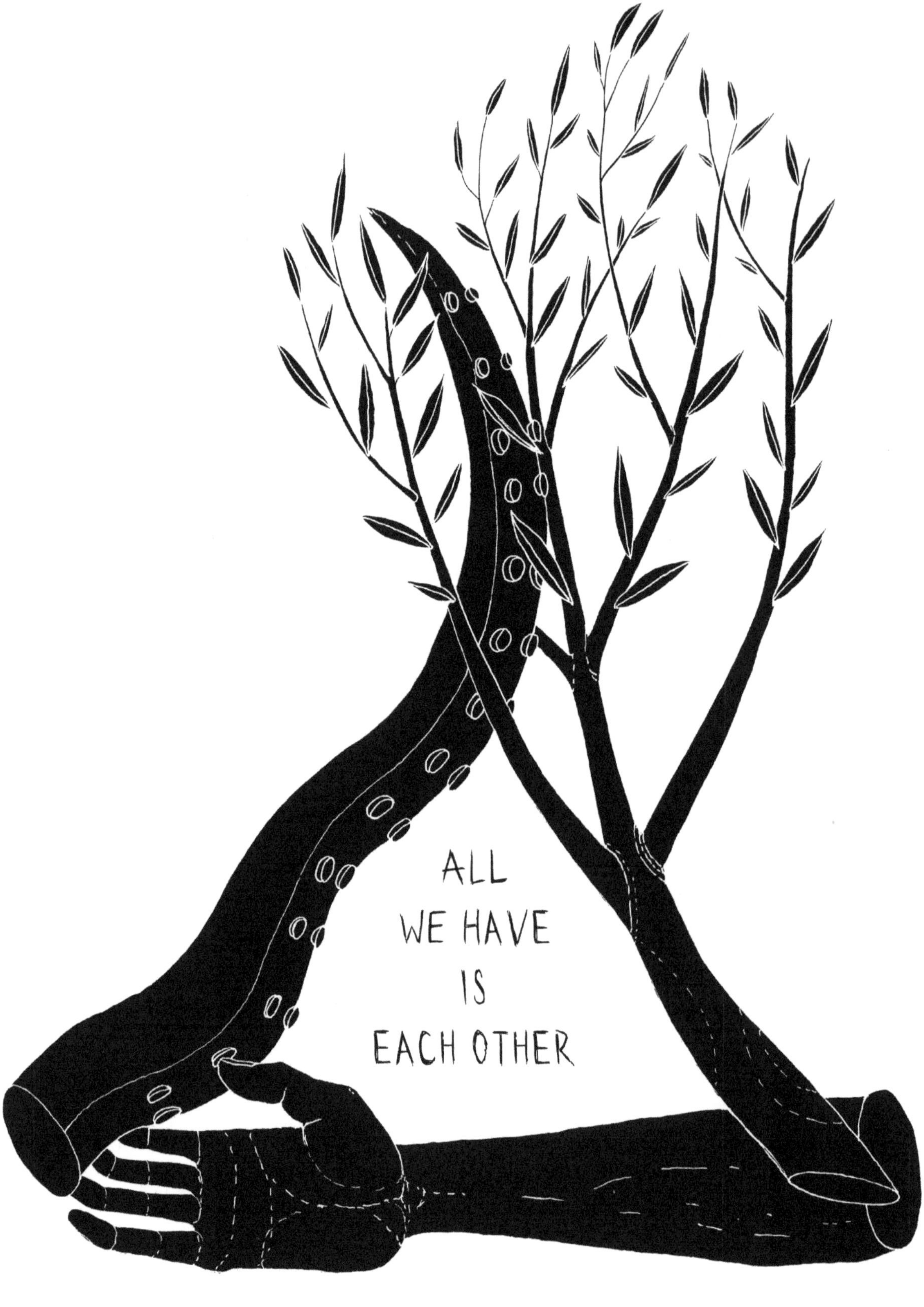

MUTUAL AID

he did a project at the end of the 80's between art and agriculture, called Agricola Cornelia, that I loved.

I am interested in the artists and the intellectuals that researched between ecology and society, they are part of my theoretical background. I am also attracted by some artists for their approach, such as Duchamp, the Cobra group and Enrico Baj, for the freedom of expression and the way they experiment with multimedia. As you mention, it is important for me to experiment with many media.

GA: It's striking how you engage with and combine different aesthetics as well as different media in ways that again seem to be very natural. I'm also curious about your interest in plants because it recurs a lot. It's obviously a subject you have talked about tonight, but you also mentioned how it is one of your main subjects.

Could tell us a little bit more about how you became interested in plants and also what role they play in your everyday life beyond your artistic engagement.

AC: My house is full of plants, of course.

GA: Mine too!

AC: Ten years ago, I took a Ph.D. on Nature Based Solution and appropriate technologies for sustainable resource management. It was peculiar at that time because, in engineering, there was no course about plants. My Post Doc, advisor Prof. Alessandra Bonoli from the University of Bologna gave me the opportunity to teach for eight years classes about two topics. The first was about Appropriate Technologies for international cooperation, which consider traditional techniques from the indigenous community as forms of sustainable water and energy management. The course now cold be called "a decolonized approach to technologies". The second was about Green Infrastructures, NBS and how plants can mitigate Climate Change effects in urban and rural areas. How important are plants in water and energy management, for the heat Island effect mitigation, the high temperature mitigation, the noise and air pollution reduction? At the time my classes were considered weird, it was uncommon to talk about plants as infrastructures in an engineering faculty. Not for me, I was always very fascinated by the plants, and in particular, some of them like the ferns.

In the last seven years I have also collaborated with biologists, such as Laura Passatore from the National Research Council, who is an expert in Phytoremediation. Engineers, we see plants on a bigger scale, as green infrastructure and we are not very expert in the biological process that happens in the different species of plants themselves, this is more a biologist's job, I learned many things from the scientists I collaborate and from the plants. I also learned by the indigenous communities I had the opportunity to meet during the time I spent in Latin America and Africa.

GA: You mentioned how working with plants until recently was unusual, or even like, contemplating the idea of working with plants was seen unusual, as unusual in institutions. Things have changed very rapidly on that front.

Luca di Vito: How do people react to your work given that communicating important issues lies at the core of what you do?

AC: People have different reactions. The Venice work is a "pointing operation" to underline an urgency. Showing the data and the scientific forecasts there, in Venice, is scary. I believe the people are worried but at the same time they unconsciously remove the problem. The Venetians know very well the sea level rise problem, better than me, they experience it. The frequency of the extreme

Andrea Conte (Andreco Studio)

All we have is each others, Interspaces mutual aid, Screenprint,made the the Kropotkin book *Mutual Aid* edited by Eleuthera, 2020 © Andrea Conte Andreco.org

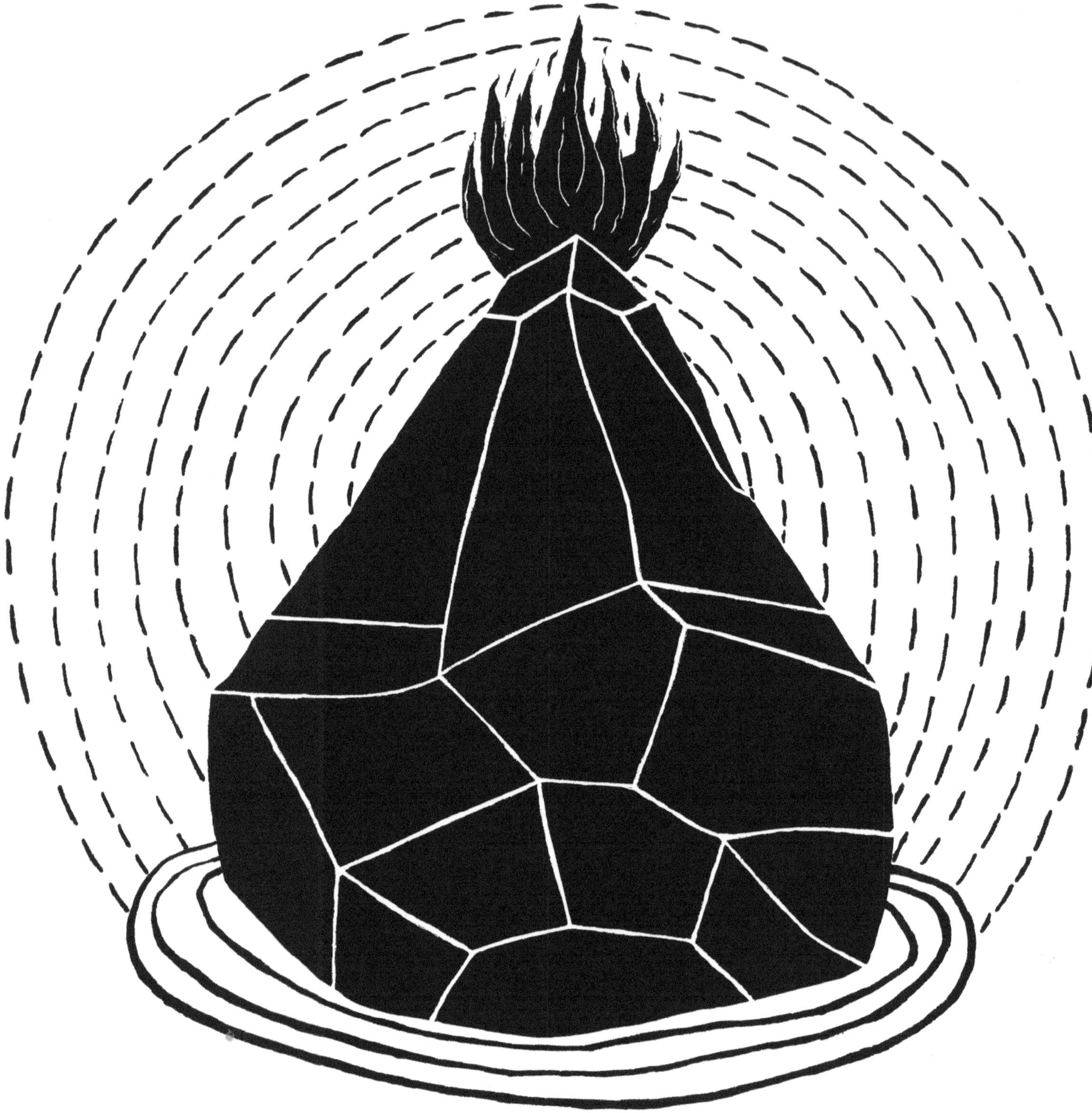

Andrea Conte (Andreco Studio)

Petra, Acrylic on Paper, 2013 © Andrea Conte - Andreco.org

climate event is every time higher. They know that in a hundred years, Venice will probably sink and disappear if we continue this way. If the trend of greenhouse gasses emission will be constant, we will head for disaster. We know this but we remove it from our minds because it's too painful to think that your city is going to disappear. It's a psychological operation that removes the problem because it's too big, and they feel it is impossible to deal with. Sea level rise as the effect of global warming is a Hyper-object, as Timothy Morton would have it. Something so largely distributed in time and space that is difficult to understand. Mentioning the Global Climate Crisis, the imminent disaster without mentioning solutions can "paralyze" the people. More the problem is bigger, the more the people feel small, useless, that nothing they can do, and nothing will save us.

This is why I also like to speak about "what we can do", what governments must do. I talk about plants and nature-based solutions, possible climate actions, best practices, and how we can envision a sustainable future.

GA: How optimistic are you in the context of climate change? I feel like all that we do truly matters and it is changing people's perspectives. I remember 20 years ago, especially in academia, that wasn't the case. Now you can have conversations about plants, animals, and climate change. There are courses on climate change, the 6th Extinction, and the panorama is changing very rapidly. What is your take on how rapidly is it changing and how do you feel the response of different governments to climate change reflects our conversations? Can we afford to be optimistic?

AC: The ecological transition, that everybody speaks about, is not happening or not fast enough. We have to hurry up, scientists say that we are running out of time. The path of change is visible, but I also see interest in making it slower. It's a big risk to slow down the process. It's time to change all the industrial sectors using renewable resources, reducing the consumption, reusing and recycling materials in a close circular economy. I believe this is needed but isn't enough to make a proper transition happen. Isn't only a technical transition; to make it happen the transition should be also cultural, philosophical, social, ecological and artistic. We have to change our ways to stay in society and on this planet. And it's not only a technical point where we must change perspective. This is why I think that also from an artistic point of view we have to completely change perspective.

Let's say that sometimes I'm optimistic, and sometimes very scared, but what I feel the most is that we are too slow in this transition process.

GA: Yes, I agree with you. Our response is too slow. Especially if, like me, you've been involved in this conversation for a long time. And when you look back and you consider that 20 years ago, there was almost no receptivity to these subjects. 20 years have gone by. And we know that the last 20 years have been terrible for the degradation of the health of the planet. So, the question really is can we afford to wait another 20? However, I have to say I was really pleased to see that your work is now featured in a college art book.

AC: This year I was mentioned in the book about international contemporary performing art by Teresa Macri', (*Slittamenti della Performance. Dal 2000 al 2022*) adopted by universities and academy of art in Italy, my work is cited in the chapter about "Social Parade" with Jeremy Deller and Francis Alÿs.

I was also mentioned in a new college art history book, *L'Arte del Mondo. Il mondo dell'Arte. 5. Dal Simbolismo ad oggi.*" by Piero Adorno and Adriana Mastrangelo. In the updated version, there is also a chapter about the 'Ecological Theme in Contemporary Art' and my work is covered with Olafur Eliasson, Ana Mendieta and Pierre Huyghe.

Of course, it's almost at the end of the book, so I am not sure that the teachers will reach the contemporary art part. I hope the students will open the book reversely, pushed by curiosity. As I used to do.

I put my hopes in the kids and I like to speak with them. As you know, in the past with the Climate Art Project we also organized workshops for kids. It's important to find a dialogue with them on ecological and social issues. Most of the time they are very creative, I always say that they should find new innovative solutions that we are not able to imagine.

GA: Yeah, I agree. I think about my history of art books. When I was sixteen or seventeen. Ecology, animals, and the environment were not a subject. One could

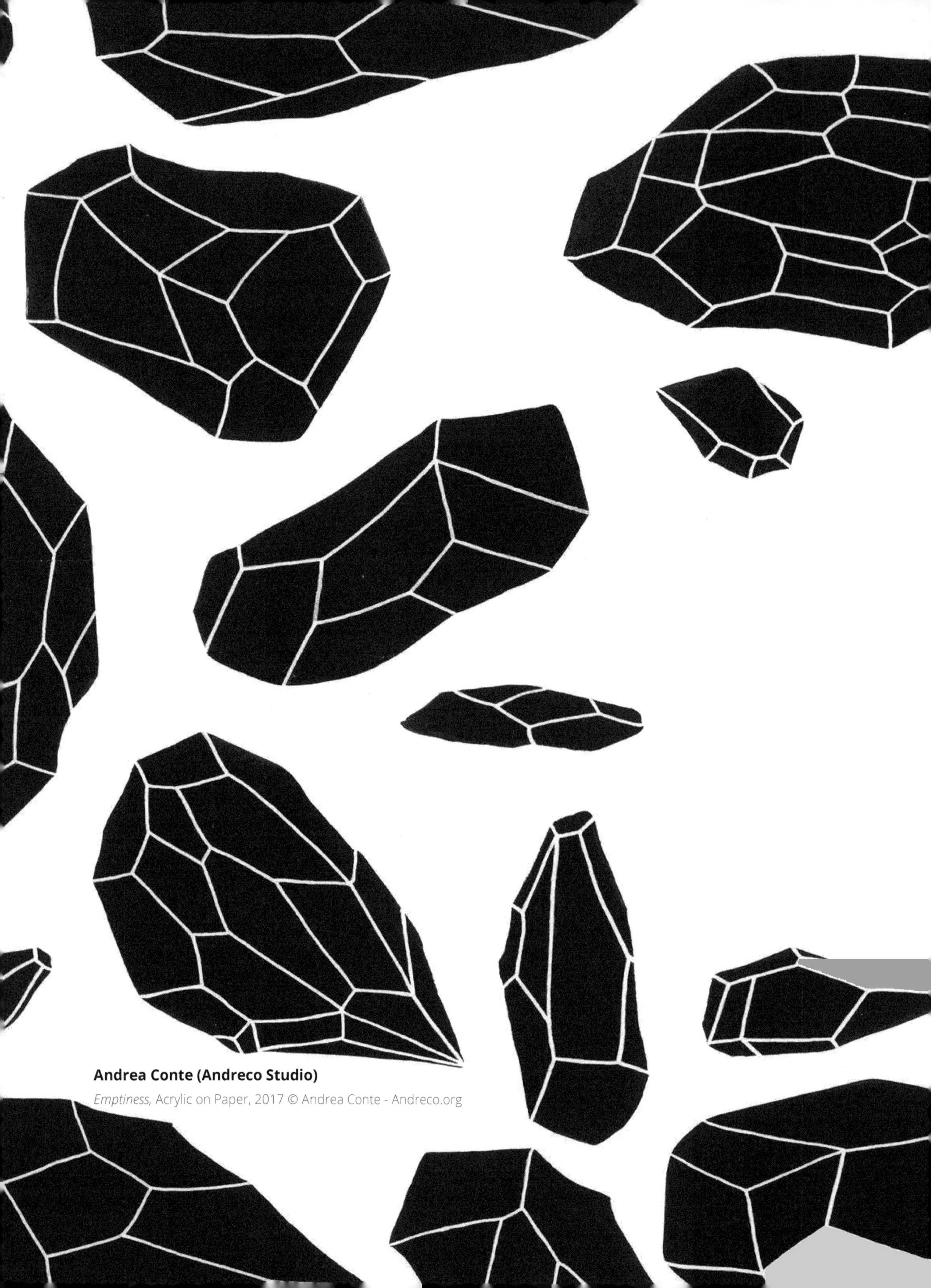

Andrea Conte (Andreco Studio)

Emptiness, Acrylic on Paper, 2017 © Andrea Conte - Andreco.org

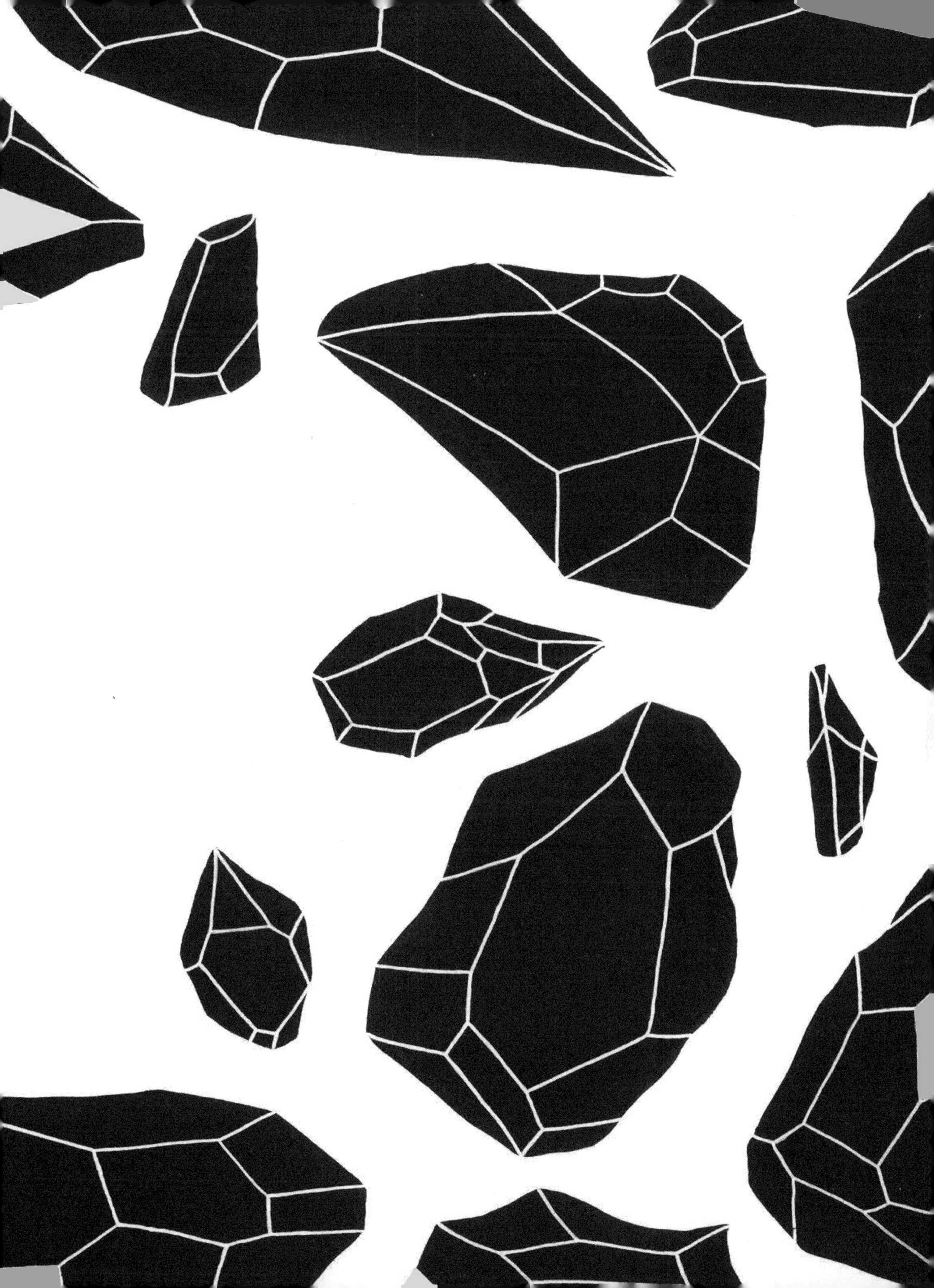

barely see works of art involving animals and plants beyond the Dutch Golden Age. And we know that the Dutch Golden Age is not about nature. The flowers are symbolic of Christian values, morals, and ethical values. So, that is a kind of false economy where one looks at nature only to see our reflection. And I think it's great that at least art books are starting to incorporate chapters on ecology, even if at the end.

AC: I believe this new generation of teachers will speak more about the present in general. Looking at these new updated books there is more space for contemporary culture. I believe it is necessary to build knowledge also about recent history and all social rights in general, everything changes fast in society and the risk is that the internet will build the recent history, a recent browser history. It is important to speak at school about the urgency of our time, we have constantly to adapt, "living with the trouble" mentioning Ana Tsing, and we must do it fast.

In *Flumen,* public artwork on rivers and riparian green spaces, we have a program based on Citizen Science and part of it is dedicated to the kids. We collaborate with schools and associations for environmental education. The schools are interested in outdoor activities. The citizen science approach transforms the kid into a scientist. During the *Flumen* workshops they learn how to take a sample soil and water, how to analyze a sample and how to analyze a river with physical-chemical and biological analysis and tests. There are many outdoor experiences for the students, many are on the ecological themes and are perfect to disseminate scientific knowledge and raise their environmental awareness.

GA: That's wonderful to hear. We need to educate children differently. We need to educate them from a very young age. I think primary school is actually one of the most I mean the whole education range is important. It is probably the most important in the sense that if we can instill some excitement for nature in these children then they probably care for it later on. Even my generation and yours probably were not really invited to look at nature and value it too much as part of the curriculum especially. It was very disconnected from what was going on with the environment and that certainly hasn't helped anybody. I think also about what you do and then we'll let you go because it's almost midnight in Italy. It's really interesting because what I see in your practice, just in your work as a scientist, and artist, working with different media performances, and two-dimensional installations in the gallery space also, we could go on for hours talking about your engagement with Bio Arts, because when you work with plants, that falls into another dimension.

The philosophical backbone that you follow. And also, this field workshop activity that you have where it's hands enthusing children and partaking into education programs. There's really to me a very interesting "artist model" of the future that luckily is also the artist of the present. In this case, it's a format that I hope other artists will take on more readily because I know you also do gallery work, I've seen some beautiful prints that you do. There is a dimension in which the more kind of old school idea of being an artist can be integrated with new ways of being an artist which entails teaching, running workshops and working in different and new scenarios. I think that's great. Just wanted to mention that to me, it's one of the most interesting aspects of how you see yourself as an artist.

AC: Art is research and artworks are applied research. Realizing a piece is like making a physical prototype of an intangible idea, a key study of a theory. I try to translate a conceptual thesis with as many as possible languages and points of views; with a multimedia and trans-disciplinary approach.

I keep experimenting all the time considering the risk of making mistakes as part of the process. When you try something new, you can go wrong. Researching and experimenting is a never-ending adventure pushed by curiosity. This is the most important part for me: building a strong, research-based, concept; from this "platform" make a jump into a vision. The vision becomes the artwork, and the jump is the artist's work.

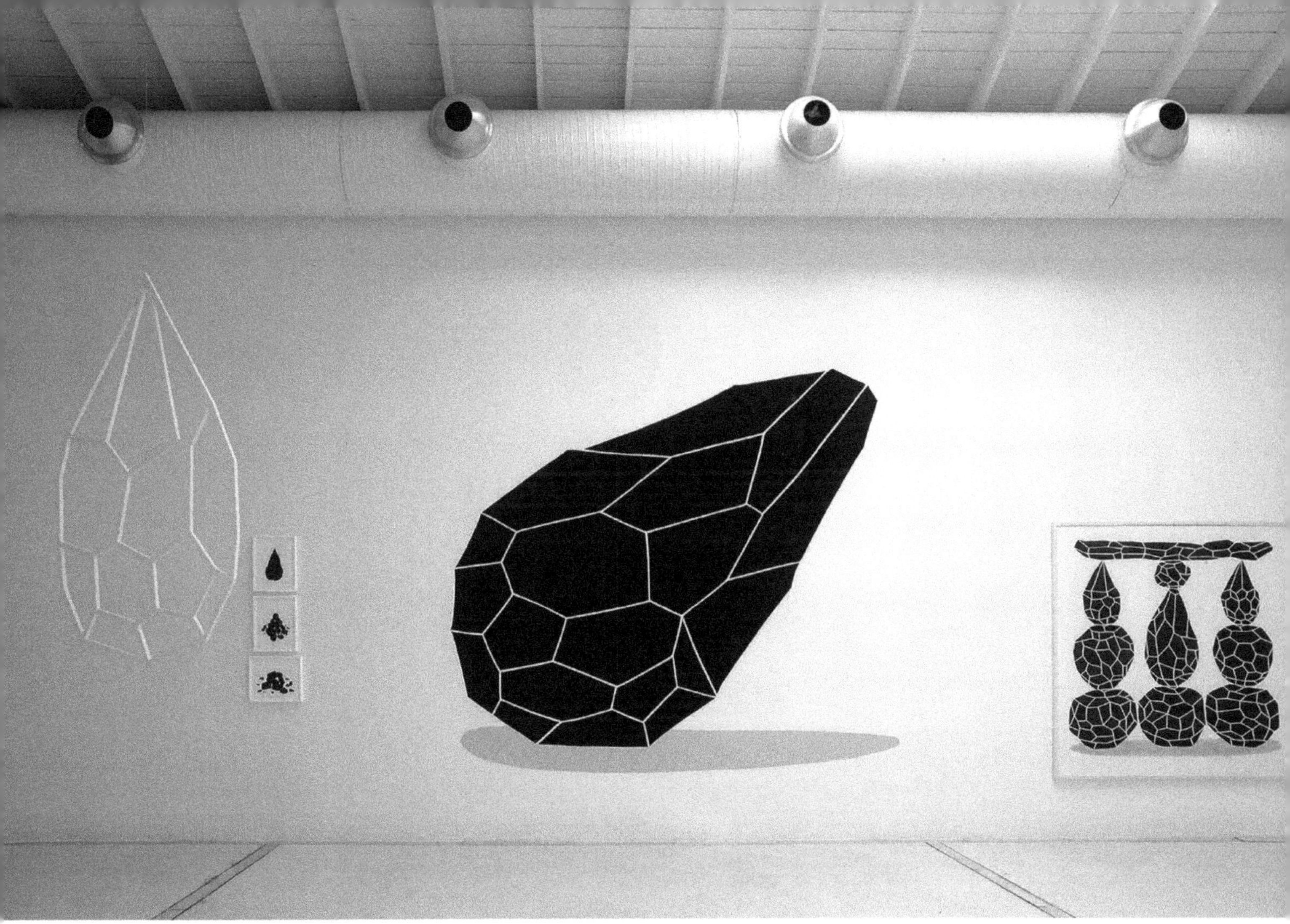

Andrea Conte (Andreco Studio)

Back to the Land, show, installation view, painting, metal sculpture, drawing and wall drawing, Studio La Città, Gallery, Verona, Photo: Pelicula snc by Sereni Michele Alberto and Barbuio Beatrice 2016 © Andrea Conte - Andreco.org

Andrea Conte director at Studio Andreco, works between art, science and environmental, social and climatic justice related themes. Andrea Conte is a visual artist and also an environmental engineer PhD specialise in sustainability and resources management in different climate conditions, he did Post. Doc researches on green technologies and Nature Based Solutions for urban sustainability collaborating with the School of Engineering and Architecture of the University of Bologna and the Columbia University of New York City. Since 2000 Andreco is researching between science, ecology, activism, urbanism, anthropology, philosophy, biology and symbolism, on the base of this transdisciplinary researches he creates a conceptual and visual language. *Climate Art Project* is one of his main projects about Art and Climate Actions. *Flumen*, is his project related to the rivers and the wetlands conservation and environmental advocacy. Both of the projects are developed in collaboration with research centers, cultural institutions, universities, environmental groups and local communities. Andrea Conte uses many techniques to represent his art, from public installations to videos, performances or wall paintings, drawings and storytelling. Studio Andreco worked for international festivals, museums and galleries; won the special price of the "Talent Prize 2017" at Macro Museum of Contemporary art of Rome, 2016, the international price for rural regeneration Jazzi, Selected Artist for the Gran Tour d'Italie of the Ministry of Culture MIBAC 2019, Selected for the Italian Oscar prize for the environmental communication 2019 related to Climate Change.

Darya Tsymbalyuk
Untitled. Drawing. 2020 © Darya Tsymbalyuk

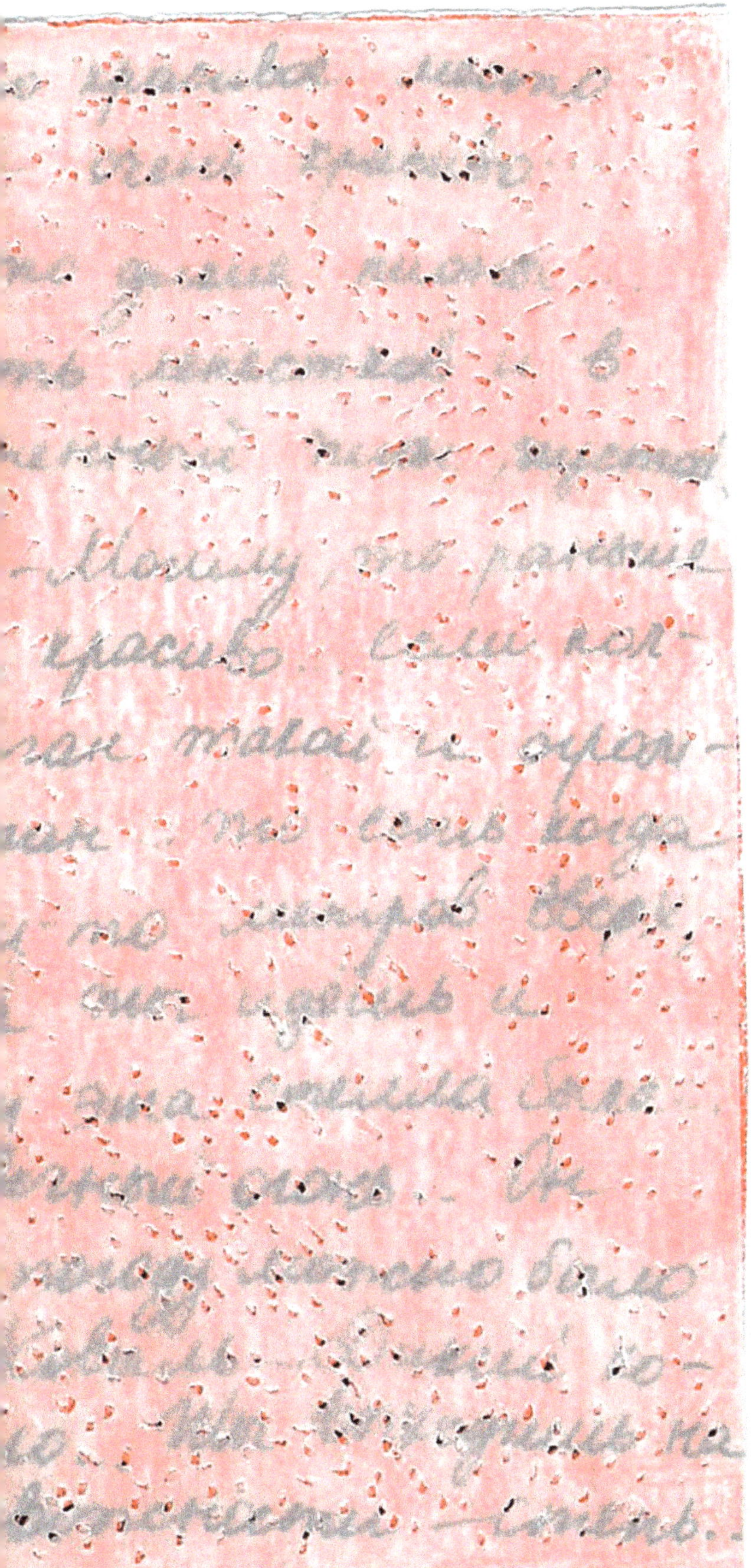

Radiant absences

This artistic research focuses on vegetal histories from and about Donbas, Ukraine, a land which once was an exemplary mining region of the Soviet Union and where in 2014 the ongoing war broke out. In order to re-examine dominant representations of the region through the frames of industrialisation and war, the study engages with scholarship in paleobotany and explores the vegetal past of coal, the fossil at the heart of Donbas' history. Through drawing and writing this research brings together plant fossils, recent interviews with internally displaced persons and critique of colonial depictions of the steppe as an empty space.

text & images: **Darya Tsymbalyuk**

Walking through bright thickets on a hot summer day, our feet slipping between an uneven path and heaps of plastic litter on the ground, our legs being hit by twigs and stems, our hands pushing the branches to make the way, we were heading to the place of the first industrial extraction of coal in the Donbas region, Ukraine. The walk was a part of a summer school that explored the industrial heritage of the region. Donbas stands for the Donetsk Coal Basin, a region in Eastern Ukraine known for its metal and mining industries, and as one of the most exemplary regions of the rapid Soviet industrialisation.[1] Often the name Donbas is used to describe Donetsk and Luhansk oblasts, even if parts of them belong to other cultural regions, such as Slobozhashchyna or Pryazovya. Here I use toponym Donbas to refer to the industrial region that developed in the Donets Basin starting XIX century. The name Donbas was given to this territory by a mining engineer Yevgraf Kovalevsky in 1827,[2] highlighting the central place mining takes in the history of the region. Recently, the name itself has seen some criticism. For example, reviewing the exhibition *Hen nepokory* (*The Gene of Disobedience*) at the Donetsk Local History Museum, now displaced to Kramatorsk, Viktoriia Grivina summarised its main message as the shift away from the toponym Donbas which implies a colonial vision of the territory solely as a natural resource.[3] Since 2014 Donbas is also known for the ongoing war, which has resulted in the emergence of two self-proclaimed unrecognised republics, supported by Russia: Donetsk People's Republic and Luhansk People's Republic, which Ukrainian government classifies as terrorist organisations. More than 13 000 people have been killed in the conflict,[4] and thousands have been displaced (UNHCR Ukraine provides a number of more than 1,4 million persons from both Donetsk and Luhansk oblasts and Crimea).[5] Therefore two grand narratives frame Donbas: industrialisation and war, both of which are narratives of masculinity, focusing on the union between Man and machine, and leaving little space for subjects that do not fall under a category of Man, whether women, minority groups, or nonhuman subjects.

Keeping in mind these two narratives, let me return to my story about the walk. We were just outside Lysychansk, one of the towns in Donbas, heading to the place of the first industrial extraction of coal in the region, first mined in 1795.[6] When I initially heard about our destination, I did not imagine it as a walk through the thickets, since my understanding of the process of coal extraction was built upon canonical depictions of men doing physically demanding labour underground, in which everything was rendered black and white, sometimes with the exception of orange helmets[7] (though even in this kind of imagery there is a vegetal trace of Lyubov Yakumchuk's contemporary classic *Apricots of the Donbas*, in which miners' helmets become apricots).[8] Many of the people on that trip joined straight from a rave night at one of the abandoned warehouses in Sievierodonetsk, where derelict sites, colloquially called '*zabroshki*' is yet another type of industrial heritage.[9] The sounds of the rave still pulsing in our bodies and our slow movements through glowing greens contributed to the feeling of sleepwalking in the woods. When we finally arrived at the coal seam, our guide Mykola Skuridin told us about sigillarias and lepidodendrons, extinct genera of arborescent plants that formed Carboniferous coal swamps. Listening to him while being surrounded by radiant green plants, it was easier to imagine abundant forests of the Carboniferous Period than a process of industrial extraction of coal. After telling us about the formation of coal and construction of the first mines, Skuridin broke off some coal pieces for us. I picked one up. As I did not have anything to carry it in, I ended up wrapping it in a big leaf I came across on our walk back: coal wrapped in vegetal matter, coal is vegetal matter, vegetal memory of coal.

This walk was organised as part of *Donbas Studies Summer School: The Plant Gave Us Everything*, which I co-coordinated in 2019 together with Dmytro Chepurnyi, Victoria Donovan, and others. The English translation of the school's name, a quote borrowed from one of the narrators in Piotr Armianovsky's documentary film *On the East* (2015), suggests a double meaning of the word 'plant', as a factory and a living organism. In the original Ukrainian this connection is not

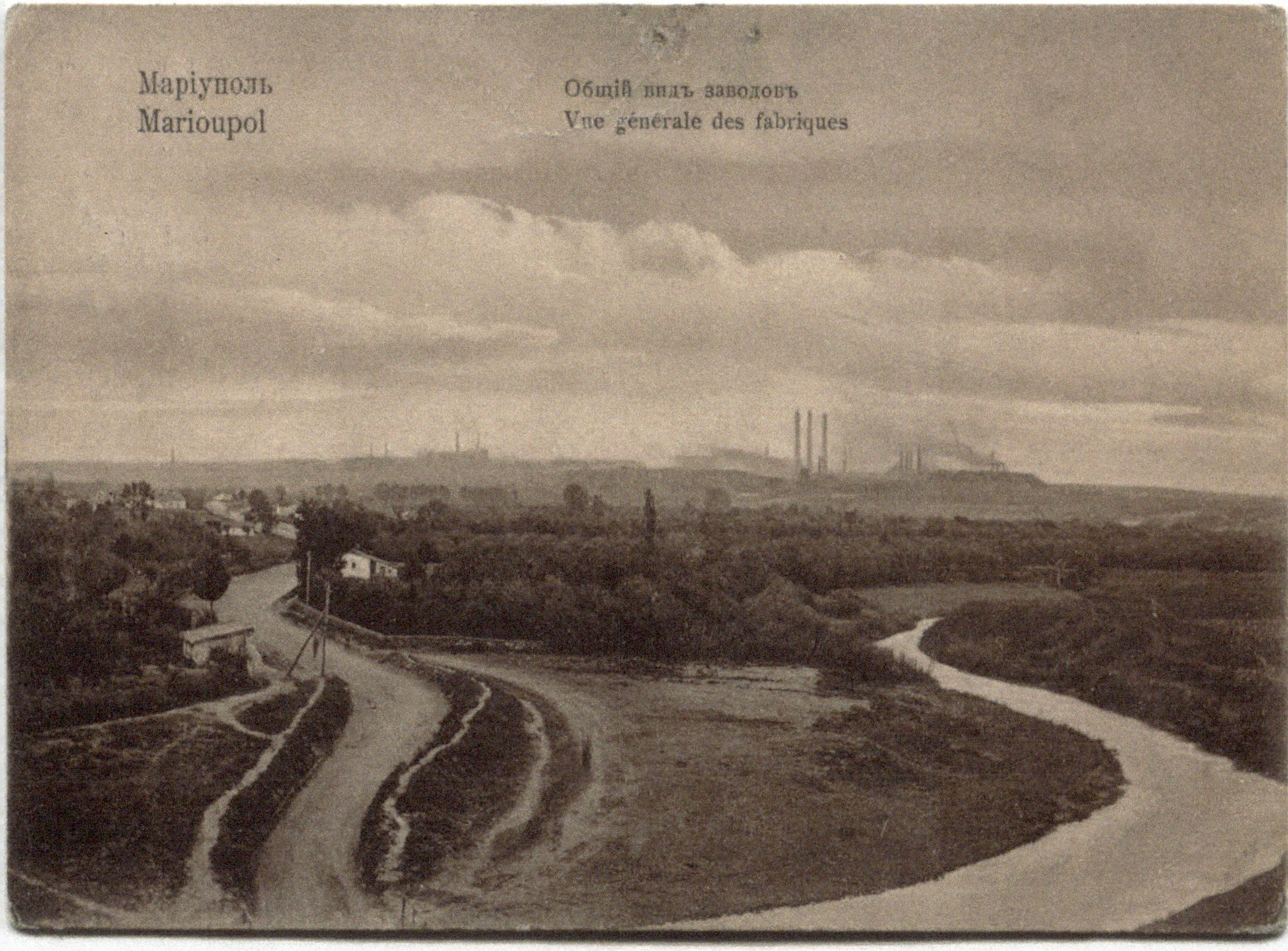

Unknown
The Kramatorsk Metallurgical Society Plant, photograph, 1900-1917, Industrial Complexes online collection of Urban Media Archive (Centre for Urban History, Lviv) © Museum of the History of Starokramatorsky Machine Building Plant

as explicit, however, the word '*zavod*' (industrial plant), does stem from the verb '*zavodyty*' (to start something, to organise)[10] which is often used in phrases like '*zavodyty roslyny*' (to get plants), '*zavodyty koney*' (to get horses), etc. The title of the summer school and the walk we did as part of it, reflect the focus of my research and this essay in particular: the process of retrieving memories of and about plants, as living organisms, in the histories about and from Donbas. Michael Marder writes about vegetal memory, as the memory within plants, where plants' bodies are the vegetal memory itself.[11] In his work, Marder develops a theory of plant-thinking, recovering 'reverberations of vegetal life in beings called "human".[12] Following Marder, I recover vegetal life within human cultures and histories, and in this study, I refer to traces of plants that made our worlds as vegetal memories.

In order to study plants at the very heart of coal extraction, looking at vegetal memories within the industry and the region, I turn to artistic research. In this paper, I present some of my drawings, which engage with scholarship in palaeobotany, a natural science concerned with plants that existed in other geological periods.[13]

Palaeobotany and artistic research

While focusing on Man and machines, colonial narratives of industrialisation and war, strategically render everything unrelated to Man and machines as an empty space, which serves as a raw material, a resource for agricultural and industrial projects, as well as military campaigns. However, industrialisation also prompted the production of histories of nonhuman subjects, as the rapid excavation of fossil fuels also exposed plant fossils and brought them to the surface, which has led to the emergence of such disciplines as palaeobotany.[14] In the Russian Empire palaeobotany developed and expanded as a science starting from the 1840s, simultaneously with the development of industries.[15] As Imre Szeman and Dominic Boyer,[16] as well as Claire Colebrook,[17] state, modernity, which includes industrial development and our current political structures and institutions, was possible because of the availability of fossil fuels. The extraction of fossil fuels was in turn possible because of systemic processes of enslavement and exploitation of Black people and colonial Others.[18] Moreover, the advancement of sciences was one of the pillars of colonisation and imperialism. In the case of Donbas, which is a part of the great Eurasian steppe belt, often referred to as the Wild Field and seen by the Russian Empire as a space for expansion, first 'military-cum-scientific' expeditions were initiated during the reign of Peter the Great.[19] Thus, the development of a more extensive knowledge about lives of organisms in other geological periods and industrial progress are interdependent, and this relationship has been discussed by many Russian and Soviet palaeobotanists whose texts I am looking at in greater depth in my research. For example, many plant fossils were discovered at mining sites because of collaborations between scientists and miners, and that is the reason we know more about the plants of the Carboniferous Period than about plants from any other period.[20]

The relationship between discovery of fossils and industrial sites is also explored in one of the memories of a protagonist of *Mustard in the Gardens*, a 2018 documentary film by Piotr Armianovsky. The protagonist, Olena returns to her native village in Donbas which is now located on the frontline between government-controlled territories of Ukraine and occupied territories. In one of the scenes Olena looks at a slag heap and remembers her childhood:

> I used to play with friends on these stockpiles, we would collect clay of all colours, yellow, red, blue, and black, and do crafts, and black clay as you know is the most radioactive one, it contains uranium. We would make clay dolls and play with them. My grandma saw us once and scolded. And also, we used to find fossilized algae and wonderful druse crystals there, my yard was full of such stuff. I thought I'd become a geologist, I collected all that stuff. It makes me feel very sad now, this situation when landmines are everywhere, fields have landmines, slag heaps have landmines. No one will demine them even if the war is over tomorrow, we still find landmines from World War II, they will be there forever.[21]

In this short quote, human and nonhuman archives come together in living memory of childhood. Olena mourns the lost access to slag heaps, manmade hills that shaped the land in the region. Slag heaps in themselves are archives of industrialisation, preserving radioactive clay and other waste, as well as containing memories of distant geological processes – plant fossils. In Olena's story, industrial waste becomes a children's game, where narratives of other geological periods, industrialisation, and childhood form entangled knots, from which just like from clay she moulds her story. Moreover, memories of wars, past and present, World War II, and the current conflict are also archived by the slag heap, containing danger of landmines, and therefore rendered inaccessible.

Just like Olena, I collect plant fossils many of which have been brought to the surface with industrialisation. For this drawing series, I work with the 1938 book *The Fossil Flora of the Middle Section of the Carboniferous Rocks of the Donetz*

Basin written by M.D. Zalessky and H.T.H. Tchirkova.[22] The book features multiple drawings of plant fossils made by the artist B.I. Sboromirsky. And just like Olena, I also place plant fossils next to memories of displacement, which I collected by interviewing internally displaced persons (IDPs) from Donbas. My interviews with IDPs focused on human plant relations, the way they were ruptured and reconfigured by experiences of migration. Therefore, these stories offer a different perspective of displacement, as well as engage with memories about Donbas, which are not structured around the dominant narratives of industry and war, Man and machines only, and which allow for multispecies stories to be told. Bringing together these different elements into a mesh of subjectivities and histories, I hope to find a multiplicity of narratives about Donbas, and transformative energy (coal is a plant fossil too!) that would prompt us to think of more inclusive imaginaries of the region.

Challenging fossils

One of the mediums of my inquiry into the vegetal memories of Donbas is drawing. In addition to making drawings myself, I also use drawings by Sboromirsky and photographs of fossils provided in the book. Plant fossils are visual objects produced through interactions of various nonhuman forces in the processes of compression and impression. Nonhuman origins of these images challenge concepts of drawing (and writing) that centre humans as the only possible producers of both. In his essay *Drawn to the Moment*, John Berger distinguishes images made by plant fossils and humans. In Berger's view, the function of any image is to 'record(s) an appearance which will disappear'.[23] Berger notes that the fossil has a potential to challenge disappearance too, but in his eyes, this challenge is 'meaningless':[24] it is random and deprived of the act of looking as a meaning-making process. Berger's reflection is based on elevating the process of looking over the process of tactile engagement, where a plant fossil is made directly through a compression and impression foregoing the mediation of the gaze. Berger's views of the meaninglessness of plant fossils can be contested by the recent theories in material ecocriticism, that offer a concept of 'storied matter' as 'a material "mesh" of meanings, properties, and processes, in which human and nonhuman players are interlocked in networks that produce undeniable signifying forces'.[25] Colebrook's provocation of extending the archive, which could be used to interpret fossils as inscriptions,[26] also provides a potential frame for reading plant fossils as drawings, and as inscriptions. This frame prompts a closer engagement with plant records and their inclusion into our histories of Donbas, which would help us rethink grand narratives that focus on Man and machines and consider other nonhuman and human lives that have inhabited the region and shaped it into the way we know it today.

While tracing plant fossils as impressions made by the pressure of matter, I think of the way these fossils impressed Sboromirsky, as he was following each curve, each line, translating them into the language of human-made drawing. The reason I started this artistic research, is the impression these images made upon me, and the need I felt to be printing, cutting, and hanging them on a board that keeps my collection of dried petals, leaves, and seaweed brought from various walks. I could not stop looking at these images and wanted to imitate them, to repeat the traces. This is the origin of reciprocity, which encouraged me to be pressing the pencil into the paper, making traces.

Punctuating absences

While cutting and copying Sboromirsky's studies, I noticed that once in a while a drawing would have a punctuated outline of space within the fossil, an absence, an invitation to imagine. Gemma Anderson highlights the interpretative nature of morphological drawing and writing about Greg Edgecombe's studies of fossils she states that he "steer(s) the viewer toward seeing biological structures and not the geological artifact".[27] Punctuated absences on the drawings left by Sboromirsky either because the original part of the matter was not preserved or because it was not clear enough for him to document it are spaces offered to our imagination. Looking at these fractured and fragmented studies of fossils, I wonder what radiant absences are there in our stories about and from Donbas? I am interested in erasure and compression, and how these processes shape our cultures and ways of remembering, where some narratives become fossilised, some become lost.

As I have mentioned, part of my research is collecting oral histories of displacement. My interviews focus on memories about homes and hometowns, and plants and gardens that make those spaces into what they are. Since they are recorded in the time of a recent displacement and ongoing military conflict, these traumatic events are mentioned in every interview, but often it is in the silences in-between where these experiences are mostly communicated. Some memories remain unspeakable, best documented nonverbally, just like plant fossils, which present nonverbal accounts of lives in other geological periods.

Researching plant stories means researching silent stories. Plants are usually portrayed as our quiet companions whose voices are present through human narrators. Plant stories are often silent in our records too, which rarely account for the loss of plant life, unless whole forests are destroyed. Absence from records can falsely lead to the assumption of absence from the landscape of life too.

While plants can sometimes be erased from human records, they are also capable of erasing human traces. In one of my interviews, a woman called Valentyna speaks of the monstrous growth of hop and other plants in her garden. Every time she comes back home, she spends hours trying to cut the thickets and save her house from being swallowed and erased by vegetal matter. I have heard similar stories before when interviewing people forcefully resettled from the Chernobyl Exclusion Zone. They would show me photos of streets and houses they had to abandon and to which they come back every other year to visit. On those photos, it was hard for me to decipher echoes of roads amidst the thickets.

Empty space

Cartographic depictions of the steppe as an empty space lend themselves to imperial, colonial, and industrial imaginaries of constructing a world from scratch. As I have already mentioned, before industrialisation, the territories of Donbas comprised the space known as the Wild Field. Results of expeditions initiated by Peter the Great provided maps of the Wild Field, in which 'the steppe was claimed by geographical science and promptly turned into a void.'[28] Colonial representations of the steppe not only erase local Cossack and nomadic populations that lived in these lands, but they also obscure vibrant ecosystems in which life was thriving, many of which were significantly altered with the processes of colonisation and industrialisation. Willard Sunderland writes that with the takeover by the empire in the seventeenth century, the 'land ownership was a matter of royal prerogative, and claims based on usage were secondary',[29] which meant that different forms of knowledge and relations to the land and its inhabitants developed by Cossacks' and nomads were substituted by new imperial frameworks. The increased number of settlers in the seventeenth century had a profound impact on local wildlife, which 'was either hunted or displaced'.[30] Agriculture became the primary way of engaging with the land until industrialisation offered a model of resource extraction.

Visions of the steppe as an empty space also feature in 19th-century photography of Donbas. Iryna Sklokina emphasises that it was photography and not painting through which first images of Donets Basin were produced.[31] Some of the examples of this early photography capture more land than industry, while converting the first one into an empty background for the second. For example, an inscription on a 1905-1909 postcard of Mariupol[32] reads 'A general view of plants/factories. Here, the factory is barely visible in the distance, while the title

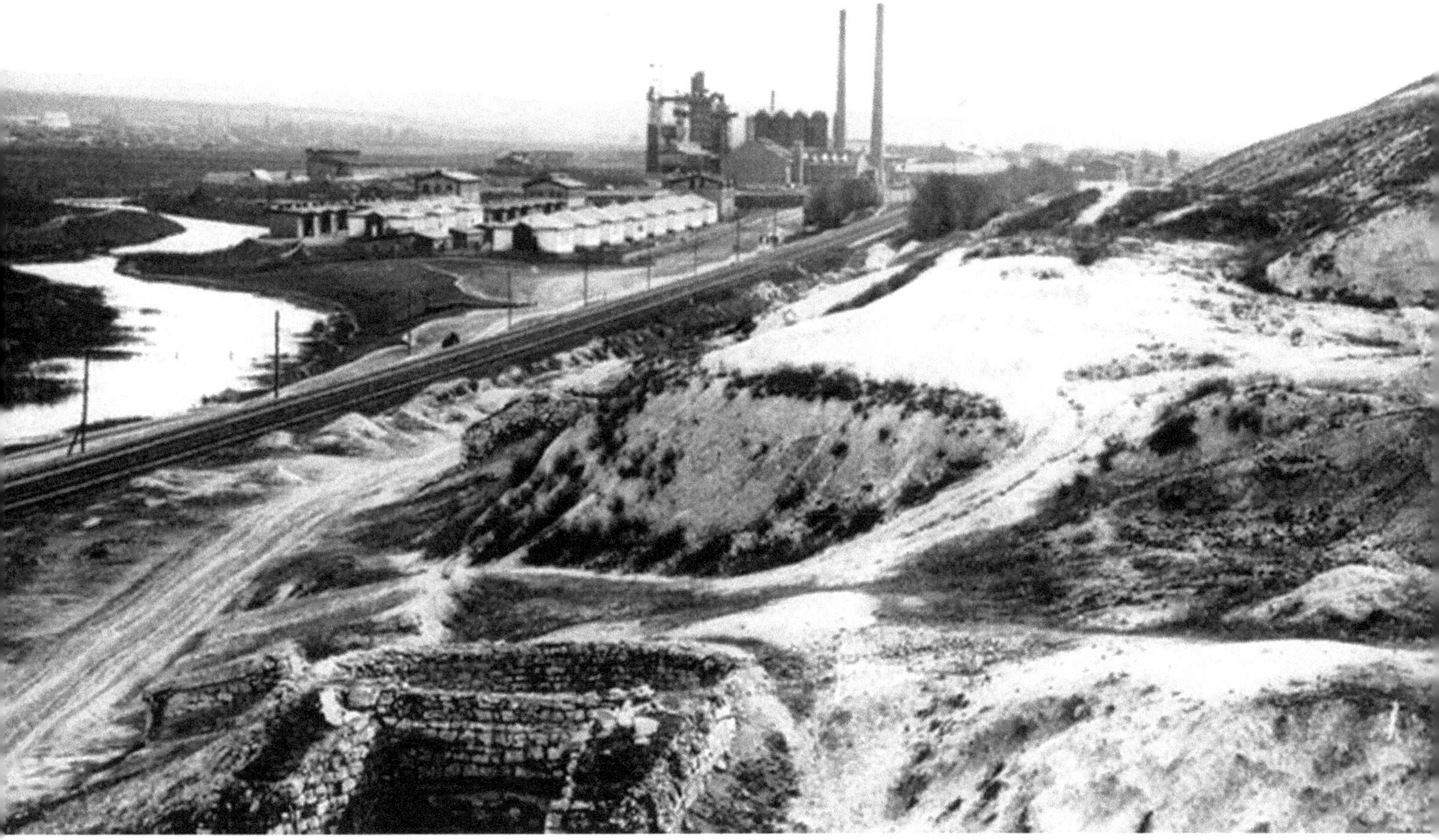

Unknown
The Kramatorsk Metallurgical Society Plant, photograph, 1900-1917, Industrial Complexes online collection of Urban Media Archive (Centre for Urban History, Lviv) © Museum of the History of Starokramatorsky Machine Building Plant

prompts the viewer to see the factory only, ignoring land that takes up most of the space. Sklokina interprets the composition of the postcard as a continuation of 'the canon of landscape painting of XIX century',[33] while also highlighting that the placement of industries 'created a feeling that the factory is the centre toward which all life in this space is directed'[34]

The second image is listed in the archive as a Kramatorsk Metal Production Plant and it was taken between 1900-1917. While both images might have been modelled upon landscape painting, their names, which are either inscribed directly on the photograph or under which they are archived, emphasise the significance of the industry depicted, where land is considered to be a mere background, and in a teleological interpretation, a space for future industrial expansion. The focus on the industry erases the land and in a gesture of plant blindness, its diverse inhabitants.

Similar images can also be found in the literature of the time. For example, Russian writer Vikentiy Veresaev who briefly visited Donbas in 1892,

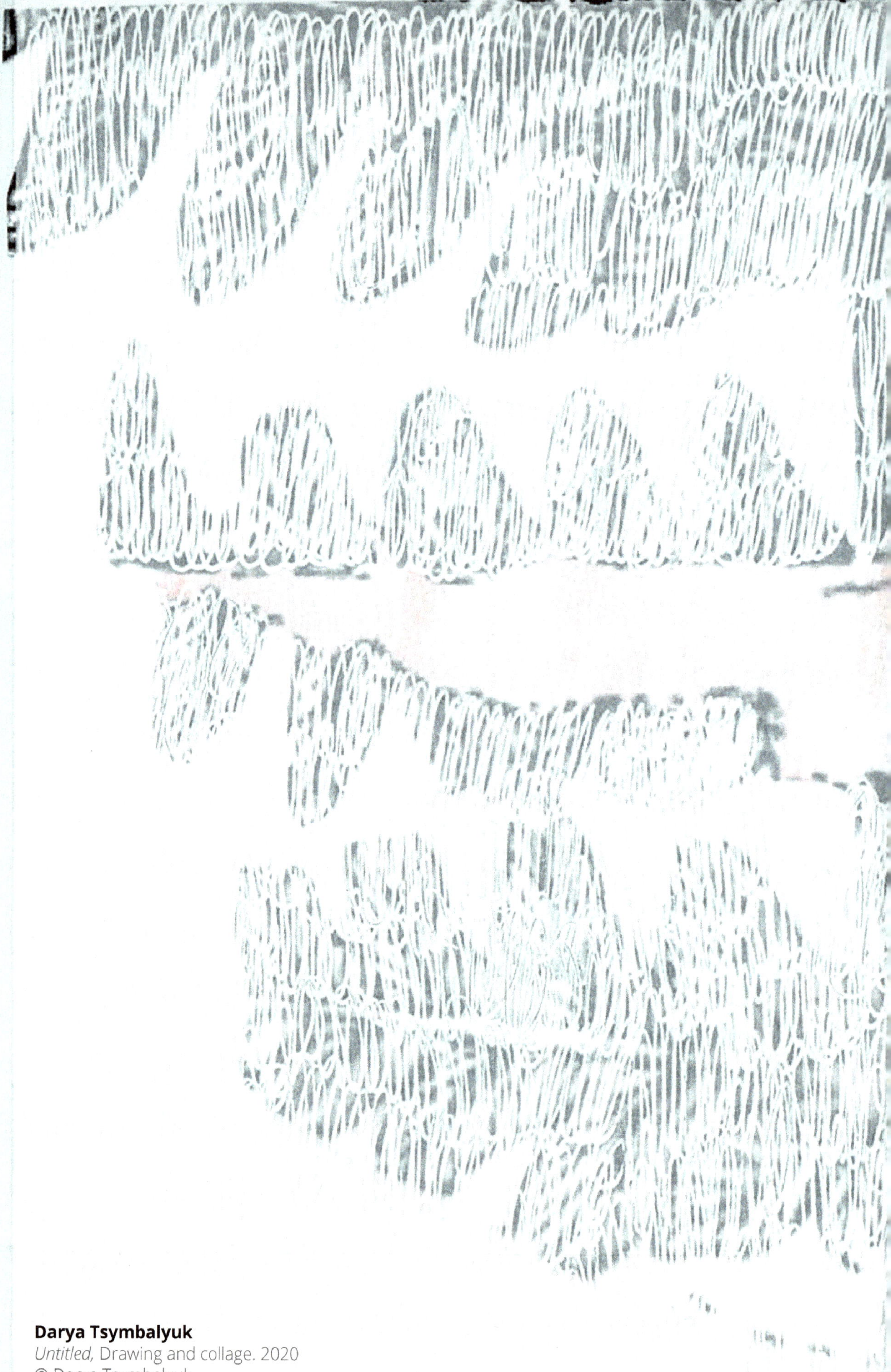

Darya Tsymbalyuk
Untitled, Drawing and collage. 2020

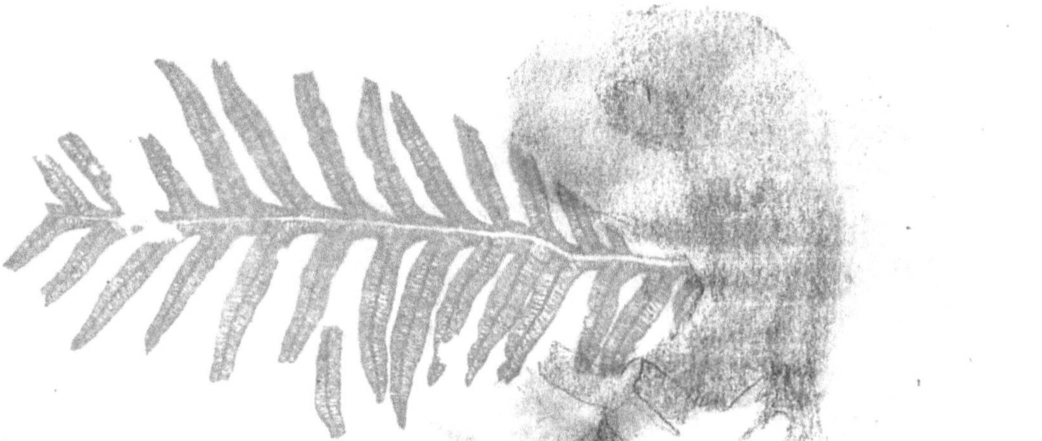

Darya Tsymbalyuk
Untitled, Drawing and collage. 2020

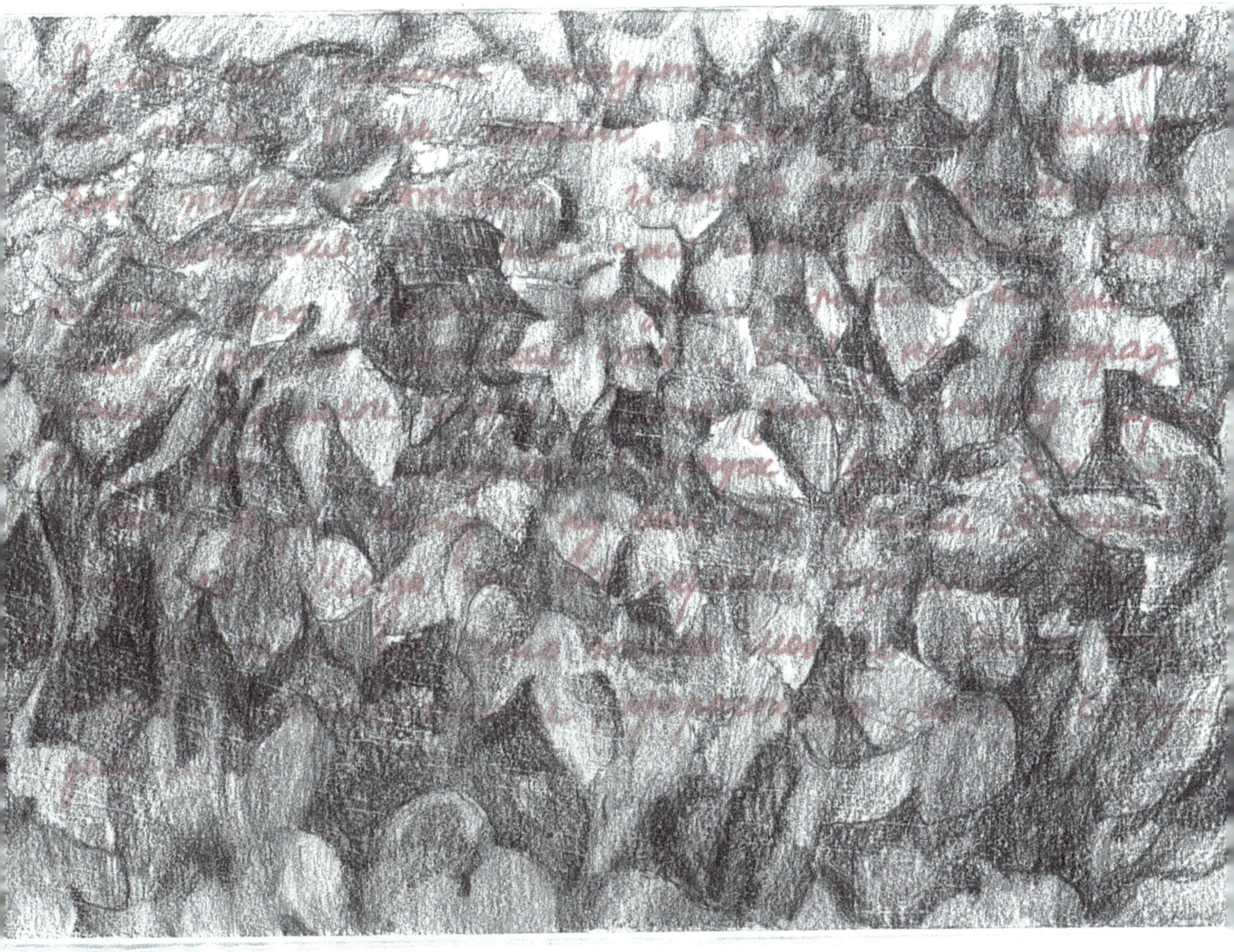

Darya Tsymbalyuk
Untitled, Drawing and collage. 2020
© Darya Tsymbalyuk

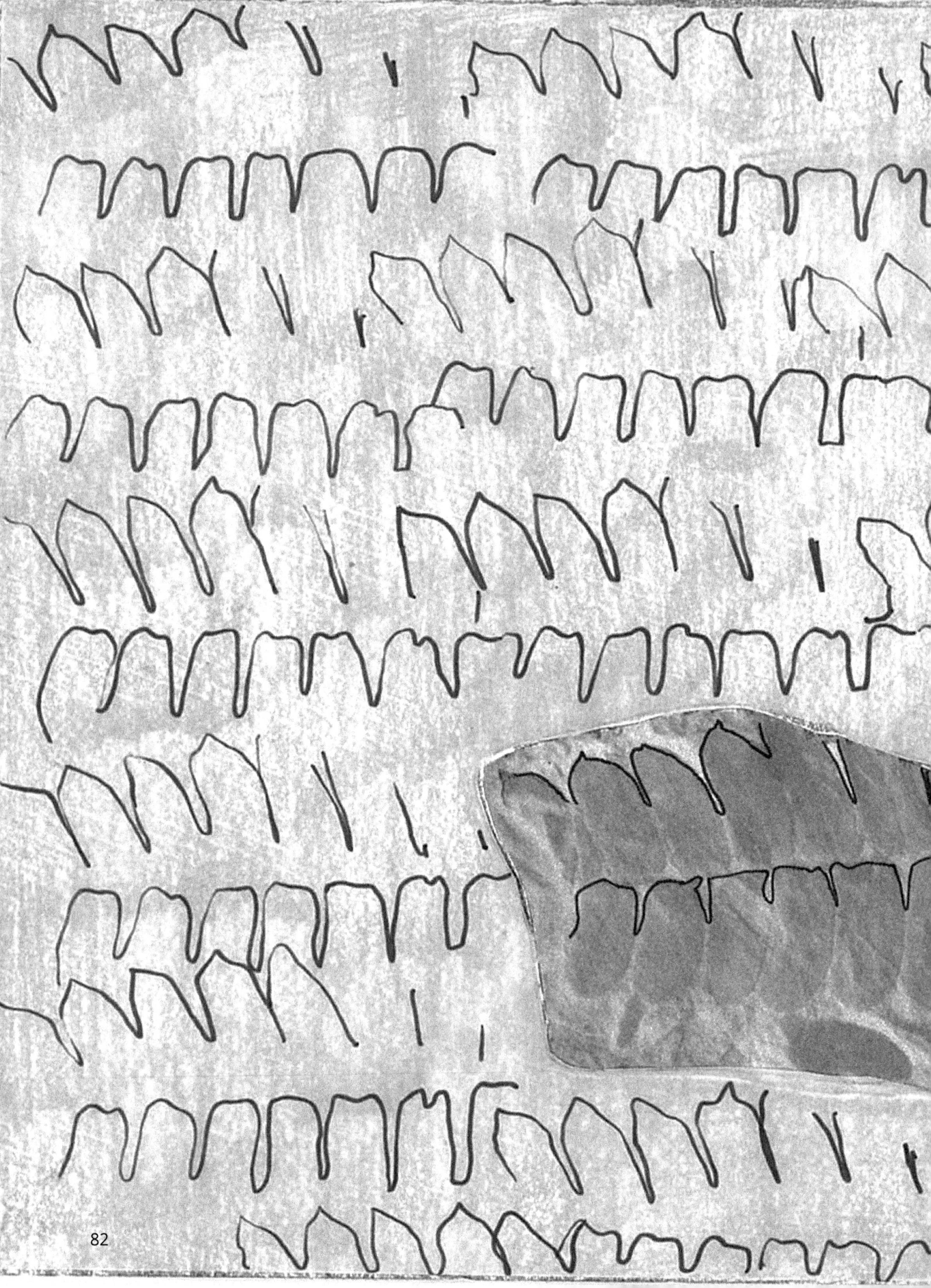

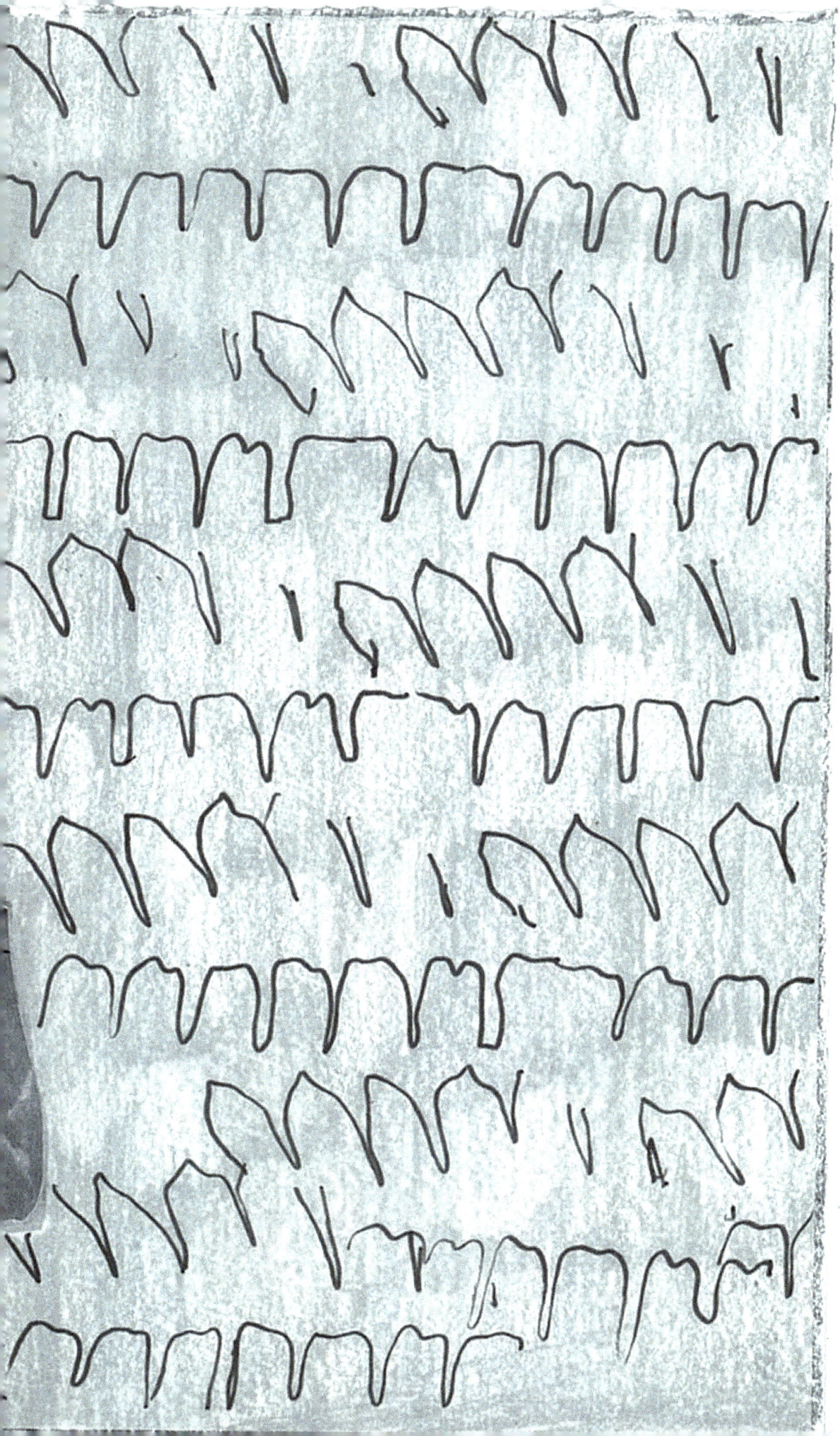

Darya Tsymbalyuk
Untitled, Drawing and collage. 2020

describes the space as 'silent, deserted (in Russian literally *bezliudnya, without people*) steppe',[35] boring place. He writes:

> Black land, black roads... All around the mine - there is not a single tree, a single bush; there is no pond, no stream. Everywhere your eye can reach, - there is a monotonous steppe, scorched by the sun.[36]

While this description could be seen as a criticism of ecological destruction and deprivation in and around mining settlements, it is also telling that the steppe itself is presented as lifeless. These kinds of images of boring nothingness are often employed to justify settler colonialism and erase local human and nonhuman histories. The tendency to see the steppe as monotonous and solid single piece exposes suppression of local knowledges, that could read and interpret these lands in all diversity of their inscriptions and manifestations. A short story collection published in 1908 by a Ukrainian writer Spyrydon Cherkasenko, who lived in Donbas for nine years, allows us to imagine what the steppe could have looked like for someone with a better knowledge of it.

> Every day, before heading to the mine, Sosnovsky stopped for a bit on the threshold [of his house] and silently, with a joyful smile admired the view in the distance, the spacious steppe that unrolled in front of him like a lush green carpet; everywhere across the steppe scarlet flowers of *vorontsi* (wild peonies) burnt like drops of fresh blood, and this made the steppe so beautiful that you could not keep your eyes off it. Invisible larks, these zealous spring singers resounded in the sky: as if an unknown giant musician stretched invisible strings and was playing unspeakably ancient praise to the spring and the sun, the majestic, ardent sun, which is the beginning and the end of life... A wonderful and sweet sorrow rose in the soul, the heart was beating more passionately from the sorrow, together with the magical music of nature, blood flowed in the veins and the whole soul was full with desire... The steppe was breathing... It was alive with each shivering stem, each inconspicuous little flower, each tiniest insect, butterfly, horse, and bird...[37]

In this passage from a story *Vesnoyu* (*In spring*) Cherkasenko presents an image of the steppe as a vibrant and thriving world, populated by all kinds of plants, birds, and other beings. In fact, the wild peonies he mentions, have been also recalled in one of my interviews by a woman called Svitlana, and I use her quote for one of the drawings. In the interview, Svitlana remembers her walks to a mound surrounded by the steppe, and just like Cherkasenko she portrays the land as a rich and living world. The mound she talks about, Savur-Mohyla, is a strategic height and it has been a place of heavy fighting. Prior to meeting Svitlana, I only imagined it as a battle place. Svitlana, however, introduces my vision of Savur-Mohyla wild peonies. "It is a flat flower with four-five petals and a yellow middle, a blank, empty peony..." - Svitlana gives me a detailed description, as I have never seen this plant. Cherkasenko's rich depictions of the steppe, as well as memories of my narrators, bring forward silent spaces around the factories featured on a postcard and a photograph discussed earlier and populate them with sounds, colors, and all forms of life. These kinds of narratives allow us to imagine Donbas and the Wild Field not as empty, erased spaces, but as vibrant ecologies. The addition of plant fossils to these accounts prompts us to think about all kinds of lives that populated the territory now known as Donbas and the way they shaped it. In this multispecies perspective of history, the narrative of industrialisation is told in relation to other kinds of narratives, such as the vegetal memory of coal and other fossils. Moreover, working with plant fossils means being constantly reminded of the processes of

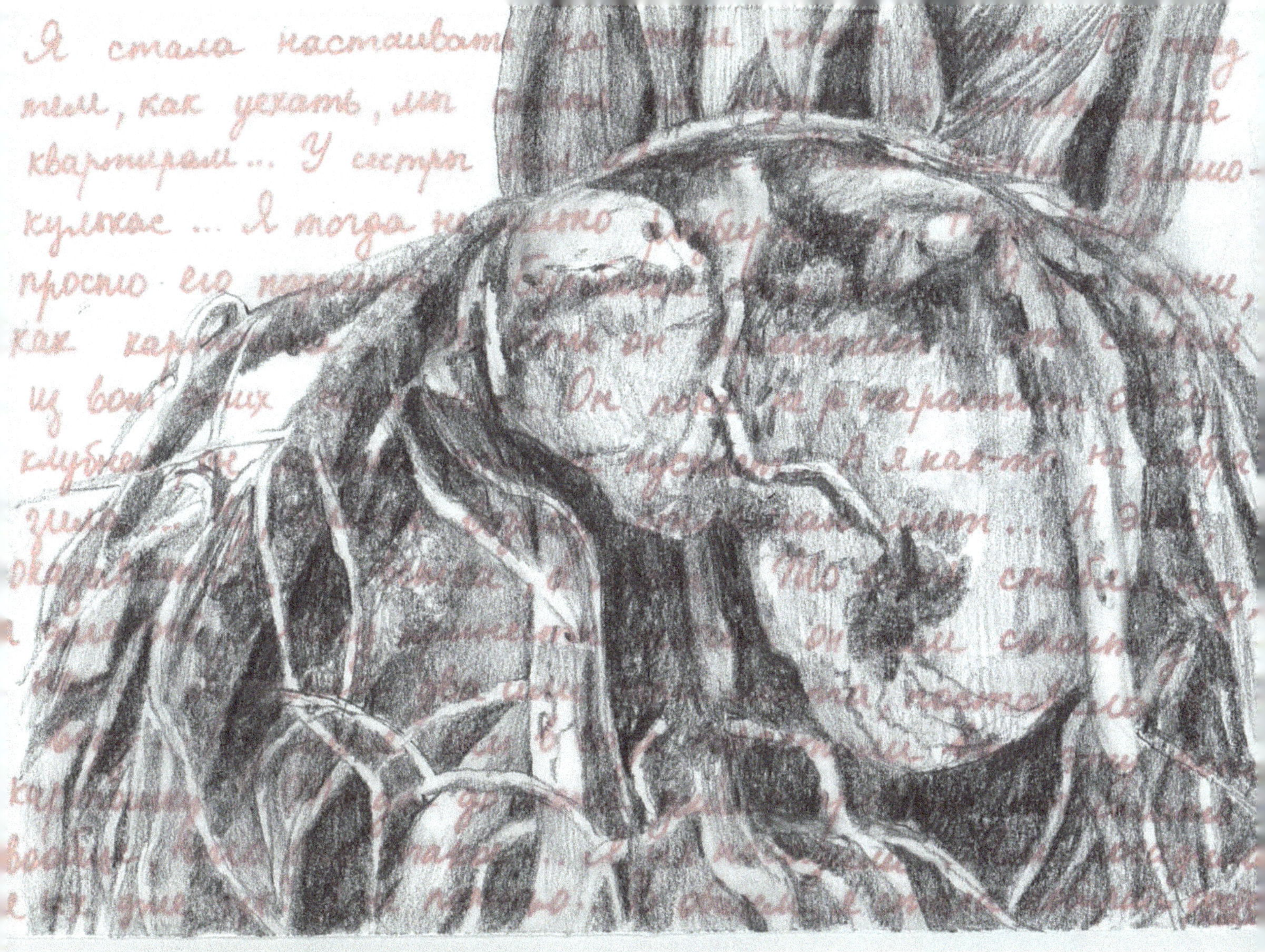

Darya Tsymbalyuk
Untitled, Drawing and collage. 2020
© Darya Tsymbalyuk

extinction and destruction. Like any other archive, plant fossils are an archive of death as much as they are an archive of life. The ongoing military conflict in Donbas produces multiple narratives of loss and destruction, erasing homes, fields, and museum collections. Studying current and past stories from and about the region means looking for radiant absences, and questioning what is missing and why. Maybe if we look carefully enough, inside the stories about military fighting and coal extraction, we can also find a trace of wild peonies and a woman who loved them.

Darya Tsymbalyuk is a PhD researcher at the University of St Andrews, Scotland. Her research explores human-plant relations in stories of displacement from Donbas, Ukraine both through analysis of oral histories and through critical-creative practices, among which are drawing and creative writing. Darya is a co-author (with Victor Zasypkin and Julia Philipieva) of a participatory art project Donbas Odyssey. Together with a team she is also working on an animation film Displaced Garden, which tells the story of displacement of humans and plants. The film is based on Darya's PhD research, and she contributes to it as a scriptwriter and an artist.

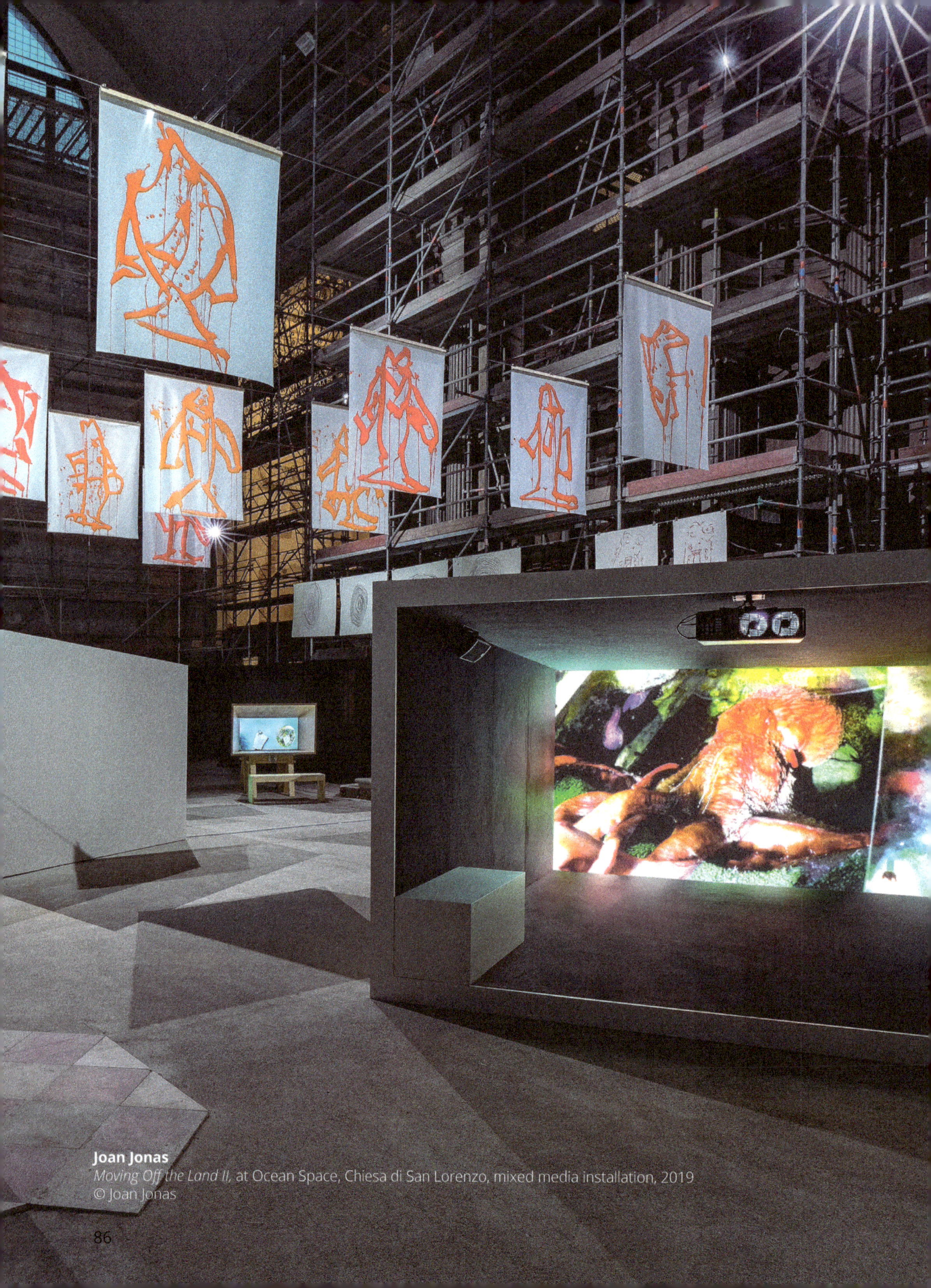

Joan Jonas
Moving Off the Land II, at Ocean Space, Chiesa di San Lorenzo, mixed media installation, 2019
© Joan Jonas

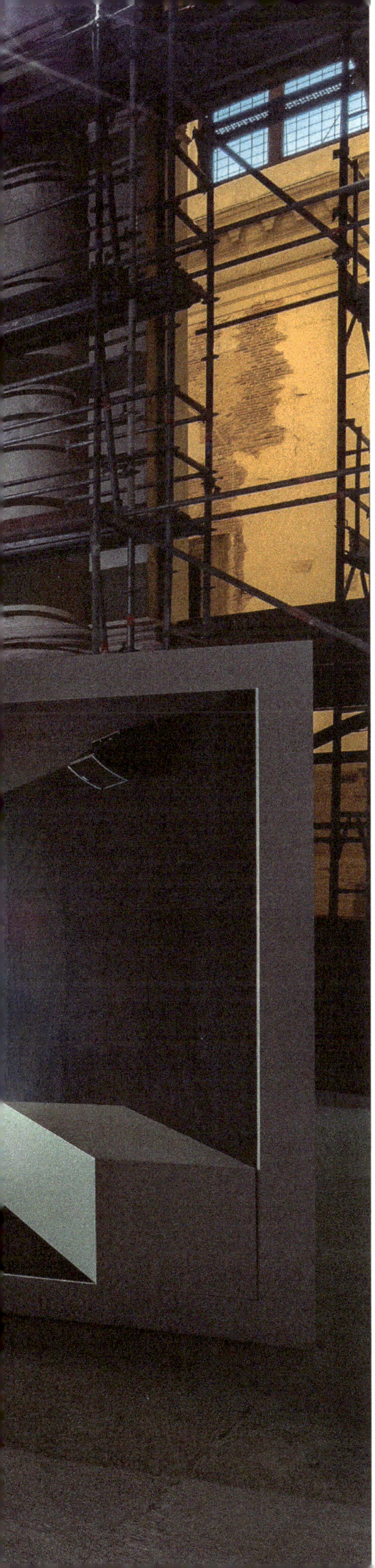

Joan Jonas, *Moving Off the Land II*, a consideration of strange strangers

Artist Joan Jonas's multi-media exhibition Moving Off the Land II transports the viewer into a liquid world where beautiful and intelligent creatures demonstrate their agency. Her approach reflects Timothy Morton's ecological thought, a way of living in the world where there is respect and connection to all living things, even "strange strangers." Jonas literally leaps over imagined boundaries into "the entangling mesh" of the ocean where she engages in metaphorical acts of symbiosis. This essay reveals how the artist accomplishes the daunting task of making us care deeply about the feelings, necessity, dependencies, and potential extinction of sea life.

text: **Cynthia Haveson Veloric**
images: **Joan Jonas**

In one episode of the satirical television series Portlandia,[1] Fred takes a walk in the forest and accidentally steps on a snail. As an uber-aware nature lover, he mourns the tiny creature. He then enters a magical forest niche where he encounters animated, talking snails. After describing his sadness at killing one of their kin, he is surprised to learn that the snails feel that their lives are inferior and that they want to be killed. They beg him to step on them too! After much protesting, he reluctantly does so. Yet later that evening he and his date are seen devouring escargot in a restaurant.

This pop culture fragment illustrates the duality of our emotional relationship with nature, on the one hand, sensitive to all living creatures, on the other, willing to sacrifice that ideological attachment and appreciation to sustain our appetites, desires, and material wants. Joan Jonas's recent traveling exhibition *Moving Off the Land II* [2] (going forward *MOTL*) considers no such ambiguity. The notion of anthropocentric hegemony over animal life is discredited here, replaced with Timothy Morton's "ecological thought"-- a way of viewing and living in the world around with respect and connection to all living things, even to those creatures he calls "strange strangers" who we will never fully know. He calls our boundless universe "the entangling mesh" and acknowledges that it can be horrific or strange, tender or loving.[3] Jonas leaps over imagined boundaries into "the entangling mesh" of the ocean where she engages in tender and loving relationships. *MOTL* doesn't just give standing to the nonhuman; it is an epic portrayal of intelligent life beneath the sea and a dreamy drama of beneficial symbioses with other species. The video, sculpture, drawing, and sound works, deconstructed from Jonas's *MOTL* performance, provide a Gesamtkunstwerk which transports the viewer into a fluid, underwater world inhabited by the "other". The installation evokes a palpable sense of vitality and connection with ocean ecology and in doing so makes us more attuned to environmental threats facing sea life. This essay reveals how the artist accomplishes the daunting task of making us care deeply about the fragility, feelings, necessity, dependencies, and potential extinction of sea life. The affective nature of the exhibition is confirmed through a reading of exhibition visitor comments.

Jonas's installation successfully simulates an external environment that evokes a sensual response in the viewer, which in turn stimulates care and attention, perhaps even action. As we move randomly through the multi-media spaces our bodies, feelings, and emotions are all engaged, leading to new types of knowledge. This confluence of forces in activating the brain is called *embodied cognition*.[4] *MOTL* strives to impart an embodied understanding of the agency of nonhuman life by employing many modes of perceptual experience at once. These include the visual, aural, tactile, and less recognized vestibular senses. Ecocritical cultural studies scholar Alexa Weik von Mossner argues that "embodied cognition is of particular relevance for environmental narratives which include any type of narrative in any media that foregrounds ecological issues and human-nature relationships, often but not always with the openly stated intention of bringing about social change.[5]

Jonas promotes embodied cognition in the viewer using five wooden viewing cubicles of different sizes, each constructed like shadowboxes, which hold videos of underwater footage shot in Jamaica and in aquariums around the world.[6] In several of the videos, water itself is a character with traits and a personality. It moves, it retracts, and it makes various sorts of noises. It is laden with philosophical possibilities. Water exists as a dramatic, enticing, dynamic space that pulls us in with its own agency, even before the sound narrative or Jonas's appearance. Our immersion there is made possible by the camera's subjective movement and pacing, like the way it lingers over the slow motion of an octopus's tentacles as it seeks food or the close-ups of swimming fish and mammals whose faces nearly touch the camera's lens. The framing of the animal's actions creates drama and this brings on feelings of anticipation in the viewer.

As soon as Jonas appears underwater or as a video projection, she becomes a human conduit to our sensory participation. As she talks, strokes, coaxes, and swims with the creatures, the viewer begins to believe in their relevance, intelli-

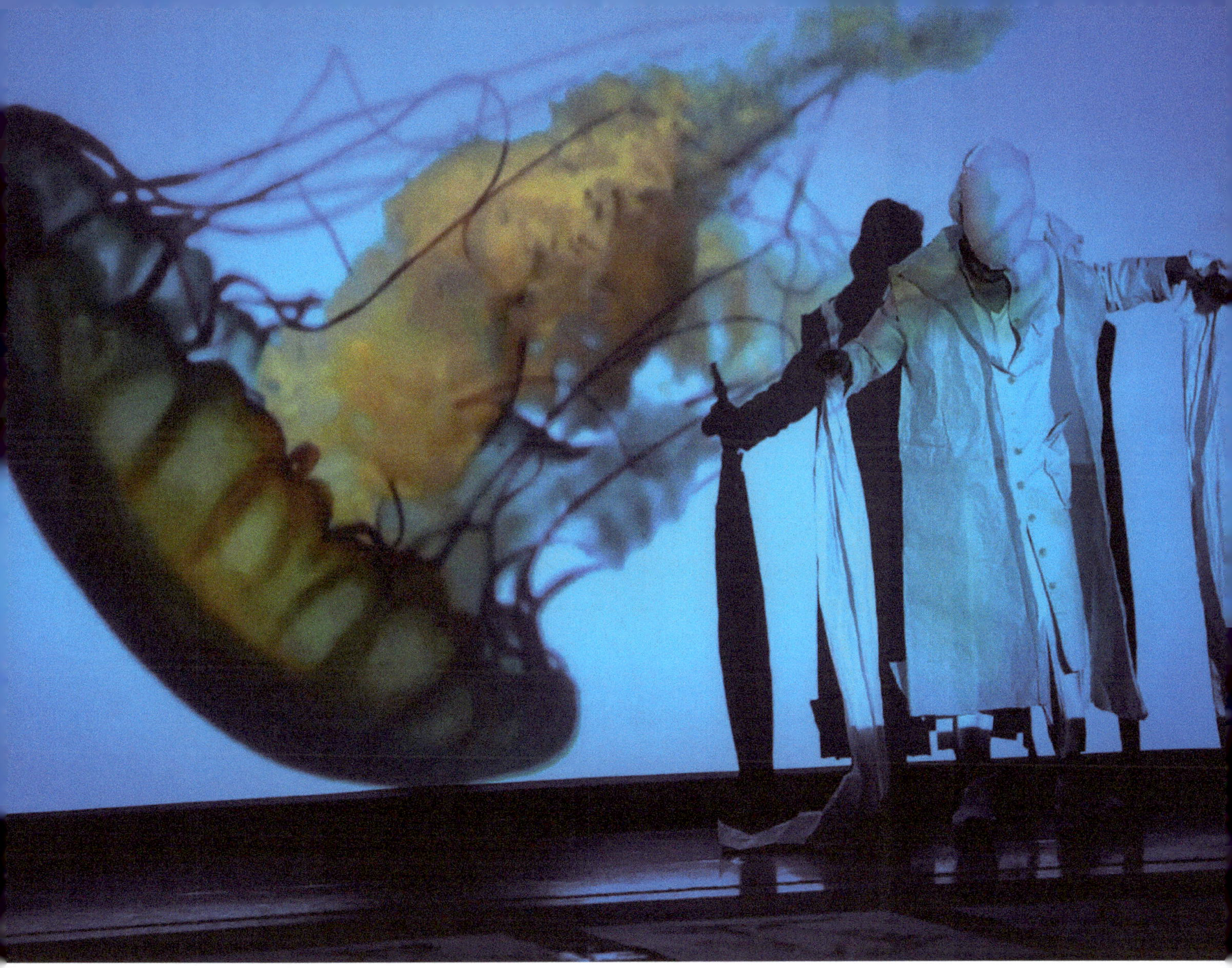

Joan Jonas
Moving Off the Land II, at Ocean Space, Chiesa di San Lorenzo, mixed media installation, 2019
© Joan Jonas

gence, grace, and openness to humans. As she reads aloud from literature, poetry, and myth about aquatic life, our consciousness is expanded and that leads to empathy. When she disguises her human form with a costume and dances with a jellyfish, she erases hierarchy and superficial differences.

Her emotional connection with land and sea has been emerging for decades, but for this project, she seems to have crossed over "My natural way of working is to get into the subject more deeply over time, so the material gradually grew. And then—actually I never had this experience before—in interacting with the projections I really did feel viscerally closer to the whole subject".[6] And so do we. Jonas serves as the intermediary and translator of the underwater world by stimulating many modes of sensory perception, particularly the tactile (accessed visually) and the vestibular through the motion of the camera. Film scholar Luis Rocha Antunes explains: "Film [video] is capable of eliciting perceptual experiences without direct sensory stimulation. Research on visual-vestibular interactions provides abundant evidence that what we call "seeing" is not just a visual but a multisensory experience".[7]

MOTL can be seen as an ecosystem with multiple parts, actors, and spaces that generate awareness, energy, and change, following theater and perfor-

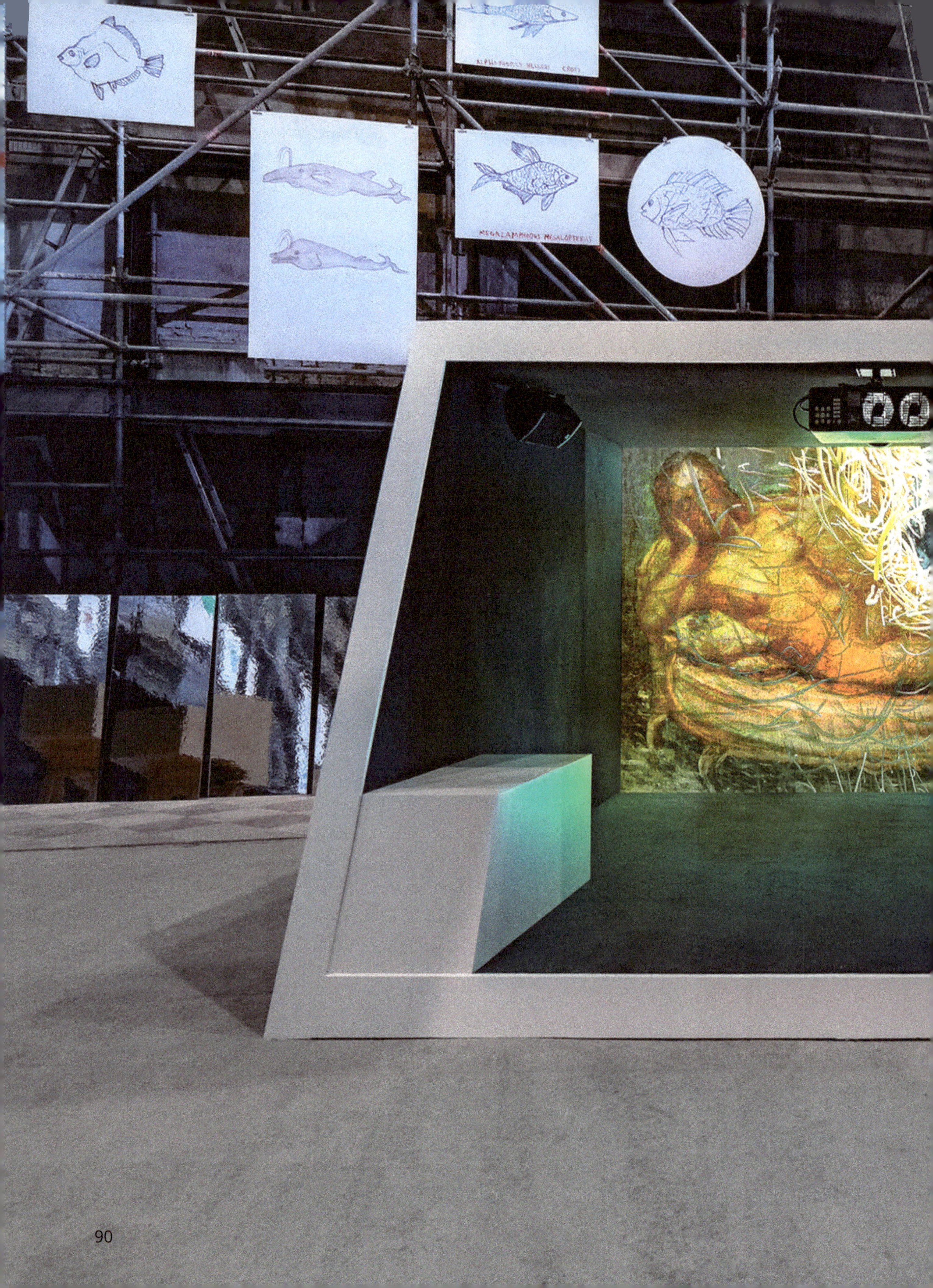
MEGALAMPHODUS MEGALOPTERUS

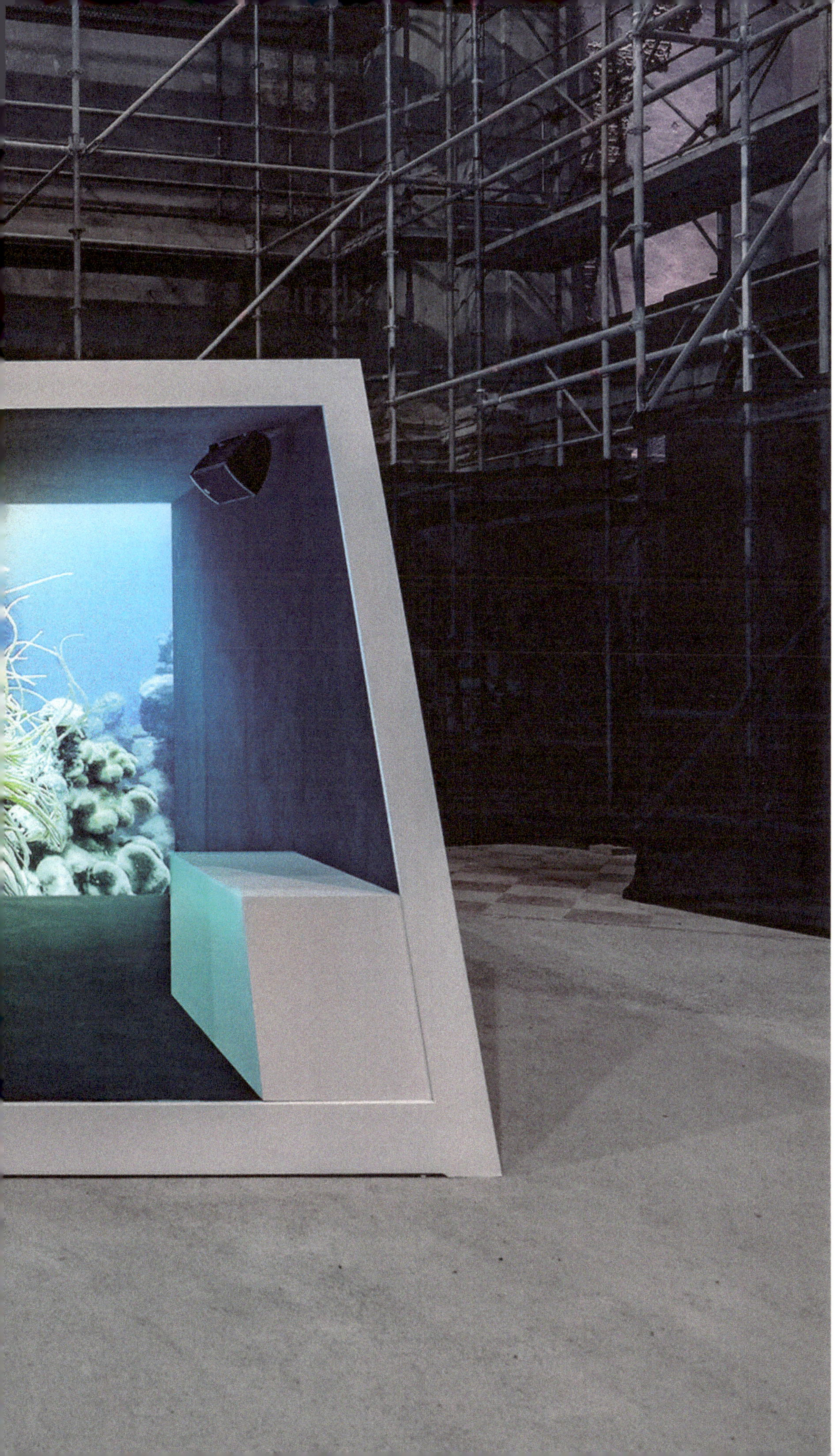

Joan Jonas
Moving Off the Land II,
at Ocean Space, Chiesa di San Lorenzo, mixed media installation, 2019
© Joan Jonas

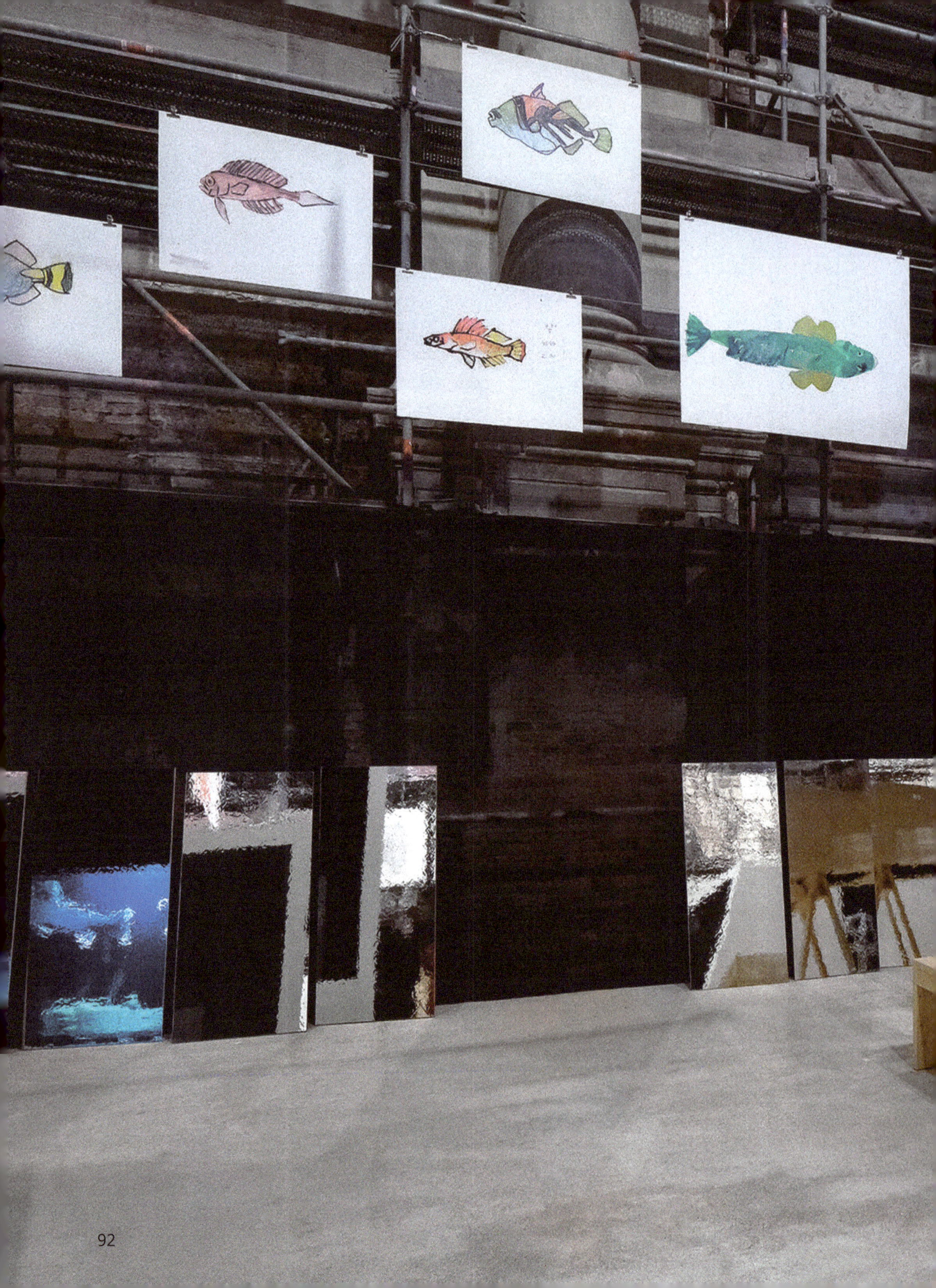

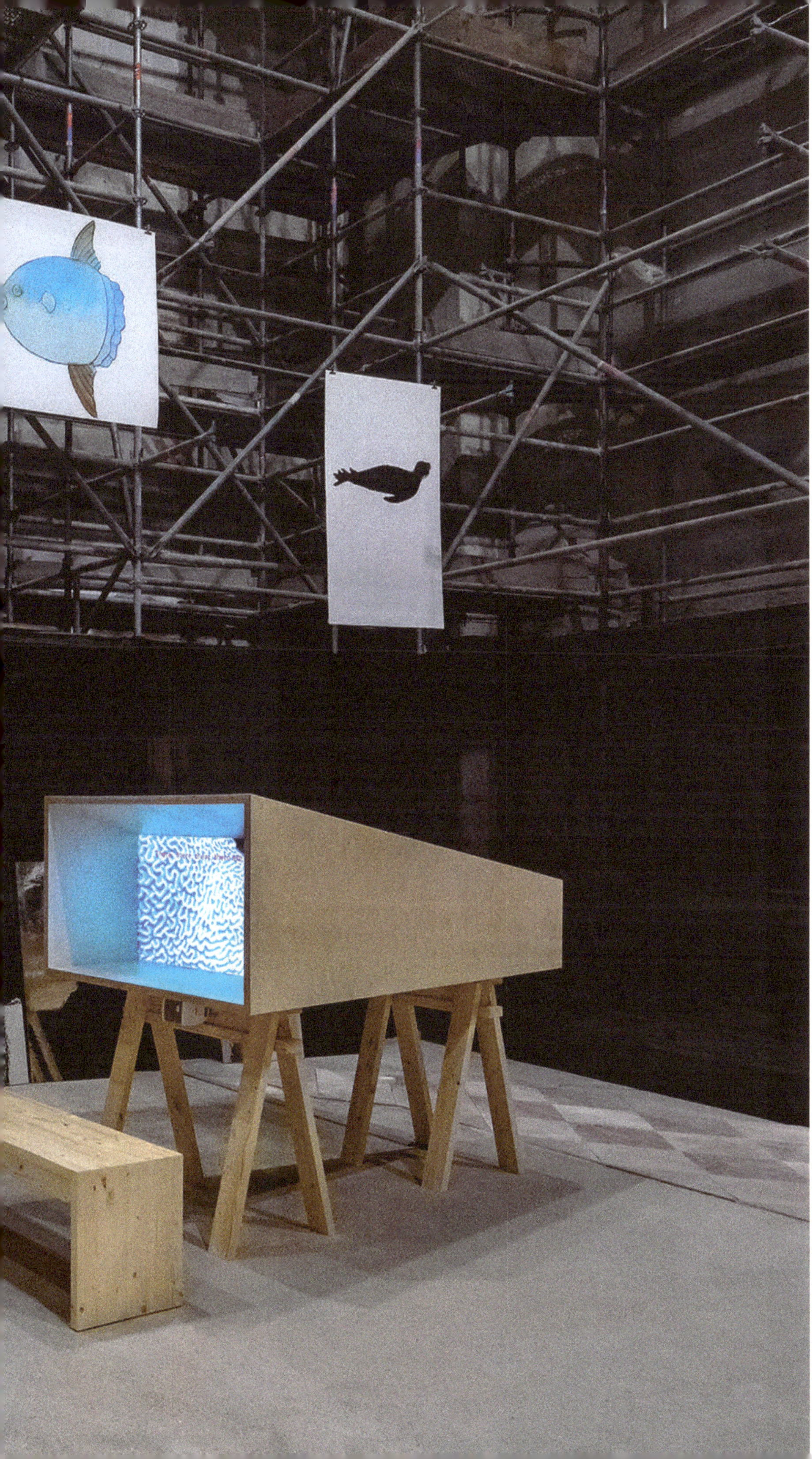

Joan Jonas
Moving Off the Land II, at Ocean Space, Chiesa di San Lorenzo, mixed media installation, 2019 Photo Enrico Fiorese
© Joan Jonas

mance scholar Baz Kershaw's notion of "theater ecologies".[8] He points out that performance systems act ecologically by providing reflexivity, feedback, adaptation, and by presenting diversity as healthy. The first instance of adaptation was the repurposing of the former Chiesa di San Lorenzo for the exhibition. The nave was filled with new ocean icons including banner-like paintings and prints of fish and sea mammals, videos of real and mythical sea creatures, and glass vitrines of ocean specimens. Mirrors line the walls of the chamber, adding visual complexity and symbolism. Whereas traditional sanctuary stained glass offered moral inspiration from Bible stories, these mirrors, placed at ground level, reflect back on the viewer's own narratives and interactions with the ocean. *MOTL* Curator Stefanie Hessler, referring to writer Jorge Luis Borges's inspiration for Jonas observed, "Mirrors throw us back onto ourselves—for Borges, this caused a feeling of horror. Today, as human actions have left their indelible mark on the environment, mirrored reflections showing us as part of our surroundings also allude to our implicated co-dependence with other creatures, and, in a wider sense, to the unsteady boundaries of culture and "nature".[9] While the mirrors provide an opportunity for introspection, they also reflect the movement of other spectators, reminding us that we are at once individuals and members of a collective whole that bear responsibility for the health of the planet. People, nature, art, and the space itself are all part of a spectacle that evolves and revolves, a space where witnesses become participants.

Jonas constructs an environment where humans and sea life commingle as equal players rather than as bifurcating forces. This reflects Bruno Latour's concept that: "As soon as we come close to nonhuman beings, we do not find in them the inertia that would allow us...to take ourselves to be agents but, on the contrary, we find agencies that are *no longer without connection* to what we are and what we do".[10] Each nonhuman creature depicted in the exhibition is presented as a life force that exists independently of our imposed categories but is open to bonding with us. Jonas even suggests that we have primordial DNA roots in mythical ocean beings like mermaids, which she features in some of her videos.

The artist aims to break down hierarchies by fostering new associations through literature and spoken word, painting, and theater. The paintings of fish are not framed or hung on walls as natural science objects waiting for the human gaze. They are oversized and placed above the spectator; many swing freely in the air, reinforcing their presence and vitality.

Jonas evokes emotion and empathy for sea life through auditory perception. Psychologist Ellen Winner has shown that music is the strongest mode of evoking emotions in people because it activates changes in the hippocampus which is involved with love, compassion, empathy, and the autonomic nervous system.[11] Non-musical sounds can also play a role in our emotions and add to our vestibular experience of the film, according to Antunes.[12] Spectators will hear sound and music within the individual videos and also wafting through the exhibition chamber. It elicits powerful feelings by enveloping us in a sort of aquarium concert that lasts for the duration of our visit.

The tone and cadence of Jonas's voice, often accompanied by music, turns each rigid video viewing box into a warm and welcoming space. The addition of other "voices" in the installation, like the clicking vocalizations of sperm whales, crashing waves, and talking mermaids move us in non-conventional ways. We get a sense that the origin of these sounds is distant in space and time. The sound work includes hydrophone recordings taken underwater by marine biologist David Gruber and the atonal music of Ikue Mori. These unfamiliar sounds may affect our nervous and vestibular systems while at the same time connecting us with the "strange strangers". They contribute to the fantasy that we are underwater.[13] The musical echoes heard around the cavernous interior convert the space into a new kind of spiritual sanctuary, one where Jonas is the priestess. Music and spirituality are gateways to universal caring.

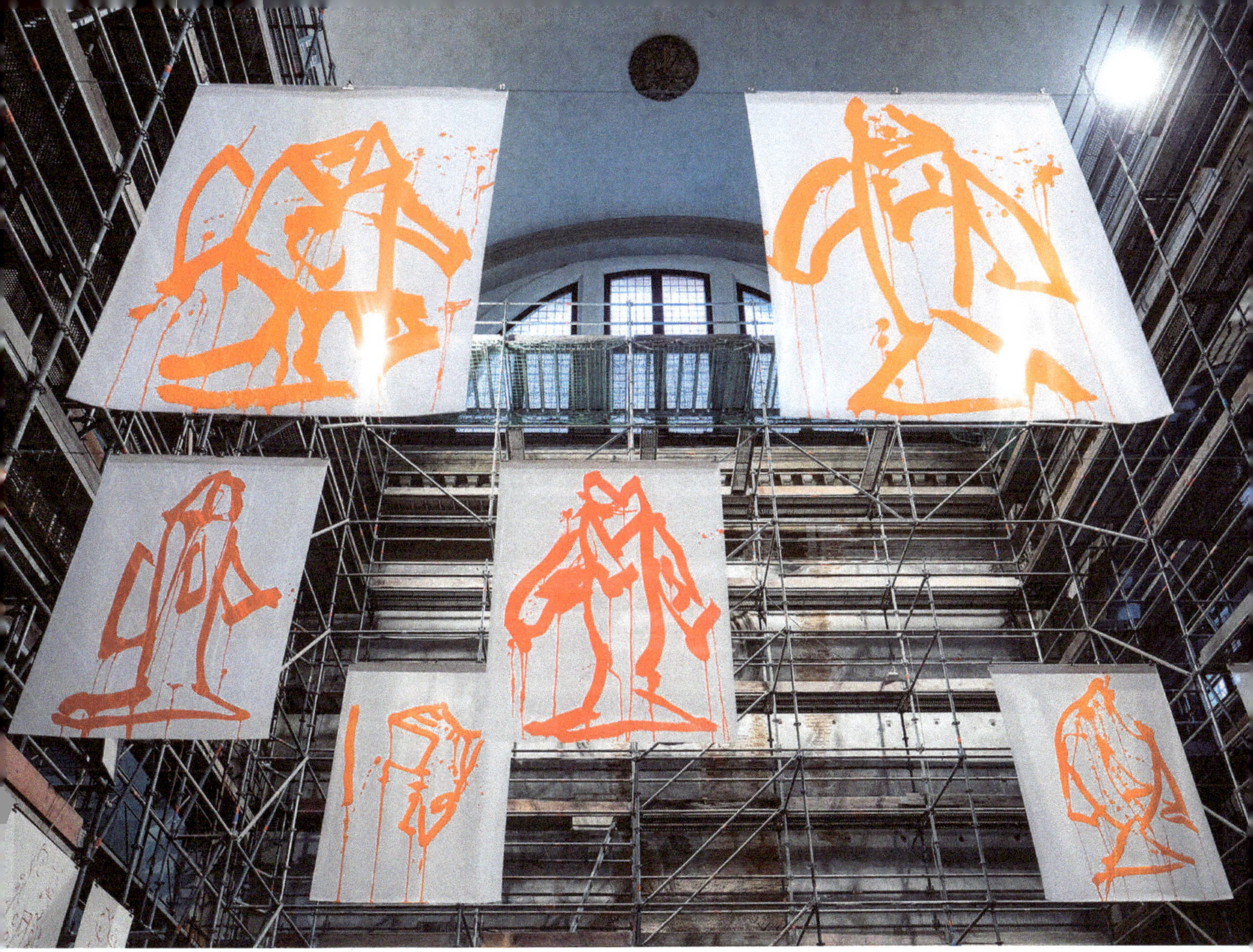

Joan Jonas
Moving Off the Land II, at Ocean Space, Chiesa di San Lorenzo, mixed media installation, 2019
Photo Enrico Fiorese © Joan Jonas

There is an advocacy agenda proffered within this installation though Jonas is reluctant to admit it "Well there is a message, but I don't think I can express it solely in words. A lot of people aren't exposed to some of these things about the ocean. It is an important issue but I don't want to be didactic".[14] In fact, in *MOTL* she is crafting a world where, as Donna Haraway envisioned "Animals are everywhere full partners in worlding, in becoming with."[15] Jonas helps us recognize the power, but also the fragility of ocean ecosystems, and inspires us to be better teammates through our actions. She brings to light beings which are hidden and endangered, like right whales, Johnson's seagrass, and coral reefs. She alerts us, through Gruber's underwater footage, to the intelligence of bioluminescent organisms, some of which can warn sea creatures of impending doom. Once we recognize this sort of intelligence and accept that it has ripple effects in the ecosystem, we are more prone to protect it.

Other forms of activism include the recruitment of teenagers for this project. They participated as learners, actors, videographers, artists, animal handlers, and writers. Gathering and showcasing a diverse group of children is an endearing and poignant gesture because we see the sincerity and optimism in their faces in spite of the fact that they will inherit our damaged ecosystem. The artist gives both participants and viewers hope that this younger generation can

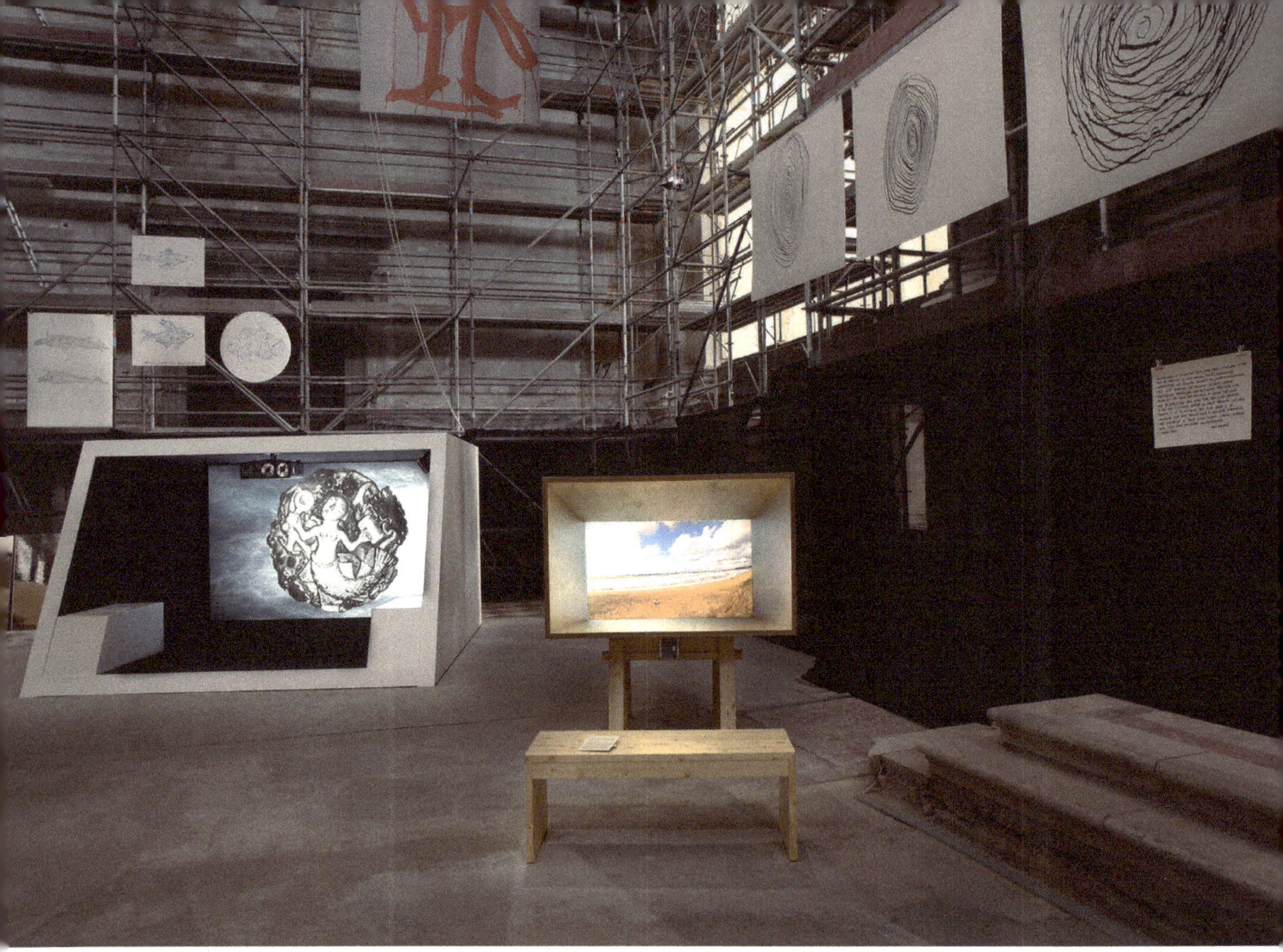

Joan Jonas
Moving Off the Land II, at Ocean Space, Chiesa di San Lorenzo, mixed media installation, 2019
Photo Enrico Fiorese © Joan Jonas

reimagine, rebuild, and sustain a more ocean-friendly world. This possibility bolsters our resolve to care as well.

This author was not the only visitor who was inspired to seek a connection with the "strange strangers" presented in the installation. The exhibition guest comment book[16] showed that the artist evoked empathy, admiration, and a sense of responsibility to sea life with visitors from around the world. Some of the most stirring comments included:

> "thank you for giving us the perception that we are responsible for life on earth"

> "You move the century forward with such beauty-wise intermediary,
> O guardian of the secret vibrations-many bows"

> "Walking through this exhibition, hosted within a disused church, feels as if I'm diving headfirst into an ocean of splendor. Thank you for curating this thoughtful mostra and bringing up a critical topic/issue of our humanity"

> "Here speaks the voice of the non-dual consciousness, to which we don't

remember we belong"

"the Water is in us, we are liquid. Thank you for this installation"

These responses indicate Jonas's success in fostering a belief in deeper and more harmonious relationships between self and the natural world. She has created an environment where Arne Naess's idea of ecosophy rules, that is, a philosophy of ecological harmony or equilibrium.

Once our emotions and sense of responsibility are triggered are we moved to action?" Hopefully yes. We know that the senses and emotions elicited by the art will circulate in the public sphere and take on an expanded social and cultural significance.[17] We have the science to prove that affect and emotion are linked to behavior and rational decision-making.[18] But empirical studies on audience response to environmental art are very limited, and nearly non-existent when it comes to viewer's subsequent actions. One important study by Sommer and Klockner,[19] made at the Paris Climate Conference in 2015, tells us something about which characteristics and styles of art caused the highest emotional and cognitive activation (which could lead to certain behaviors). That group of art was labelled "the awesome solution" and it displayed "beautiful and colorful depictions of sublime nature, created a personal connection, engaged audiences in a positive way, and offered solutions to environmental problems".[20] Jonas's aesthetic, durational, and immersive work provides an opportunity for reflection, ongoing dialogue, and short-term engagement with the "strange strangers" in our universe.

Endnotes

[1] *Portlandia*, Season 8, episode 5, 2018

[2] Joan Jonas, *Moving Off the Land II* premiered at Ocean Space, Chiesa di San Lorenzo, Venice March 24 - September 29, 2019, and travelled to the Museo Nacional Thyssen-Bornemisza, Madrid February 25-September 13, 2020. My essay refers to the Venice venue only. The exhibition at Ocean Space was the first in a series of shows, performances, symposia, concerts, screenings, and other events organized by Thyssen Bornemisza Art Contemporary that explore the oceans from different perspectives over the coming years. Commissioned by TBA21-Academy and curated by Stefanie Hessler.

[3] Timothy Morton, *Ecology without nature: rethinking environmental aesthetics* (Cambridge, Mass: Harvard University Press, 2009) and *The Ecological Thought* (Cambridge: Harvard University Press, 2012). This concept finds earlier expression in Alexander von Humboldt's "web of life".

[4] See the origin of the term in Antonio Damasio, *Descartes' Error: Emotion, Reason and the Human Brain* (New York: Penguin, 2005).

[5] Alexa Weik von Mossner, *Affective Ecologies: empathy, emotion, and environmental narrative* (Columbus, OH: Ohio State University Press, 2017), 3

[6] Footage recorded by Jonas in the following aquariums: the Lofoten Aquarium in Norway; the New England Aquarium in Boston, MA; the New York Aquarium in Coney Island, NY; the National Aquarium in Baltimore, MD; the Aquarium in Genoa, Italy; the Mystic Aquarium in Mystic, CT; and various Aquariums in Tokyo, Japan

Biofluorescent sea animals and Cape Breton footage recorded by marine biologist David Gruber. Underwater swimming footage recorded in Jamaica by Cynthia Beatt. For full credits see MOTL curator Stefanie Hessler's website http://stefaniehessler.com/entries/joan-jonas-moving-off-the-land-ii.

[7] Sonia Shechet Epstein, "A Conversation with Joan Jonas Moving Off the Land", "Museum of the Moving Image website", *Sloan Science and Film*, August 9, 2018 http://www.scienceandfilm.org/articles/3129/a-conversation-with-joan-jonas-moving-off-the-land

[8] Luis Rocha Antunes, "Slow TV: The Experiential and Multisensory Documentary," in *Cognitive Theory and Documentary Film*, ed. Catalin Brylla, and Mette Kramer (Palgrave Macmillan US, 2018), 206, 213. https://doi.org/10.1007/978-3-319-90332-3_12

[9] Baz Kershaw, *Theatre Ecology: Environments and Performance Events* (Cambridge: Cambridge University Press, 2007), 15, 53.

[10] Stefanie Hessler, *Joan Jonas: Moving Off the Land II*, 2019, exhibition labels.

[11] Bruno Latour, *Facing Gaia, Eight Lectures on the New Climatic Regime* (Cambridge: Polity Press, 2017), 62

[12] Ellen Winner, *How Art Works: A Psychological Exploration* (New York, NY: Oxford University Press, 2019), 32-44.

[13] Antunes, "Slow TV," 215.

[14] For an excellent sound recording visit the virtual tour in Madrid. https://www.youtube.com/watch?v=-eaR6j_UBAo

[15] Epstein, ibid

[16] Donna Haraway, *When Species Meet* (Minneapolis: University of Minnesota Press, 2008), 301

[17] See digitized version of the guestbook from *Moving Off the Land II* at Ocean Space, 2019. There is also an analysis of visitor data accumulated from questionnaires completed by visitors to the exhibition. Courtesy of Mark Ferkul, Archivist, TBA21–Academy, Vienna

[18] See discussion of affect theory as it relates to literature and film in Weik von Mossner, "Affective Ecologies," 11.

[19] See the "somatic marker hypothesis" in Antonio Damasio, *Descartes' Error: Emotion, Reason and the Human Brain* (New York: Penguin, 1994), Martha Nussbaum, *Upheavals of Thought: The Intelligence of Emotions* (Cambridge, U.K.: Cambridge University Press, 2003), and Ellen Winner, *How Art Works, A Psychological Exploration* (New York: Oxford University Press, 2019)

[20] L.K. Sommer and C. A. Klockner, "Does Activist Art Have the Capacity to Raise Awareness in Audiences? A Study on Climate Change Art at the ArtCOP21 Event in Paris," Psychology of Aesthetics, Creativity, and the Arts. Advanced online publication (July 1, 2019) https://doi.org/10.1037/aca0000247

[21] Sommer and Klockner, ibid, p.12.

Cynthia Haveson Veloric is an art historian, independent curator, and environmentalist. She received her PhD in Creativity from the University of the Arts, where she is an adjunct professor. Her dissertation analyzed how contemporary artists, using diverse mediums and methods, provoked strong emotional, visceral, or cognitive responses to the climate crisis. In 2018 she curated the exhibition *Repairing Our Earth, Diane Burko Artist/ Environmental Activist*. In 2022 she curated the group exhibition *Risky Beauty: Aesthetics and Climate Change* which is touring the Philadelphia region. Veloric has chaired and presented at the College Art Association, and at the International Environmental Communication Association. Her recent public service includes the inaugural Pennsylvania Climate Convergence, the Clean Air Council of Philadelphia, the Brodsky Center for Printmaking, and the Board of the Main Line Art Center. Her writing has appeared in *19th Century Magazine, Pennsylvania Heritage, Afterimage*, and two essays are forthcoming with Vernon and Bloomsbury Press.

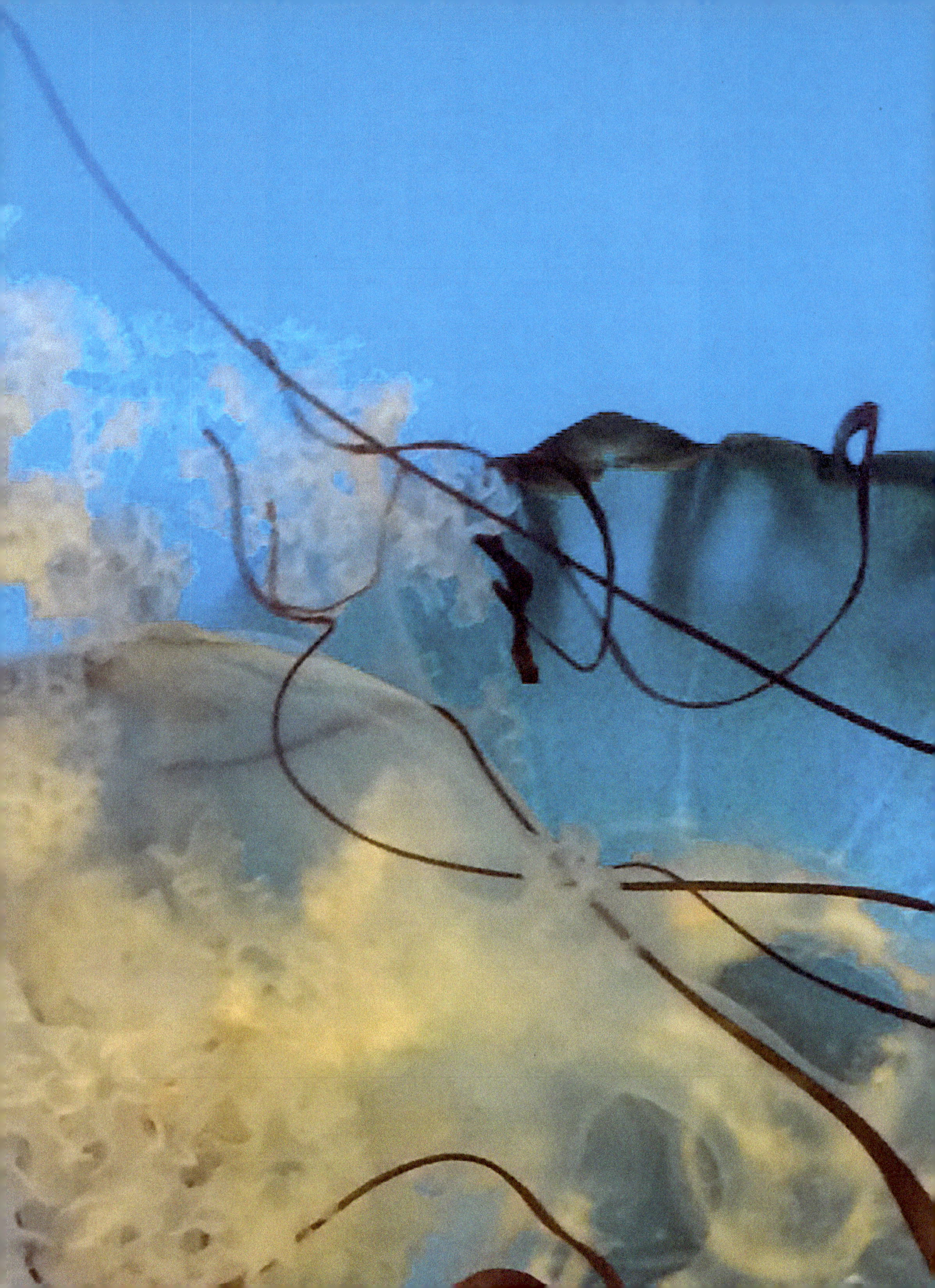

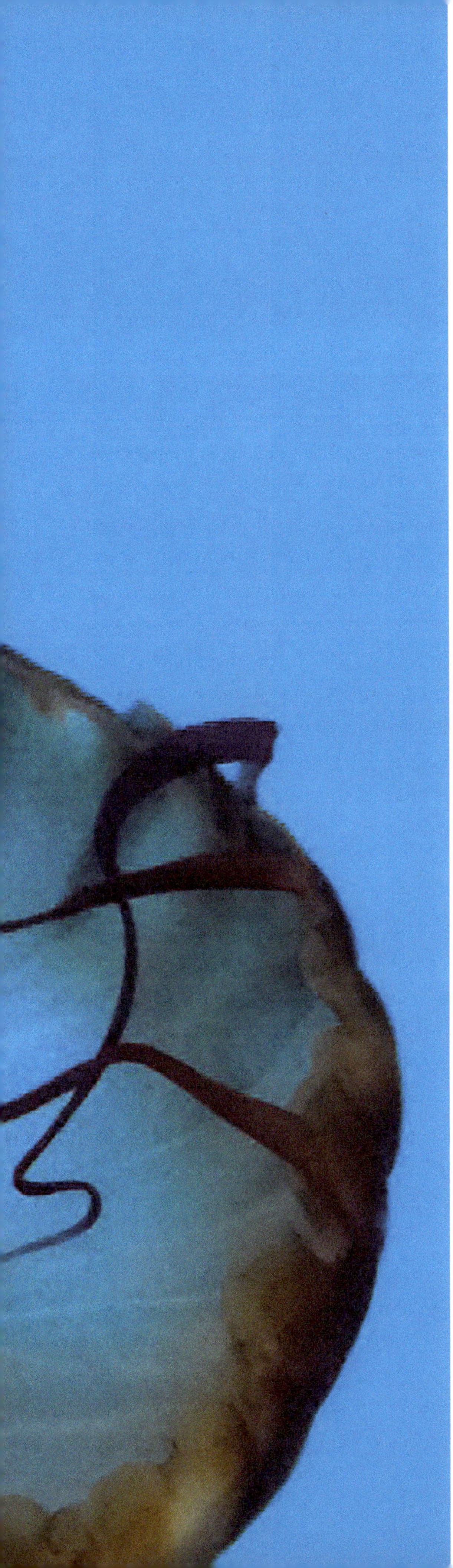

Circulatory entanglements

This dialogue has emerged from a project funded by the Leverhulme Trust called "Circulatory Entanglements: Marine Biomaterials and Paradoxes in Ocean Governance." The project explores how marine organisms figure in contradictory narratives of ocean futures. Horseshoe crabs, jellyfish, and shrimp all feature in concerning stories of depleted and damaged oceans. But they also enliven narratives of a prosperous blue economy. Throughout the project and inspired by Helen's contributions, we have begun to interrogate our own entanglements with the subjects of our research. Through a series of interlaced reflections, we weave personal histories together with the political economies and imagined resource futures in which our research is embedded. Circuitously, we collectively arc toward a more "blended inquiry" and new ways of knowing.

in conversation: **Elizabeth Johnson, Kristoffer Whitney, Hannah Dickinson, Helen J. Bullard**

Helen J. Bullard: What *is* "blended inquiry"? My mind springs immediately to moss slurry: a puree of moss and buttermilk blended to spread the spores and brushed across the rocks around my pond's tiny waterfall. An effort to create an environment where something might germinate: an open suggestion. It's a hypothetical experiment because I'm vegan. And because, somehow, I could never bring myself to hit blend. But beyond the slurry that's growing miniature dairy farms in some other world, "inquiry" is such a sterile word to me (a sterile *world*, as my dyslexic brain writes) of police investigations and perfect laboratory experiments. Add "Entanglements", and now I'm thinking of bodies - bodies entwined, bodies of water, bodies of plants, forests, legs, and arms. And the bodies and body parts of our case studies: jellyfish, shrimp, and horseshoe crabs. The way their stories tangle - through their "uses", their histories, their industries, their promises. Add *"Circulatory"*, and I'm freed again - it gives permission for the freeing. Free to move, free to think, free to swim around in this three-year project called *Circulatory Entanglements: Marine Biomaterials and Paradoxes in Ocean Governance*. Free, until the circulating materials *become* the bodies - become food, harvest, waste, enemies, and saviors. Become "potentially inexhaustible", and now I'm entangled again. And trapped. Trapped in a paradoxical loop of promises, solutions, endless abundance, and simultaneous collapse. Of profit and loss in this Blue Economy.

This direction of blended inquiry wasn't always the plan. We were forced by COVID away from our fieldwork, away from our separate worlds of production, and plunged instead into thick conversations and, at times, uncomfortable entanglements with each other; with our stories, with our pasts, presents and futures. And so, we find ourselves - two geographers, a historian of science, an artist - moving with the waves that overwhelm us, ebbing, and not flowing right now in the world. We four are in the amplitude of the wave, somewhere between the origin and its crest. And now, we want to hold open this space, this open-endedness, not to unite behind one voice, one shared method, and one shared direction, but to share a space that *remains* open and multivocal. It's become a form of care for us; caring for each other, caring for the world, and carving intentional safe spaces for messy discomfort.

We are swept back and forth, back, and forth, through time - deep time - through our methods, through our memories and into the shallows sometimes, into the pools where we converge, and tangle, awkwardly considering the future. Where we hunker closer together - closer, and further, closer, and further - and seek refuge.

We have become perplexed with our methods, our expectations of engagement, our scales of inquiry. We have become our inquiry. Along with the cycles of matter and life, death, rebirth, and record. Our personal histories have followed us here, pitched up on the crests above us, and trailing across the rippling sands beneath.

In wondering where to begin, where our origins are (the four of us - our four species, our four selves), we could start with our beginnings, our earliest memories as researchers. Or we could sweep further back into our pasts - ourselves as curious children - we've talked about that. Or, further back, still, across the sand bars, and into the pasts of our ocean selves, our ocean animals... our research animals, the collective deep times of us all. "We don't see things as they are, we see them as we are", wrote Rae Theodore in a piece called *Scrimshaw*. So, how am I? *Who* am I? Who are we?

I am the kid staring into the rockpools and out to sea (I have frequently started with fieldwork).

I am the small hands that reached high for the old and yellowing books (I love to be in the archives!). I am the kid, wrapped tight in the safety and stories of family, of history, of travelers (I love anecdotes - I'm a storyteller). I'm a listener. A gatherer. A thinker.

Is it radical, and not just academic to imagine a personal connection to research? Like really personal? What if you live a paradoxical life – just like the animals you study – in their liquid and... sedimentary worlds that are ever-shifting, just like your own? What if you study a fish that isn't a fish, a crab that isn't a crab what if you are not perceived as you are, either? What if the crab has gills – like a fish – that flip like the pages of a book? What if the fish is gelatinous and slips away too quickly, and strands itself on the beaches from your childhood – from my childhood, like I do – forever – forever and ever stranded on those beaches, where shrimp flicked in the rockpools, inside their transparent shells. The illusion of protection. Three case studies, four people, well, three and an artist, you know what I mean: "Hi Helen, this doesn't fit the Federal definition of Research". Hmm. Okay. So, how do we navigate this, then?

We're sharing a virtual conversation around a virtual table across three different time zones, and four different lives. What separates us, now, is a virus. I've become pedagogical. Distantly theoretical. Philosophical... We're teasing our methods into tentacles, into boxes and shells, and out of shells.

How do *you* see things as *you* are?

Hannah Dickinson: How do *I* see things as *I* am?
How do *I* make sense of the intersecting methodological and personal questions that are entangled within my research, within *our* shared project?

Let me start with the virus. Covid-19 has stopped me in my tracks and tethered me to my desk in Sheffield since beginning this research. My birthplace, the city I love, but about as far away from the ocean as anywhere else in the UK. Gritty, industrial, so far removed from these marine species that we think with and talk about together. I long to untether myself from this desk, to do some fieldwork, to feel better connected to these species, to oceanic spaces, and other people. And so, I often catch myself thinking back to past times when I felt deeply and irrevocably connected to the sea, its forces, and its inhabitants.

Sometimes I reminisce – almost fondly – about the time I got a jellyfish sting whilst swimming in Sicily. It was September 2020, a brief and welcome reprieve between covid lockdowns, and coincidentally I was spending my evenings during that holiday writing an application to join this project and this team. Sitting on our terrace overlooking the sea, traces of the jellyfish tentacles lingering as welts on my arm, I typed and felt hopeful about the future, imagining the possibilities for following shrimp, horseshoe crabs, and jellyfish. There's something curious about how that jellyfish sting aligned with the start of my personal inquiry, my deep dive into the circulation of marine biomaterials. I somehow feel corporeally connected to this project now.

And these organisms that we study have in their own way become corporeally connected to covid. Horseshoe crab blood used for vaccine production; luminescent components from jellyfish to detect covid in the air; PPE coated with chitosan derived from shrimp shells. The drive to combat this virus has held all of *us* in place at home for so long, yet moves these organisms from their respective watery homes into unfamiliar terrestrial spaces, entangling them with human bodies and circuits of capital.

But what about moving these organisms into extra-terrestrial spaces? Some scientists say that maybe the answer to our collective earthly woes – to avoid future pandemics – is to jump ship: to move to Mars. And they even promise that shrimp and their biomaterials will help us to build our future homes on Mars.

I've tried to imagine this, but somehow I can't believe it. Martian shrimp? Well no, it's not believable.

We can't farm shrimp on Mars, there's no water there. Shrimp on Mars is just a fantasy, one of the co-authors of the paper[1] admits: "It's a sci-fi imagination, we're just trying to prove a concept". Black soldier flies will be the answer, shrimp were just the start.

I keep finding myself at these crossroads where the material and the immaterial, the real and the imagined intersect. I begin by following apparently real things to real places: shrimp shells, shrimp-derived chitosan, chitosan bioplastics, chitosan innovators, and biotechnology companies. But these real, material configurations of people, places, objects, and ideas keep dissolving into broken promises before re-emerging as novel iterations of the same fantastical stories of salvatory shrimp shells. How can I make sense of these tensions and thresholds between reality and fantasy?

So, here I am, momentarily floating adrift, untethered, treading water, trying to work out how to move forward from here. The world is opening up again, I feel an urgent need to move away from my desk to *really* follow the circulatory entanglements of shrimp and chitosan. We'll start in Louisiana, but will we find anything real to follow? Or is this story of circulation one that demands new methodologies which are attuned to fantasies as 'things' to follow?

This is the task that confronts me now. It's staggering to think how far I've come since that jellyfish sting nearly 18 months ago, and yet I've hardly moved anywhere at all.

Elizabeth R. Johnson: Where do I begin? Where does all of this—these circulatory entanglements of human and nonhuman matters and ecologies—begin? There are, of course, too many starting points to propose an actual origin, so we have to start somewhere in the muddy middle, as Donna Haraway suggests.

My inclination, nearly always, is to begin in a bioscience research laboratory, where the pursuit of some form of knowledge engages in intimate encounters with nonhuman organisms, where bioscientists curiously ask of a body that is not their own: "Now, how does *this* work"? "What is the nature of *this* life"?

My mind invariably returns to the same laboratory, the same interview, the same bodies. It was an event, in my life at least. It took place in 2009, in the course of my PhD research. I can still hear the salt water running through the pipes that ringed the room; still smell the damp, slightly salty air, tinged with mildew that threatened to corrode the walls. The saltwater traveled across petri dishes that housed jellyfish polyps, through beakers where jellyfish ephyra pulsed, and into four kreisel that housed fully grown medusae. Above the noise, a postdoctoral researcher explained that the single most crucial ingredient in his research was his love of jellyfish. I was - and still am - struck by this declaration.

Such love is, in many ways, incomprehensible. Yes, the research required caring—constantly—for the jellyfish. But it also involved dismembering them. What was I to make of this form of love that was also a form of violence? It was incomprehensible. But perhaps it was also fitting. The jellyfish themselves seemed to remain inscrutable despite the post-doc's efforts. For over a century, bioscientists have struggled to describe the nervous system of jellyfish. A neural net stretches across the bell of their body. Nerve clusters concentrated at the edge initiate movement. But how those clusters coordinate and communicate with one another remains something of a mystery. After two years of research, this careful, loving postdoc was still short of answers.

Over a decade later, bioscience communities are still only learning how little they understand jellyfish bodies and their role in ocean ecologies. So, I keep returning to jellyfish and the laboratories where they are encountered and knowledge about them made.

But, I have to confess that I've been disingenuous. This laboratory, this interview...wasn't the starting point at all. Yes, I want to see and experience the encounter between the curious minds of bioscientists and the nonhuman subjects of their research. But it was the shape of their questions that had taken me there. If early twentieth-century jellyfish researchers asked, "Now, how does *this* work?" or "What is the nature of *this* life", twenty-first-century bioscientists are asking a different set of questions: "Now, what can *this* body do"? and "How can I put this body to *work*"?

The questions—of both eras—were animated by histories that stood pres-

Elizabeth Johnson
Live Jellyfish © Elizabeth Johnson

ent in my moments of laboratory inquiry. My jellyfish lover's research was funded by one of the world's foremost oil well companies. They were hoping insights into neural nets would lead to new sensory array technologies. Their histories—of wanting to know what lay beneath the surface of the earth, of perfecting the art of petroleum extraction—could not be disentangled from the utterances of love or that circulation of saltwater, Petri-dishes, kreisels, and jellyfish in various stages of development.

My pursuit of jellyfish research today is leading me to laboratories where jellyfish collagen, mucus, stem cells, and toxins are studied to spark biotech and biopharmaceutical innovations. Those early twentieth-century researchers who seemed driven by some innate curiosity about the world? They used knowledge of jellyfish neurology to justify their advocacy of eugenics. Certainly, I can follow Bruno Latour to suggest that from the laboratory, I can raise these worlds of late capitalism, colonialism (neo and otherwise), and racism.[2] But the laboratories are neither a beginning nor an end of such entangled stories. I will return to them again nevertheless, but always wary of what worlds are being raised in advance of and following them.

Kristoffer Whitney: I'll start with memory and the places of policy-making. Like Hannah, like all of us, I spend most of my days tethered to a laptop in my home, COVID-bound. I made hopeful promises to visit the sites where horseshoe crabs are caught, where they are bled, and where their unique blood is transmogrified into a toxin-detecting substance. But here, too, COVID has made itself felt. Not only in the sense that the vaccine injected into my arm was tested with this substance but that the ongoing pandemic has nixed these hoped-for site visits.

I wanted to see this biomedical miracle in action and reconnect with long-ago experiences of horseshoe crabs. In the absence of travel, I find myself straining to remember. Over twenty years ago, now, I first discovered these creatures in person. In late spring, they pour onto Delaware Bay beaches in numbers too large to convey in language (I suppose one could use the language of mathematics, but we don't seem to have a head for large numbers). This spawning event has to be seen, perhaps captured visually - photos can convey a rough approximation of its magnitude. But I wanted to be there and to remember, more than just the visual. Assuming connections matter - in research, in life - I wanted the opportunity to reach back out to horseshoe crabs in all senses. So I try to remember.

I can sort of bring Bay beaches covered in crabs back into my mind's eye. Although, it's hard to separate what I saw from the innumerable photos I've seen since. I can almost hear the waves, and soft scratching of *Limulus's* legs on the sand and each other's carapaces. Birds too, of course. What's a beach without the screaming and laughter of seagulls? I can even, indistinctly, recall picking up horseshoe crabs. Righting them when they've flipped over. Allowing their legs to play over my fingers. I've never tasted a horseshoe crab, thank god, but taste's close relative 'smell' is another matter. Of my memories, this is probably the strongest. The smell of a salt marsh, and the brackish rot surrounding these beaches, are unforgettable.

As tenuous as these memories seem, and as disappointed as I am that I will not find my way back to the crabs and the beaches any time soon, I wonder what - if any - connections the people who decide these creatures' fate have to them. Presumably, the people who capture and bleed the crabs have a direct, sensory experience of them. The wildlife managers keep an eye on the harvests and the beaches, as well. Does it matter? What happens when one works their way up through the agencies in charge of setting limits on crab harvests, or the rules governing how they are treated? What about those who deliberate over using animals like horseshoe crabs in biomedicine, versus the use of synthetic compounds that don't rely on blood "donations" from one of the world's most ancient creatures?

I don't know. The people occupying the boardrooms of the multinational conglomerates that use the crabs' blood almost certainly have no direct experience with them. I've been assured by one marine biologist that "they don't give a fuck about horseshoe crabs." Maybe a bit harsh, maybe likely. The experts at wildlife and fisheries agencies, the FDA, and the Pharmacopeia, at least when they talk to me, seem more interested in their models, their chemicals, and their experiments than in Bays, beaches, and biology. I can't blame them, exactly. That's their job, maybe even their calling. But I feel like it should matter - direct experience, connection, and care. I have at least one example of it mattering, in the most unlikely of places: a technician in the biggest of big Pharma has led the charge to replace horseshoe crab blood in our public health infrastructure with the synthetic replacement.

So, I try to remember. Hoping that a direct connection to horseshoe crabs matters, or will matter, for this research, for those whose decisions directly affect the crabs, for all of us who benefit - unwittingly or not - from horseshoe crab blood, and for *Limulus polyphemus* themselves. We'll see.

HJB: Yes. It matters. And, we benefit. It's all *so* messed up, though.

When I sat in that building, people being labeled and controlled like cattle, and felt the first needle sink into my arm, I couldn't help thinking of them, and thanking them; the horseshoe crabs. I was in England at the time, *so far* away from any of it.

Yes. I know that feeling of *incomprehensible* love, of *unconditional* love. And I focused *so hard* on that box of disposable gloves in front of me to stop crying. I see you. I hear you. All of you! Stuck in the muddy middle. I can feel my skin itching as my feet sink into the mudflats of Kitts Hummock. I can smell the dried, cracked salt on the backs of the horseshoe crabs crowning out of the baked mud-like rocks. I *long* to be there, Kristoffer. I *long* for it!

I hear you, Elizabeth, recounting Latour, and it takes me back to one of my own beginnings, a science-art residency in Brighton, called Lab. Life.: the first time I considered medicine and transgenics in my practice.

I, too, hear the saltwater rushing through the open loop system. This time, in Massachusetts, I hardly knew where to start: horseshoe crabs, jellyfish, squid, dogfish... And I remember the sounds of the lab space I was promised in New York. He was standing there in his suit, sweating, and explaining the marine water system. He paused, for just a second too long, as he looked me up and down, and smirked, and said "You can grow pot in here if you like."

I hear you, Hannah, *longing* to be untethered from this endless present. It's even worse now, in the dullness and ice and wind, and I don't even bother to dress myself most days. I'm dreaming only of the past, lately where nothing is real, and everything dissolves upon waking, leaving me exhausted.

Interesting, about the not giving a fuck. I've never met anyone in the field who wasn't deeply moved: industry or otherwise. Now that's the power of lived experience, right? *Study nature, not books.*

And yet, here we are, not in nature. Yes. It's *so* much harder to get there now: to care, I mean.

I find myself bouncing back and forth between sheer emptiness and total fulfillment. In so many ways things matter *more* now. But also, less.

I hear you. I remember those sounds, the touch, the smells: I walked for miles in the rain, with blisters, trying to get to that workshop called Green Eggs & Sand. That technician, Kristoffer, had made his announcement just days earlier: he's an ornithologist, critically. We discussed it, eventually, as a group, after that first uncomfortable night in a dorm-room bunk.

Those moments, on the beaches, are the closest I have *ever* come to a spiritual experience; a rapture.

KW: I think, now, reflecting on my initial reflection, I've conveyed care. In my frus-

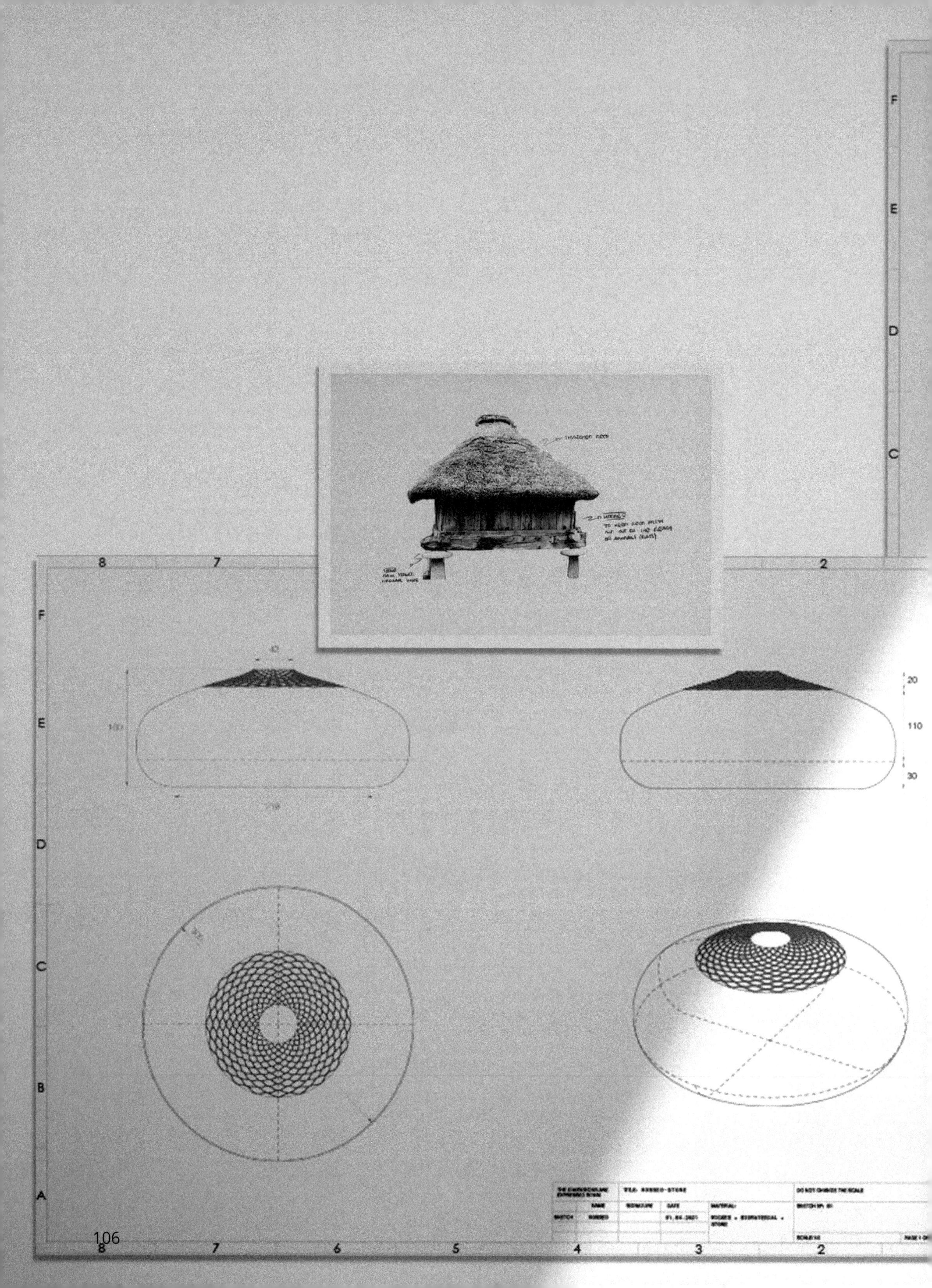
20
110
30

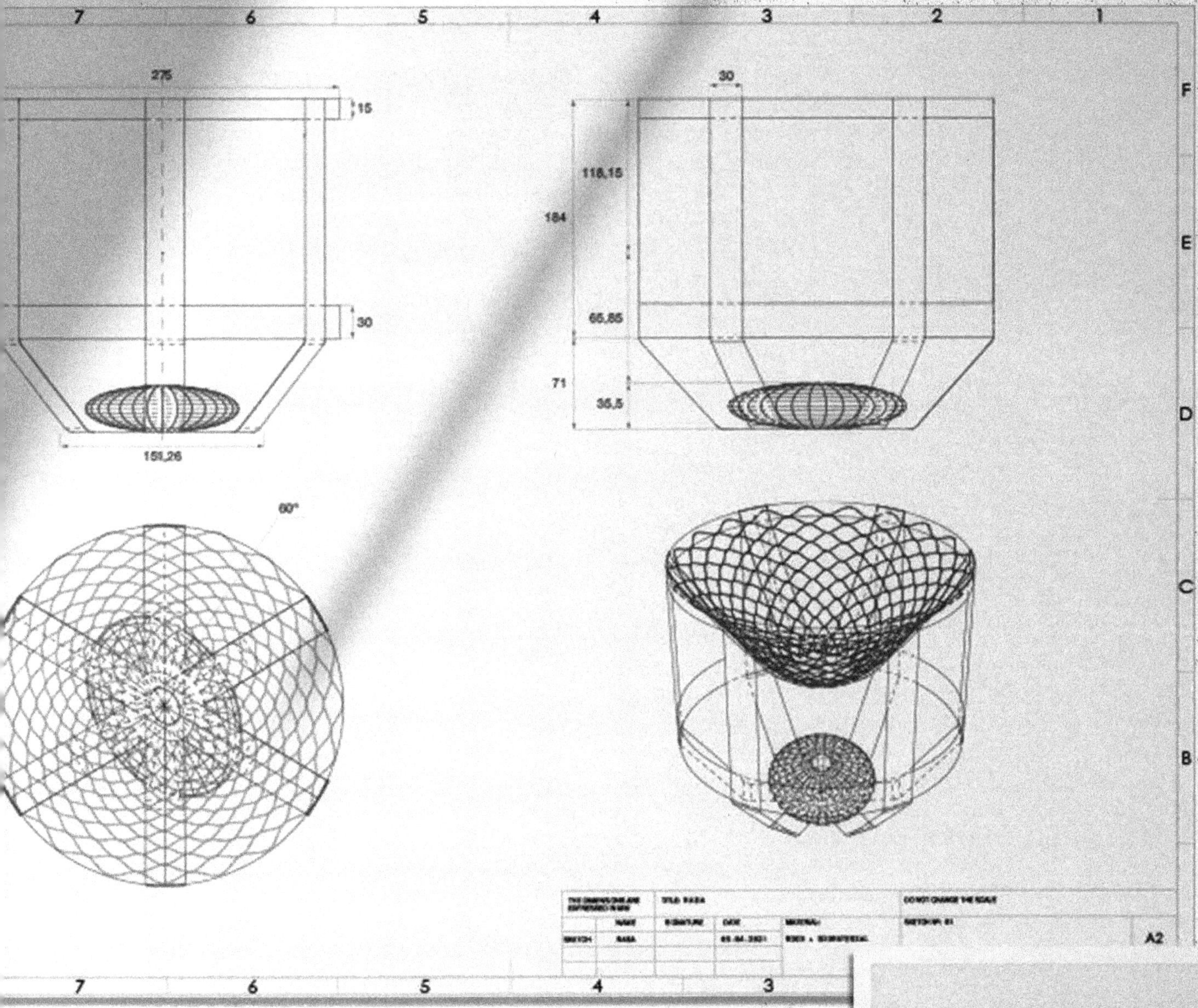

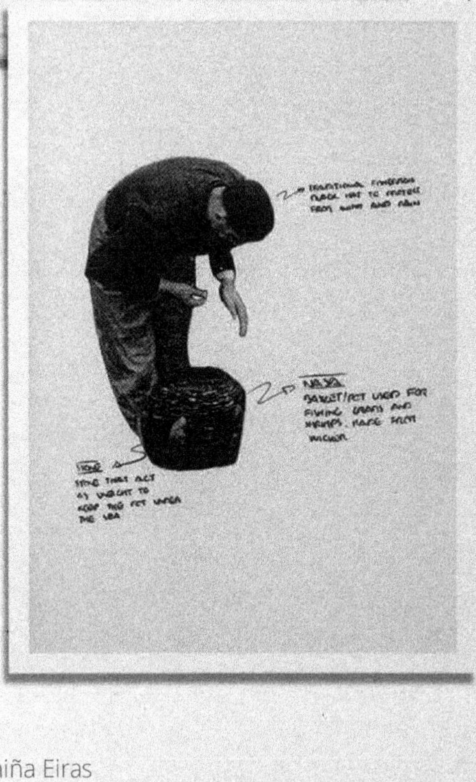

Paula Camiña Eiras
Design Concept for Galician wooden fishing trap re-interpretation, 2021 © Paula Camiña Eiras

tration that I can't go back to Delaware Bay anytime soon, I've reinforced for myself that I care about creatures like horseshoe crabs – care about how they are treated, how they are used, and *that* they are used at all. About framing any nonhuman animal as "natural resources" for big-C Capital. Not that I'm prepared to go down the slippery slope of eschewing the use of life to sustain my own. Let's remember once again the vaccine we can all thank bled horseshoe crab for.

But care. Respect for nonhuman life. That's different, I think. A reflection on us. So what do I do? I know what I said I would do – said to myself, to my funders. I want to engage in the policy debates over horseshoe crab blood. Keep the political in ecology – figure it out, take a stand, write a paper, give a talk. But I feel a long way from that. From the dilemma of method in the time of COVID, I move to the dilemma of analysis. I've found a dim, slim silver lining in pandemic research: informants think nothing of jumping on Zoom and talking to me for hours about what they think is going on with horseshoe crabs. So many people, so many economic and political entities, so many perspectives.

Most of the horseshoe crabs pulled from the water for human use are used as bait – used to catch other organisms, that in turn are shipped to seafood markets halfway around the world. Is that sustainable? Allowable? The "crabs" used for biomedicine largely, as far as anyone can tell, survive the process. So that's fine, right? But why continue this practice when there is a synthetic alternative waiting in the wings that promises to make questions of threatened species and animal rights related to this fishery moot? What's the holdup?

I could say let's just look at the numbers – the populations and models of horseshoe crabs and fisheries – and trust the experts. But that's cheating. Humanistic science studies is meant to critique knowledge production, not lean on it. Approaches like standpoint theory are great for adopting more perspectives and diversifying voices. Maybe less helpful for making decisions? I don't know. I cast about for ways to make sense of our reliance on horseshoe crabs for myself, much less inform policy (not to mention deal with the conceit that policymakers care what I think). Hmmm, this reflection has turned sour. But I do hope, I do want to understand. Still looking for a way to parse the interests and perspectives of everybody that uses these creatures. Is it hopeful or apocalyptic to realize that species that were around before the dinosaurs are likely to be here long after the Anthropocene?

HD: Helen's almost spiritual experiences on the beach have reminded me that our collective conversations about our personal histories, engagements, and entanglements with the ocean and oceanic beings, have *often* evoked a semblance of the spiritual. By spiritual, I mean experiences that affect our human spirit, our understanding of what it means to be human, to be *us* as individuals. Moments that make us stop and ask, who *am I*?

Admittedly, however, I never really anticipated finding others' spirituality - even religion- lurking within this science of transforming shrimp shells into chitosan. A chemist told me his commitment to chitosan stems from his biblical vocation to be "a steward of the materials in our world that no one else wants: the pollutants". From a different, albeit connected perspective, famed material scientist Neri Oxman speaks about her shrimp-chitosan inventions as "a realization of the ancient biblical verse 'From Dust to Dust'"; or in this case "from water to water".

I'm still not at all sure what to make of these seemingly paradoxical relationships between the bio-sciences, biotechnology, spirituality, and religion. Surprising, uncomfortable, taking on different guises, yet seemingly everywhere. I'm reminded of anthropologist Nils Bubandt, who calls our era the Anthropocene Uncanny. This epoch, he says, is a "melting pot of political doubt, scientific truth, and religious morality". Thinking about it, I've seen this muddle of politics, bioscience, and religion circulating amongst the wealthy, Western masses for whom dieting of all things, has become something of an uncanny Anthropocene religion.

Indeed, hordes of people are popping millions of chitosan diet pills as part of modernity's doctrine of self-improvement.

Of course, this is all so far removed from spiritual moments on beaches... it's hardly fair to contemplate them in the same breath. Nevertheless, there does seem to be *something* about chitosan – a synthetically produced biomaterial - that inspires spiritual conversations, adulation, and reverence from people. It's *so* strange, *uncanny* even. How do I pinpoint this intangible something? How do I put my finger on it? Here it is again, this dilemma of analysis that haunts me: the tensions between the material and the immaterial.

This makes me ponder... if Kristoffer is locating ways to keep the *political* in ecology, then I, on the other hand, seem to be continually searching for the 'ecology' in my data. What I mean is, where are those elusive shrimp? Informants discuss chitosan with fervor, but rarely do they stop... pause for thought... to think, let alone talk, about the shrimp for whom chitin provides a natural armor. When asked, many don't even know where the shrimp were harvested, or where the shells were processed to make their chitosan. Do they care? Not always, and maybe not often. Clearly, to care about chitosan does not necessarily entail caring about shrimp, their habitats, and oceans. But it does to *me*.

And so, there are big, glaring ecological gaps in my data and my knowledge. And these gaps reflect a growing chasm, disconnection, and distance that I'm witnessing emerge between many chitosan biotechnologies, their innovators, and the ocean. Whilst the liveliness and oceanic ecologies of jellyfish and horseshoe crabs loom large in my collaborators' reflections and practical engagements with their research participants, for me, shrimp and their watery habitats come in and out of focus: they are abstracted, sometimes out of reach, ghostly figures even.

But returning to those informants who spoke about chitosan in almost spiritual or religious ways... it seems for them the ecological is ever present in their work. They may not explicitly dwell on shrimp, but they believe in chitosan as an ecological force: that this marine biomaterial will build better, more sustainable, socio-ecological futures. Isn't it funny then, how following a story of techno-scientific and capital circulation has become entangled with the circulation of 'ancient biblical verse'. I'm repeatedly struck by the paradoxes embedded within humanity's efforts to produce biomaterial futures; and by extension, the paradoxes in my own efforts to make sense of chitosan circulations. What futures do *I* hope for or believe in when I think about this biomaterial?

ERJ: At this point, I'm not sure what exactly I'm feeling. Am I feeling trapped? The layers of entanglement that my collaborators reference... have me feeling the unbearable weight of personal, political, spiritual, and more-than-human social histories amid which we are all deeply ensnarled. But I also have the opposite feeling: that I'm lost; that all it takes is the shake of my head and I've forgotten about having been connected to the ocean, horseshoe crabs, jellyfish, or the politics of settler colonialism and capitalist extraction that guide inquiry into these organisms. Rather than tracing these entangled connections, it would be all too easy to forget and dwell apart from the ocean, in the everyday of my seemingly terrestrial life. That all of this weight of being, as Milan Kundera wrote, is unbearably light after all.

All of us are writing this document together, passing it around to see what stories and ideas our words will spark. Earlier today, I talked with Hannah, but I hadn't read her latest installment. She too was frustrated, and confused. Unsure of where all of this was going, how long we would let these meandering thoughts unwind, whether it would amount to anything at all. As our conversation unfolded, she reminded me of a concept that I often find comforting when faced with this pull between too much and nothing at all: Abyss. As a metaphor for the deep sea, the word conjures watery darkness; a world so impenetrably distant that it might

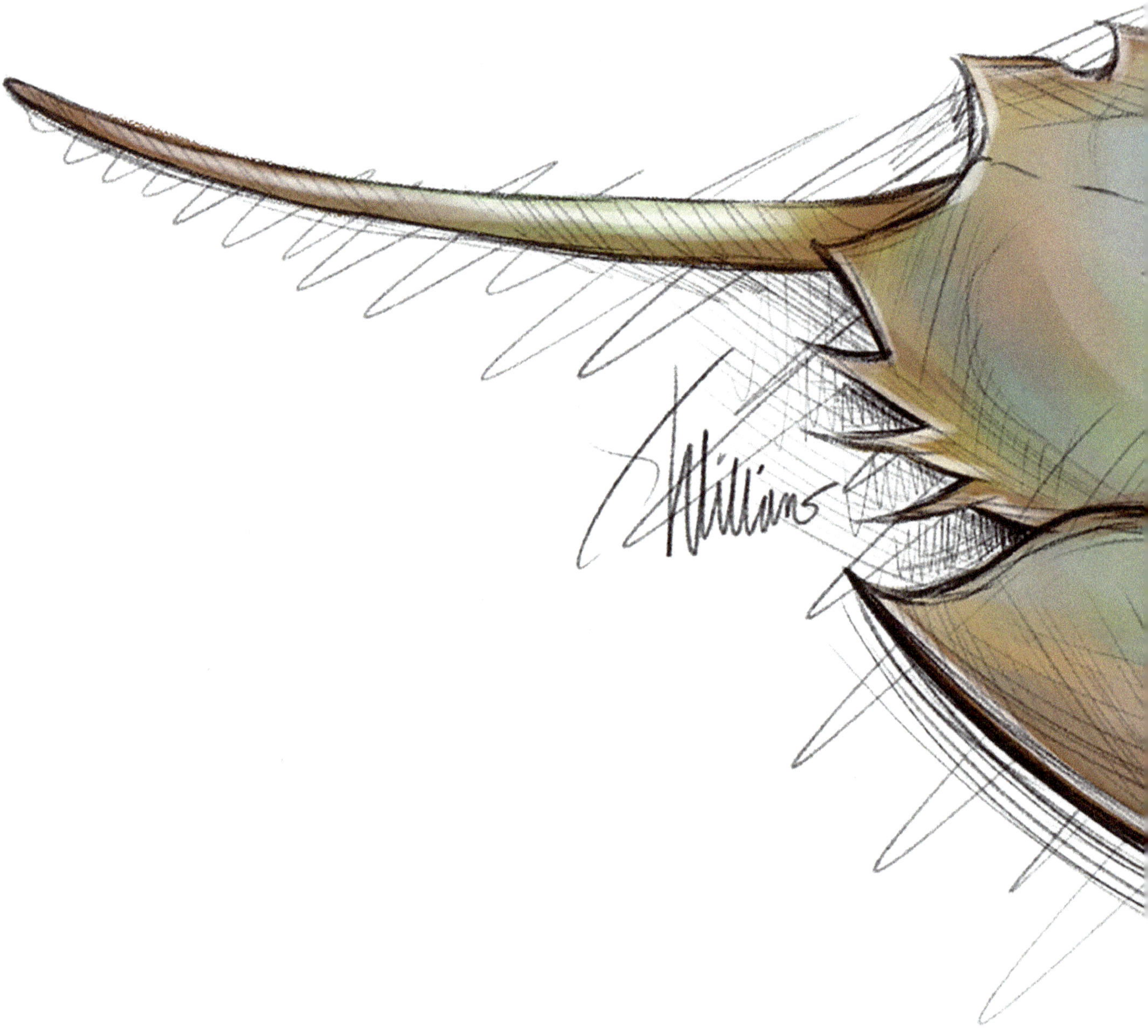

Xavier Williams
Horseshoe crab illustration, 2022

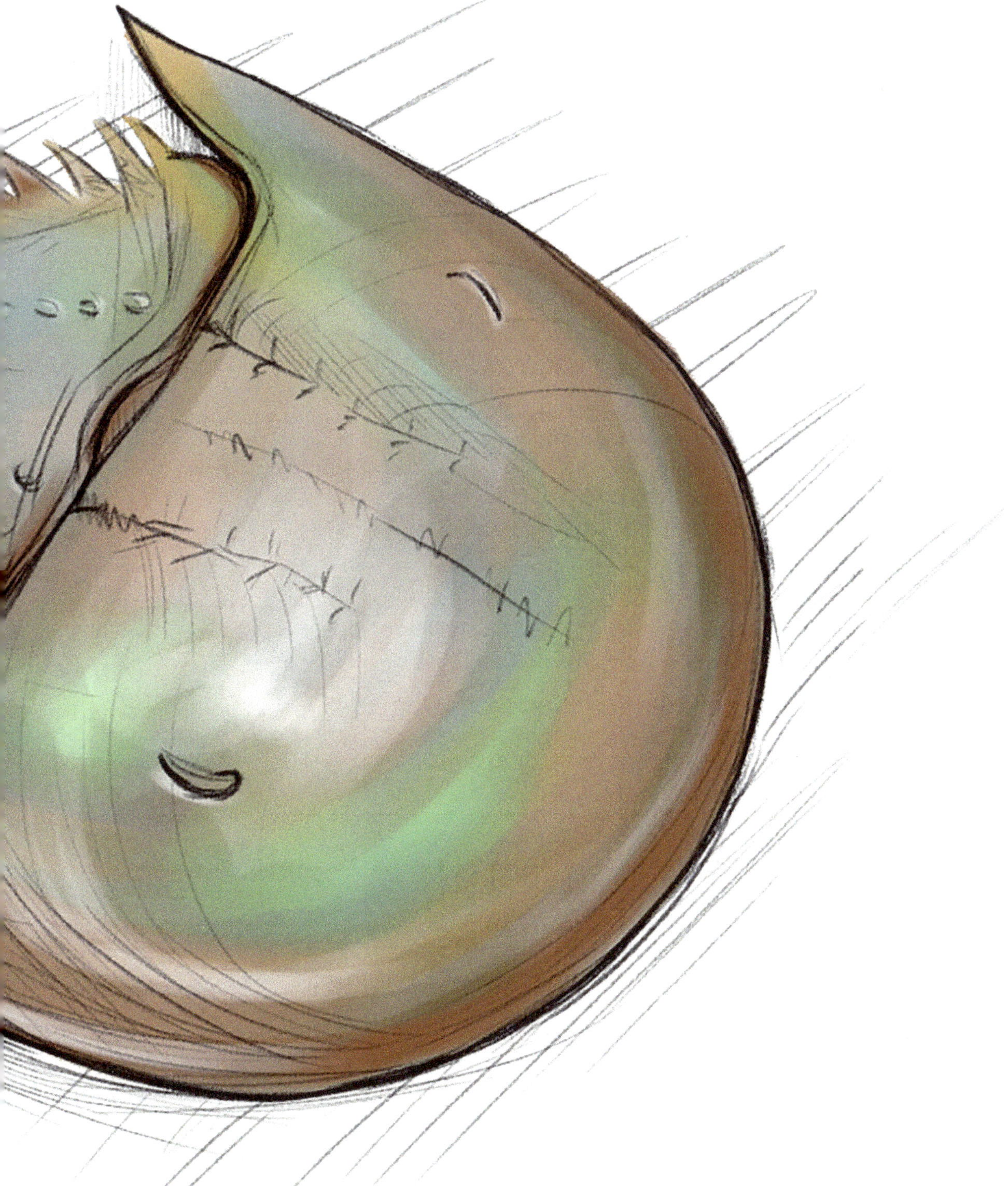

as well be another planet. The deepest dive on record by a human is 328 meters, a small fraction of the ocean's depths, which reach over 10,000m in the Mariana Trench. Below 300m, the weight of water becomes unbearable. We can send robots, sonar, and other sentinels into it to plumb the deep sea, but it's a space we can only experience by such proxies. So, an abyss that is impossibly distant from our immediate experience.

But the abyssal may also be used to describe more than this planetary space accessible only through technology and imagination. In an article on Hesse Honneger's large format paintings of the deformed leaf bugs of Chernobyl's exclusion zone, STS scholar Astrid Shrader uses the notion of "abyssal intimacy" to think about the practice of caring for "seemingly irrelevant" nonhuman organisms.[3] Drawn from Jacques Derrida, "abyssal intimacy" suggests a paradoxical relation. It is characterized by an unbreachable difference/distance and, at the same time, identification and physical proximity. For Scrader, "abyssal intimacy" undoes the "opposition between sameness and difference". Even more, it troubles the dichotomies "between temporal continuity and discontinuity", "activity and passivity" and "attachment and detachment". This leads Schrader to contemplate care and compassion in ways that are not bound to plans of action, responses, or a series of immediate solutions, as these paradigms suggest temporal limits to our capacity to care. If we have only so much time in the day for enacting ethics and politics of care, we must choose what subjects are deserving of our attention, time, and life activity. Such a model of care, hemmed in by time limits, suggests that to care about Ukrainian leaf bugs, especially today, is not only a distraction but a rather horrific injustice given the weight of suffering currently carried by Ukrainian people. But such a calculus, Schrader suggests, is misguided. In its place, she advocates for an "unlimited compassion" fueled by shared vulnerability. Such an unlimited compassion is not the basis for action, but for a curiosity that seeks to "know differently."

If there's a sense of spirituality that drives my work, I think it resides in this space of abyssal intimacy, where unbearable weight and lightness collide in ways that might drive a desire to know differently.

I'm reminded again of that first laboratory encounter where the love of jellyfish seemed so full of contradiction. I would try to offer my modest and often inept help in the lab. One day, I was invited to clean the jellyfish kreisels. It would be my first time touching the jellyfish and I wanted to know exactly how to proceed. The post-doc again surprised me. To begin, he said "make friends with them. Talk to them. Tell them you won't hurt them". There was a playful insincerity in his tone. He said these words with a sardonic smile. I thought he was teasing me. Jellyfish, as far as humans know, don't have ears let alone language. But later, I discovered that he often talked to the jellyfish, even as he would dismember them. In my political ecology inquiries, I often want such tensions to resolve. I, like many, am driven to tell stories of winners and losers, of human oppressors and animal victims. But perhaps these are narrative guide rails that are better overturned so that we might begin to know differently.

HJB: Okay, I'm adding something. But I'm not sure about this. I'm struggling with work at the moment (all of it) because of the world. I find it hard to see why *any* of this matters, especially when the sun is out and all I want to do is fit myself into the slither of light on the floor, like a dog. But, here goes.

To know differently. Yeah, I wish I'd been armed with those words. Because when the "weight of it all" is *not* unbearably light, when you live it every moment of your life when the forced binary choice is between "too much... and nothing at all", for most of my life I've chosen nothing at all. It's how I've coped.

I really don't know where to go from here. I've been staring at my screen for days. How do we shift this? *How* do we move towards hope, towards justice towards a more *just* future? What is the currency?

I think I've decided it's everything we bring: *everything* we have: belief, religion, family, identity, our work, our research, our *lives*.

And it can take a long time to know those things. To trust your knowledge that you're *not* lacking, just because you check "alternative". Because... if I'm *your* "alternative" then *you* are *mine*. And I don't want that. I am my data: that's what I give. My animal has *always* been me. In my shell, with the ocean crashing inside. We need "unlimited compassion", a shared vulnerability. But it's idealistic and *that's* the problem. And, while we've been writing this, the world has changed – again– and I'm changed, with it.

After *all* these conversations: objects and animals, memories and politics, the virus, the war, the heartache... isn't the biological *too hard* to separate from the social? What I mean is, I don't think we can.

And so, I'm with the leaf bugs *and* the people of Ukraine.

How can we talk about justice – just-ness – when the currency is: life and oil, bodies and sand. Blood and water and kreisels – circles. The moon.

And the currency is... the currency is... the currency is...

KW: Not to make glib etymological comparisons, but that word. I can't help but notice that 'currency' itself bridges human and nonhuman worlds – the 'running' root of both water and money. Not unlike the ecosystem and economy, which share a home. Or specie and species: whether coins or 'natural' kinds. I don't know if that's important, but maybe there's an idea there for assessing the political, for potentially connecting academic research with more just policy?

Let me get more and less specific (there's the root of species again!), thinking out loud with horseshoe crabs. It seems to me that justice for these creatures, and for people who depend on them or care for them, gets bogged down when the focus is on species. Or even, in the language of ecologists, 'functional groups' within species. The hyper-specific attention of technocrats abounds with difficulties. Fisheries are managed species-by-species, missing the proverbial forest for the trees. Species that have economic value and come to the attention of managers at all, that is. And soon after, those species – or manageable groups within those species – are subject to attempts at optimization across ecological and economic worlds. The elusive "sustainable yield" of dozens – hundreds? – of historical, collapsed fisheries.

So too with horseshoe crabs. The crabs' populations are modeled, along with those of shorebirds that depend on their eggs for sustenance, and the ever-expanding needs of bait and biomedicine. Add in some statistical stochasticity, and the future-oriented models will churn out the optimum number of crabs that can be harvested to keep everyone happy. The result? Stalemated political processes in which no one is happy. And population crashes that can never be ruled out.

But what if our concentration was shifted from the level of species to something larger? I don't just mean so-called "ecosystem", "bioregional", or "holistic" approaches to management – though surely those are better than species-based conservation. But what if, instead of asking "How many of these animals can we ideally use", we ask whether we need to use them at all? Eschewing the kind of politics of "what can we get away with" that bedevils a host of just aims.

There are models for this. I asked someone at the U.S. Pharmacopeia why the EU had approved a synthetic replacement for horseshoe crab blood in their medical infrastructure so much more quickly, while the U.S. dragged its collective feet. He had a ready answer. He told me, "Europe is driven by the European Commission's mandate, legislative mandate, to replace all animal tests, okay? FDA doesn't have that..." That is, a mandate to eliminate animal tests wherever possible, rather than to ask how much of this or that animal is permissible to harvest, mangle, and employ. No doubt the European Pharmacopeia is its own scientific and policy quagmire. But this mandate, it seems to me, is at least at the right scale. Do nonhuman 'others' (or any 'others') need to be caught up in our

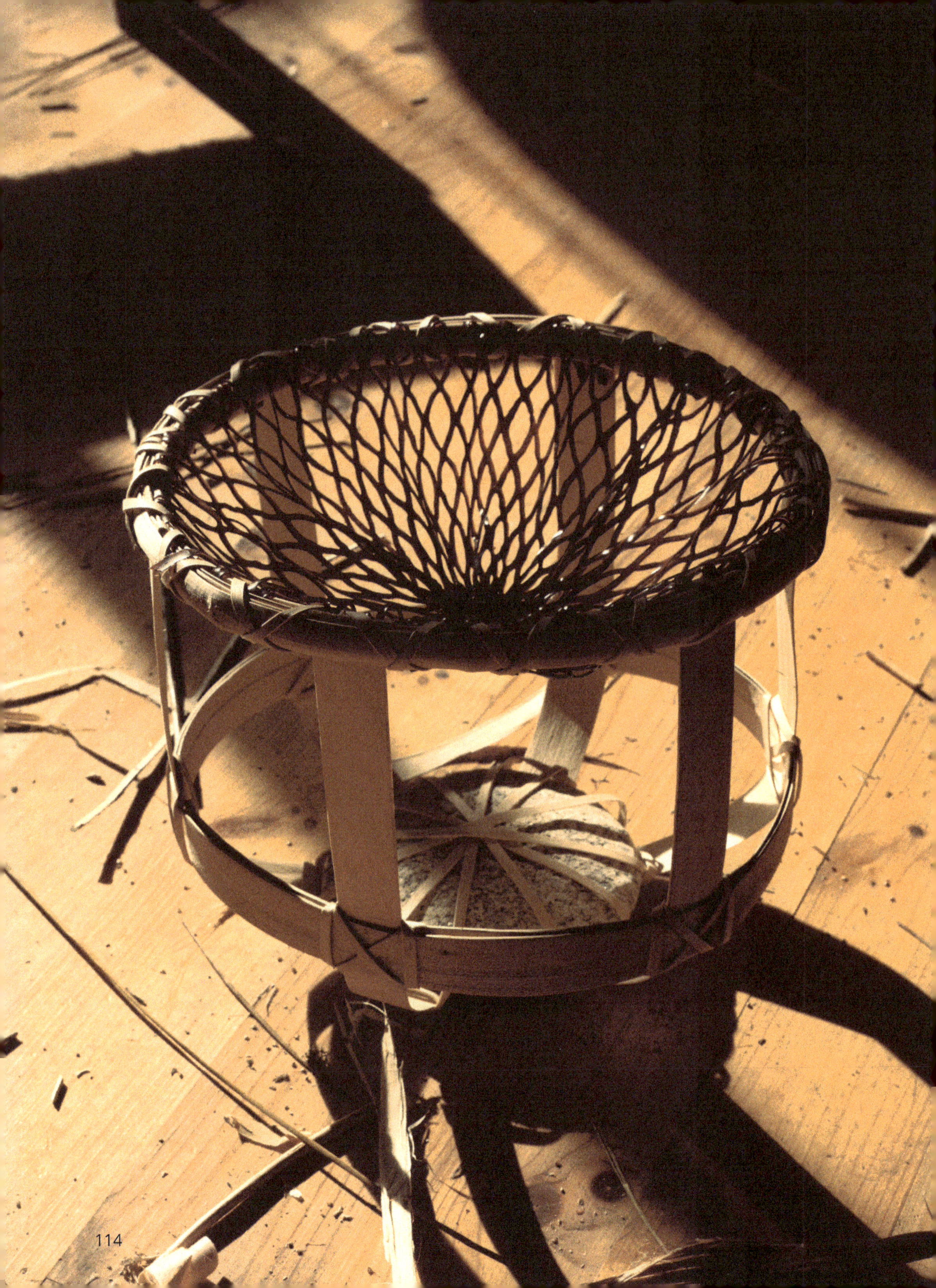

economic machinations at all?

And here's the kicker: we (the U.S. FDA and all Federal agencies, that is) *do* have this mandate. It's called Public Law 106-545, enacted and signed over 20 years ago. And the language of the law is remarkably similar to the EU Directive on the protection of animals. The difference? While it is true that this Act has fewer "teeth" than its EU counterpart, it is also curiously overlooked. This Act is almost nowhere to be seen in the interviews and documents I've collected. Even conservationists hell-bent on stopping horseshoe crab harvest by any legal means necessary seem unaware that endotoxin detection came under the scrutiny of this Law, decades ago.

This, then, might be something useful. Pointing this out. Holding technocrats, regulators, and industry accountable to their own standards. For horseshoe crabs, for ecosystems, and for humans and nonhumans more generally, regardless of species or economic value. At least, that is where the current of my thought is taking me, and I see some hope there.

HD: I'm thinking about weight: the weight of these discussions; the weight of the decisions we make; the weight of expectation that we can move towards more hopeful and abundant more-than-human futures.

And sometimes the massive weights we are dealing with are more than emotional or psychological, they're also resolutely material. Just think about the 6-8 million metric tons of shellfish waste produced globally each year. Piles of shells going to landfills, piles waiting to be incinerated, piles dumped into coastal waters: shrimp-shell graveyards.

These growing piles of crustacean waste are one of many Anthropocene masses which we need to find ways to digest. While chitosan may provide a seemingly sophisticated way to recycle these shells, is it the *right* kind of answer to this problem? Or are chitosan futures particularly narrow in their promise? Offering linear progress, techno-fixes, and abundant (read economically prosperous) futures for a minority? Rather, will these trajectories of innovation reinscribe inequality and injustice for already marginalised more-than-human collectives? How thorny the question of biomaterial innovation becomes when we consider it through the lens of ecological justice.

This brings me to another material, perhaps the most obviously hazardous material polluting our oceans and weighing our collective psyche down, infiltrating our bodies and minds: plastic. We've all heard it said that by 2050 there'll be more plastic than fish in the oceans. So how can we locate solutions to resolve the weight of our ecological plastic crisis, our plasticized oceans? Scientists and biotech innovators have eagerly taken up this task, identifying ways to mobilize plastic-eating microbes, creating microplastic filters using jellyfish mucus, and developing novel biodegradable bioplastics from seaweeds, chitosan, cellulose, and more.

All of these innovations offer promise that we *can* digest the mass of planetary plastics suffocating our seas. But at the same time they rely upon capitalist systems of extraction and processes of putting nonhumans to "work": revealing methods and motivations which fit somewhat paradoxically within visions for progressive ecological futures. Which begs the question, if marine biomaterials and plastic-targeting biotechnologies can never be fully extricated from the grip of capitalist currency and colonialism, then where do they fit in a just and radical future?

We might turn to artists and designers for inspiration, to consider what worlds, scales, and temporalities they are conjuring up with these materials. One project in Galicia, Spain sees biodesigner Paula Camiña Eiras work with traditional basketmakers, creating chitosan from waste shells from the local seafood industry and using this chitosan to create biomaterial baskets combined with vegetable fibers, woven in a traditional method. Where cheap, imported plastic baskets previously displaced Galician cultural crafts and ended up strewn on the shore in fragments; modern biomaterials can reconnect the basketry and sea-

Enrique Táboas
Galician wooden fishing trap re-interpretation net made in chitosan, 2021, Sabela Andrés
© Enrique Táboas

food community with a dying cultural heritage and also with their local ocean ecologies. This is an entanglement of sustainable circularity: uniting ecological pasts, presents, and futures in the form of a woven basket.

Amidst the unbearable weight of the world - and despite some of their failings - perhaps in particular situations and at smaller scales, biomaterials like chitosan *can* be radical. Maybe then, marine biomaterials to quote Hannah Stark, Katrina Schlunke, and Penny Edmonds, can "offer a hopefulness that other orders of existence can be practiced that might not necessarily lead into extinction".

ERJ: I love this notion that we might find ways to practice "other orders of existence". As I turn to the marine organisms that we collectively think with, I find myself returning, always to the question I posed earlier: how can we–as a collective, as academics and artists, as those bearing the weight of (in our cases) settler colonial histories of extractivism–begin to know differently? There are multiple ways that academics and others have approached such a question. There are growing conversations around the so-called decolonization of knowledge production in the West; the imperative to engage with Indigenous forms of knowledge; to create the space for more expansive endeavors (I suppose like this one) that take us beyond publication metrics whether through "slow scholarship" or by defending the conditions of research and teaching in higher education.

Hannah and I are currently engaged in a struggle to defend those conditions. By the time we deliver this presentation, we will have just concluded yet another week of strike action against our employer at Durham University (alongside over 80 other UK institutions). Our union has gone on strike four out of the five years that I have worked at Durham as part of efforts to resist devastating pension cuts and the continued erosion of pay and job security in higher education. Rightfully, I think, the University Colleges Union has represented the dispute as a defense of higher education from the encroachment of aggressive neoliberal policies and the overall devaluing of the sector. The pension cuts, stagnating salaries, increased workloads, continued rise of contingent positions, particularly across the humanities, and race and gender wage gaps are all at odds with universities' strident efforts to enhance diversity and equality as well as "decolonize" curricula and higher education practices. The cuts all but ensure that those without family support or intergenerational wealth will find the prospect of careers in research and teaching too precarious to pursue. Even many of us who have such support are eyeing exits as low morale sets in and the costs of high workloads, distance from family and loved ones, or the pressures of promotion criteria no longer quite seem worth the joys that accompany a career of lifelong learning.

Against such cuts, defending institutions of higher education–where the opportunities to think beyond our existing worlds seem most plentiful–is absolutely necessary. If our goal is to expand our capacities for world-making, our institutions need to continue to expand, widen, and be more rather than less inclusive. But inaugurating other orders of existence and beginning to "know differently" may also require questioning the infrastructures of learning that currently exist. In his book, *Beyond Education: Radical Studying for Another World*, Eli Meyerhoff levels several critiques at institutions of education in the West. Among them, Meyerhoff argues that the seeming necessity of formal education in K-12 schools as well as higher education creates "an epistemology of educated [and academic] ignorance".[4] Existing academic institutions drive an ideology that they are the only way to better oneself and the world. This exception, he writes, delegitimates and obscures alternative modes of learning and world-making. The romanticization of education as *the* pathway toward enlightenment creates the conditions for a narrowing of knowledge forms, even as formal education creates pockets of expanded epistemes. As an antidote, Meyerhoff recommends first a critical genealogy of institutions of education and their roles in maintaining white supremacy and capitalist modes of world-making. Second, he suggests exploring

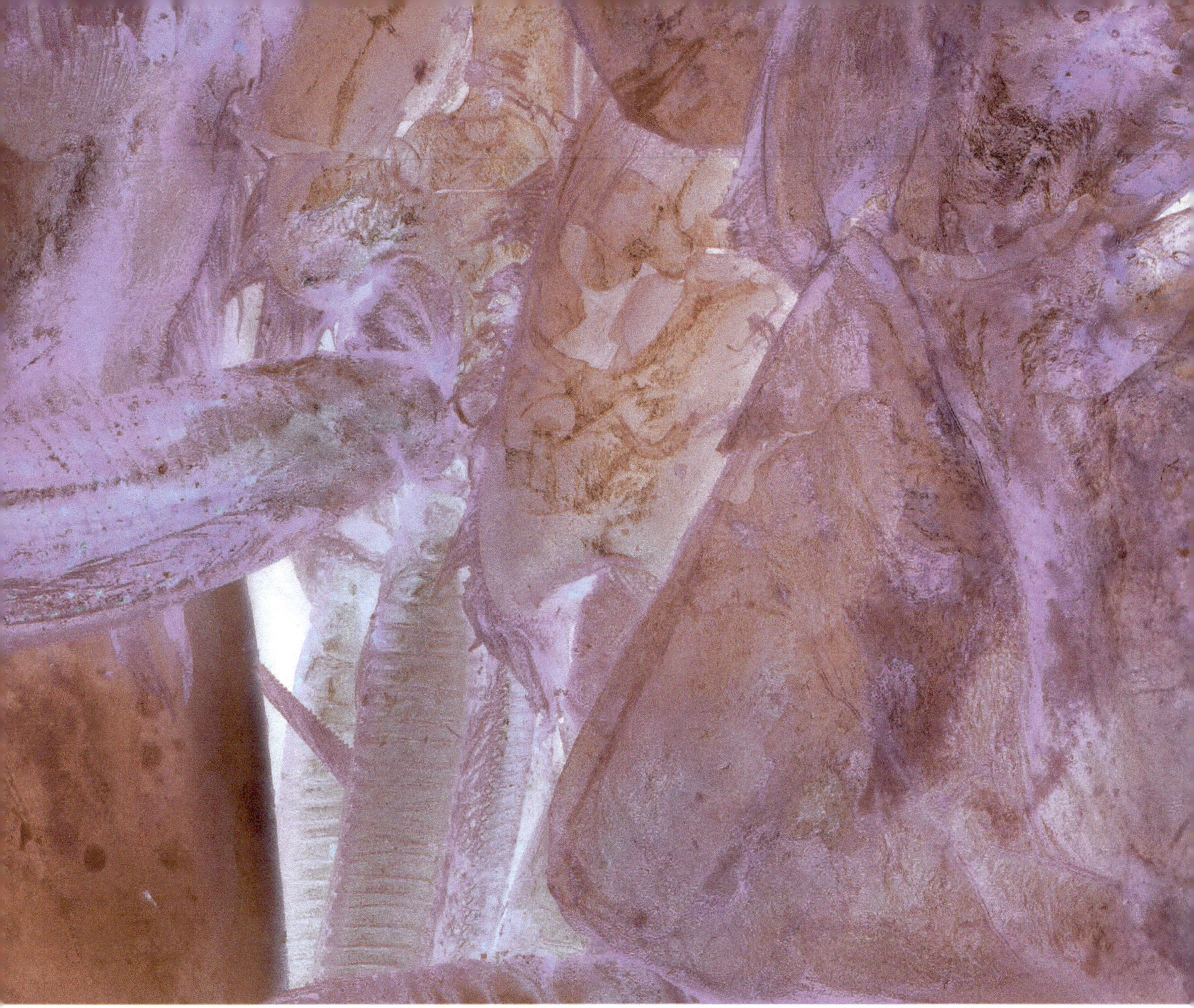

Paula Camiña Eiras

Prawn exoskeleton under microscope E20X50, 2021 © Paula Camiña Eiras

alternative modes of study in the historical record, including Indigenous forms of knowledge production, the maroon networks of former slaves, Third World liberation movements, and Black freedom struggle.

I like to think that our research exploring the genealogies of marine biology and illuminating their political and social contexts offers yet another avenue for exposing how regimes of extraction produce epistemologies of knowledge twinned with ignorance. But perhaps we might better link these to an even more reflexive analysis. Much of our work, after all, is funded by the endowed wealth of the Unilever corporation, a wealth accumulated in part in King Leopold's Congo, through a brutal regime of extraction and genocide. Those histories have already been well documented.[5] But it is certainly worth continuing to recognize their role in the shaping of knowledge production today.

All of this leaves me wondering if we might expand how and where we engage in practices of research and learning. In my first remarks, the post-doctoral researcher I spoke of and continue to think with, that lover of jellyfish, ultimately abandoned an academic career path. He returned home to Japan, where he now works as a technician for the Okinawa Institute of Science and Technology. With that one foot (or perhaps, I should say tentacle) remaining within higher education institutions, in 2013 he founded an organization called the Okinawa Basic Science and Research Laboratory. They offer 'nature experiences,' run a children's science program and provide laboratory equipment and guidance for experimental citizen science. I cannot say with certainty how successful the institute is, but it may be a model for how to create alternative ways of engaging with organisms–human and nonhuman–beyond extractivism and the pressures of academic life. Though undoubtedly modest, such experimental sites of entanglement may be necessary for exploring alternative modes of learning and creating other orders of existence.

HJB: And so, we find ourselves moving with the waves, struggling and ebbing, and-holding space for change. Holding conversations, and discomfort, turning them over in our hands to find new paths. Looking for the courage to pursue a future where openings might never close, or close just enough to become siphonophores. Just enough to become an alternative mode of thinking, of learning, of being. It's easy to say, isn't it? But where to from here?

Endnotes

[1] N Shiwei, S Dritsas, JG Fernandez, "Martian biolith: A bioinspired regolith composite for closed-loop extraterrestrial manufacturing". *PLoS ONE* 15, no. 9 (2020): e0238606.

[2] Bruno Latour, "Give Me a Laboratory and I Will Raise the World," in *Science Observed: Perspectives on the Social Study of Science*, edited by Karin Knorr Cetina and Michael Mulkay (London: Sage, 1983), 141–70.

[3] Astrid Schrader, "Abyssal Intimacies and Temporalities of Care: How (Not) to Care about Deformed Leaf Bugs in the Aftermath of Chernobyl," *Social Studies of Science* 45, no. 5 (October 1, 2015): 665–90.

[4] Eli Meyerhoff, *Beyond Education: Radical Studying for Another World* (Minneapolis: University of Minnesota Press, 2019), 5.

[5] Jules Marchal, *Lord Leverhulme's Ghosts: Colonial Exploitation in the Congo* (London New York: Verso, 2017).

Helen J. Bullard is a gardener, paddler, listener, reader, writer, artist, and storyteller, among other identities. They use the arts (including social practice) and the sciences (including social science) as their mediums. They are faculty in Service Learning and Writing at Milwaukee Institute of Art and Design (MIAD), with the intention of supporting the local community, far beyond the classroom. Their work is often collaborative, working with artists, scientists, writers, political and critical thinkers, academic-creatives, and people of observant, parental and minority experience to consider topics including oceans and queerness.

Hannah Dickinson is a geographer and political ecologist based at Durham University, UK. Hannah lives in Sheffield in the UK and spends as much free time as possible in the nearby Peak District: walking, swimming, and adventuring with dog and husband in tow. Although living far from the ocean, the ocean is never far from Hannah's mind; and she devotes much of her academic life to studying and thinking with ocean creatures, marine spaces, and the human impacts on these organisms and ecologies. The rest of Hannah's academic time is often spent talking and working with others to cultivate spaces of kindness and community in academia.

Kristoffer Whitney has lived near forests, oceans, deserts and plains, but has settled in the U.S. Great Lakes, working in the Science, Technology & Society Department at the Rochester Institute of Technology. He spends most of his time playing outside with his family, but does find the time to research and think scholarly thoughts about the animals we share the planet with. He used to live on a sailboat in the Delaware Bay, where he first encountered, and was awed by, horseshoe crabs.

Elizabeth R. Johnson is a human-environment geographer whose work and life spans two sides of the Atlantic Ocean. Her work explores how new ties between the biosciences and technological innovation are changing how we understand life in the context of environmental precarity. Over time, her research has gravitated toward to study of marine bioscience and ocean imaginaries. She teaches human and more-than-human geographies at Durham University in the UK. Outside of term time, she can be found with her partner in the Finger Lakes of New York State, which connect to the world's oceans via the Erie Canal system.

Earth my body, water my blood

Will there be rooted belonging if home was a colony built on reclaimed land fill? If connecting with the earth is seeking support for healing, are nature-based therapies "resourcing" the earth just like the colonists? "Earth my body, water my blood" is a call and response inquiry where an expressive arts therapist wrestles with social trauma, the ecological sense of selfhood, her own cultural belonging and our aesthetic responsibility in decolonizing/healing the earth and ourselves. A settler of colour in Canada responds to the call to returns to her land of origin Hong Kong- a former British colony -after the city has been through months of civil unrest, social wounding and flight.

text & images: **Gracelynn Chung-yan Lau**

This inquiry began with the call to work with social trauma in the land of my origin. After months of civil unrest, thousands of families have been wounded, torn apart by conflict or fleeing to the UK- the former colonizer. This land itself was once colonized, and the colonial project has never ended. I was born in a "satellite town" built mostly on reclaimed landfill. If the sense of who we are is beyond political identifications, the land, the earth, the mineral world might have something to say about us. They have witnessed our ancestors, and they have known us from our bone memories.

I started collecting soil and water from ten urban parks, wondering if painting with soil could help people to let the earth touch us intimately, to remind us of our ecological belongings. But I found barely any soil. Trees were growing in rocky and sandy dirt, covered and surrounded by bricks. As my concern for topsoil's well-being grew, I found myself drawn to the natural shapes and ways that roots and the edges of water touch the surface of the earth, so I started photographing their interactions. "Do not fight against gravity. Do less. Let gravity does its thing," became my motto when I realized I was positioning the earth as healing resource, letting the earth beings to speak through the images.

My studio practice is rooted in a juxtaposed exploration of my poiesis and my therapist's responsibility. In expressive arts therapy, poiesis is the act of art-making and is always an art-based inquiry. To engage in the phenomenon of poiesis is to return to my innate aesthetic response-ability to shape what has been given to me in the immediate environment where I find myself, while being shaped by that. The studio is right here, nowhere and everywhere. I arrive with the questions and get out of my own ways. I have to leave behind self-expression, meaning-making and the desire to find the answer so that I can hang out in not-knowing. I am most often lost in the process, feeling the liminal discomfort of not-knowing, while at the same time following my curiosity to engage with the emerging materials until I find my aesthetic response. How I respond, act, create, and shape in the creative process informs my being in the world.

My role as a nature-based expressive arts therapist is always to open and deepen poiesis. My aesthetic responsibility is to shape the play space for others to experience their poiesis. I engage them with materials and their immediate environment as the studio. The studio is right here, nowhere and everywhere. But I have very little to do with the healing. Healing happens when images and surprises arrive in their creative process, and when they experience a new sense of who they are, a spaciousness and unexplored capability to respond and act in

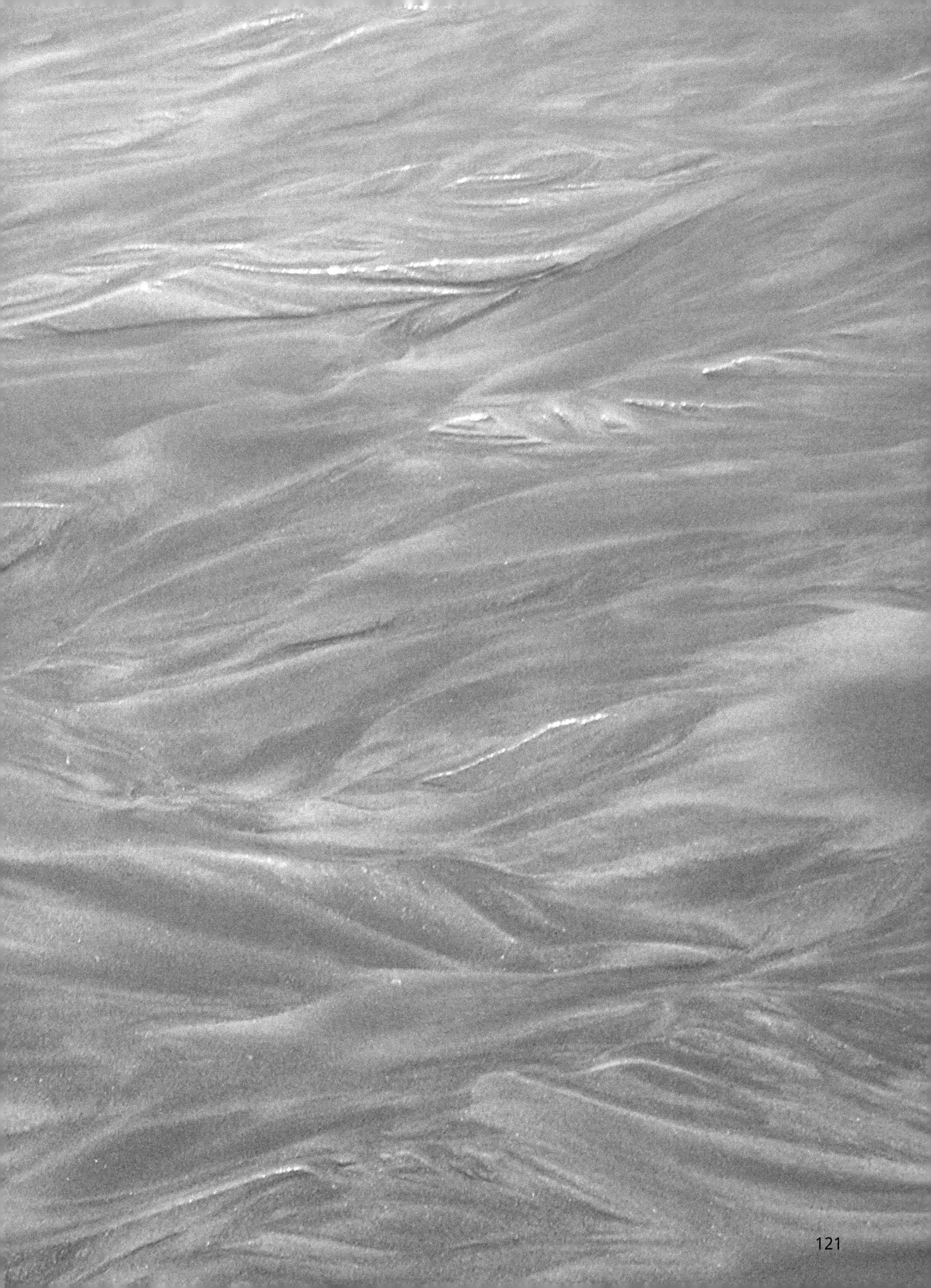

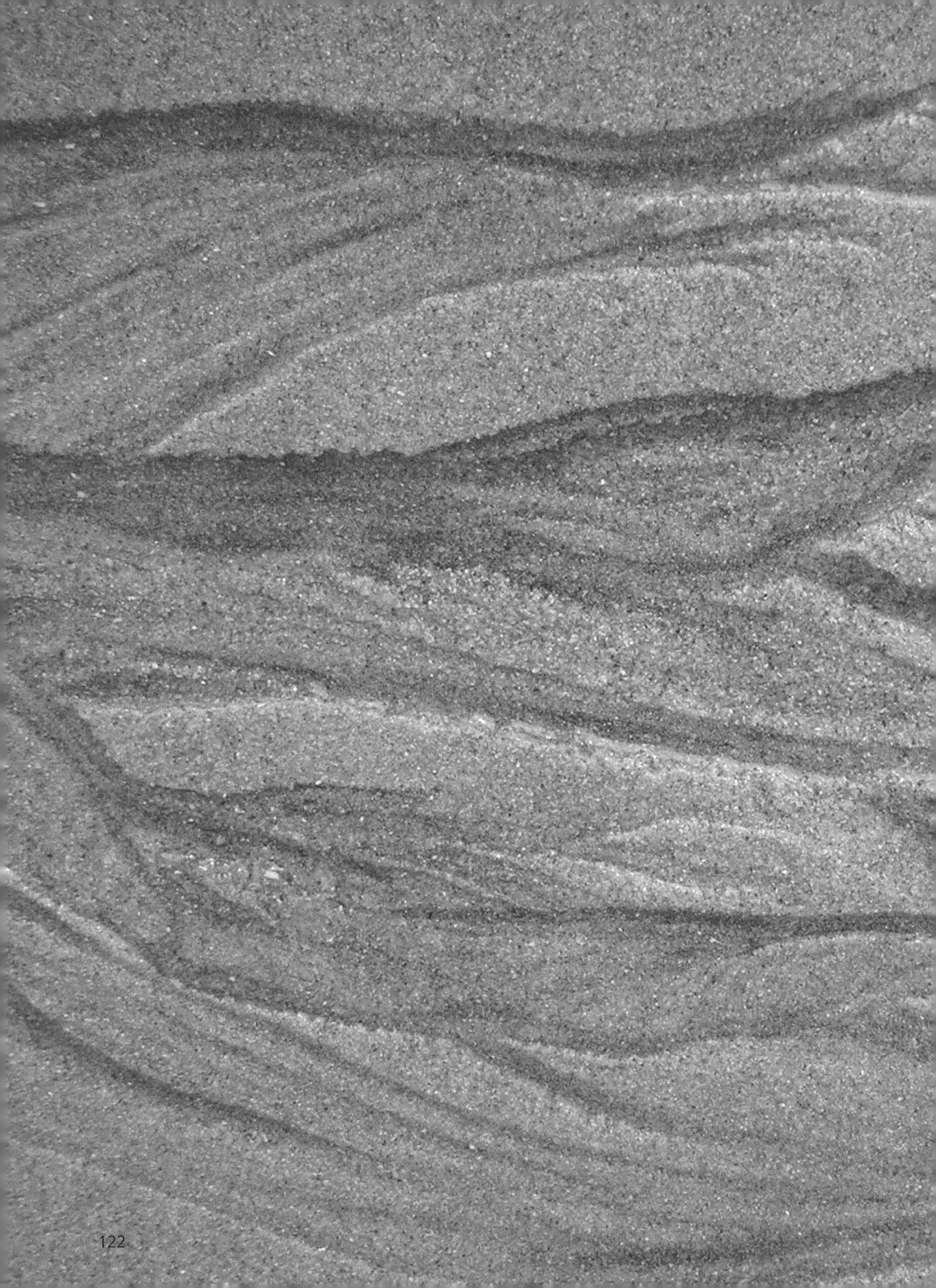

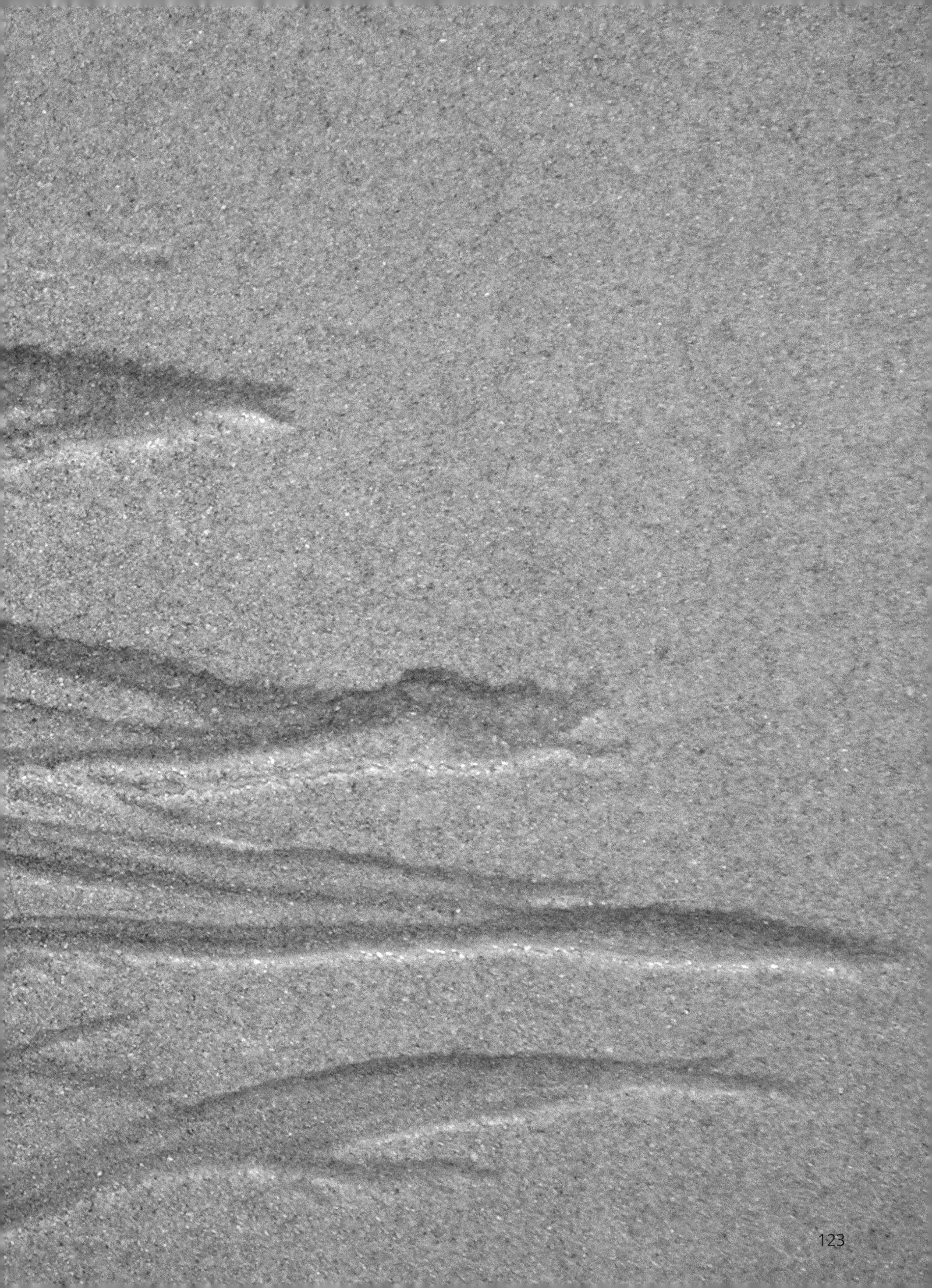

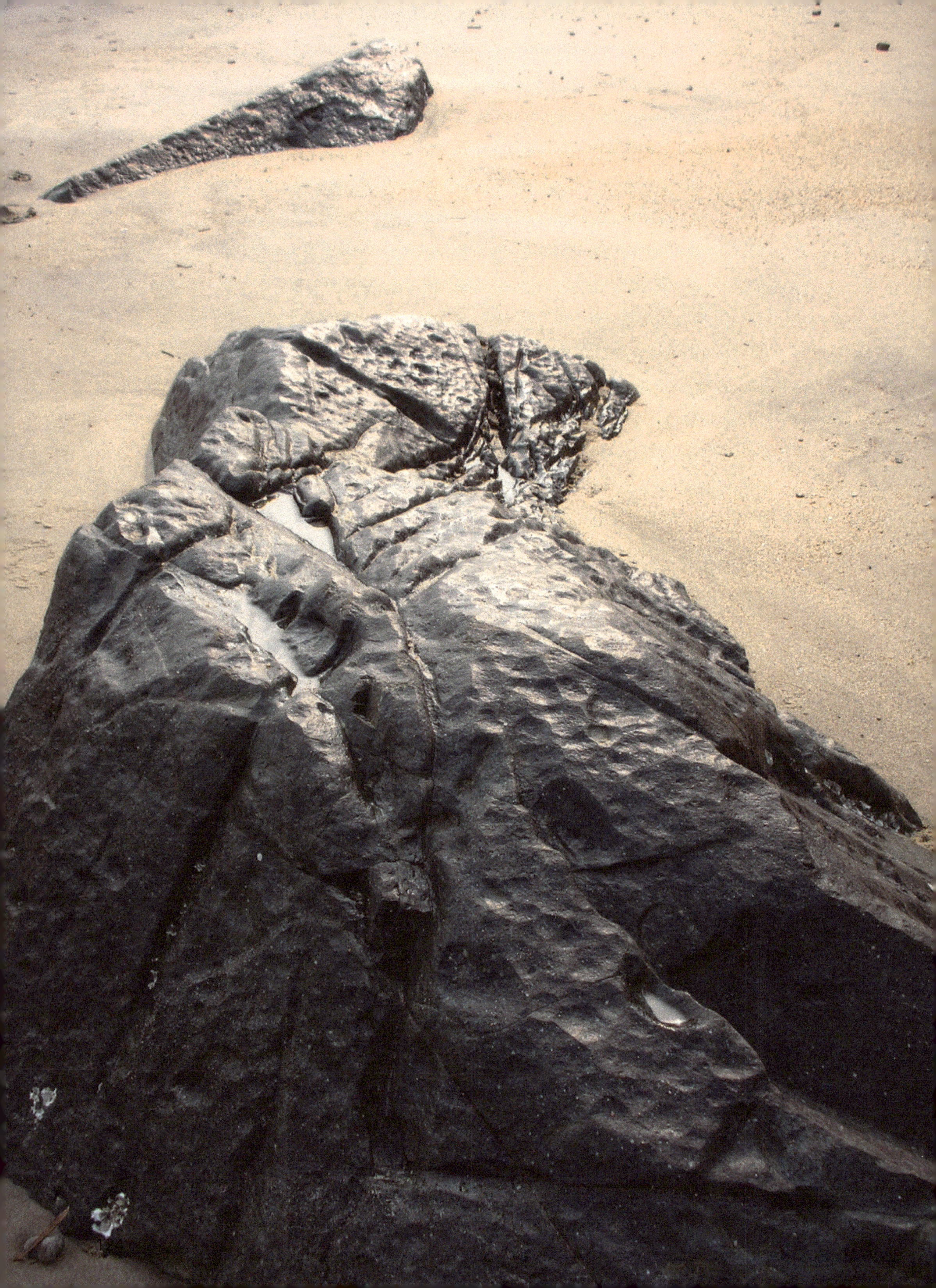

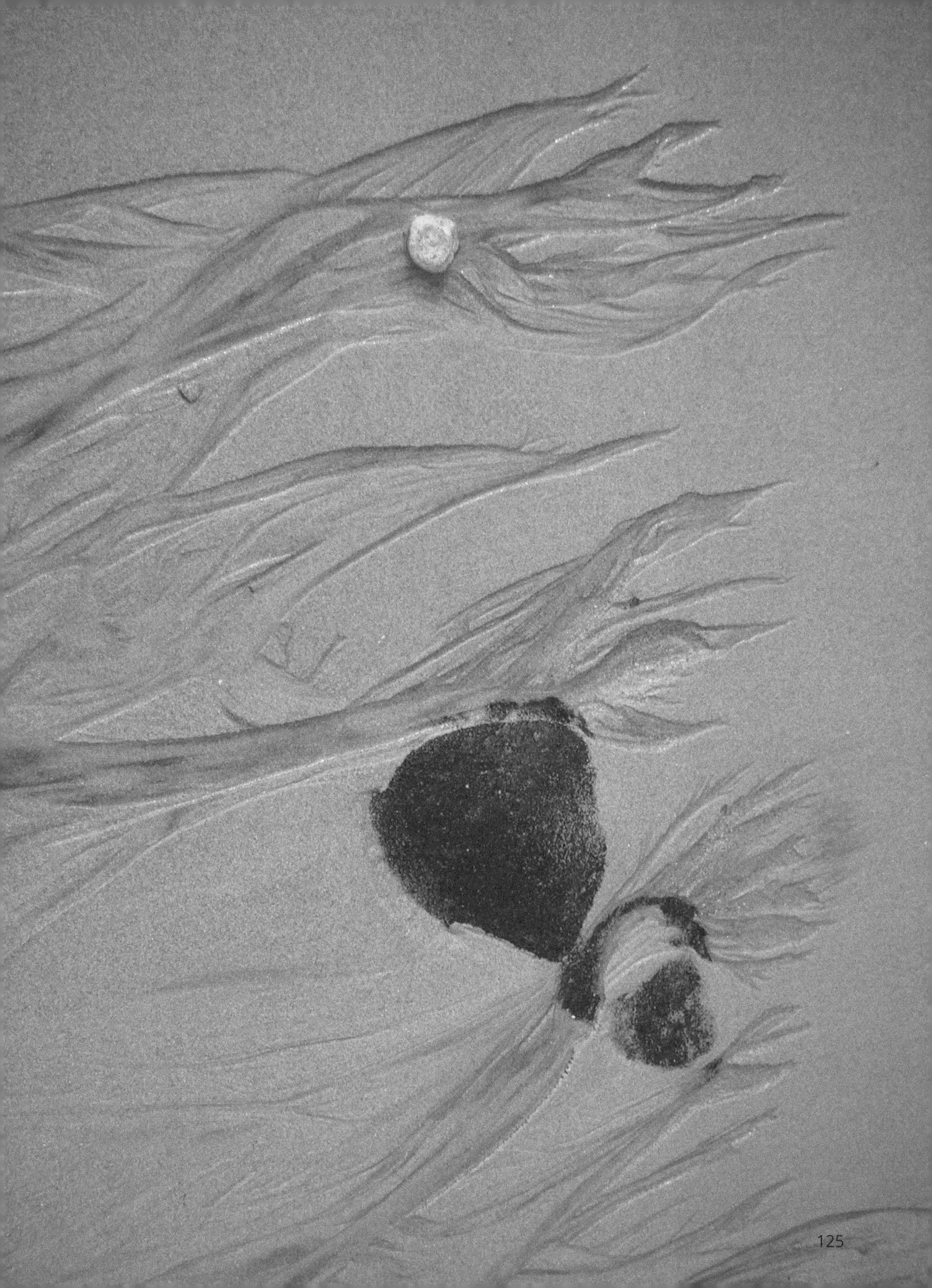

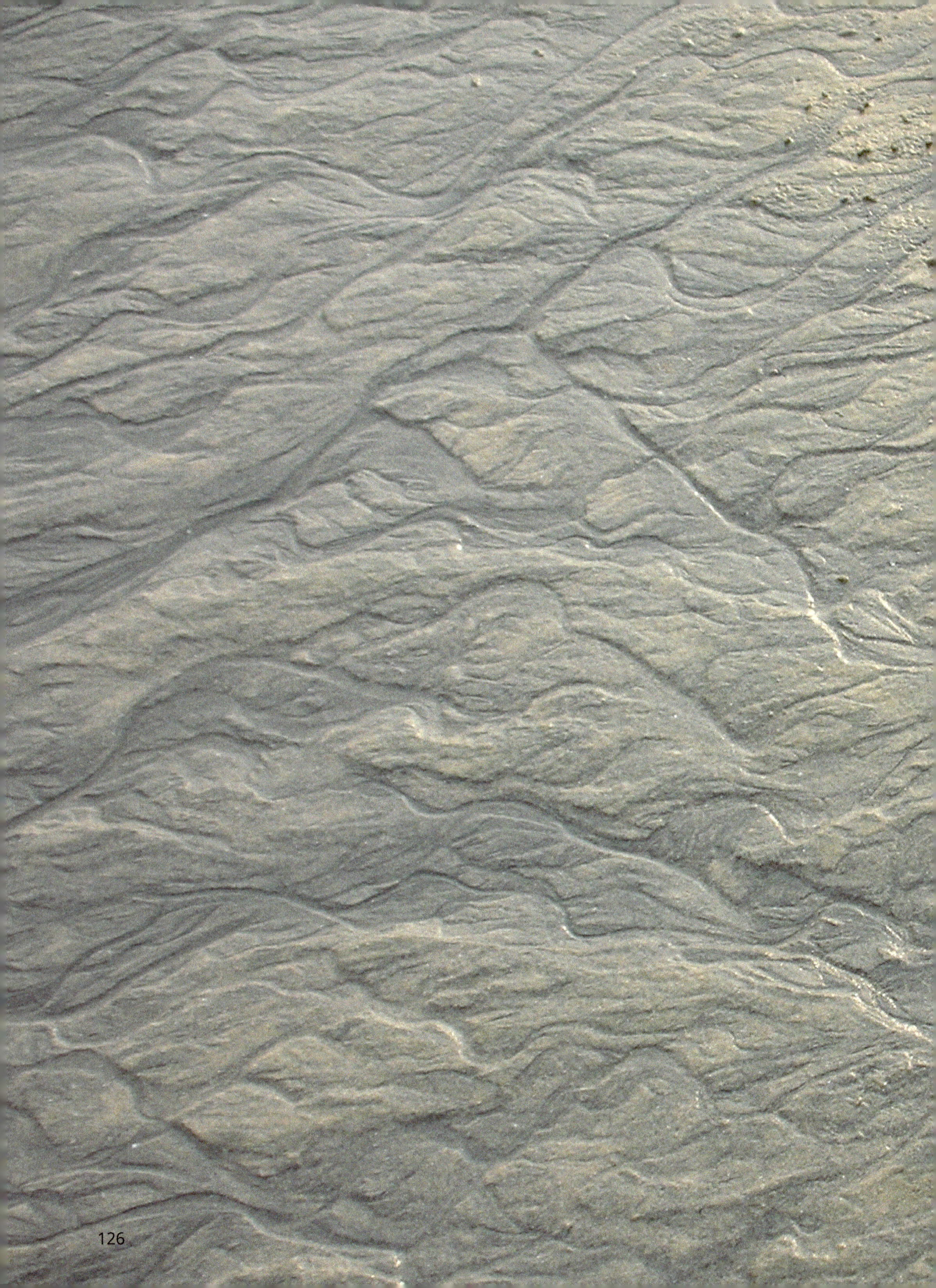

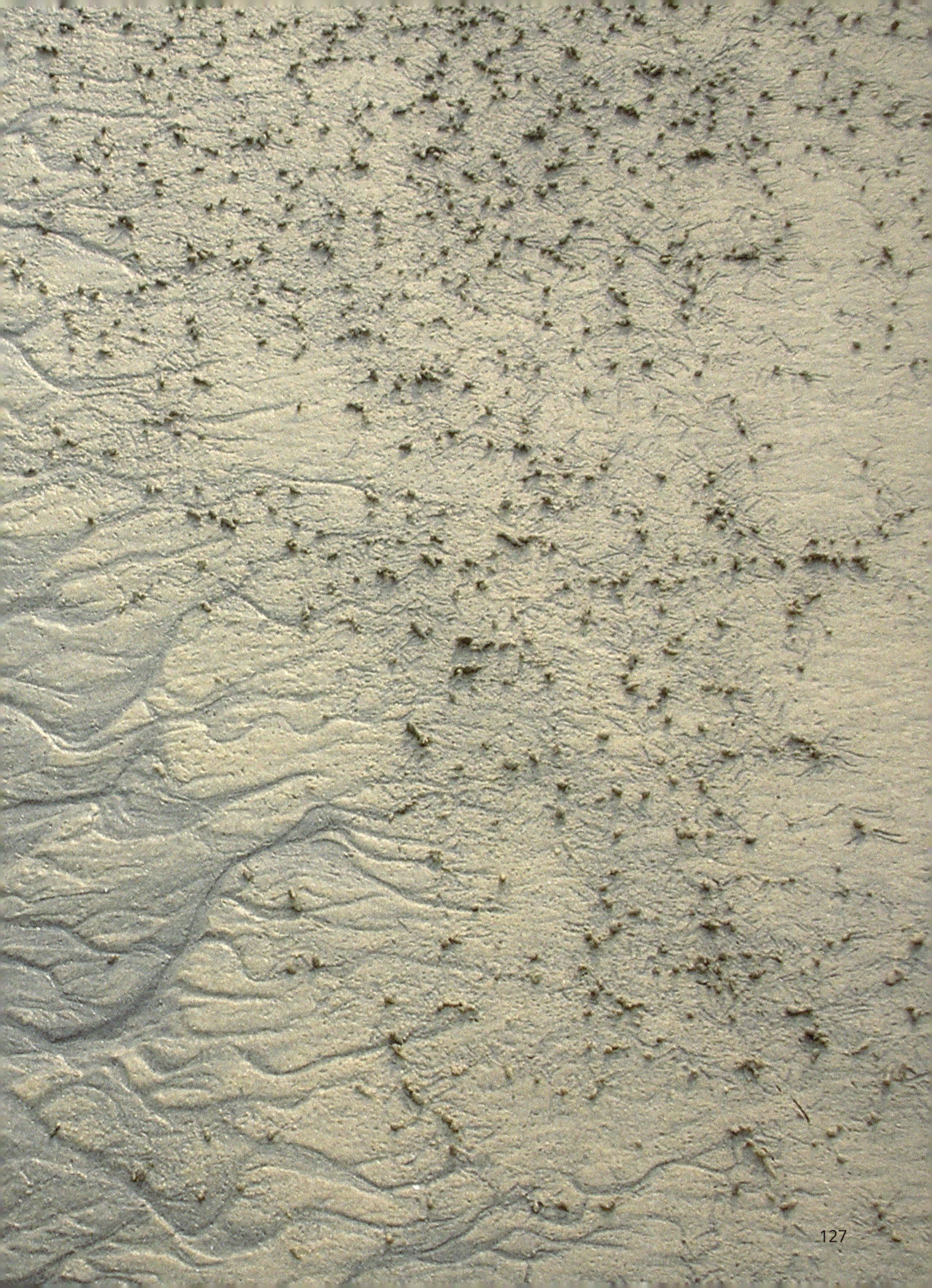

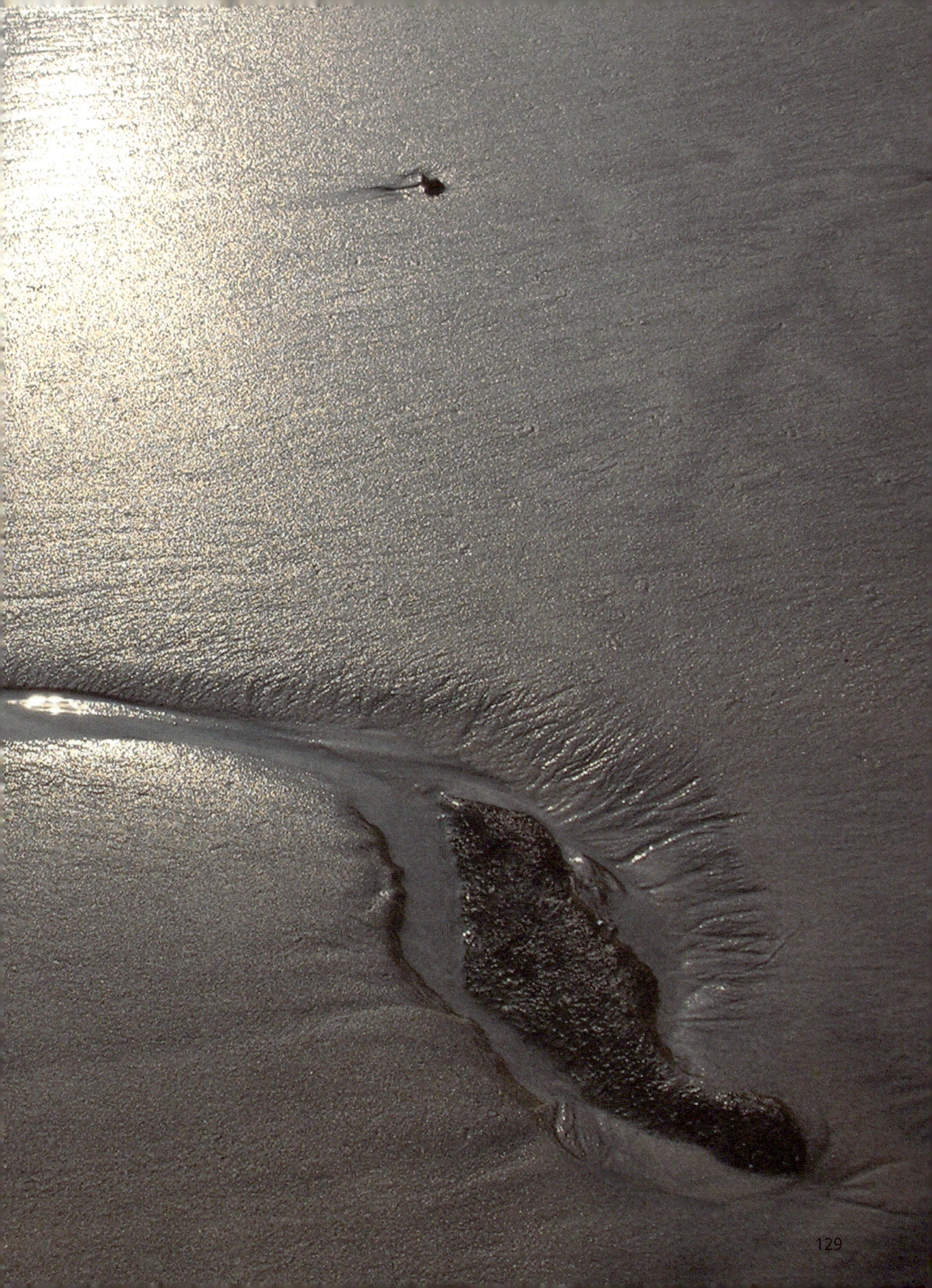

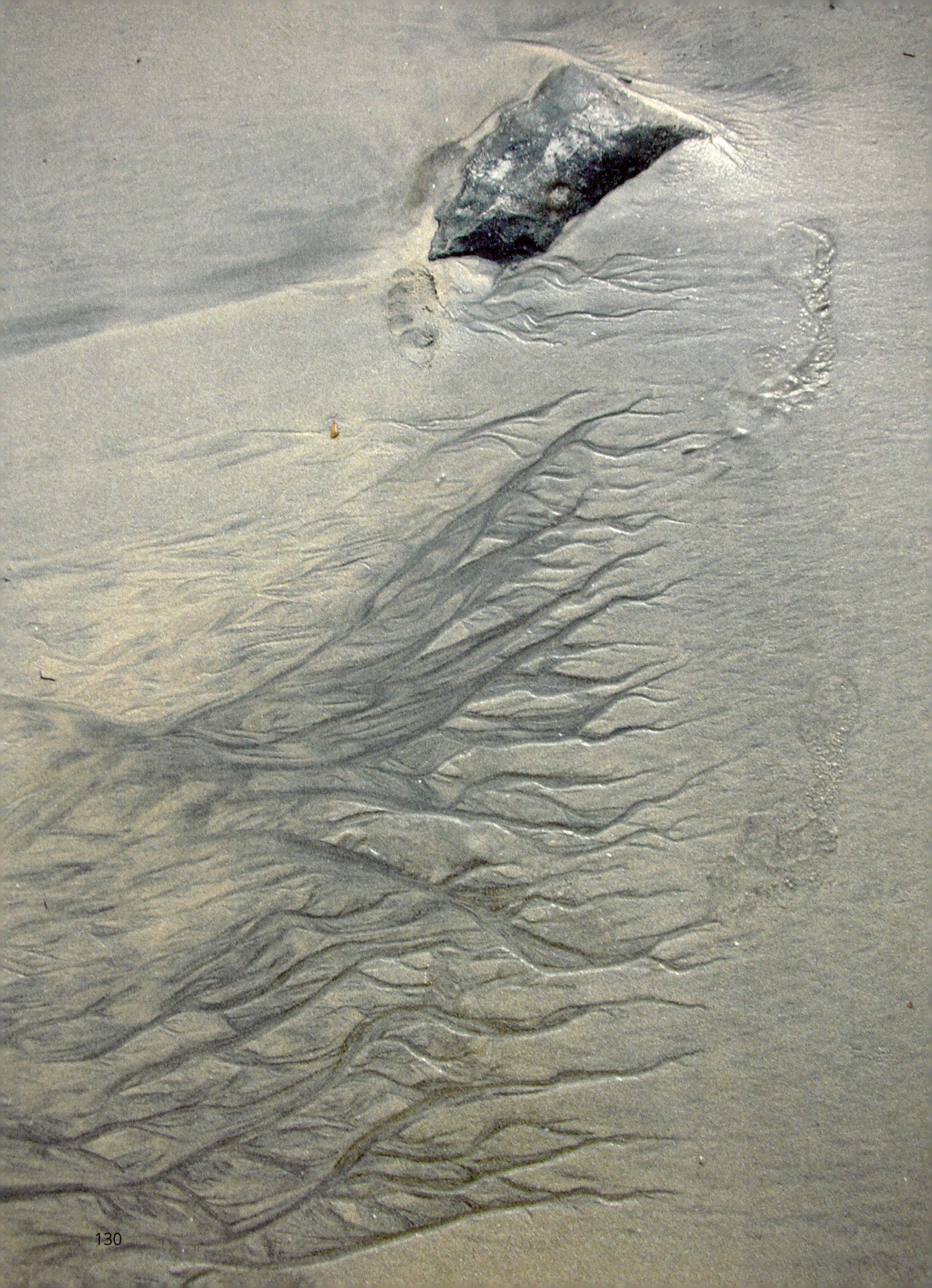

difficult or heartbreaking situations.

When the therapist steps aside and stops "commodifying" nature, then the earth, the mineral world, the water step in to speak. My job becomes shaping the play space for response to happen. The best way to explain my findings from this inquiry is to create an experience for you, the readers of this journal, now. What if what you are reading is the poiesis play-space? I invite you to engage with the images from the land of my ancestors, the shapes crafted by the edges of water and the minerals touching the earth. This is my call to you:

-Leave your device. Pick up a piece of paper. Give yourself 10 minutes to free write continuously in response to these questions: what is your relationship with the earth? how do you form such a relationship? how does the earth carry you? Use rich and descriptive language to describe the relationship and its impact on the shaping of your identity and the world around you. Do not worry about spelling or grammar, or even finding the right word. No one will see your writing. Let your thoughts and feelings arrive on the paper.

- When you feel you have done this, look at the words you have written. Highlight three sentences or phrases that speak to you at this moment.

- Put the paper aside. Return to your device. Follow your intuition to choose one image from this series.

- Enlarge the image to full screen on your phone/tablet/laptop. Carry the image with you, explore the physical space where you find yourself at this moment. Walk around if you are indoor. Feel free to go outside.

- Let the image encounter a more-than-human being in your surroundings. It or they might be mineral, vegetative, earthy, smoky, airy or thingy. Let them find each other, allow them to connect in their own ways. See what other beings in the space would like to join in. You participate by physically arranging them together in ways that they prefer. Until the arrangement feels complete.

- Witness this three dimensional constellation/installation from a distance. If it has a name or title, what would it be?

- Now if the image on your device has to leave the constellation/installation and you were to replace it with something else you see or can gather right now, what would it be? What wants to come in? Make it happen.

- Look at this constellation/installation again. Does it have a different name/title now? If so, what is it?

- If this being has something to say about your relationship with the earth, what is it saying to you? Does what it is saying to you have any consequences for thinking or acting in relationship to the earth? How would you respond?

-Find your way to return this installation back to the earth.

Images

p.106-107- 林, 2020 @ Gracelynn Lau
p.108-109- 根, 2020 @ Gracelynn Lau
p.110-殖, 2020 @ Gracelynn Lau
p.111-浮, 2020 @ Gracelynn Lau
p.112-113-游, 2020 @ Gracelynn Lau
p.114-115-直, 2020 @ Gracelynn Lau
p.116-移, 2020 @ Gracelynn Lau

Gracelynn Lau was born and raised in Hong Kong when it was still a British colony. Since moving to Canada in 2005 for her Master in Worldview Studies, ecofeminist theology has changed her world "downside up." Self-identified as a settler of colour who is deâling with a triple-colonized past, Gracelynn had lived in communities with orphans and earthquake survivors in rural China before joining the ecovillage movement.
She is a nature-based expressive arts therapist (Ontario Expressive Arts Therapy Association). Since 2017, Gracelynn has been co-facilitating EDE in BC, Canada where she facilitates school programs, internships, women's circles and sustainable wellness retreats. Currently, a PhD candidate in cultural studies at Queen's University, her research focuses on community-led intercultural healing initiatives and Indigenous-settler relationships through arts-based inquiry, but her real intention is to increase more "biodiversity" within the academic ecosystem by being part of it.

In-human appetites and mineral becomings

The landscape, environmental and aesthetic, is constituted in and by transformative alliances, where witnessing becomes wit(h)nessing. The reparative potential of environmental justice to attend to world-wounds, evokes a shared horizon staked in the process of destabilizing a singular gaze. Sharing-in-difference through earthly wit(h)nessing, is only possible in the interstices of in/humans and Non/Life. Caitlin Berrigan's speculative renderings metabolize plosive transformations, which are read diffractively through Karen Barad and Bracha Ettinger's writings. This text creates waves and non-vacuous holes in its encounters with geology, orifices, memory and time.

text **Callum Bradley and Georgia Perkins**

images: **Caitlin Berrigan**

"...I entered
The stomach of indifference, the wordless cupboard.

The mother of pestles diminished me.
I became a still pebble.
The stones of the belly were peaceable,

The head-stone quiet, jostled by nothing."

Sylvia Plath, 'The Stones' in *The Colossus and Other Poems*, 1960

Caitlin Berrigan's body of work *Imaginary Explosions* (2018-ongoing) layers volcanology, "geological consciousness" and "radical planetary transformation", with speculative fiction.[1] Berrigan links the subsurface of magma cores, to the minerals which conglomerate into stones within our bodies. The lithic cavities of rocks are in a process of mineralizing, causing *plastic*[2] and in/animate "movements and expansions of its magma chambers".[3] Creating what Donna Haraway would call unlikely "transformative merger practices",[4] Dr. Karen Holmberg in episode 2 of Berrigan's series describes how rock formations and sea lions mutually shape stomachs and magma chambers:

> It appears these deep black rocks were swallowed by sea lions as ballast to weigh down their buoyant fat and were smoothed in the chambers of their stomachs. When sea lions were brought to the caves to be eaten, the stones fell out of their bellies and piled on the floors along with the remains of other animals.[5]

The "shared aqueous kinship"[6] in which the indigestible rock sits within the sea lion's stomach, co-constitutes the depths in which they can collectively plumb deep waters. Here is an example of what Donna Haraway calls *messmates*, in which "eating one another and developing indigestion [...is a] kind of transformative merger practice; living critters form consortia in a baroque

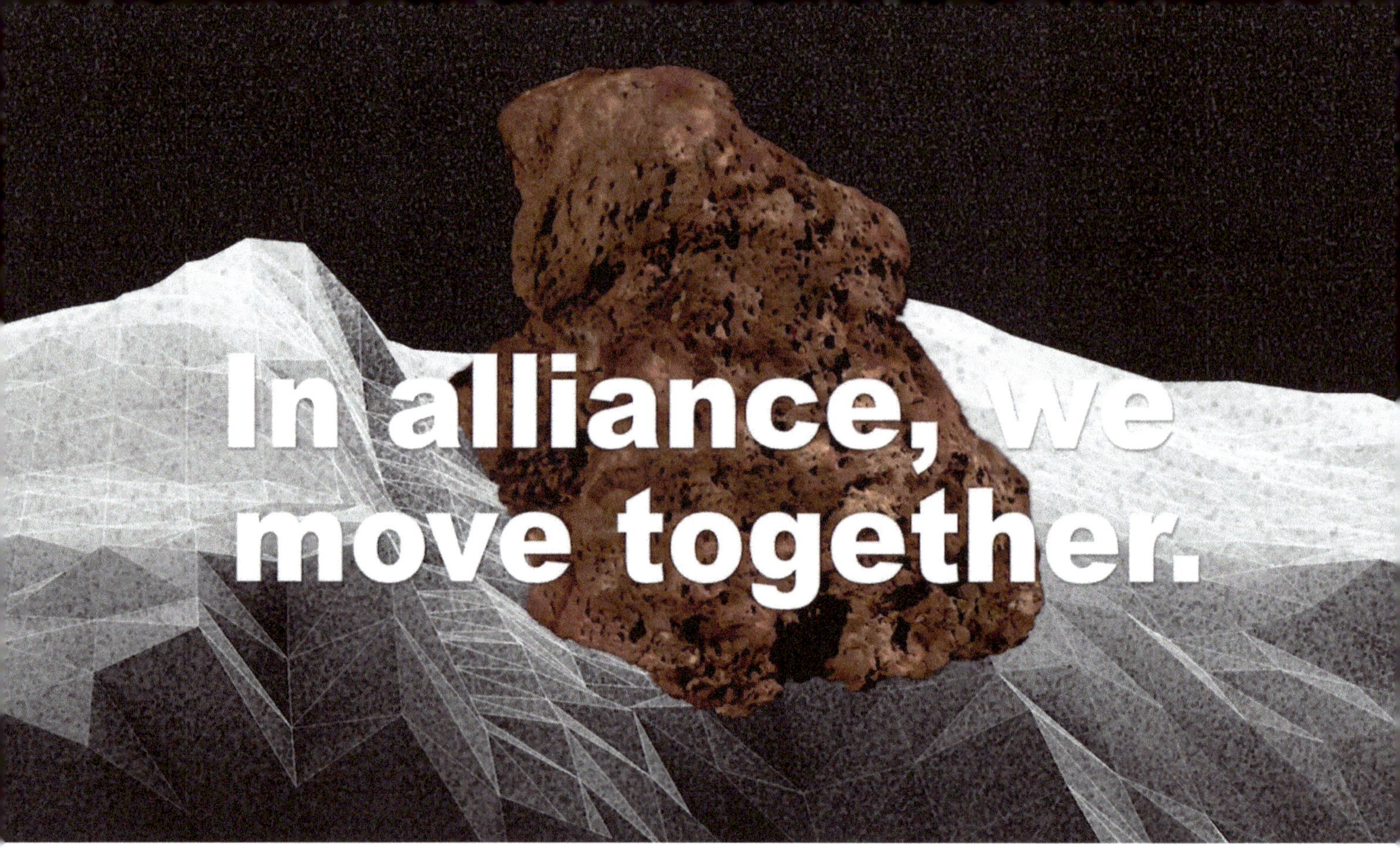

Caitlin Berrigan
Becoming Mineral, moving image still, 2018 © Caitlin Berrigan

medley of inter- and intra-actions".[7] The in(di)gestable *diffractive* patternings of sea lion-rock entanglements, create a rippling emergence of changes in co-buoyancy. Eating does not constitute full absorption of another, or produce a kind of sameness, but rather attends to the "patterns of differences that make a difference".[8] In Karen Barad's essay *Nature's Queer Performativity*, she argues that "a classic diffraction pattern is the one produced by the interfering disturbances of water waves when two stones are dropped simultaneously into a pond. That is, it is a pattern of alternating regions of intensity".[9] As the stones are 'dropped' into the hold of the sea lions' stomachs, different intensities in bodily waters or waves are produced, as well as differences in how they (multi-)navigate bodies of water.[10] Diffractive watery movements pull in different directions between bubbles and subsurface magma cores rising, in conjunction with sea lion-rocks plunging into deep waters, stomachs and cave chambers.[11] Orienting the space differently becomes a space of alliance, resistance, and earthly transformation in the water column, which goes beyond the boundaries of a terrestrial and aquatic divide.[12]

Staked in similar differentiating processes to those voiced by Barad, artist and theorist Bracha Ettinger reconceptualises the structuring of "subjectivity [so that it] becomes both diffracted and assembled, both dispersed and partial, and part of an alliance".[13] Subjectivity is emphasised as being constituted by diffractive alliances, as transformative practices, always already merging in/humans and Non/Life. This (de)constructs the self with-in the other in the same stroke as (re)structuring the other with-in the self. The stones in the sea-lions' stomachs parallel an instance of pregnancy, of carrying with-in an-other. These are watery, rippling differences, carried across terrains, scales, and reiterating intensities. Stone is swum down into the depths of sea with-in the stomach; the mineralised anti-floatation tool resurfaces, dredged up, and deposited on the cave floor, becoming a part of its carpeted sea of stones. The translations of pregnancy across transgressions of inside/outside and self/other boundaries relay with processes of eating and being eaten, along with living and dying. In(di)gesting stone, returning (to) earth, then stories intra-actions that cut through in-difference, transforming relations with displaced and assimilated matter. For Ettinger, not only is "our consciousness linked to and is a part of the consciousness of the earth" from birth, but these archaic links can be threaded through "artistic engagements", tracing a "spiralic movement of transformational eventing" between artworks and witnesses.[14] Berrigan's video work not only diffracts stones through seas, stomachs, and caves as transformed molten cavities, but the space of the screen itself and its bringing together of witnesses might also figure as part of this in(di)gesting economy, *metabolising rock*.

Reading diffractively through Barad and Ettinger's writing, this text creates waves and non-vacuous holes in its encounters with geology, orifices, memory and time. Berrigan's speculative renderings metabolize plosive transformations, (e)merging in/humans and Non/Life. This reverberates in the aesthetic dimension, as well as between Barad and Ettinger's quantum and psychoanalytic thoughts.

Metabolizing Rock

The space of Berrigan's video works intimately *in*-human. The artist's onscreen writing asks, "who is to say, that stones are exempt from metabolism?"[15] Witnesses of the 'lithic choreography'[16] in *Becoming Mineral* are suspended in an aesthetic assemblage that resonates beyond demarcations of interiority and exteriority, in-between human and inhuman, before any splitting of *geos* and *bios*. The *metabolizing rock* has a "warping surface",[17] which distorts the "material imaginaries"[18] of rock formations as monolithic concretions. The three-dimensional rock at the heart of the image moves; audiences encounter something *in*human, in themselves, when approaching the rock that spirals in random rotational patterns, anchored to an invisible axis in the middle of the screen. We follow Berrigan's moving image and resonate with her words, "in alliance, we move together, we mineralise".[19] The seemingly inert minerals which are ingested into the body, complicates, as Elizabeth Povinelli argues, the 'geontopowers' of the dualistic dynamics between Life and Non-Life, according to Western metaphysics and imaginaries.[20] Invited in, the rock relays geometrical precision to the gaze that is fixed dead centre, between Life and Non-Life, holding the rock as it precariously swirls and loops in place. Its permeable, spongy texture further leads the gaze in-between its strata, into imaginaries that implicate witnesses of the rock within its formation and vice versa.[21]

Void of monolithic scale and monumentality, the rock is staged as an unassuming and microcosmic object constituted as much by its originary materiality as the assistive technologies resourced for its videographic representation; geo-metric witness working in the measure between Life and Non-Life. Its porosity bores passageways between the material and discursive, through technical figurations of rock that are held in tension at the heart of the screen. We are invited to ingest the rock as if it is a mediational morsel that might feed geontological relations. Displacing styles of popular food advertisement, the rock is abstracted, emerging out of a dark background and rotating in space as if on a platter; fit for video consumption, invitingly lit and precisely placed. The morsellithic rock tempts our desiring, indigesting economy into exchange. Words layered over the image appear on screen; the artist is "reporting a shared mutual desire to erupt".[22] An in(di)gesting economy of metabolic intra-actions is figured through *geos* becoming food for thought in *bios* becoming mineral. Material-

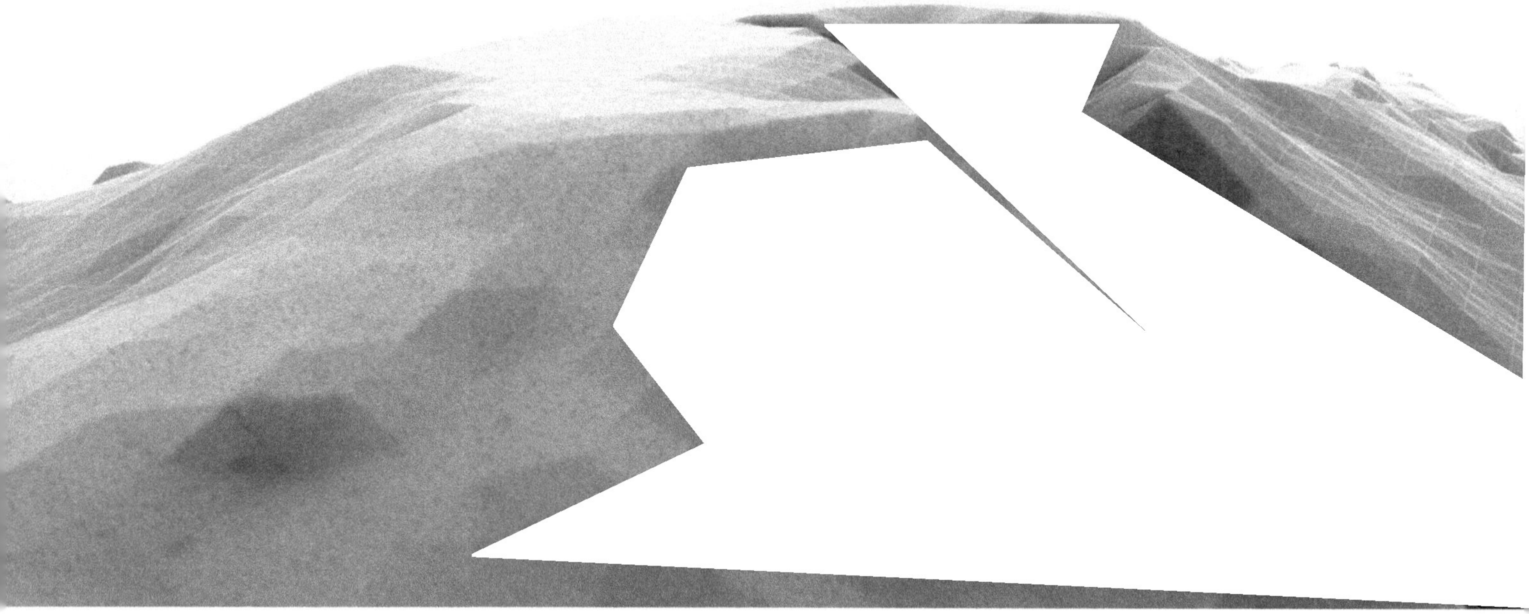

Caitlin Berrigan

Imaginary Explosions, episode 1, Eyjafjallajökull, moving image still, 2018 © Caitlin Berrigan

semiosis works through the pores of the aesthetic eruption on screen; the reproduction of rock relays *in*-human witnesses.

Beneath the rock, line drawings of mountainous landscape flash across the screen in split-second intervals, producing a sense of infinite webbing that cannot possibly be held by the frame. Computational radar topographies are blown up, zoomed into and panned across. The moving background transports witnesses across space whilst refusing any kind of anthropo-scenic view from above that might grasp and map out the landscape in its entirety. Witnesses are drawn into and across the depths of the land and dwell with-in the porous rock simultaneously. They are moved by the diffractive rhythms of the multiple representations of *geos*, the rock rotating in place composited with mountainous topographies that will not stay in place. A particular aesthetic-ontology suspends audiences between juxtaposed representations of *geos* in the space of the screen - a kind of situatedness in-situ – where witnesses feature as nonexhaustive components in metabolic relation with geological agencies and technological figurations in an aesthetic stasis.

Ettinger discusses "working-through and passing-through artistic pregnant dwellings...with-in the Other and with-in the Cosmos".[23] Here, interest in pre-birth relationality and differentiation is taken up and mapped onto earthly relations where the human is always already co-constituted *with-in*-human others. A sense of *differences that make a difference* are located by Ettinger in the originary patternings of becoming-child and becoming-mother that are blueprinted during intrauterine development. These patterns refigure subjectivity as originating with-in an-other, and return from out of repression via engagements with aesthetic works, in "encounter-events".[24]As with Barad's diffraction, Ettinger's difference between "*I* and *non-I*" rests on alternating intensities and reiterative agencies.[25] In-utero mother-child symbioses is refused as much as any complete contradistinguishing of child and mother, instead instating a pattern for "sharing-in-difference" between partial, hybrid and co-emergent *transsubjects.*[26] Ettinger's sibling term, *transject*, figures a kind of horizontal ontology that does away with the hierarchical grammars indexing sub- and ob-ject. Manifesting in and by a web of *wit(h)nessing* stringing together transsubjects in shared aesthetic encounters, the

> transject (patterned upon the figure of archaic m/Other to which the I is transconnected...) subjectivizes and differentiates by connecting between humans, between the human and the non-human, as well as between formations and expressions of Life and of Non-Life with-in the human... the artwork as a transject provides such an occasion.[27]

The blueprinted patterns grounded in the womb instate the rhythm of the other in the heart of the self. *I* and *non-I* always already carry and are carried with-in each-other. Ettinger's term, co/in-habit(u)ation "with-in the other echoes bodily pregnancy, understood not as containing but as resonating together...while habituating to one another".[28] This is facilitated by transsubjects and transjects engaged in (e)merging practices, opening up to hospitality and co-response-ability as "expressions of communicaring in a womb-like neighbouring".[29]

In Berrigan's words, "renewal" is sought "from the erosions and hollows of patriarchy".[30] Toward facilitating ways of flourishing on a damaged planet[31] - with Haraway's observance that "the fetus and the earth are sibling seed worlds"[32] - an-other difference can be situated from the womb, through Ettinger, *in*-human. This locates an originary proto-ethics constituted by a sharing of situations in-difference, which might be returned in artworking, stitching the world-wounds that cut persons from relation through geographic displacement according to dominant geologics.[33] Following the words onscreen, "we are attuning to ...metabolic transformations".[34] In Berrigan's art, the counterflows of the Anthropocene - as an event marked by anthropogenic effects in the geosphere is as much as an event affecting geontological stirrings in the heart of anthropos - is manifest in the engagement between *Becoming Mineral* and its witnesses.

Projections from the gaze touch at a transsjective rock; we in(di)gest the heart of the screen turning (us to) stone. This transformation is not passive viewing; much like Michael Marder's writing on misconceptions of what it means 'to vegetate' - in likeness of wit(h)nessing stone or plant - is "to flourish" and be animate as opposed to lacking movement or vitality.[35] At stake is an embroiled and imbricated material-discursive metabolics between *bios* and *geos*. Further imaginaries for such intra-actions are shared through Berrigan's longer narrative-based video series, *Imaginary Explosions*, episodes 1 and 2. Swallowing an egg and being swallowed in explosions caused by Eyjafjallajökull in Iceland generates a phenomenon that interweaves material agencies in unexpected ways, feeling out the tensions of in(di)gestion. This is rendered doubly unexpected in the register of Berrigan's speculative fictioning, storying differences onscreen before, beyond and between symbolic and stratospheric surfaces.

Swallowing Egg

In *Imaginary Explosions,* episode 1, another encounter embodies the felt tensions of in(di)gestion, as described by an off-screen voice assumed to emanate from the network of earthly alliances that scaffold Berrigan's speculative fiction: "When I feed an egg to my stomach, I sense it disappears down a dark, long, shaft into a molten cavity that is still mineralizing".[36] The speaking character along with the egg form an imageless presence throughout Berrigan's work, which is not an erasure through its absence, but rather a calling to *what can not be seen* in the in/visible of the 'absent real'. The egg is drowned in the depths of the stomach, in more than a repetition of impregnation as the impregnable bounds between in/humans are broken through. Viviparous gestation enfolds appetites attached to oviparous reproduction; becoming vivi/ovi-porous. The networking voice follows their *in*-human sensing with an indeterminate counter; "maybe egg is not the right food for this inhuman appetite".[37] When ingesting an egg, the matter moves through numerous pathways of chemical processes including constructive/destructive metabolism, involving the building and breaking down of bodily energy stores. Ingestion is seen as fundamentally swallowing the outside in, and in contrast, egestion is the expelling movement from inside out of the body. Berrigan's representations of oscillating in/ex-gestions resonate with Ettinger's argument that "when a world, internal and external... becomes shared with-in-difference via artwork, this world is... the process of making a difference" and marks "the opening of a space at the heart of the border".[38] The oval matter of invagination through ingesting seeds, pips and eggs, combines the process of inner and outer fleshy/shell bodies enveloping another. The explosive stories of trees growing from seeds *in*-human bodies come to mind here, as a speculative investigation into the potentiality of bodies manifesting within other bodies through this co-metabolic openness. As Barad writes, through interstices of exchange "we are always already opened up to the other from the 'inside' as well as the 'outside'".[39] Thus, an 'inhuman appetite' can be read as the following: the desire to eat and become in/organic matter; of being otherwise; and to acknowledge, and bring together alternative knowledges; in a way that does not also absorb and consume an-other.

Thus, maybe egg is not the right food as porous links are sought beyond biologies of the living, mapping the scaling between egg and earth, (e)merging with-in non/living geologies. Maybe earth is better than egg for decentring humans in the ripples and radiations of an enfolding eruption. Maybe egg too readily feeds Ettinger's warning, "if I expel or swallow the stranger it is me who will be reduced...who will freeze the becoming-threshold" creating "fixed frontiers".[40] Ettinger recognises that we in fact reduce ourselves in the consumption and appropriation of the other, realising an absent real in our h/eart/h, in place of "the stranger without whom *I* will not co-emerge".[41] Maybe eruption is better than ingestion for decentering the centre, too, preventing "a retreat beyond the scope of shareability".[42] Frontiers thaw out when they're erupted, when exploding and swallowing are locked in the oscillations of unsettling indigestion. Becoming "raging hot all of a sudden", the networking voice is further connected to "desires [they] never knew [they] could have", where egg is sensed as maybe not the right food, where inhuman appetite is thought as inhuman desire.[43] In/human desires reverberate from the "erotic antenna" of each psyche as "an impulse toward the other" which for Ettinger "does not receive a human sense" though "does not remain inhuman" either.[44] This transgressive desire is paralleled in Barad's attempt to "confron[t] our inhumanity... [or] lack of compassion", by asking how we might reconfigure and turn to the inhuman as a way of coming "to feel, to care, to respond".[45]

With Barad, inhuman desire acquires a new resonance with reparative potential, pertaining to ethical imperatives attached to ecological (in)justices. As the off-screen voice in *Imaginary Explosions* swallows an egg, they "ingest [an] event like radiation"[46] in Barad's words, becoming material-discursive food for thought in an explosive desiring that enfolds (e)merging inhumanities; "to take [this egg] into your gut, to feel it leach into your bones, mutate your innards, and reset your cellular clocks".[47] Materialising differences *within*-humans is, for Barad, "about the im/possibility of metabolising the trauma"[48]

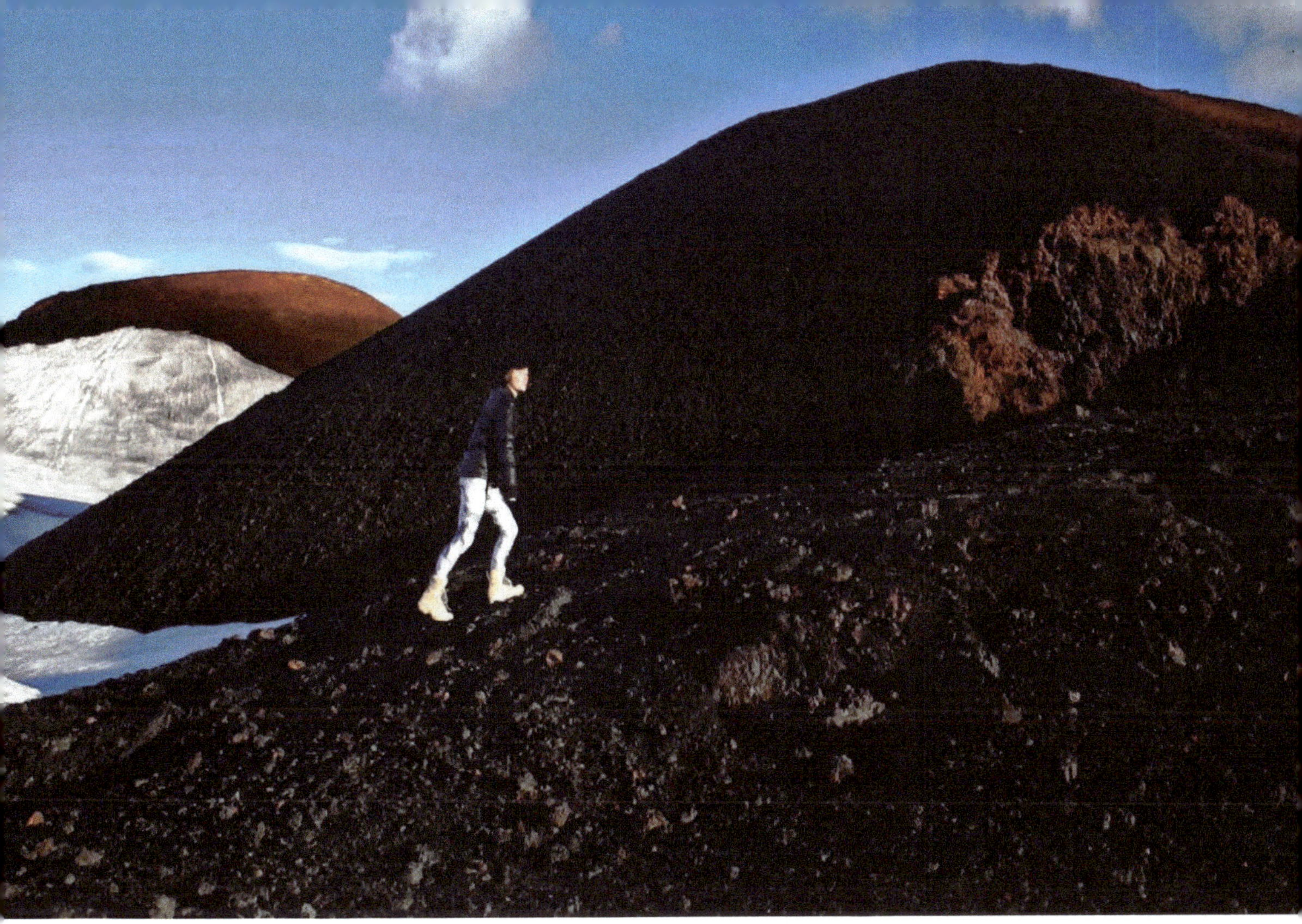

Caitlin Berrigan
Imaginary Explosions, episode 2, Chaitén, field photograph, 2018 © Caitlin Berrigan

stemming from planetary destruction and the absent real of an earth going/gone extinct. Radioactive decay "frays time's coherence".[49] Our own inhuman histories have severed our relations to the other, however Berrigan's speculative indigestions confront this *in*-humanity, reworking relations inside-outside the body as well as the space of the screen. In this way, with Ettinger, Berrigan facilitates "wit(h)nesses to the trauma of the Other...and of the world," retracing this "unforgettable memory of oblivion" through the earth and the work of art.[50] For Barad, "violence tears holes in the very fabric of the world in its sedimenting iterative intra-activity".[51] Wounding and tearing re-configures the landscape. Filling holes or gaps, as Berrigan suggests, can be enacted through imaginative processes or "material[...]data".[52] In more depth, "like breathing", filling lungs with oxygen, "the deformation of its surface tells us some things about the movements and expansions of its magma chambers".[53] Through Berrigan's affective embodiment across inhuman temporal scales, and Barad's inward and outward "trac[es] of [...] embodied [...] re-membering",[54] there is a "material reconfiguring of spacetimemattering in ways that attempt to do justice to account for the devastation wrought as well as to produce openings, new possible histories by which time-beings might find ways to endure".[55] Open wounds and openings made for "justice-to-come" confronts the environmental in/justices and severed potentialities of *being with* those that cease to erupt.[56]

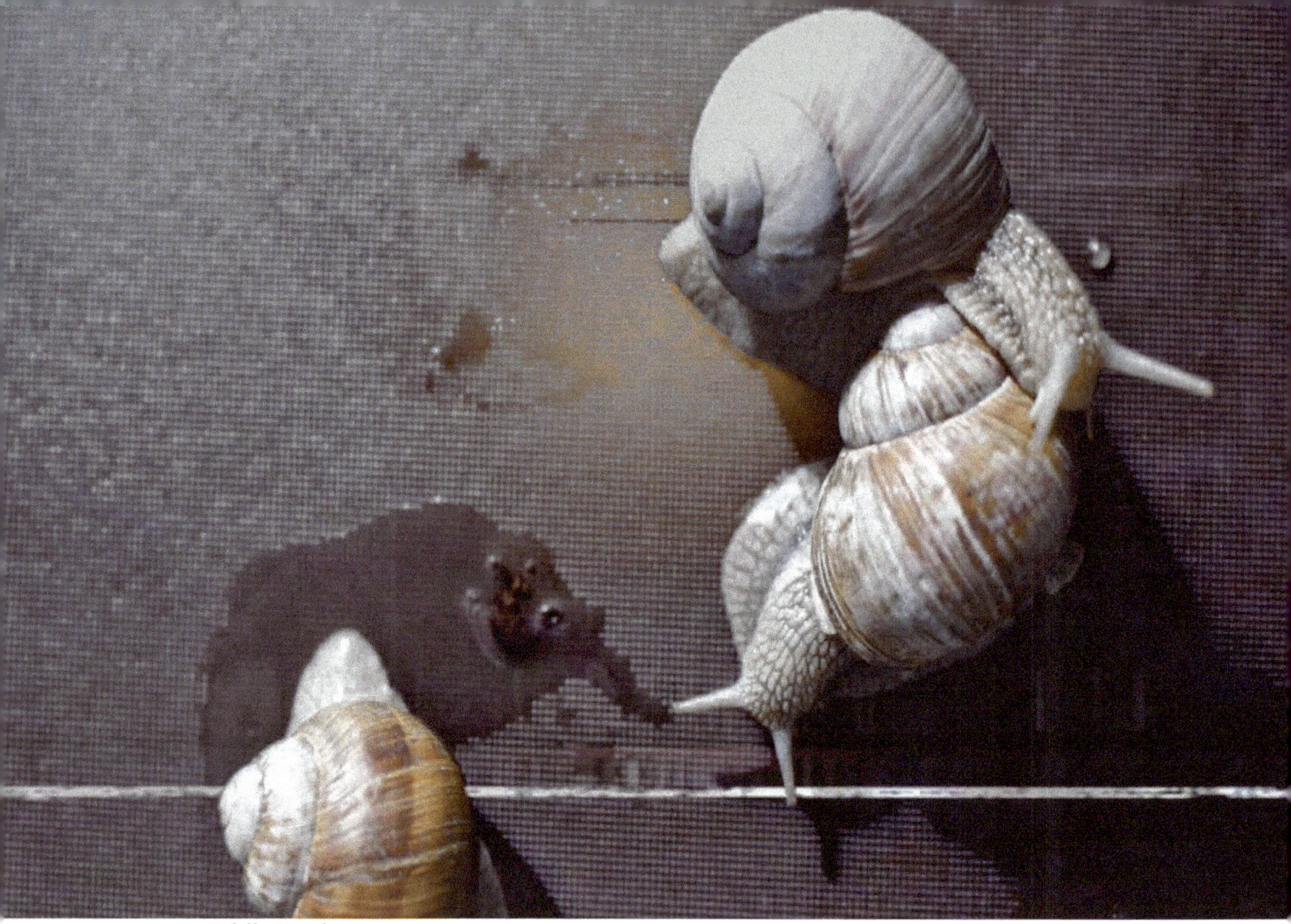

Caitlin Berrigan

Imaginary Explosions, episode 1, Eyjafjallajökull, Moving Image Still, 2018 © Caitlin Berrigan

Earthly Interruptions

The Eyjafjallajökull eruption in Iceland (2010) was witnessed across micro- and macro-cosmic scales. The (sm)othering of vast ash clouds, created conflicting dynamics in air time(-/)travel, and generated an in/visibility of the surrounding area. The obstructive flows of lava and smoke, engendered the turbulent momentum of news reports across the globe, as well as restricted motions of worldwide air travel, in which approximately 100,000 passenger flights were cancelled. Beyond the statistical data of postponed flights, the eruption enveloped the holey flows and fleshy worldings of lived experience. The volcano's inhuman smog was both ingesting and being ingested by multiple bodies; it subsumed multi-orifices, excretions and passageways. As the thick smoke seeped out into the atmosphere from the mouth of the volcano, it was indeterminately regurgitated across multispecies ecologies. Reports from the Shetland Islands described the mephitic sulphurous smell of the eruption, sniffing out the divide between Life and Non-Life further, as being similar to that of rotten eggs.[57] A miasma of decomposition, decay and sulphur fumes fill the atmosphere and fray the always-already incoherent times.[58]

> *Newscaster 4*: Satellite pictures track the clouds. What's hard to calculate is exactly how dangerous it is.

> *Engineer:* Speaking as an aeronautical engineer, I wouldn't want to be putting a big airplane up there at the moment. Uh... there's a lot of fairly nasty stuff there.[59]

The seismic eruptions communicated across the network of multi-species ecologies, and affected the impetus of la(r)va(l) subjects' diffractive waves of becoming. To become mineral: the impulse for activation, of breaking into an-other, and transformation. Tracing 'mineral becomings'[60] across multiple bodies (of rock), involves an attunement to the particularities of those instances of transformation beyond a critical and objective distance. At the beginning of the film, as the camera pans in and follows the textural ridges of the ash and rock, the tactile quality of the image produces an empathetic exchange between the viewer and volcano. Berrigan develops this intimate encounter of *being with* the volcano, specifically with-in the hold of the magma chamber, attuning to the volcanic patterning of eruptions with-in her stomach:

> Inside I'm changing and massively hungry – like an acid gas has imploded, disintegrated my organs, and left behind hardened deposits of sharp rock.[61]

Further witnesses to volcanic communications appear in episode 2 of *Imaginary Explosions*, in relation to Chile's Chaitén volcano. Chaotic and ecstatic representation of Eyjafjallajökul erupting is mirrored by the intimate, in-static encounters filmed with-in the Vilcún cave complex at the base of Chaitén. Berrigan collaborates with archeologist and volcanologist Dr. Karen Holmberg, who researches sustainability and conservation in "the linkage of the prehistoric caves" with "contemporary sites of volcanic disaster" following Chaitén's 2008 eruption.[62] Holmberg locates archeological interests in common between the prehistoric caves and the contemporary landscape, where returning economic and geographic stability to the region rests on their shared "geoheritage" and preserving their ongoing alignment and alliance. Berrigan bears witnesses inside the Vilcún cave complex, in-forming a space with-in the heart of the eruption that is staked in ongoingness and facilitates generative alliances.

Becoming mineral, then, is not indicative of solely collapsing outwardly (erupting/exploding/being ingested) across a planetary dimension, but also of folding inwardly (imploding/ingesting) on a more localised, phenomenal or molecular scale. In(di)gesting rock and its gassy im(aginary ex)plosions, describes the inward and outward pull of the diffractive (e)mergence between geological aesthetic layers within and out of the body and the landscape. The layering envisaged, creates a stark contrast to the ways in which monolithic strata layers have come to define linear, geological epochs. The spongey, porous layers of rock, space and time, are aligned to Neimanis' argument: after "capturing all the time in the world in a single stratigraphic snapshot...we need a different kind of archive. *We need to talk about our feelings*".[63] How does the body (of rock) feel and re-collect as it is witnessed across multiple scales breaking into an-other? Ettinger writes on "co-emergence" from "feeling-knowing": "I feel in you, you think in me",[64] this entails a "shareable memory"[65] of pain and wounding which resonates across multispecies ecologies. Not only to 'construct or deconstruct memory',[66] in a similar vein to how metabolism is not only *constructive* or *destructive*, this alludes to the transformative and energetic forces which extend our 'inhuman appetite' and settle in the future, as much as they do in the past.

Though not directly referenced in Berrigan's video work, the Icelandic *huldufolk* stir up geontologies and question the status of absented ecologies, repopulating the landscape and specifically its molten cavities with speculatively charged, in/human, in/visibility. The hidden or 'absent[ed] real' of *huldu-*

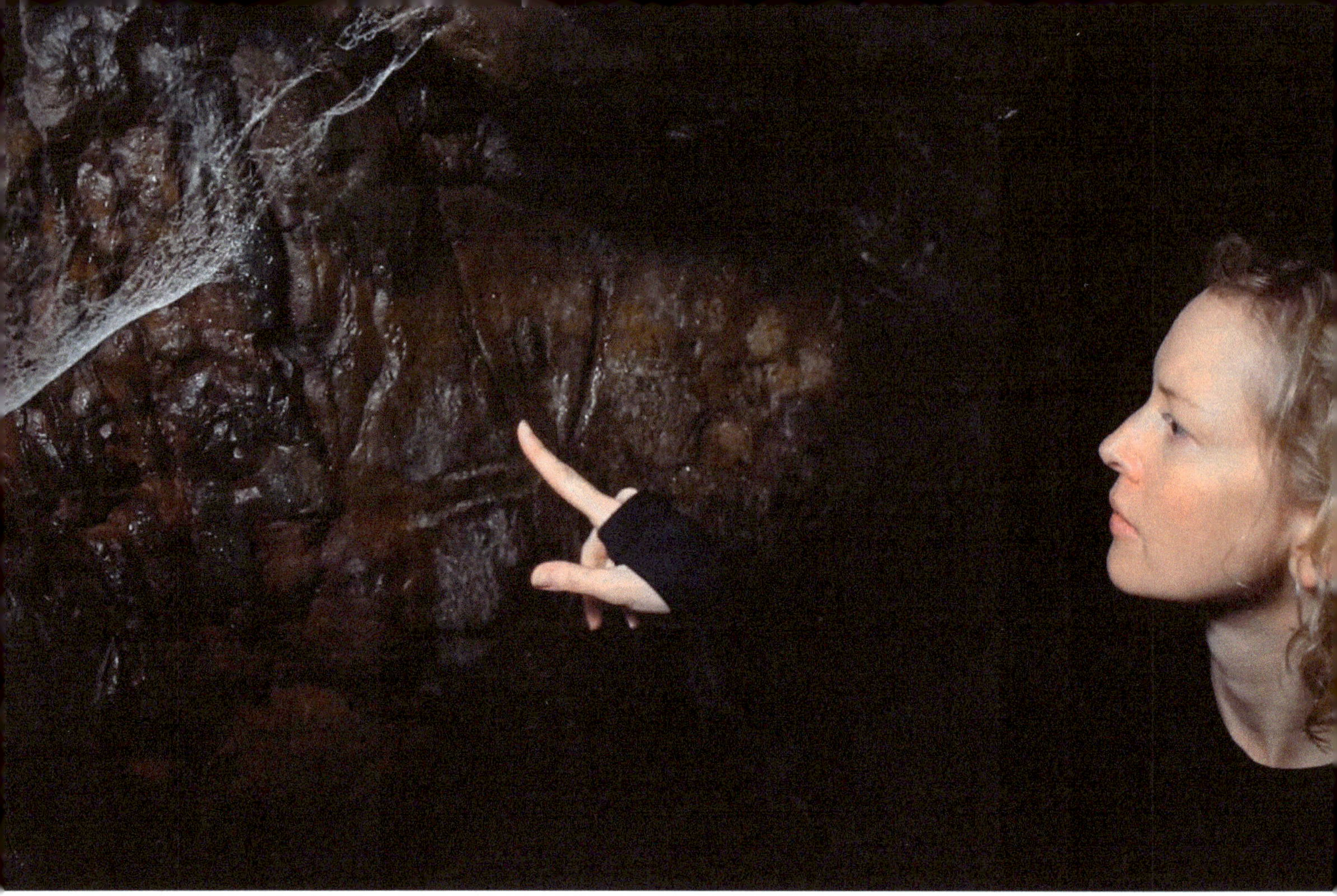

Caitlin Berrigan
Imaginary Explosions, episode 2, Chaitén, moving image still, 2019 © Caitlin Berrigan

folk stitch the Icelandic landscape, implying a kind of absent presence in the act of becoming mineral. As Jon K Shaw writes: "the *huldufolk* (literally hidden people) ...often dwell in the gnarled volcanic rock formations that jut through the island's ashen topsoil".[67] This knotted fabric of a landscape stitching molten rock-dwellers must remain undisturbed. Following Shaw, there is an emphasis on the way in which destructive anthropogenic effects, extending an homogenising anthropo-scenic gaze, are realised along "routes threaten[ing] the natural environment of the *huldufolk*".[68] The figure of the *huldufolk*, resisting scopic capture and camouflaged with-in the landscape, undoes the scopophilic and xenophobic mechanisms of the Anthropocene in the same stroke as their being seen as other. Their wavering in/visibility indicates a negative ontology from which in/human wit(h)ness to ecological injustice becomes possible. Seeing (with) the *huldufolk* returns the absented real of an environment destroyed; our sharing-in-visibility opens up landscapes (not-)seen as lacking out of which uncommon alliances might generate. Transformative (e)merging is not only stirred up in the transsubjective domain, *with-in*-human and *huldufolk* others, but also affects the landscape and the work of art as transjects. Diffractions differently map onto a landscape that re-collects absent presences as spatiotemporal deepenings in the knotted fabrics of earth. As in the temporal drag of disrupted air time(-/)travel caused by Eyjafjallajökull erupting, following Barad, we are tasked with "re-cognising material kinship with this exploded/imploded moment in time'.[69] Re-con-figurations of snails

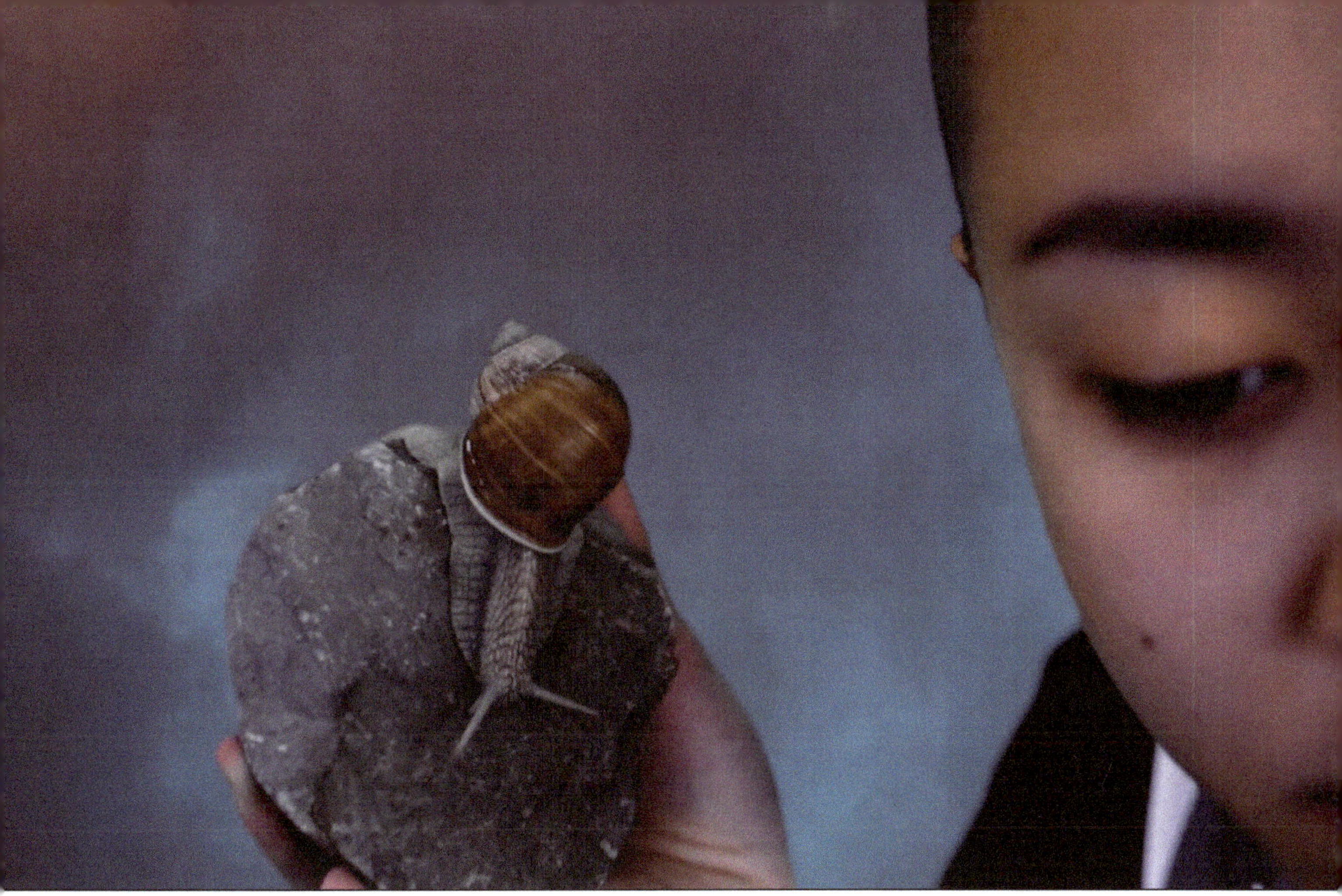

Caitlin Berrigan
Imaginary Explosions, episode 1, Eyjafjallajökull, moving image still, 2018 © Caitlin Berrigan

and sea lions along with spiders and manifold hidden others opens up alternate technologies, temporalities and cosmologies for earthly wit(h)ness.

Sounding Sibilant (Multi-)Species

Speculative figurations of sibilant, sibling (multi-)species others populate Berrigan's films. The subtle forces of snails, sea lions, and spiders stir up hybrid in/human con-figurations, attuned to alternate signals and sounds for networking with-in earth. Specifically, episode 1 features "Helix pomotia (big fat hermaphroditic snail humans like to eat)".[70] Footage of the snails sliming over stones remembers our own enfolding encounter with rock in Berrigan's *Becoming Mineral.* Wit(h)nessing as (e)merging practices between snails and viewers is instated, settling in the future, as we trace our shared secretions across stratospheric surface, deepening a space and time out of which in/humans and Non/Life might continue to reassemble. Mineral deposits are diffracted in their tropic figuration with snails in excess of our appetites and spatiotemporal limits. The big, fat snails are not only attractive when ingested *in*-human but, imploding desires, we in(di)gest with-in wit(h)ness of their own mineral becomings, expanding a shared horizon, feeling out tensions and tenses. As Barad writes:

> "Past" and "future" are iteratively reconfigured and enfolded through the world's ongoing intra-activity. [...] Even the 're-turn' of a diffraction

> pattern does not signal a going back, an erasure of memory, a restoration of a present past. Memory—the pattern of sedimented enfoldings of iterative intra-activity—is written into the fabric of the world. The world 'holds' the memory of all traces; or rather, the world is its memory (en-folded materialization).[71]

Memory indeterminately implodes and collapses inwardly, into the 'past'; and concurrently explodes outwardly into the 'future'. We are wit(h)nessing explosions with-in the artist and artwork, through Berrigan's speculatively imag(in)ed deep time. This is traced through the mineral deposits of memory settling into the worldly patterning and fragmenting of rocks assembling, making alliances, and continuously *re-membering*.[72] Doubling crossings at the in/human divide, this is traced in snails sliming over rocks, further *re-membering* diverse populations and biochemical interactions with-in mineral deposits. The superposition between a hereness and thereness of memory-sedimentation, bridging the diffractive tempos, scales and distances between our disrupted air time(-/)travel and the snail's pace traversing rock, moves beyond the linear-archival framework of plumbing waters or capturing earth. In/human and non/living assemblages might intra-actively ally themselves, re-collecting bilateral and horizontal archives with-in the landscape as it im/ex-plodes with-in us.

Following Ettinger and Barad, a landscape materialised in and by acts of wit(h)nessing itself constitutes re-membering. The affective co-emergence between agents in an aesthetic encounter promises to re-turn otherwise repressed and absented transsubjective affects that support the co/in-habit(u)ation of reiterative agencies with-in both rock and screen. In *Imaginary Explosions*, the off-screen voice senses "communications" but they do not know "how to translate them into human language". In the second person, viewers are addressed directly by this networking voice, bringing them indirectly into communion with the snails: "Are you getting the signals? And the snails, are they sensing something, too?"[73]

An extended shot follows this questioning, showing snails moving over a dark, textural background. Green-screening allows for the compositing of multiple images; the background appears to be a piece of fabric, perhaps it is rock, or a television screen on standby. Aesthetic horizons are adjusted by the snails, becoming co-constitutive actors with-in the art(net)work itself. Their figural, tropic agency is emphasised in the trails they trace across the screen, impacting the compositing of the image they occupy as they move through it. These "queer co-workers" produce a thickness to the material exchange, oozing amorphous inseparability against linear causal impressions as a way of introducing a series of more-than-human modes of communication.[74] Slime becomes another aesthetic layer, only partly visible through the outline of darkened patches smeared onto the background; the slime materially affects technological changes in the process of green-screening, participating in the post-production of visual effects. The shot features further flashes of an ambiguous light, emanating from the centre of the screen, from beneath the snails. These intermittent overexposures of light reflect the problem of the in/visibility of snails, or *huldufolk*, who become subject to anthropocentric scopism in the same stroke as signalling the instability and ultimate self-destruction wrought by this gaze. The dark background becomes a television lacking a sensible signal; cracks appear in the composition as visual effects of static electricity streak across the image, rearticulating the snail's slimy trails through technologies of the screen.

In *Imaginary Explosions*, episode 2, Berrigan bears witness to the 'agential cuts'[75] in stone of spider and vulva communicators across the 'unconnected' network of caves, which risk being submerged by rising sea levels.[76] The unsegmented, invaginating alliance-network spins an heterogeneous transmission which loops and folds back in on itself across multiple locations. The multi-patternings of petroglyphs on Vilcun's cave walls produce a "hybrid spider vulva" which are reverberated and imaged by the shape of the caves themselves.[77] Their image, as Berrigan states, "make us uncomfortable: the too-close-proximity of these mirrored shapes with their simple, metonymic alignment".[78] Becoming mineral in episode 2 can be said to be a form of "proximate sensing" in which our "current embodiment" sounds a "non-linear movement across materialities".[79] The space of the cave itself, its geo-metric metonymic alignments, in-forms the net(art)work that is followed by "an affiliation of transfeminist scientists" throughout Berrigan's narrative, "cooperating with the desires of the mineral earth to simultaneously erupt all volcanoes."[80] These desires follow in the metonymic footsteps of cave and vulva cross-inscriptions, rendering "landscape as birth canal".[81] The integration with-in and of geological and aesthetic networks emphasises our responsibility as wit(h)nesses in co-birthing ecologies of co-in/habit(u)ation between in/humans and Non/Life. Berrigan's speculative network follows signals across lithic stratas in a kind of oro/ero-genous mapping of zones that stir desires for earthly wit(h)ness. Becoming mineral in and by metonymies of networking; invaginating appetites, turning inside-out, becoming-with-in manifold others across shared aesthetic and geological stratas, bearing "witness to impressive scenes of eruptions".[82]

The landscape, environmental and aesthetic, is constituted in and by transformative alliances, where witnessing becomes wit(h)nessing. From the limits of our own singular perspectives, a shared horizon staked in processes of ongoingness is marked by the frayed edges, knotted centres and indeterminate tenses thread through lithic layers as well as that of the screen. Earthly wit(h)ness is only possible in the porous diffraction of the limits between in/humans and Non/Life. The reparative potential of environmental justice to attend to world-wounds arises in the aesthetic dimension when our own landscape is destabilised in relation to the disruption of our singular gaze, encountering the other and sharing-in-difference the diffractive rhythms resonating a third space, in/ex-gesting from the h/eart/h of the work of art. Through co-metabolic openness, Berrigan writes: "The work finds its way into the bodies of the audience, resolving the material and conceptual transfer to create a third space in which the boundary between the artwork and the audience is itself permeable and indistinct".[83] The net(art)working promises a third imaginary explosion, imminently with-in-human. Berrigan's upcoming episode 3 transmits the network's reach through a signalling of infrasounds, an artificial, miniature of Vesuvius from the 18th century, and through creative modes of environmental sensing, inviting us as active participants to continue in our earthly wit(h)ness of the "collective desire to erupt".[84]

Endnotes

[1] Ania Szremski, 'Caitlin Berrigan: Art in General', *Art Forum*, 2019 https://www.artforum.com/print/reviews/202001/caitlin-berrigan-81705 Accessed 25.1.21

[2] Catherine Malabou, *The Ontology of the Accident: An Essay on Destructive Plasticity*, (Cambridge and Malden: Polity Press, 2012)

[3] Caitlin Berrigan, *Imaginary Explosions, episode 2, Chaitén*, Moving Image, 2019

[4] Donna Haraway, *When Species Meet*, (Minneapolis and London: University of Minnesota Press), 2008, p.31

[5] Caitlin Berrigan, *Imaginary Explosions, episode 2, Chaitén*, Moving Image, 2019

[6] Astrida Neimanis, *Bodies of Water: Posthuman Feminist Phenomenology*, (London and New York: Bloomsbury Publishing), 2017. p.142

[7] Donna Haraway, *When Species Meet*, (Minneapolis and London: University of Minnesota Press), 2008, p.31 [Found in Tarsh Bates, 'Cutting Together-Apart The Mould,' Antennae: the journal of nature in visual culture 32, 2015, p. 61]

[8] Karen Barad, *Meeting the Universe Halfway: Quantum Physics and the Entanglement of Matter and Meaning*, (Durham and London: Duke University Press), 2007, p.72

[9] Karen Barad, 'Nature's Queer Performativity,' Qui Parle 2(19), 2012, p.157

[10] Astrida Neimanis, *Bodies of Water: Posthuman Phenomenology*, (London and New York: Bloomsbury Publishing), 2017

[11] Caitlin Berrigan, *Imaginary Explosions, episode 2, Chaitén*, Moving Image, 2019

[12] For more see: Melody Jue, *Wild Blue Media*, (Durham and London: Duke University Press),

2020, p.6, and Astrida Neimanis, *Bodies of Water: Posthuman Feminist Phenomenology*, (London and New York: Bloomsbury Publishing), 2017
[13] Bracha Ettinger, 'Art as the Transport-Station of Trauma,' Interdisciplinary Handbook of Trauma and Culture, Springer, 2016, p.157
[14]Bracha Ettinger, 'Fragilization and Resistance,' Studies in the Maternal 1(2), 2009, p.26
[15] Caitlin Berrgian, *Becoming Mineral*, Moving Image, 2018
[16] This creates parallels to the artist Sam Smith's ongoing project *Lithic Choreographies* and recent film *Lithic Coda* (2020), which depicts touching strata layers of human-more-than-human intimacies where bodies of rock and human communicate and mirror one another, as they float and rotate. The layered image gives the impression that the human is inside the rock. https://www.samsmith.net.au/projects/lithiccoda.php. More on 'lithic choreography' in Nicolas Sassoon, Rick Silva, Elise Hunchuck, Jussi Parikka, *CORES: Eight Fragments on Eight Stones, s-i-g-n-a-l-s*, 2020, https://s-i-g-n-a-l-s.com/cores Accessed 25.1.21
[17] Caitlin Berrigan, *Imaginary Explosions, episode 2, Chaitén*, Moving Image, 2019
[18] Nishat Awan and Zahra Hussain, 'Conflicting Material Imaginaries', *e-flux*, 2020 https://www.e-flux.com/architecture/new-silk-roads/312609/conflicting-material-imaginaries/ Accessed 25.1.21
[19] Caitlin Berrgian, *Becoming Mineral*, Moving Image, 2018
[20] Elizabeth Povinelli, 'When rocks speak,' Countersign Podcast, July 8 2020 https://countersig-nisapodcast.com/podcasts/ Accessed 25.1.21
[21] Povinelli suggests "even now, my hand is potentially rock holding a rock". Elizabeth Povinelli, Mathew Coleman and Kathryn Yusoff, 'An Interview with Elizabeth Povinelli: Geontopower, Bio-politics and the Anthropocene,' *Theory, Culture and Society*, 34(2-3), 2017, p.178
[22] Caitlin Berrgian, *Becoming Mineral*, Moving Image, 2018
[23] Bracha Ettinger, 'Fragilization and Resistance,' Studies in the Maternal 1(2), 2009, p.25
[24] Bracha Ettinger, 'Fragilization and Resistance,' Studies in the Maternal 1(2), 2009, p.12
[25] Bracha Ettinger, 'Fragilization and Resistance,' Studies in the Maternal 1(2), 2009, p.2
[26] Bracha Ettinger, 'Fragilization and Resistance,' Studies in the Maternal 1(2), 2009, p.12
[27] Bracha Ettinger, 'Fragilization and Resistance,' Studies in the Maternal 1(2), 2009, p.18
[28] Bracha Ettinger, 'Fragilization and Resistance,' Studies in the Maternal 1(2), 2009, p.28
[29] Bracha Ettinger, 'Fragilization and Resistance,' Studies in the Maternal 1(2), 2009, p.28
[30] Caitlin Berrgian, *Becoming Mineral*, Moving Image, 2018
[31] Anna Tsing, Heather Swanson, Elaine Gan, Nils Bubandt, Arts of Living on a Damaged Planet, (Minneapolis:University of Minnesota Press, 2017).
[32] Donna Haraway, *Modest_Witness@Second_Millennium. FemaleMan©_Meets_OncoMouse™*, Routledge 1997, p.174
[33] For more see: Kathryn Yusoff, 'Geology, Race and Matter', *A Billion Black Anthropocenes or None*, (Minneapolis: University of Minnesota), 2018.
[34] Caitlin Berrgian, *Becoming Mineral*, Moving Image, 2018
[35] Michael Marder, 'Plant-Soul: The Elusive Meanings of Vegetative Life,' *Environmental Philosophy* 8(1), 2011, p.84
[36] Caitlin Berrigan, *Imaginary Explosions, episode 1, Eyjafjallajökull*, Moving Image, 2019
[37] Caitlin Berrigan, *Imaginary Explosions, episode 1, Eyjafjallajökull*, Moving Image, 2019
[38] Bracha Ettinger, 'Art as the Transport-Station of Trauma,' Interdisciplinary Handbook of Trauma and Culture, Springer, 2016, p.160
[39] Karen Barad, 'On Touching -The Inhuman That Therefore I Am,' differences: A Journal of Feminist Cultural Studies 3(25), 2012, p.217
[40] Bracha Ettinger, 'Metramorphic Borderlinks and Matrixial Borderspace', *Rethinking Borders*, Palgrave Macmillan, 1996, p.154
[41] Bracha Ettinger, 'Metramorphic Borderlinks and Matrixial Borderspace', *Rethinking Borders*, Palgrave Macmillan, 1996, p.154
[42] Bracha Ettinger, 'Metramorphic Borderlinks and Matrixial Borderspace', *Rethinking Borders*, Palgrave Macmillan, 1996, p.154
[43] Caitlin Berrigan, *Imaginary Explosions, episode 1, Eyjafjallajökull*, Moving Image, 2019
[44] Bracha Ettinger, 'Art as the Transport-Station of Trauma,' Interdisciplinary Handbook of Trauma and Culture, Springer, 151-160, p.160
[45] Karen Barad, 'On Touching -The Inhuman That Therefore I Am,' differences: A Journal of Feminist Cultural Studies 3(25), 2012, 206-223, p.216
[46] Karen Barad, 'Troubling Time/s and Ecologies of Nothingness: re-turning, re-membering, and facing the Incalculable', New Formations 92, 2017, 56-85, p.82
[47] Karen Barad, 'Troubling Time/s and Ecologies of Nothingness: re-turning, re-membering, and facing the Incalculable', New Formations 92, 2017, 56-85, p.82
[48] Karen Barad, 'Troubling Time/s and Ecologies of Nothingness: re-turning, re-membering, and facing the Incalculable', New Formations 92, 2017, 56-85, p.82
[49] Karen Barad, 'Troubling Time/s and Ecologies of Nothingness: re-turning, re-membering, and facing the Incalculable', New Formations 92, 2017, 56-85, p.63
[50] Bracha Ettinger, 'Art as the Transport-Station of Trauma,' Interdisciplinary Handbook of Trauma and Culture, Springer, 2016,151-160, p.160
[51] Karen Barad, 'Troubling Time/s and Ecologies of Nothingness: re-turning, re-membering, and facing the Incalculable', New Formations 92, 2017, 56-85, p.83
[52] Caitlin Berrigan, *Imaginary Explosions, episode 2, Chaitén*, Moving Image, 2019

[53] Caitlin Berrigan, *Imaginary Explosions, episode 2, Chaitén*, Moving Image, 2019
[54] Karen Barad, 'Troubling Time/s and Ecologies of Nothingness: re-turning, re-membering, and facing the Incalculable', New Formations 92, 2017, p.62-63
[55] Karen Barad, 'Troubling Time/s and Ecologies of Nothingness: re-turning, re-membering, and facing the Incalculable', New Formations 92, 2017, p.76
[56] Karen Barad, 'On Touching - the Inhuman That Therefore I Am', *Feminist Theory Out of Science* 23(3), 2012, p.215
[57] Robert Booth and Severin Carrell, 'Iceland volcano: First came the floods, then the smell of rotten eggs', *The Guardian*, 2010 https://www.theguardian.com/world/2010/apr/15/iceland-volcano-eruption-ash-earthquake Accessed 25.1.21
[58] Karen Barad, 'Troubling Time/s and Ecologies of Nothingness: re-turning, re-membering, and facing the Incalculable', New Formations 92, 2017, p.63
[59] Caitlin Berrigan, *Imaginary Explosions, episode 1, Eyjafjallajökull*, Moving Image, 2019
[60] For more see: Giles Deleuze and Felix Guattari, *A Thousand Plateaus*, Bloomsbury, 2013
[61] Caitlin Berrigan, *Imaginary Explosions, episode 1, Eyjafjallajökull*, Moving Image, 2019
[62] Karen Holmberg, 'the vilcun caves and volcanic landscape of chaiten, chile: a transdisciplinary conservation study of coastal patagonian archaeology and geoheritage', Blog, 2018 http://karenholmberg.com/blog/2018/3/23/the-vilcn-caves-and-volcanic-landscape-of-chaitn-chile-a-transdisciplinary-conservation-study-of-coastal-patagonian-archaeology-and-geoheritage Accessed 25.1.21
[63] Astrida Neimanis, 'Water a Queer Archive of Feeling' in *Tidalectics: Imagining an Oceanic worldview through Art and Science*, ed. Stephanie Hessler, London, England and Cambridge, Massachusetts: TBA21 Academy and The MIT Press, 2018, p.192
[64] Bracha Ettinger, 'To Feel the Word's Pain and Its Beauty': Brad Evans interviews Bracha Ettinger', *Los Angeles Review of Books*, 2017 https://lareviewofbooks.org/article/feel-worlds-pain-beauty/ Accessed 25.1.21
[65] Bracha Ettinger, 'Fragilization and Resistance,' Studies in the Maternal 1(2), 2009, p.22
[66] Bracha Ettinger, 'To Feel the Word's Pain and Its Beauty': Brad Evans interviews Bracha Ettinger', *Los Angeles Review of Books*, 2017 https://lareviewofbooks.org/article/feel-worlds-pain-beauty/ Accessed 25.1.21
[67] Jon K Shaw and Theo Reeves-Evison, *Fiction as Method*, (Berlin: Sternberg Press), 2017, p.16
[68] Jon K Shaw and Theo Reeves-Evison, *Fiction as Method*, (Berlin: Sternberg Press), 2017, p.16
[69] Karen Barad, 'Troubling Time/s and Ecologies of Nothingness: re-turning, re-membering, and facing the Incalculable', New Formations 92, 2017, p.82
[70] Ania Szremski, 'Caitlin.Berrigan: Art in General', *Art Forum*, 2019 https://www.artforum.com/print/reviews/202001/caitlin-berrigan-81705 Accessed 25.1.21
[71] Karen Barad, 'Nature's Queer Performativity,' Kvinder, Køn, Forskning 1-2, 2012, p.44
[72] Karen Barad, 'Troubling Time/s and Ecologies of Nothingness: re-turning, re-membering, and facing the Incalculable', New Formations 92, 2017, p.84
[73] Caitlin Berrigan, *Imaginary Explosions, episode 1, Eyjafjallajökull*, Moving Image, 2019
[74] Karen Barad, 'Nature's Queer Performativity,' Kvinder, Køn, Forskning 1-2, 2012, p. 33
[75] Karen Barad, *Meeting the Universe Halfway: Quantum Physics and the Entanglement of Matter and Meaning*, (Durham and London: Duke University Press), 2007, p. 175
[76] Caitlin Berrigan, *Imaginary Explosions, episode 2, Chaitén*, Moving Image, 2019
[77] Caitlin Berrigan, *Imaginary Explosions, episode 2, Chaitén*, Moving Image, 2019
[78] Caitlin Berrigan, *Imaginary Explosions, episode 2, Chaitén*, Moving Image, 2019
[79] Caitlin Berrigan, *Imaginary Explosions, episode 2, Chaitén*, Moving Image, 2019
[80] Caitlin Berrigan, 'Imaginary Explosions (Episodic)' https://caitlinberrigan.com/ Accessed 25.1.21
[81] Caitlin Berrigan, *Imaginary Explosions, episode 2, Chaitén*, Moving Image, 2019
[82] Caitlin Berrigan, *Imaginary Explosions, episode 2, Chaitén*, Moving Image, 2019
[83] Caitlin Berrigan, 'The Life Cycle of a Common Weed: Viral Imaginings in Plant-Human Encounters,' *Women's Studies Quarterly* 40 (1), 2012, p. 112
[84] Caitlin Berrigan, *Imaginary Explosions, episode 2, Chaitén*, Moving Image, 2019

Georgia Perkins is a tutor and doctoral candidate in the Visual Cultures Department at Goldsmiths, University of London, visiting lecturer at Winchester School of Art, and curatorial fellow at SIRIUS, Cork. Her research critically examines the molecular scale, indeterminacy and the sensible.

Callum Bradley is a PhD researcher in the Visual Cultures Department at Goldsmiths, University of London. His research turns to Bracha Ettinger's theories for extending an ecological thought. His work has been published with *The International Journal of Human-Computer Studies* (2021), and *The Journal of Queer Studies in Media and Popular Culture* (2023), as well as presented at 'Earth(ly) Matters' (Sheffield, 2020) and 'Forms of (More-Than-)Human Relationally' (Amsterdam, 2023).

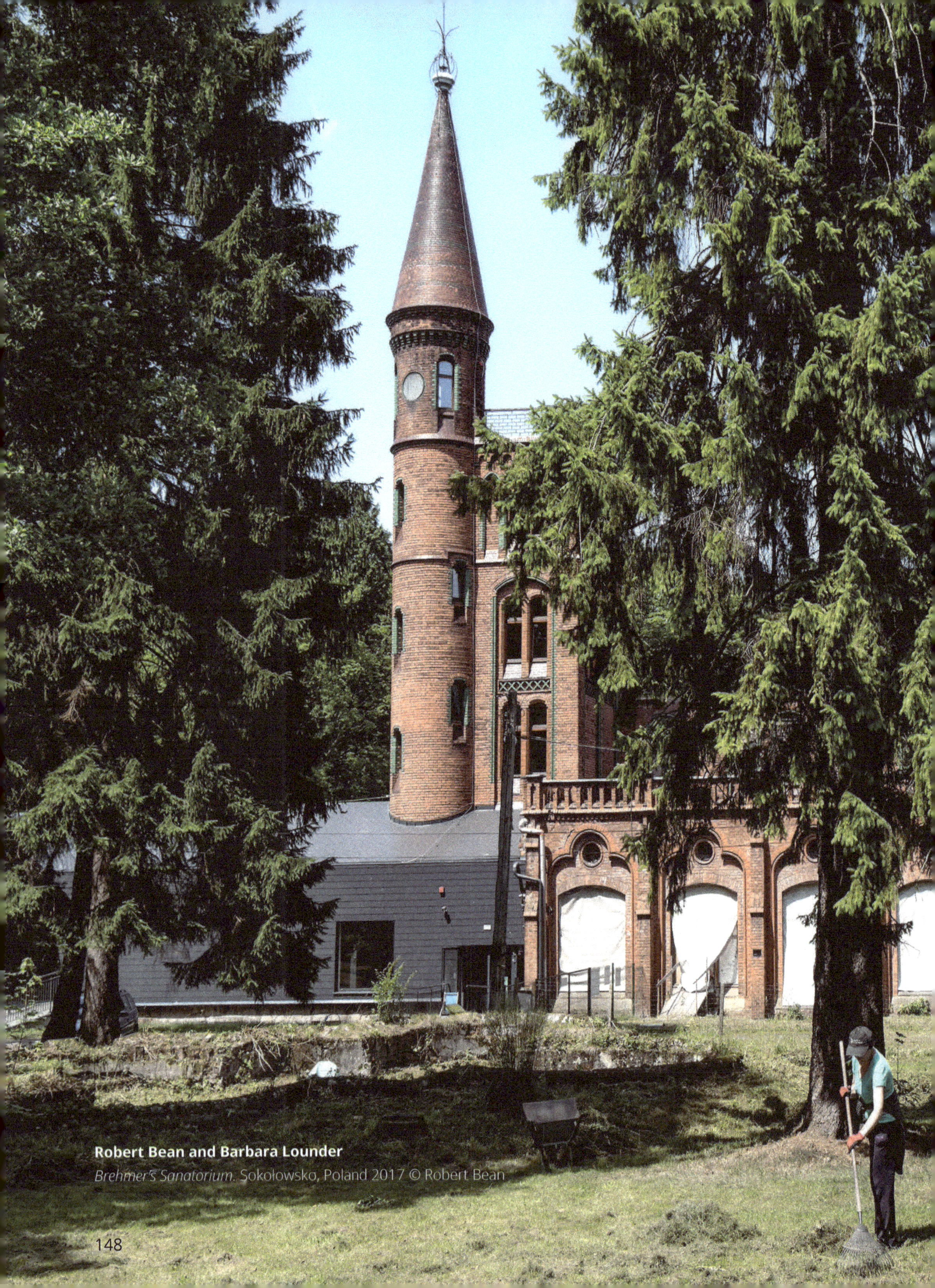

Robert Bean and Barbara Lounder

Brehmer's Sanatorium, Sokołowsko, Poland 2017 © Robert Bean

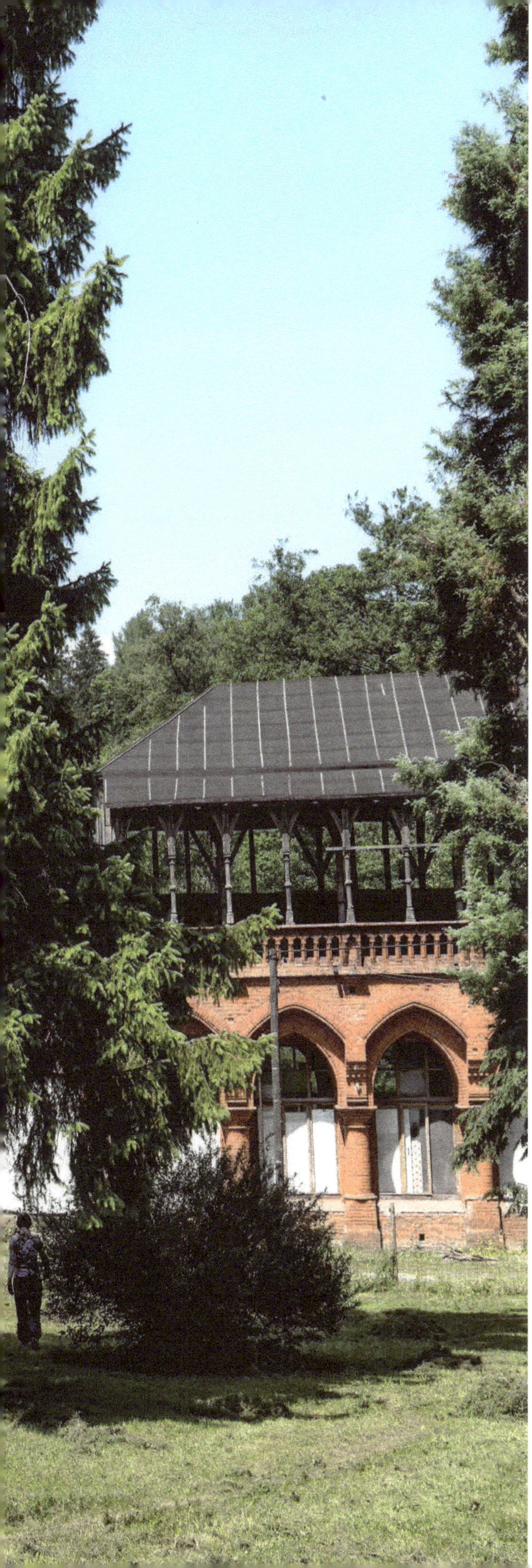

Being-in-the-breathable: atmospheres of the Anthropocene

Being-in-the-Breathable, a collaborative artwork by Robert Bean and Barbara Lounder, was introduced in 2017 for the *Contexts International Festival of Ephemeral Art* in Sokolowsko Poland. *Being-in-the-Breathable: An Annotated Walk* responded to the earth's atmosphere as the last Commons shared by human and non-human entities. Their 2018 work, Being-in-the-Breathable: Weathering, was based on walks in the Lake District, UK. In 2019 they created *Being-in-the Breathable: The Commons* and the fourth work in the series, *Being-in-the Breathable: 44.649589,-63.574150*, which took place in the immediate aftermath of Hurricane Dorian. This visual essay is about the first two works in the series.

text and images: **Robert Bean and Barbara Lounder**

1. Air conditioning[1]

Peter Sloterdijk used the term "Being-in-the-Breathable" to describe "atmoterror", how the atmosphere was made explicit by the use of gas warfare during the First and Second World Wars. He referred to this phenomenom as "air conditioning". The weaponizing of the atmosphere, or "atmoterror", continues to be utilized in warfare and is visible in the inequities of climate change. Taken at the site of the Majdanek concentration camp near Lublin, Poland, 35 still photographs of the sky, clouds, birds and atmosphere were counterpoised against a topography of unspeakable trauma. Exhibited in 2017 as one large contact sheet on the wall of the ruined sanatorium in Sokolowsko, Poland, the Majdanek images invited an affective response to difficult histories.

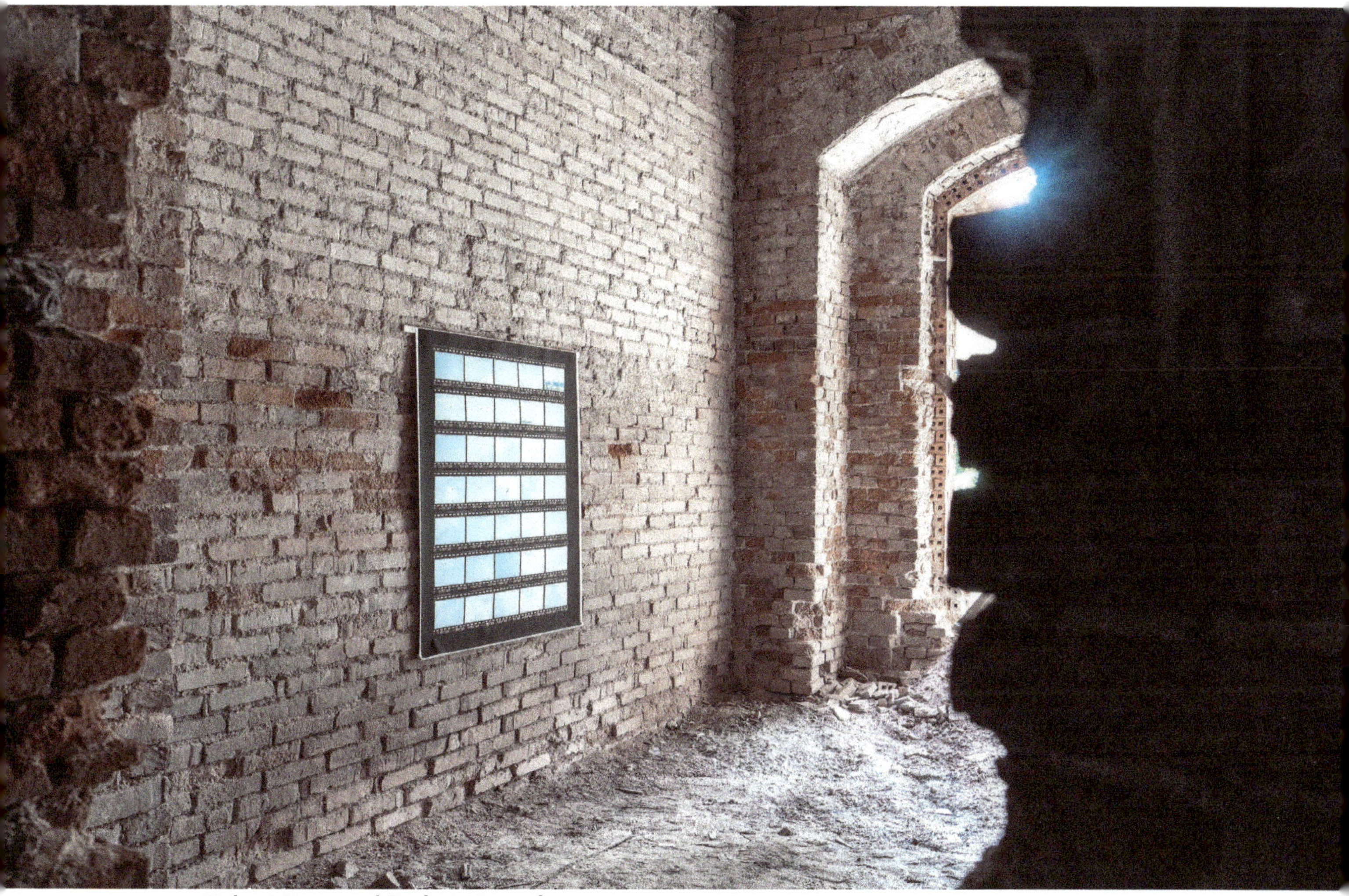

Robert Bean and Barbara Lounder

Majdanek, 1988 (2017). Ink Jet Print, Sokołowsko, Poland 2017 © Robert Bean

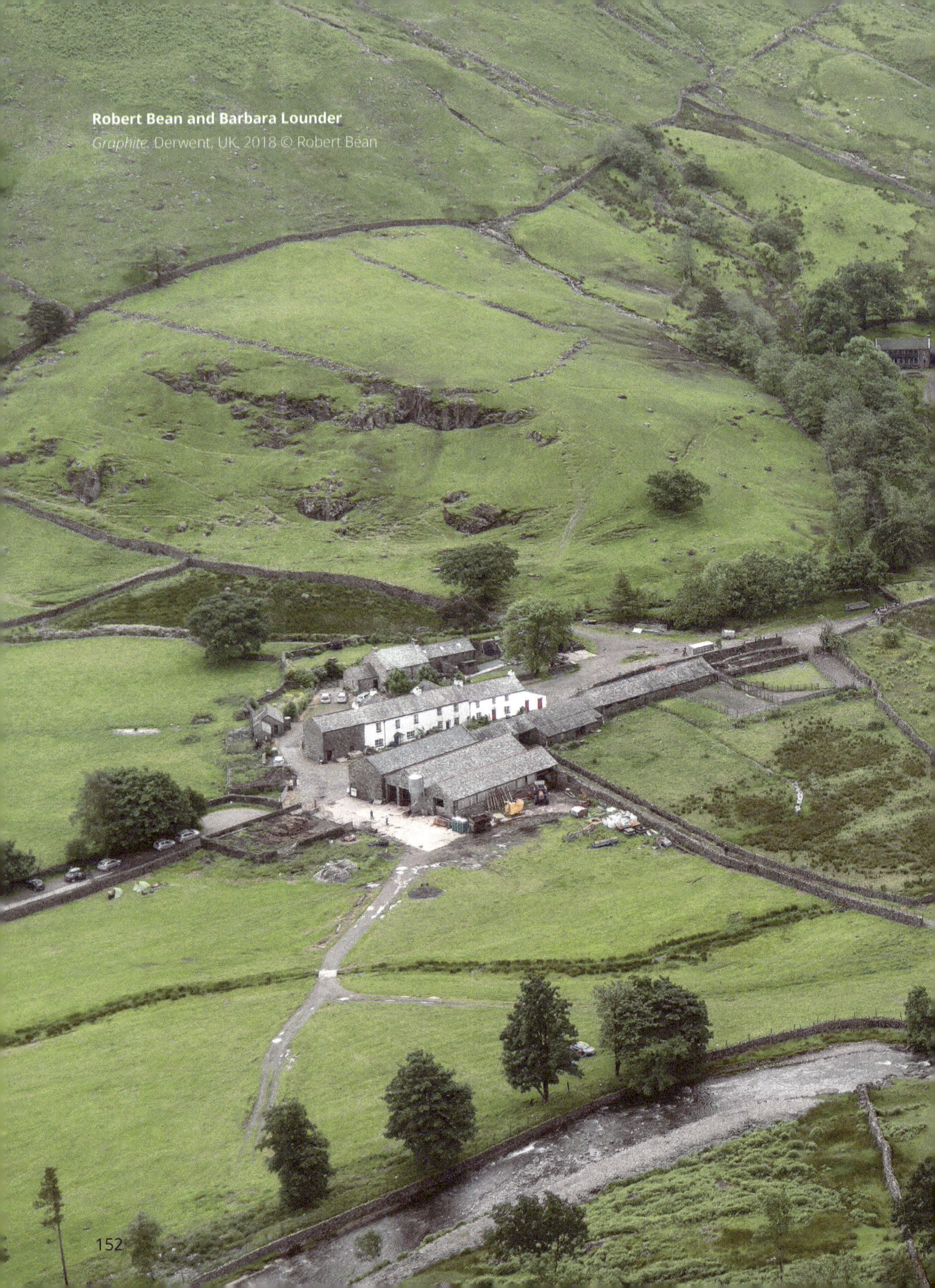

Robert Bean and Barbara Lounder

Graphite, Derwent, UK, 2018 © Robert Bean

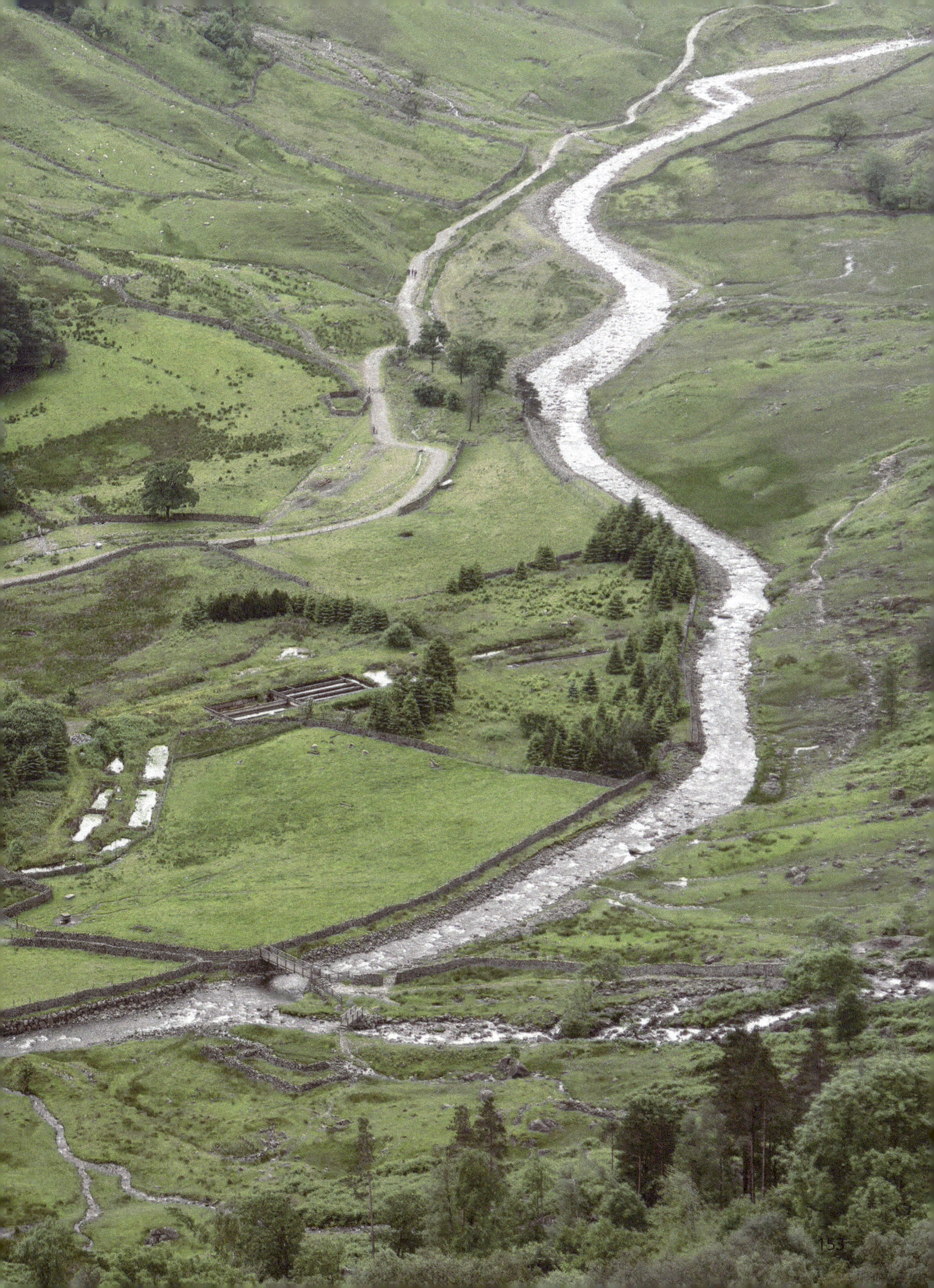

2. Quarantine: quaranti giorni (40 days)

> ...air is the medium and breathing the mechanism through which the outside environment is embodied. Air carries the weather, climate and particles from the environment into the body. Humans embody the climate of their environment through air, just as fish embody the climate of their environment through water.[2]

We began the walk by establishing quarantine, distancing participants in space according to the criteria used to prevent the spread of disease. Each person performed the quarantine by pivoting slowly in a circle, arms outstretched, establishing an empty space isolated from others. This recalled the quantification of breathing that influenced the design of Brehmer's sanatorium in Sokolowsko; each body breathes 15 litres of air per minute, and in the sanatorium, each patient in the chest ward was provided with 75m3 of air and a 5m3 area of light. This is understood today as social distancing.

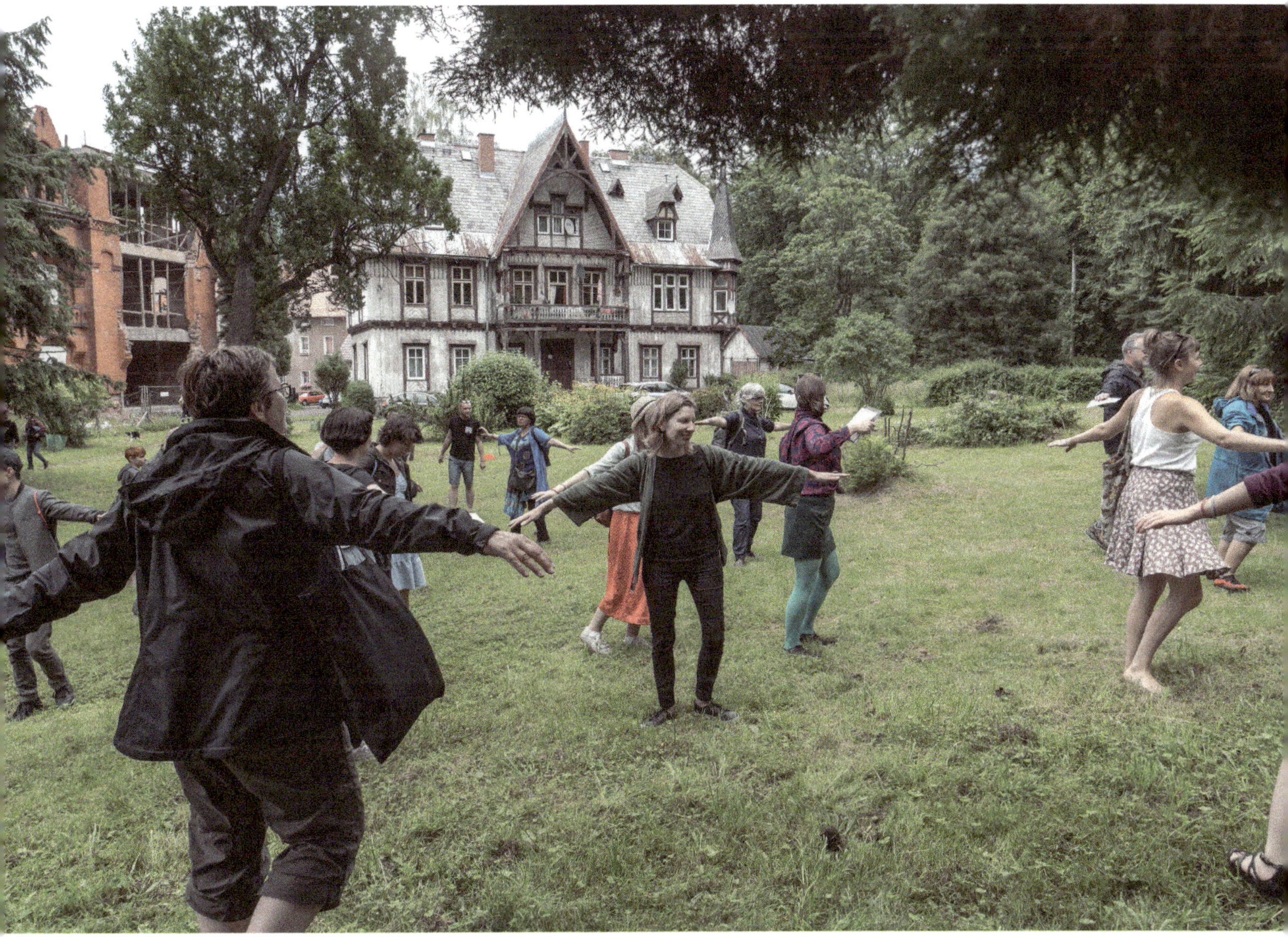

Robert Bean and Barbara Lounder

Quarantine: Quaranti giorni. Sokołowsko, Poland 2017 © Robert Bean

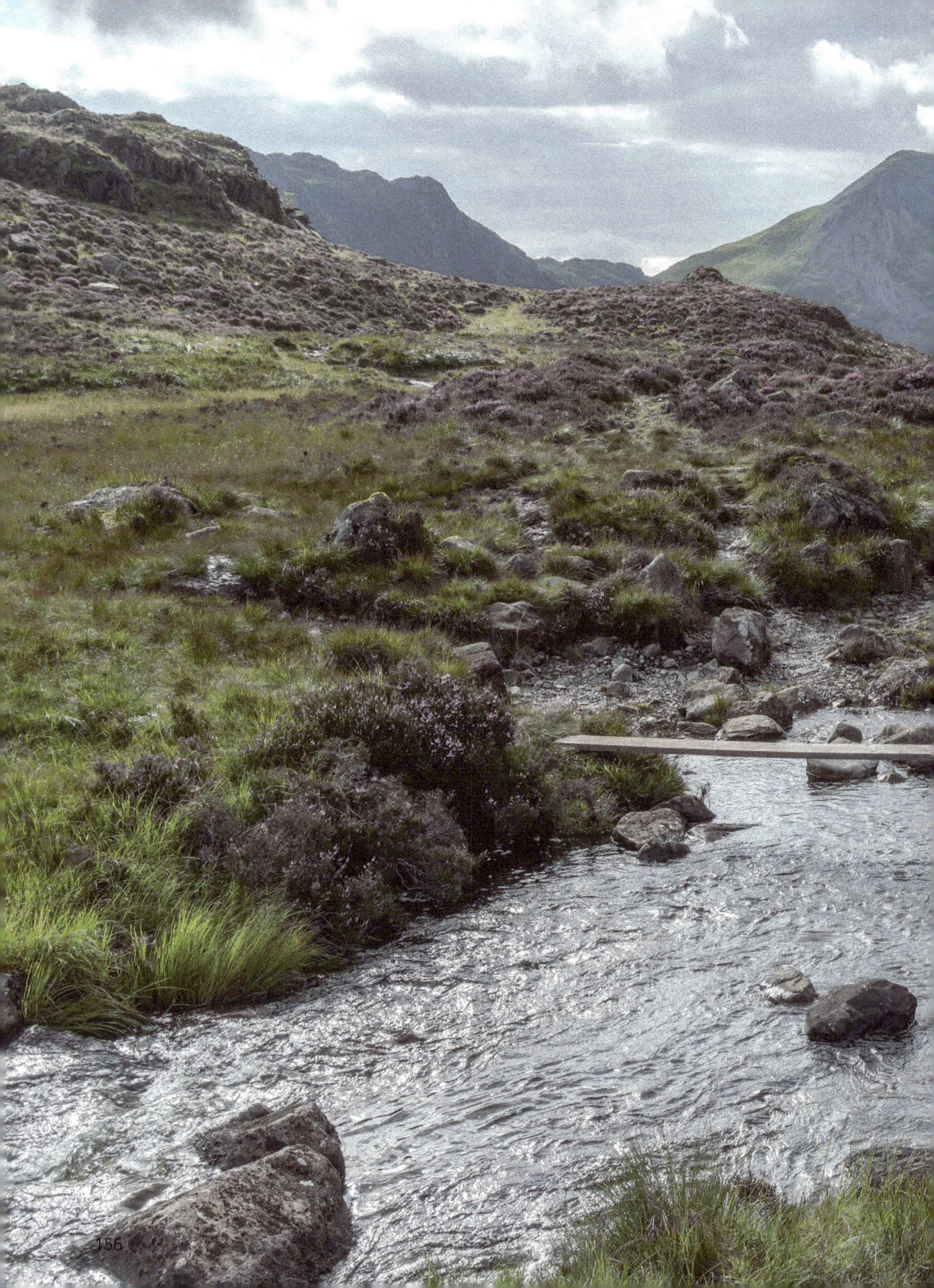

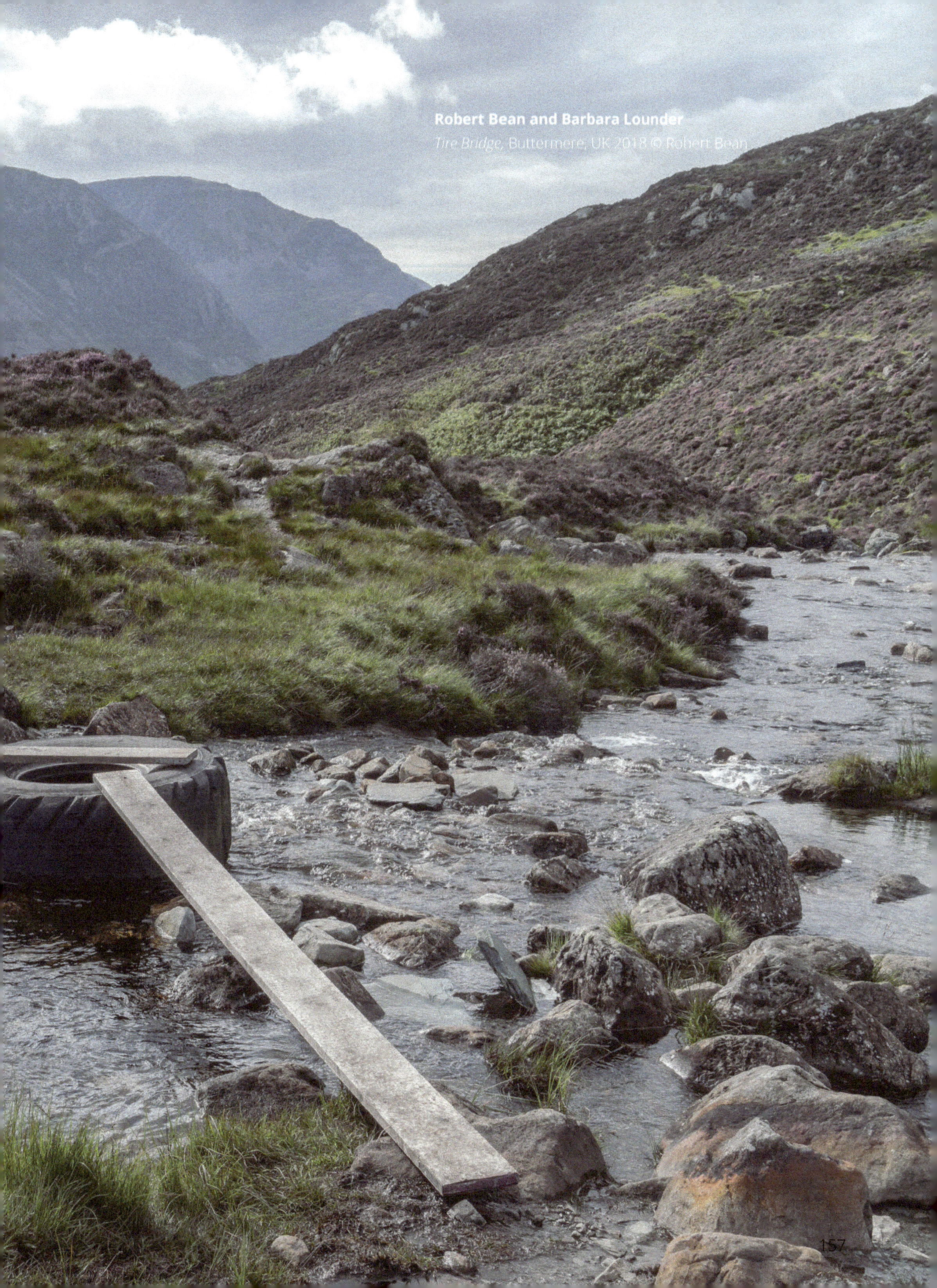

Robert Bean and Barbara Lounder
Tire Bridge, Buttermere, UK 2018 © Robert Bean

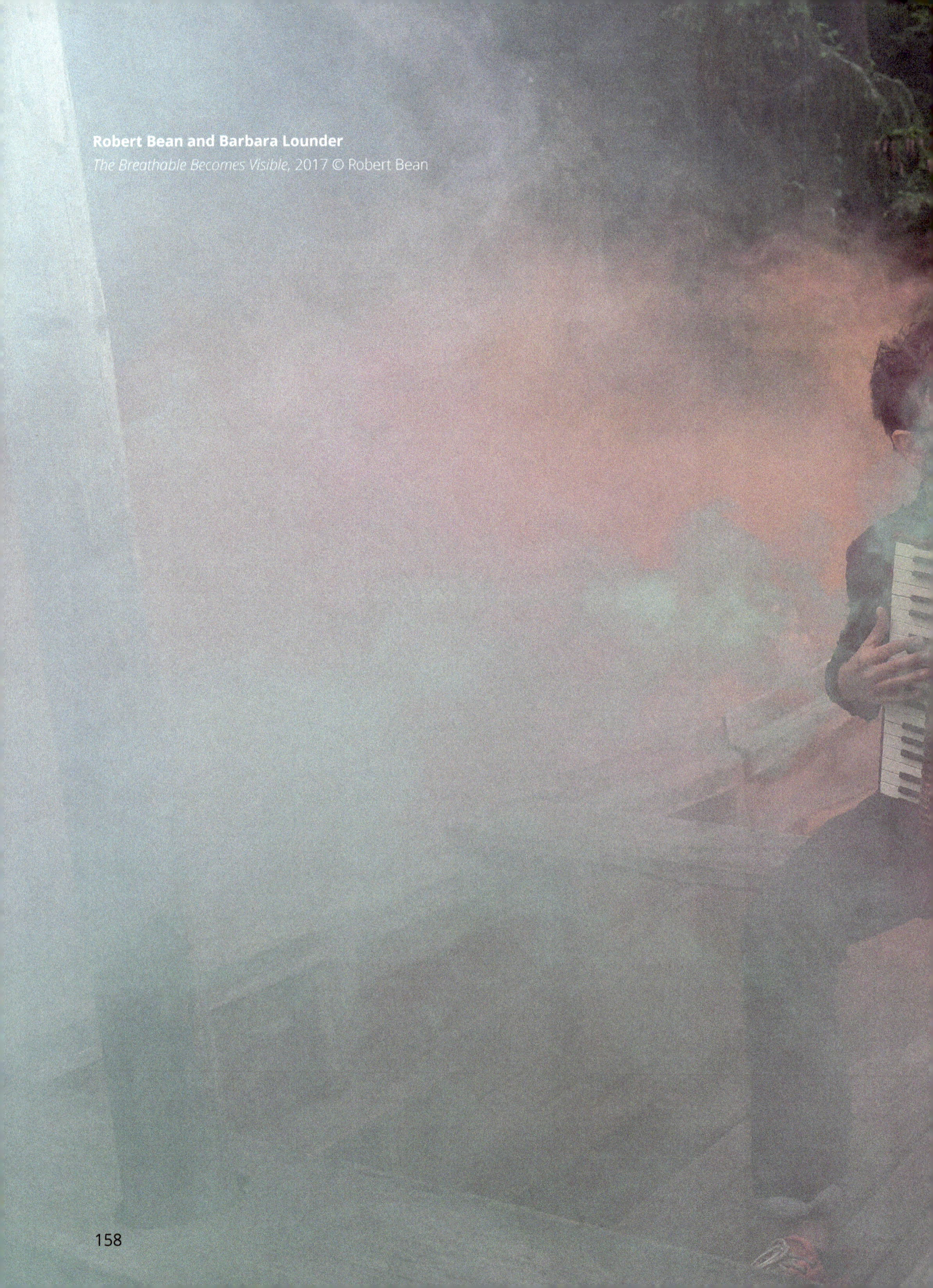

Robert Bean and Barbara Lounder
The Breathable Becomes Visible, 2017 © Robert Bean

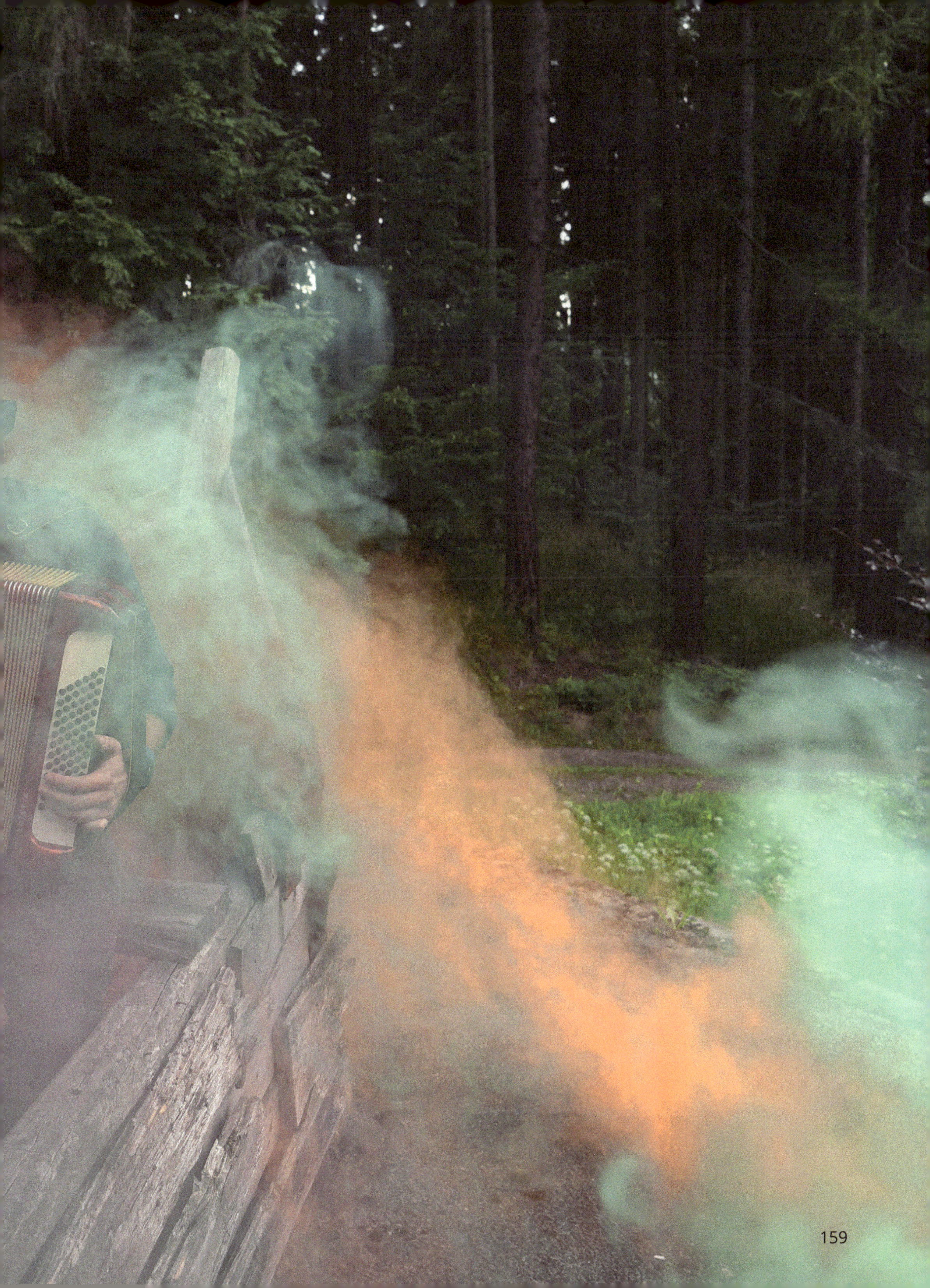

3. Walking in the fresh air

The tire and planks assisted in our wayfinding as we descended Haystacks, Buttermere, UK. The tire, a broken tool, revealed its thingness. In the image, it continues to form part of an assemblage that gathers fossil fuels, carbon emissions, rubber trees, rainforests, acrid fumes, extractivism, asphaltum, ancient and modern technologies of mobility. Walking has the potential to simultaneously disturb histories, ideologies and habits while creating new meshworks of meaning spanning temporal frames, spaces, disciplinary boundaries, and embodied sensorial modalities. Passing through the fresh air of the forest surrounding the sanatorium in Sokolowsko, walkers paused, doubled back, turned, inscriptive movements, proceeding in a roughly linear fashion while inviting deviation and improvisation.

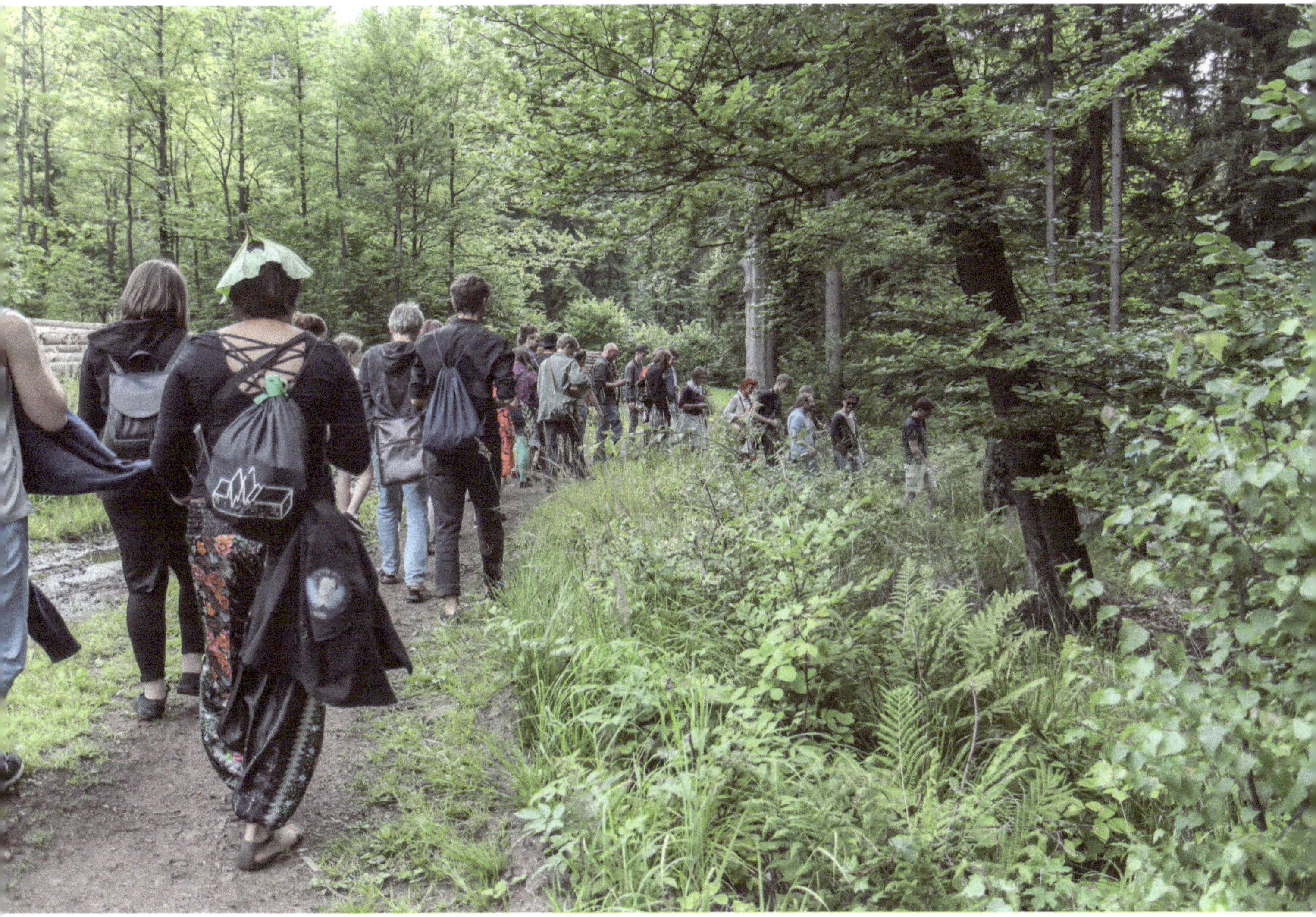

Robert Bean and Barbara Lounder
Fresh Air: Sanatorium Walking, 2017 © Robert Bean

4. Scar and scree

> Dust forms part of this extended discussion, and though it is not given more space than any other substance, its role in stimulating an emergent forensic imagination is evident.[3]

Being in the breathable is not just about atmospheres, but about particles and droplets in the air: dust stirred up by wind passing over drought-dry barrens; ash and carbon released through burning and tilling; industrial pollution; water vapour, haze and storm clouds; toxic contaminants and pathogens. On the hillside above Seathwaite, near Derwent in the Lake District, we walked to the abandoned sites of medieval graphite mines. Now depleted, the Derwent graphite was used as a mould-release in casting cannonballs and other ordnance for the Royal Navy. *Derwent* is also the trade name for a notable brand of artists' pencils. The Lake District was deforested and scarred by centuries of sheep farming and mining but became a popular destination for recreation and respite for workers from the industrial centres nearby. Their vacation postcards provide phatic observations of weather, sites, vistas, terrain and walking excursions.

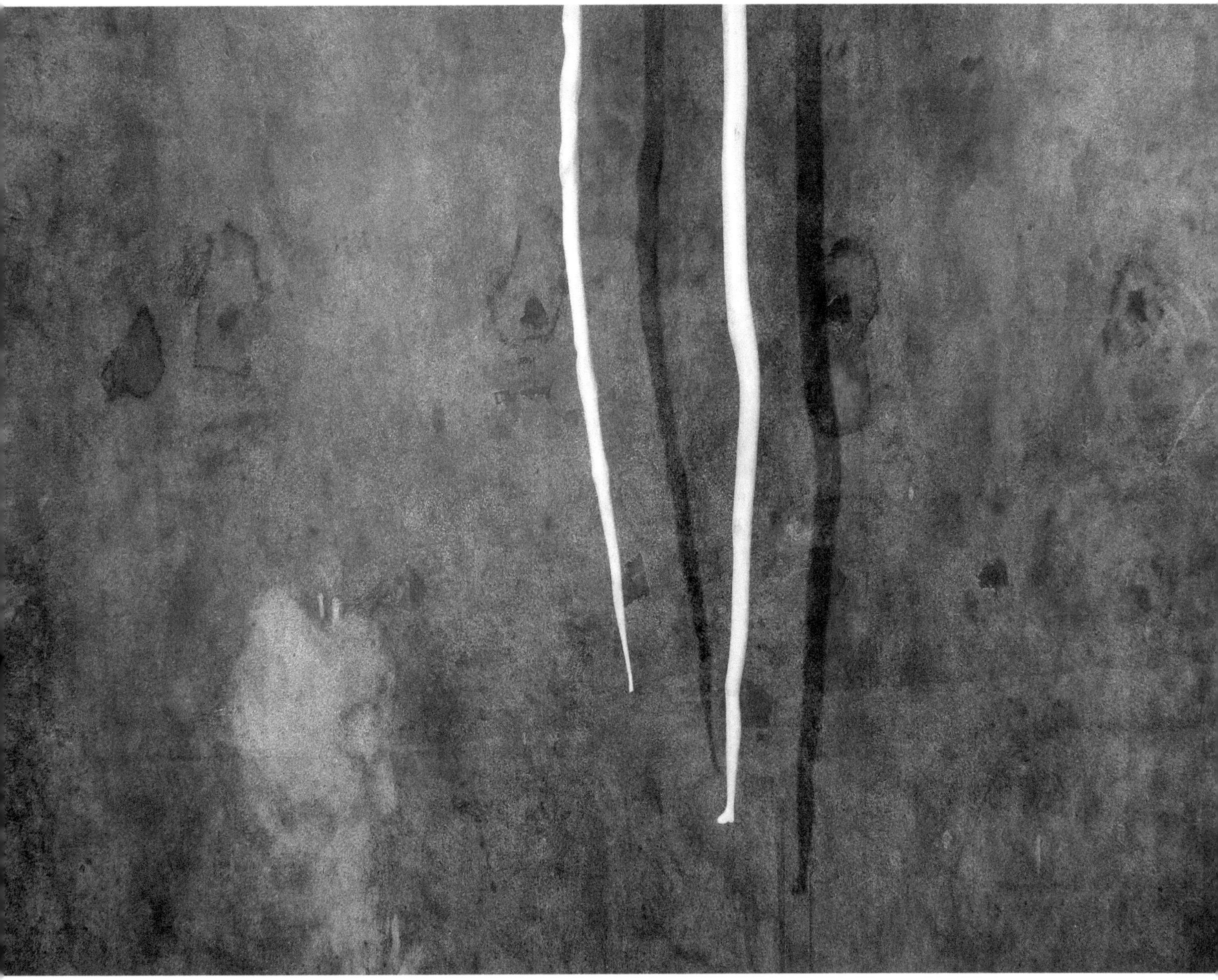

Barbara Lounder
Dorothy and William Walking Sticks, graphite, carved and painted sticks, 2018 © Robert Bean

5. Graphite

Movement leaves a trace. Graphite is smeared on the backs of the sheep, on wheel axles and gears, and inside the moulds. An artist sketches a picturesque landscape with it or drags it across the bare wall of the gallery. The walker uses it to note her observations, and later to make journal entries. Her famous brother relies on her notes for his poems. The words are, like walking sticks, prosthetic devices that impress the walking subject into the topography.

> While it is Dorothy holding the pen, the memories and sensations she records are a peculiar mixture of her own independent recollections and her brother's, as well as fragments from their shared experiences. Here 'we' slips into 'I', and back into 'we', making it difficult to disentangle which feelings or memories belong to which individual. The act of retracing this route makes indistinct the boundaries between the siblings, and brings multiple pasts into the shared present.[4]

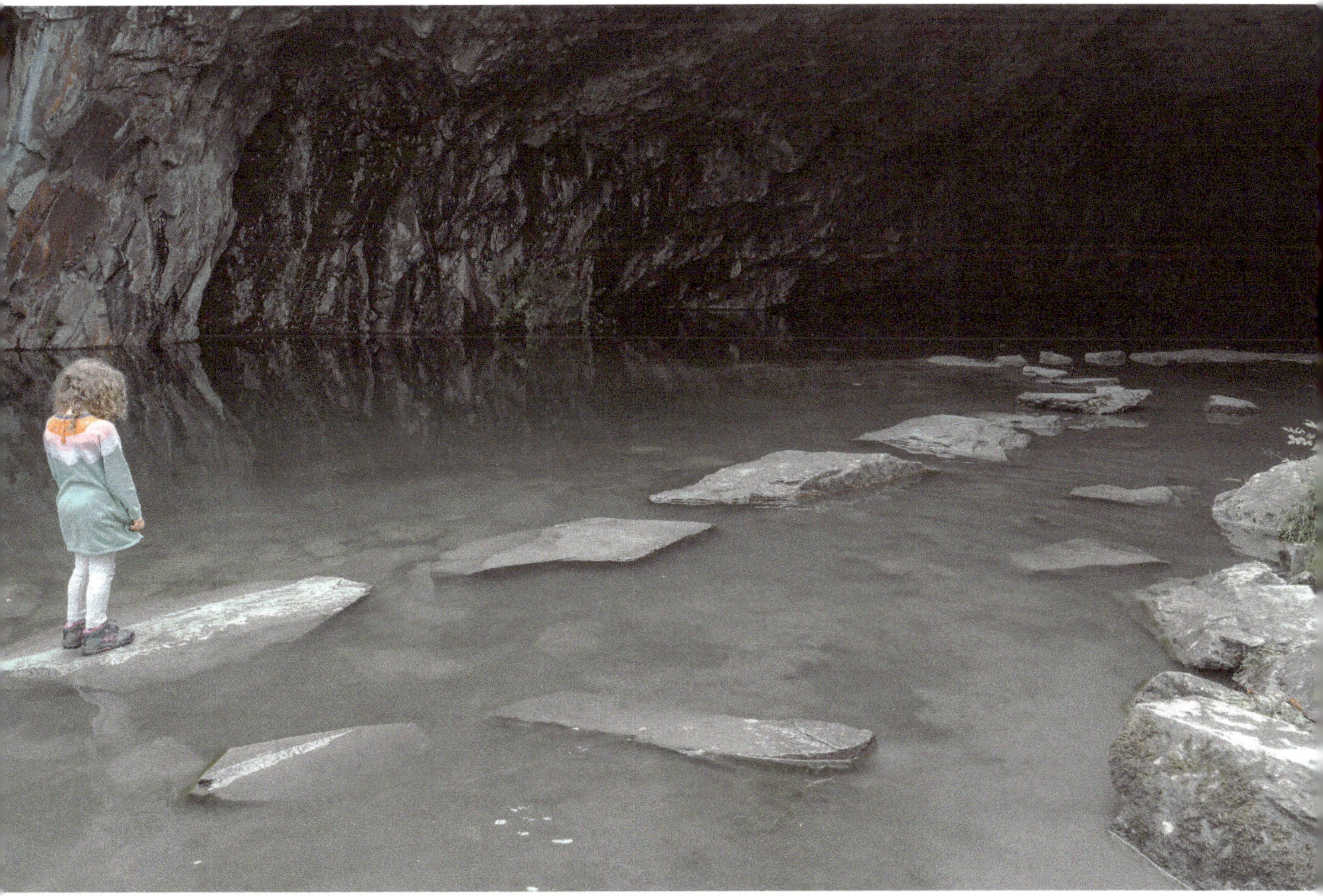

Robert Bean and Barbara Lounder

Cave at Grasmere, Grasmere, UK 2018 © Robert Bean

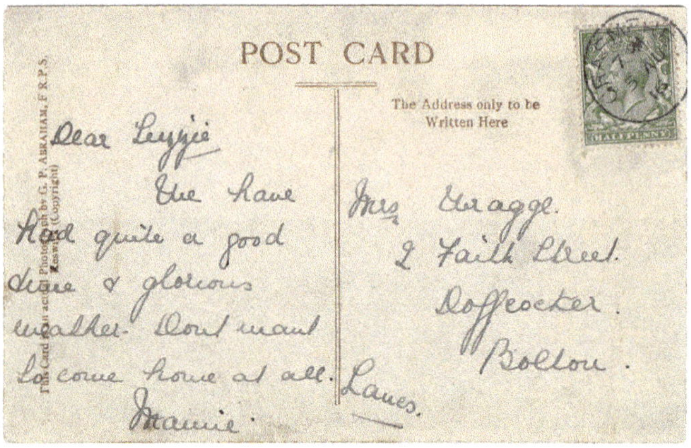

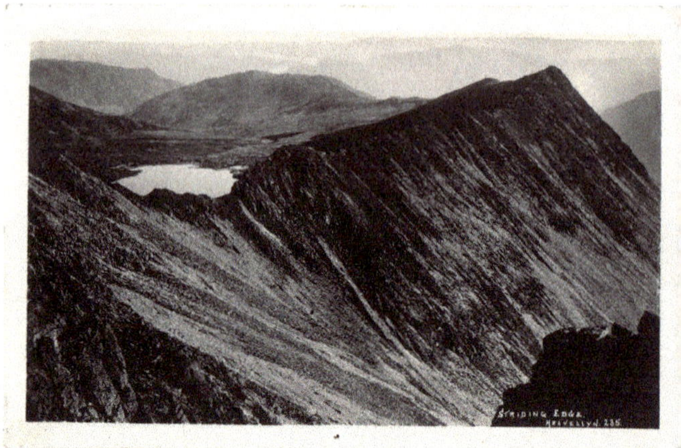

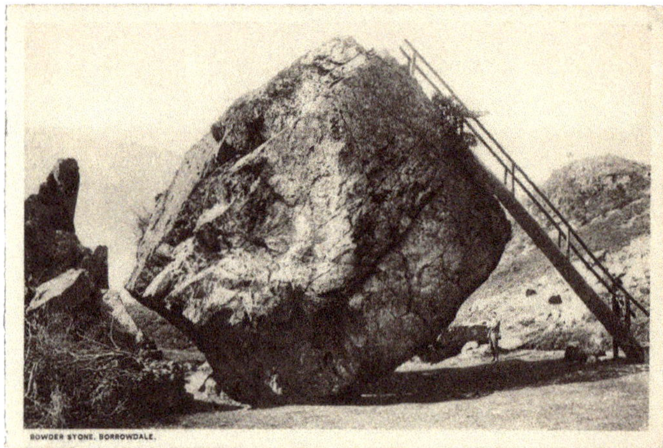

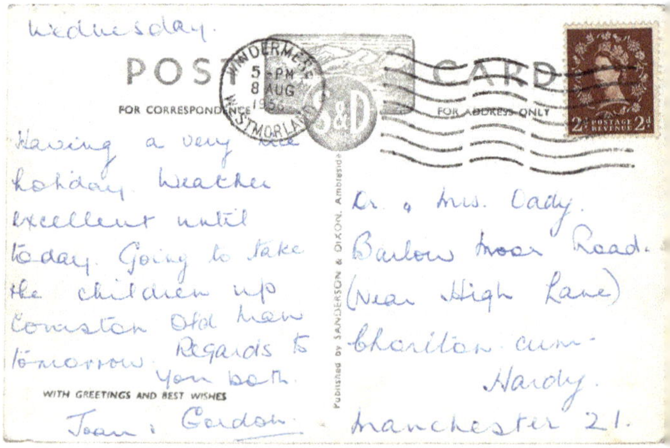

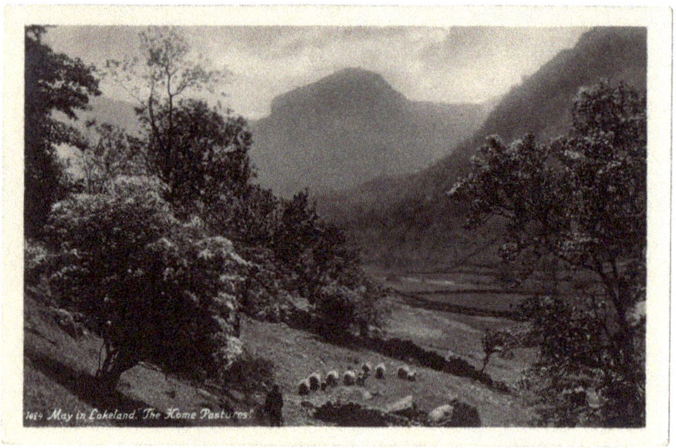

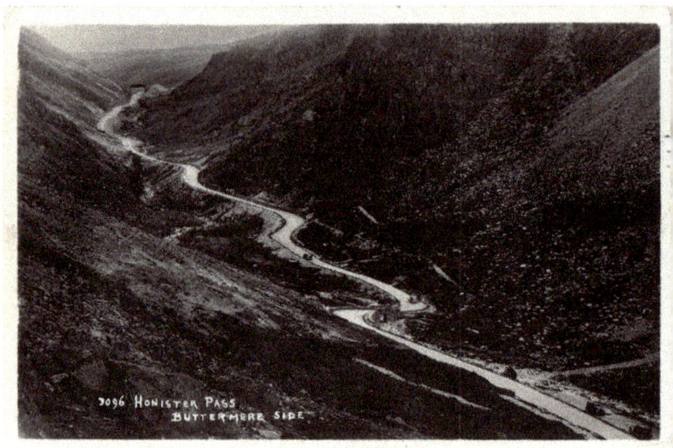

Robert Bean and Barbara Lounder

Cave at Grasmere, Grasmere, UK 2018 © Robert Bean

6. Improvisations

The girl appeared apprehensive, she paused on the steppingstones, doubtful of her path. The steps seemed like dotted lines on an established route, but there was no map for this journey. The water at her feet was cloudy, full of silt and sediment washed down from the slate mine above the cave. The stone is weathering and will eventually form earth. At the conclusion of his walk on the sanatorium grounds, the accordion player sat and improvised a circular breathing song by Joan La Barbara. Breathing notes and chords, the sounds from the accordion were sustained for a duration of inhalations and exhalations. The atmosphere was visible as colours drifted around him. He was briefly veiled in a dense haze of beautiful smoke.

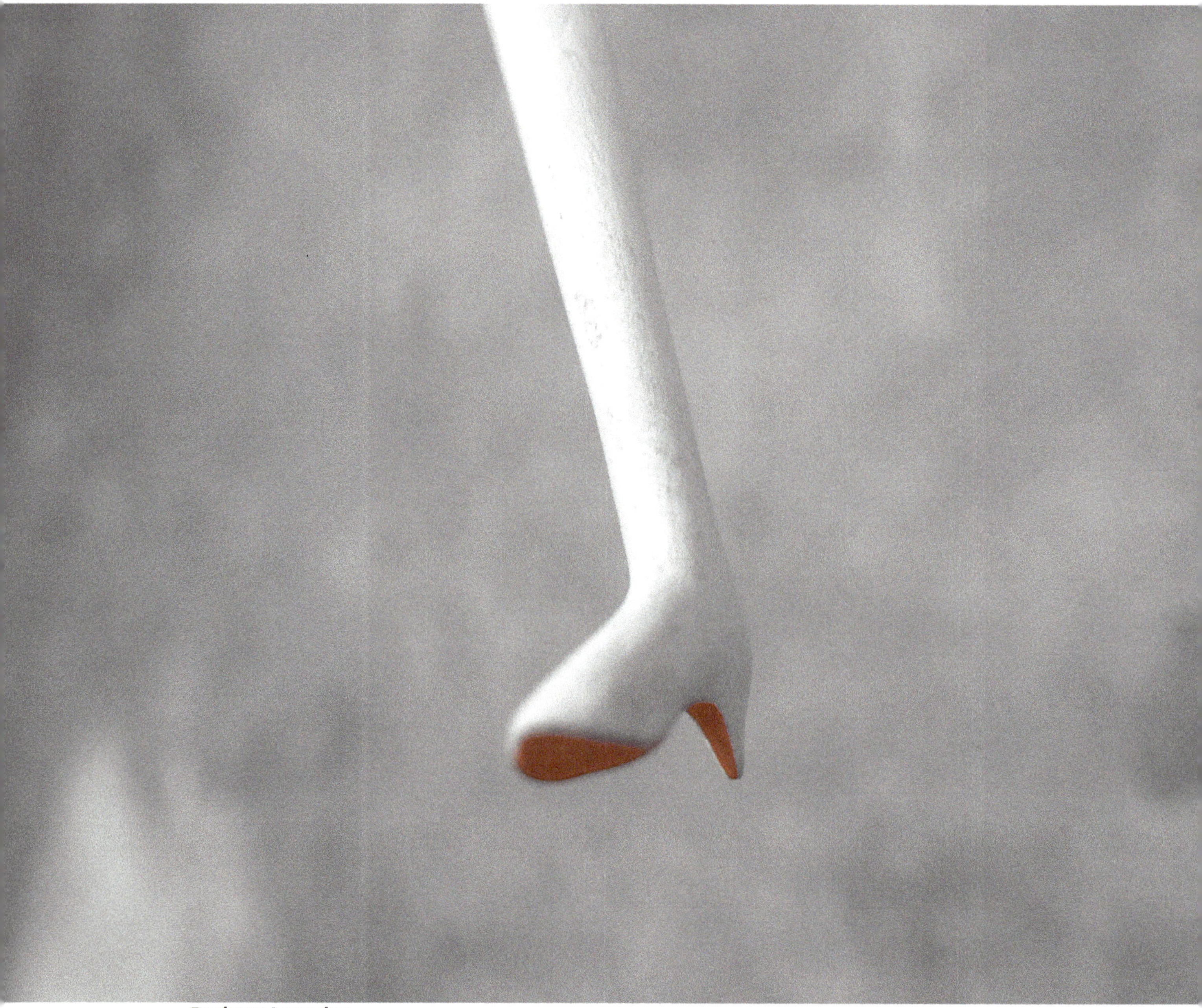

Barbara Lounder
Dorothy (detail), graphite, carved and painted sticks, 2018 © Robert Bean

Endnotes

[1] Sloterdijk, P. *Terror from the Air*. Los Angeles. Semiotext(e), 2009, pp.9-46
[2] Wainwright, M. *Sensing the airs: the cultural context for breathing and breathlessness in Uruguay*, Medical Anthropology, 36:4. Retrieved May 1, 2017, p.11
[3] Burney, I. *Our Environment in Miniature: Dust and the Early Twentieth-Century Forensic Imagination*, Representations. Berkeley. Winter 2013, p.37
[4] Andrews, K. *Wanderers: A History of Women Walking*. London. Reaktion 2020, p.63

Robert Bean and Barbara Lounder live and work in Nova Scotia and have collaborated on art and publishing projects since 1983. Bean is an artist, writer, curator and Professor at NSCAD University (Nova Scotia College of Art and Design). His artworks have been exhibited at the Contact Photography Festival, (Toronto), ZKM (Karlsruhe), the National Gallery of Canada, Festival Contexts 2017: International Sokolowsko Festival of Ephemeral Art (Sokolowsko Poland, and elsewhere. Barbara Lounder is an artist and educator, now retired from her position as Professor at NSCAD University. Her situated works engage the public in carefully designed walking activities and have been presented in Canada and internationally. Lounder writes and speaks on topics related to contemporary art, walking, social activism and education.

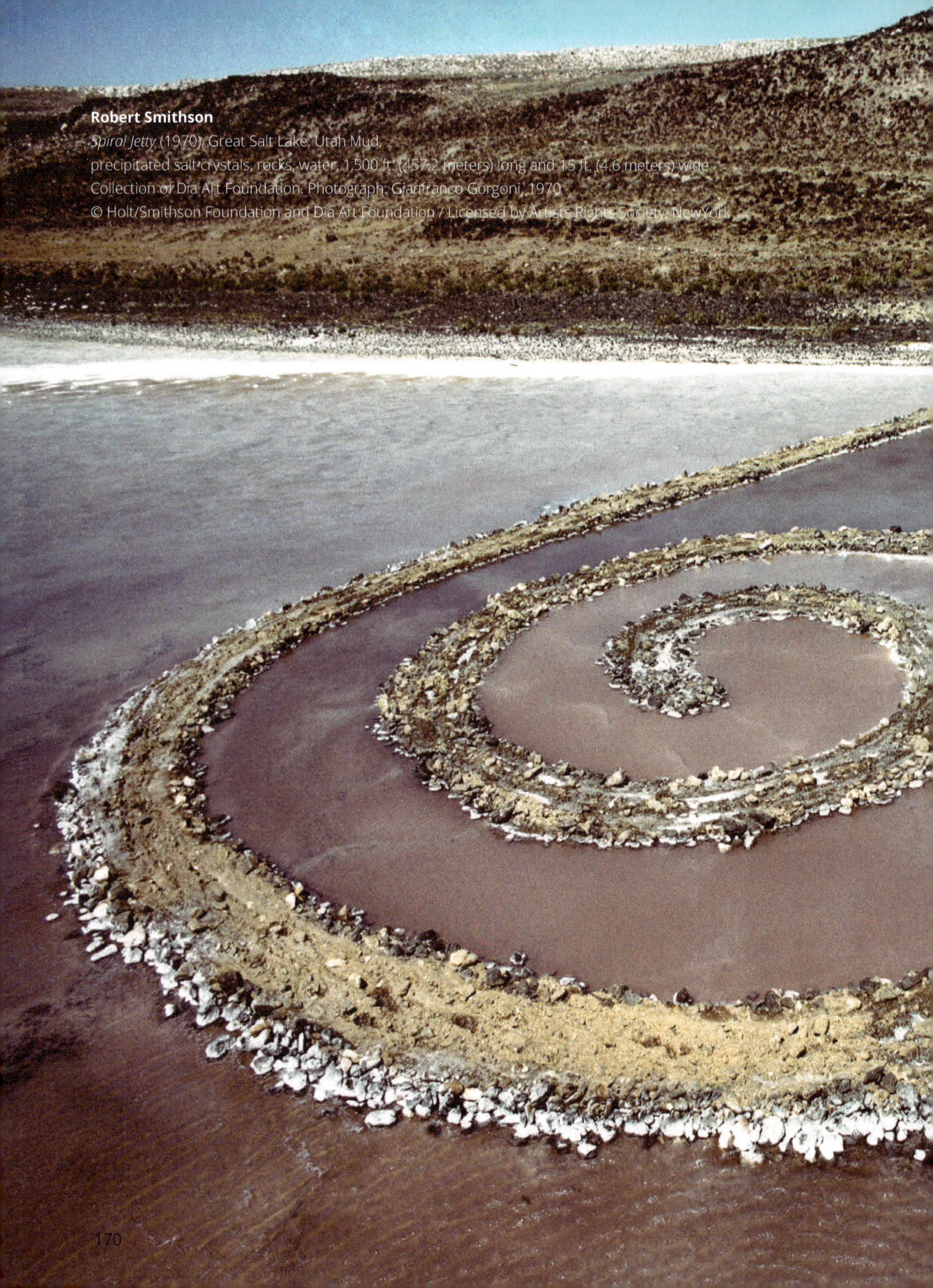

Robert Smithson
Spiral Jetty (1970), Great Salt Lake, Utah Mud,
precipitated salt crystals, rocks, water, 1,500 ft. (457.2 meters) long and 15 ft. (4.6 meters) wide
Collection of Dia Art Foundation. Photograph: Gianfranco Gorgoni, 1970

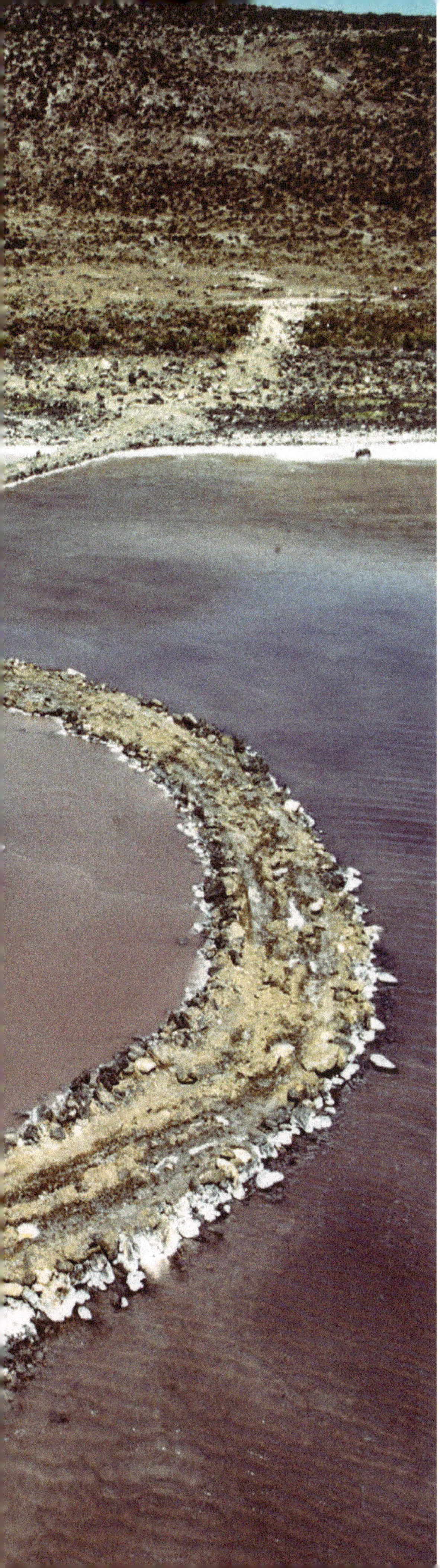

Robert Smithson: becoming geological

Robert Smithson envisioned art as a "catastrophe of mind and matter," a physical metaphor that moves one beyond the abstract grids of intelligibility into an abyssal materiality. Operating in the space between an intensified perception of the earth and the constructs that represent it, Smithson defamiliarizes anthropocentric conceptions of the real to reveal an undifferentiated state of matter. This essay aims to reconcile the artist's materialist and metaphysical tendencies through the speculative concept of the infraphysical, a hidden order of reality revealed through the dislocation of the viewer into the nonhuman geological past and entropic future.

text **Rory O'Dea** images: **Robert Smithson**

Robert Smithson envisioned himself to be a "geologic agent".[1] While this self-fashioning of the earth artist as an actual *force of nature* might evoke the grandiose sense of human agency that has wrought the catastrophe of the Anthropocene, Smithson's geological conception of the creation and experience of art, in fact, represents a radical rejection of this human-centered logic. To Smithson, the (il)logic of modern metaphysics is rooted in the idea of *separation*, which he saw as a "convenient fiction" that convinced humans that both subjects and objects can be distilled and fixed from the primary processes of the earth.[2] Consequently, Western modernity's teleology is towards absolute material transcendence, a desire currently apotheosized in Silicon Valley's vision of a dematerialized and disembodied future lived in the formless ether of the cloud. To be fully human, in this sense, is to be fully separate from the earth.

While the prophets of the Space Age in Smithson's time and those of Eco-modernism in our own promise us technological transcendence, Smithson's art aimed to plunge humans back down to earth. Rejecting the modern metaphysics of transcendence, Smithson proposed the novel concept of *infraphysics*, which he used to describe the awareness of an unfolding order of material reality *below* the earth rather than an immaterial ideal *beyond* it.[3] Smithson's infraphysics resonates deeply with what Deleuze and Guattari describe as "geophilosophy," which takes as its (non)object of study the elements from which humans emerge, flow, and return, unendingly.[4] For Smithson, the vision of the artist as a geological agent thus meant using art as a means to attune humans to their inseparability from the earth's material processes. By rendering humans and their culture geological, his art reveals the porous fluidity and ecological entanglements of the human and nonhuman world, and in so doing, speculatively proposes that we have *never been human* in the modern sense of that term.[5]

The Terrestrial Sun

Sun, stone, blood, dust, oil, mud, salt, and water. The metamorphic materializations of Smithson's *Spiral Jetty* (1970) ebb and flow through these elemental mediums. Composed of a monumental sculpture made of basalt stone that extends into the Great Salt Lake, an essay comprised of text and images, and a film, the conceptual and phenomenological experience of *Spiral Jetty* requires a complex movement—actual and metaphorical—between the site and the nodes of its mediations. While the text, photographs, and film frame the earthwork—it is likely that most spectators will experience *Spiral Jetty* only in these forms—Smithson perceived this array of mediations to be materially continuous with the elementality of the site. And their unexpected terrestrial qualities make the viewer aware of their own as well, and so trigger an awareness of one's trans-corporeal enmeshment with the site of *Spiral Jetty* rather than separation from it.

Smithson's film and essay begin with a solar meditation. In the film, the opening sequence casts the spectator into the red phosphorescence of the sun's molten sphere, and the cosmic resonances of this primordial image of raw creative force are amplified by the essay's epigraph by G.K. Chesterton: "Red is the most joyful and dreadful thing in the physical universe; it is the fiercest note, it is the highest light, it is the place where the walls of this world of ours wear the thinnest and something beyond them burns through".[6] The effect of these cinematic and literary establishing shots is both materialist and mystical in nature, and together they intensify the molten fluidity of the sun while also intimating its capacity to exceed the limits of rational thought. Given the anti-metaphysical nature of Smithson's art, the celestial sun—an enduring symbol of transcendence in Western philosophy—may seem an incongruous medium for the translation of humans back into the geological matter of the earth. But in Smithson's hands, the sun is desublimated into a force of entropic metamorphosis that liquefies the philosophical grounds of metaphysics and dissolves the boundaries between the human subject and the more-than-human world.

The evocative imagery and hallucinatory reveries of the sun permeating *Spiral Jetty* attune one to the multiplicity of ways that the natural and human history of the Great Salt Lake is shaped by the forces of a solar economy. We begin with human history. In many ways, *Spiral Jetty* is a counter-monument to the Golden Spike, a nearby historic site that commemorates the point where the transcontinental railroad was unified in 1869. Read in relation to this monument, the convulsive coils and inversions of Smithson's earthwork subvert the linear model of history symbolized by the railroad's inexorable progress across the American frontier.[7] Crucially, this history was determined by fossil fuel, as the development of the transcontinental railroad was inextricably bound to coal. While the steam engines of the trains themselves were powered by coal or oil, the routes they carved across the land were often determined by the location of coal deposits. Consequently, the trains were instrumental in driving the accelerating and expanding cycles of extraction and consumption. And this history flows into the present. In 2021, representatives of the coal industry pushed to rehabilitate a section of the old railroad that traverses the Great Salt Lake—which is now on the cusp of disappearance due to climate change and unsustainable water use in the region— to facilitate the transportation of Western-mined coal to the California coast. And exploratory oil drilling in the lake continues unabated.[8]

The residues of the fossil fuel industry litter the site of *Spiral Jetty*, lingering as viscous material shadows of human history layered upon the site. Smithson describes how,

> The mere sight of trapped fragments of junk and waste transported one into a world of modern pre-history. The products of a Devonian industry, the remains of Silurian technology, and all the machines of the upper Carboniferous Period, were lost in those expansive deposits of sand and mud. ...A series of seeps of heavy black oil more like asphalt occur just south of Rozel Point. ...Pumps coated with black stickiness rusted in the corrosive salt air. ...A great pleasure arose from seeing all those incoherent structures. The site gave evidence of a succession of man-made systems mired in abandoned hopes.[9]

The hyper-salinated waters of the Great Salt Lake—it is a kind of dead inland ocean— and the desert that surrounds it casts the site of *Spiral Jetty* as an implacable wasteland, a deliquescing space where the law of entropy made itself known through the nullification of capitalism's black-blood lust. The site has been subject to devastating ecological damage, and the ruinous remains of the oil industry stand as portentous anti-monuments to the catastrophic terrestrial fallout of human industry.

While these vestiges of fossil fuel index the past, present, and possible future of human endeavor at the site of *Spiral Jetty*, oil is also a fossil record of time scales that radically exceed those of human history. Here, we return to the golden spike, but now consider it as a monument of an entirely different order of temporal magnitude. In the earth sciences, a golden spike is a term that describes the demarcation between two geological epochs. The still-speculative golden spike of the Anthropocene, for example, is variously placed at the years 1452, 1610, and 1800—dates that implicate Western histories of colonization, enslavement, and industrialization as the catalysts of humanity's evolution into a geological force.[10] And there is a multiplicity of golden spikes planted in the material depths of the site of *Spiral Jetty*. To cross the threshold of subterranean golden spikes at *Spiral Jetty* is to open oneself to the possibilities of speculative time travel. When encountering the work, we enter the Archeozoic, the Cambrian, and the Pleistocene.

The various temporalities conjured by the term golden spike attune one to the porous strata of human and natural history within *Spiral Jetty*. Oil also embodies the simultaneity of such radically different time scales. While its presence

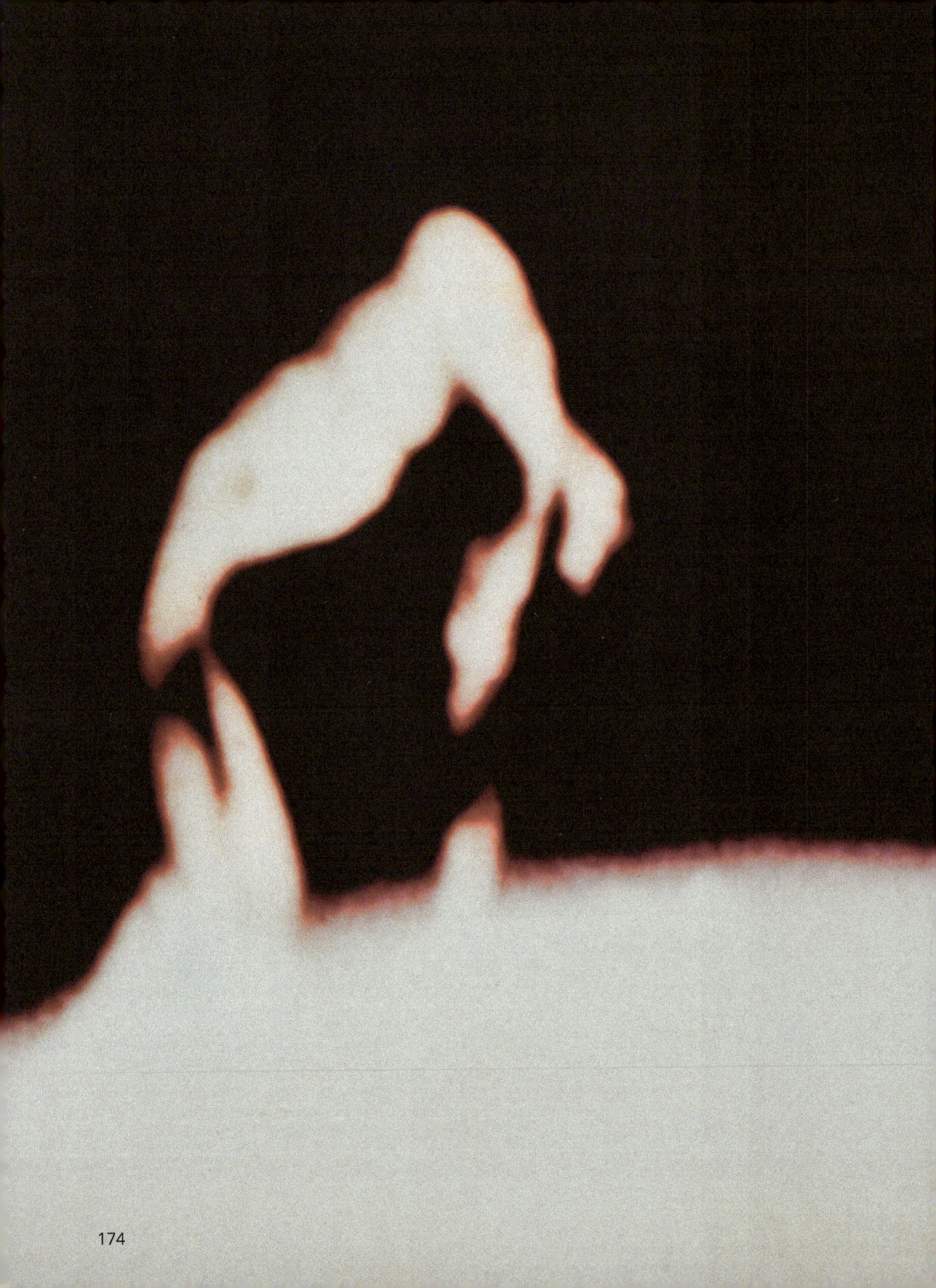

Robert Smithson
Spiral Jetty [still]
(1970) 16 mm film
Duration 35 minutes
Color, sound
© Holt/Smithson Foundation / Licensed by Artists Rights Society, New York. Distributed by Electronic Arts Intermix, New York

around *Spiral Jetty* indexes the site's history of extraction, oil is also a material transmission from the far deeper reaches of the geological past. And its origin story returns us to the sun. In essence, oil is what Georges Bataille arrestingly described as the *black* or *rotten sun*.[11] Formed via the compression of solar energy trapped in decaying organic matter and sedimented within underground reservoirs, oil is a subterranean monument to entropy, the archival record of solar rot over vast stretches of time. Once extracted and burned, however, the solar energy materialized in fossil fuels over the course of millions of years is instantaneously and irreversibly dispersed. The abyssal prospects of this transformation are described by Reza Negarestani in darkly poetic language. In *Cyclonopedia,* he imagines oil to be the "buried terrestrial sun which must be exhumed, a rotting sun oozing black flame, the black corpse of the sun".[12] The burning of fossil fuel thus represents the erasure of vast and slow stretches of geologic temporality through the acceleration of time catalyzed by human consumption.

As a material incarnation of the deep time of geology, oil indexes a past anterior to human history, and *Spiral Jetty* is saturated with such dislocating temporal traces. The earthwork itself is, of course, made of geological matter, and its spiral form traces the metamorphosis of basalt from its origins as subterranean molten magma to the mineralized stones used as building blocks by Smithson. Uranium is another resonant example. Utah was an epicenter for uranium mining—in the 1950s and 60s Salt Lake City was known as the "Wall Street of Uranium Stocks"— and the desert landscape of the Southwest was infamously exploited as the proving grounds for the United States military's nuclear testing.[13] While not visible in *Spiral Jetty*, the radioactive fallout of uranium pulses through Smithson's film in the auditory form of a Geiger counter's unnerving staticky pulse. With a half-life of 24,110 years, plutonium—which is uranium transformed into weapons-grade nuclear matter—is detectable in sedimentary deposits for over 100,000 years, and the temporal scale of its material persistence is a signal from the post-human future.

By animating the geological time embedded in the material strata of the sites he worked within, Smithson aimed to dislocate the spectator from the historical present. The ontological implications of this idea are clarified by his series of "hypothetical continents" and "earth maps". In these works, Smithson uses natural materials to re-create—or, perhaps, *reenact*, given his emphasis on *processes in time*—human-scaled materializations of long-vanished landmasses. We might understand these works as fictional fossils conceived on a continental scale. Describing his *Earth Map (White Limestone) of the Hypothetical Ice Cap of Gondwanaland* (1969) installed on the Yucatán peninsula, he reflects how,

> Reconstructing a landmass that existed 350 to 305 million years ago on a terrain once controlled by sundry Mayan gods caused a collision in time that left one with a sense of the timeless. ... Gondwanaland is a kind of memory, yet it is not a memory, it is but an incognito land mass that has been *unthought* about and turned into a Map of Impasse.[14]

What is the *impasse* Smithson has in mind, and what does it mean to *unthink* about something? Despite the material presence of the hypothetical continents, the actual ancient continents of Cathaysia, Gondwanaland, and Lemuria to which they refer were witnessed by no human, and their prehistoric existence is thus "fugitive and uncertain".[15] The deep time of their geological history is absolutely prior to the existence of thought itself, and the reality that Smithson's work indexes is consequently *unthinkable* in human terms. Smithson's speculations on the geological past anticipate what the contemporary philosopher Quentin Meillassoux theorizes as the *arche-fossil*.[16] In *After Finitude*, Meillassoux describes the arche-fossil as a material trace of an "ancestral reality" anterior to the emergence of the human, and therefore, human thought. Lumps of coal and rays of light from long-dead stars are stimulating examples.

Meillassoux's thought experiment is equally provocative when temporally reversed. If the abyssal blackness of the buried sun in *Spiral Jetty* points towards the *pre-human* past, the work's entropic allusions to the ultimate heat death of the universe signal a *posthuman* future. Smithson famously stated that the future will be prehistoric, and his vision of a pre-and posthuman universe merges in *Spiral Jetty's* cinematic sequence in the Museum of Natural History's "Hall of Dinosaurs". Saturated in a field of blood-red light, the fossilized bones of long-extinct dinosaurs project viewers into their future annihilation symbolized by the image of "dying suns" Smithson conjures via the museum's light bulbs.[17]

Rather than a beneficent source of eternal light, Smithson envisioned the sun to be a "portent of entropy"— an arche-fossil in the future tense— and its ineluctable presence in *Spiral Jetty* forecasts the solar catastrophe that will cause the extinction of humans and the planet Earth itself.[18] If we accept the inevitability of this future catalyzed by the law of entropy, we are consequently forced to imagine a posthuman world without us. But this is an impossibility, as the end of humanity cannot be known empirically by any human being. Cast into the throes of such entropic speculations, we must ask ourselves, in the words of Ray Brassier, "How does thought think the death of thinking?"[19]

Meillassoux locates the profound power of the arche-fossil in its potential to liberate humans from what he calls "the correlationist circle" that marks out the boundaries of an anthropocentric ontology. In essence, the correlationist circle describes an extreme anti-realist point of view from which there can be no reality outside the horizon of human thought. In terms analogous to Meillassoux's, Smithson often criticized the "conceptual fallacy," by which he meant the erroneous human belief that the material earth corresponds to the concepts of the human mind. But "physical reality isn't like that," Smithson insists,

> People are convinced they know what reality is, so they bring their own concept of reality to the work...they never contend with the reality that is outside their own, which might be no reality at all. The existence of "self" is what keeps everybody from confronting their fears about the ground they happen to be standing on.[20]

Trapped within the correlationist circle, humans will never know the nature of the ground beneath their feet. For Meillassoux, the consequences of the circle are calamitous, as its rigid anthropocentrism separates humans from "the *great outdoors*, the *absolute* outside of pre-critical thinkers; that outside which was not relative to us ... existing in itself regardless of whether we are thinking of it or not; that outside which thought could explore with the legitimate feeling of being on foreign territory—of being entirely *elsewhere*".[21]

Smithson, fittingly, imagined the penumbral zones he worked within as ontological *elsewheres*, and the attraction of these sites arose from the way that their earthly materiality exceeded human frameworks—what Smithson defined as "rational categories".[22] Reflecting on the Pennsylvania slate quarry where he collected the material fragments for his *Nonsite* (1968), he recounts how, "All boundaries and distinctions lost their meaning in this ocean of slate and collapsed all notions of gestalt unity. The present fell forward and backward into a tumult of 'de-differentiation.'"[23] For Smithson, the experience of de-differentiation ruptures the solid philosophical ground of anthropocentrism and reveals the fluid earth that rumbles beneath it. Slipping into the subterranean, infraphysical realm of the earth, Smithson describes how "your mind loses its boundaries and a sense of the *oceanic* pervades".[24]

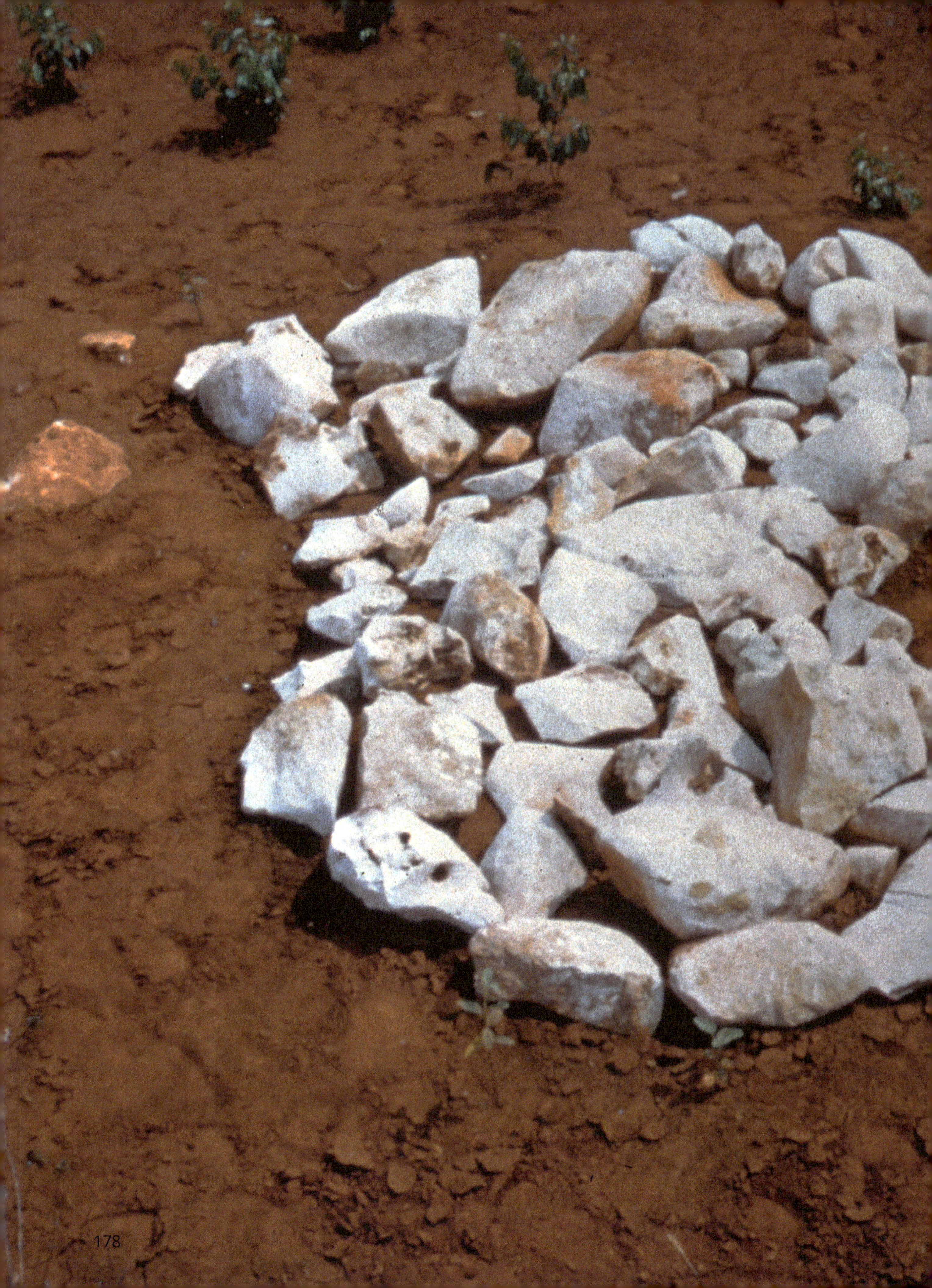

Robert Smithson
Hypothetical Continent of Gondwanaland—Ice Cap (1969)
126 format, chromogenic-development slide

The Oceanic Earth

What does the ocean have to do with the earth? Apart from the obvious fact that the planet is seventy-one percent water, the point of geophilosophical interest is that the remaining twenty-nine percent is far more dynamically fluid than we commonly imagine. Smithson insisted that, "one pebble moving one foot in two million years is enough action to keep me really excited," as a "mere" pebble is a microcosmic compression of the tectonic shifts, erosion, sedimentation, and churning of the sea that brought it into being.[25] The most obdurate and impenetrable stone dissolves into liquid when perceived within the sublime duration of deep time. The geologic is oceanic to the core.

The images of the molten sun at the outset of Smithson's film *Spiral Jetty* are simultaneously speculative images of the earth's core. Despite the illusion of solid ground provided by the planet's thin crust, an infernal abyss always roils below. Georges Bataille's recollection of his experience atop Mt. Aetna in Italy darkly illuminates the ontological implications of the earth's oceanic fire. Peering into the "gaping wound" of the volcano, he describes how "One could not possibly imagine a place which demonstrated more clearly the fearful in-stability of things."[26] Like the sun, the primordial magma of the earth is a sublime arche-fossil, and to Smithson's mind, the experience of it causes one to be "Dislocated by the molten condition".[27]

In a series of vivid passages in "The Spiral Jetty" essay, Smithson offers a mesmerizing account of his oceanic and molten experience of the Utah desert, and the hallucinatory language he uses to conjure it into being invites citing at length:

> As I looked at the site, it reverberated out to the horizons only to suggest an immobile cyclone while flickering light made the entire landscape appear to quake. A dormant earthquake spread into the fluttering stillness, into a spinning sensation without movement. The site was a rotary that enclosed itself in an immaculate roundness. From that gyrating space came the possibility of the Spiral Jetty. [...] solid and liquid lost themselves in each other. It was as if the mainland oscillated with waves and pulsations and the lake remained rock still. The shore of the lake became the edge of the sun, a boiling curve, an explosion rising into fiery prominence.[28]

While Smithson's evocations of a vortex allude to the mythic belief that the Great Salt Lake contained a whirlpool providing passage to Pacific Ocean, the greater geophilosophical implications of this natural phenomenon lies in the way it *ungrounds* the earth and offers a metaphor for the planet's perpetual state of becoming.[29] In *Philosophy of Nature* (1799), F.W.J. von Schelling describes a whirlpool as "something constantly transforming—but reproduced anew at each moment".[30] In *The Ethics of Earth Art*, Amanda Boetzkes expands upon these resonances spun out by the whirlpool via Walter Benjamin, who proposed that a whirlpool has no beginning, end, or center, and instead "emerges from the process of becoming and disappearance. Origin is the eddy in the stream of becoming, and in its current, it swallows the material involved in the process of genesis".[31] The question of origins is vital to Smithson, and he frequently alludes to the primordial aspect of the sites he worked within. By returning, speculatively, to its inorganic beginnings, Smithson's art pursues the question of how the human becomes geological.

In *Spiral Jetty*, the "crushing light" of the sun's rays possesses an earthly gravity that seems to trigger a shift from the organic to the inorganic, from the biological to the geological:

> I closed my eyes, and the sun burned crimson through the lids. I opened them and the Great Salt Lake was bleeding scarlet streaks. My sight was saturated by the color of red algae circulating in the heart of the lake, pumping into ruby currents, no they were veins and arteries sucking up the obscure sediments. My eyes became combustion chambers, churning orbs blazing by the light of the sun. All was enveloped in a flaming chromosphere. [...] I was on a geologic fault that churned within me. [32]

In this passage, Smithson describes the metamorphosis of the sun into the ocean, as well as the exteriorization of his body into the elemental matter of the site. In an iconic scene in the film, Smithson is filmed from the vertiginous vantage of a helicopter as he travels inward along the spiral, and as the camera pulls away, he appears to disappear into the antediluvian sea:

> I was slipping out of myself again, dissolving into a unicellular beginning, trying to locate the nucleus at the end of the spiral. All that blood stirring makes one aware of protoplasmic solutions, the essential matter between the formed and the unformed, masses of cells consisting largely of water, proteins, lipids, carbohydrates, and inorganic salts. Each drop that splashed onto the Spiral Jetty coagulated into a crystal. Undulating waters spread millions upon millions of crystals over the basalt.[33]

Meditating on his own fluid and embodied relationship to the Great Salt Lake, Smithson describes how, "Chemically speaking, our blood is analogous in composition to the primordial seas. Following the spiral steps we return to our origins, back to some pulpy protoplasm".[34] Humans, of course, evolved from the sea, and our bodies are aggregates of their material composition. The stream of calcium, potassium, and sodium that circulate through our veins is composed of the near-exact proportions of seawater, and the skeletal support of the human body is a mineral armature formed from the calcium-rich waters that flowed in the Cambrian period. Astrida Neimanis poetically describes this primal oceanic state of being as the "onto-logics of amniotics".[35]

The elementality of *Spiral Jetty* unfolds on a vast micro- and macro-cosmic scale. Blood. Water. Sun. Salt. Crystals. Smithson's bloodstream is a tributary that leads back to primordial seas, and the crystalline structure of the lake's supersaturated waters reverberates through the site's scales of time and space. Due to the sun's evaporation of the lake's water, salt proliferates at the site and often envelopes Smithson's earthwork in encrustations, producing an alchemical transformation of volcanic basalt into icy crystal. To Smithson's mind, "Each cubic salt crystal echoes the Spiral Jetty in terms of the crystal's molecular lattice. ... The Spiral Jetty could be considered one layer within the spiraling crystal lattice, magnified trillions of times".[36] Like the centripetal and centrifugal movements of the earthwork, the crystalline structure that forms the infraphysical order of the site contracts and expands infinitely, stretching from the lake's waters to the spiral realm of the galaxies.[37] In this way, the multiplicity of the crystalline works as a kind of scalar arche-fossil that displaces the human as the measure of all things. More broadly, Smithson perceived crystalline structure to be a boundaryless condition—an oceanic field within which there is no figure, only ground. At the same time, crystals express the strange duality of geologic matter's dialectic of stasis and flow. As Esther Leslie makes clear, "What is liquid cannot be crystal. What is crystal is not liquid. But there are liquid crystals".[38]

Earth as Medium

Smithson's accounts of *Spiral Jetty* foreground an intensified phenomenological experience that borders on the mystical, within which the artist's subjective ego is absorbed into "the magma of the other".[39] Yet, a paradox emerges. While some may visit the site, spectators largely come to know the radical materialism of *Spiral Jetty* via the mediations of Smithson's language, film, and photography. Despite Smithson's privileging of the elemental matter and processes of the earth, is his art ultimately limited by the way it circumscribes these via the representational structures of the human mind? The answer is yes and no, and the tension created by this contradiction remains unresolved. Though Smithson intentionally foregrounds the ways his work mediates the elementality of the site through multiple registers of discourse, the result is nevertheless an act of containment and framing. Framing

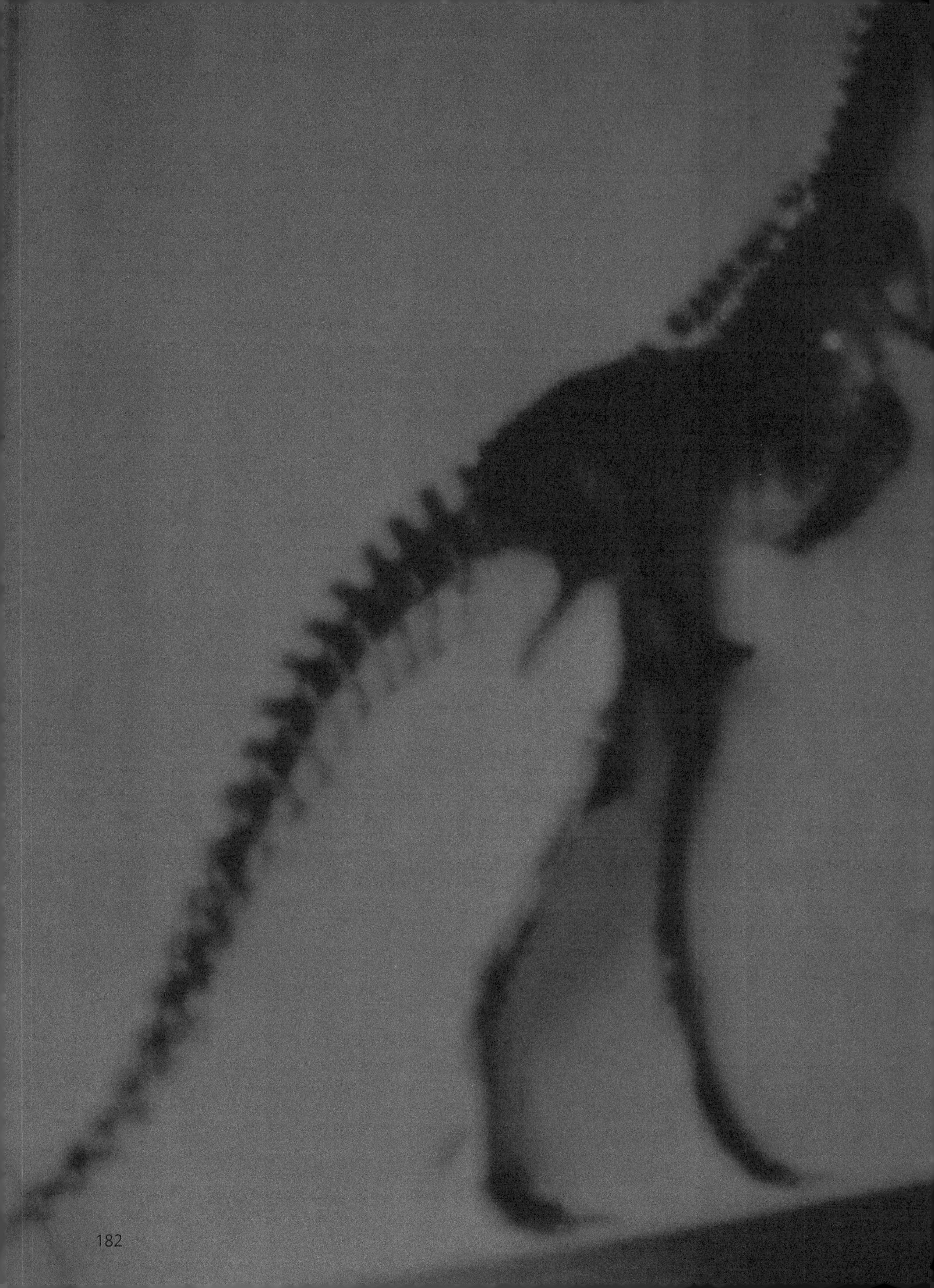

Robert Smithson

Spiral Jetty [still]

(1970) 16 mm film

Duration 35 minutes

Color, sound

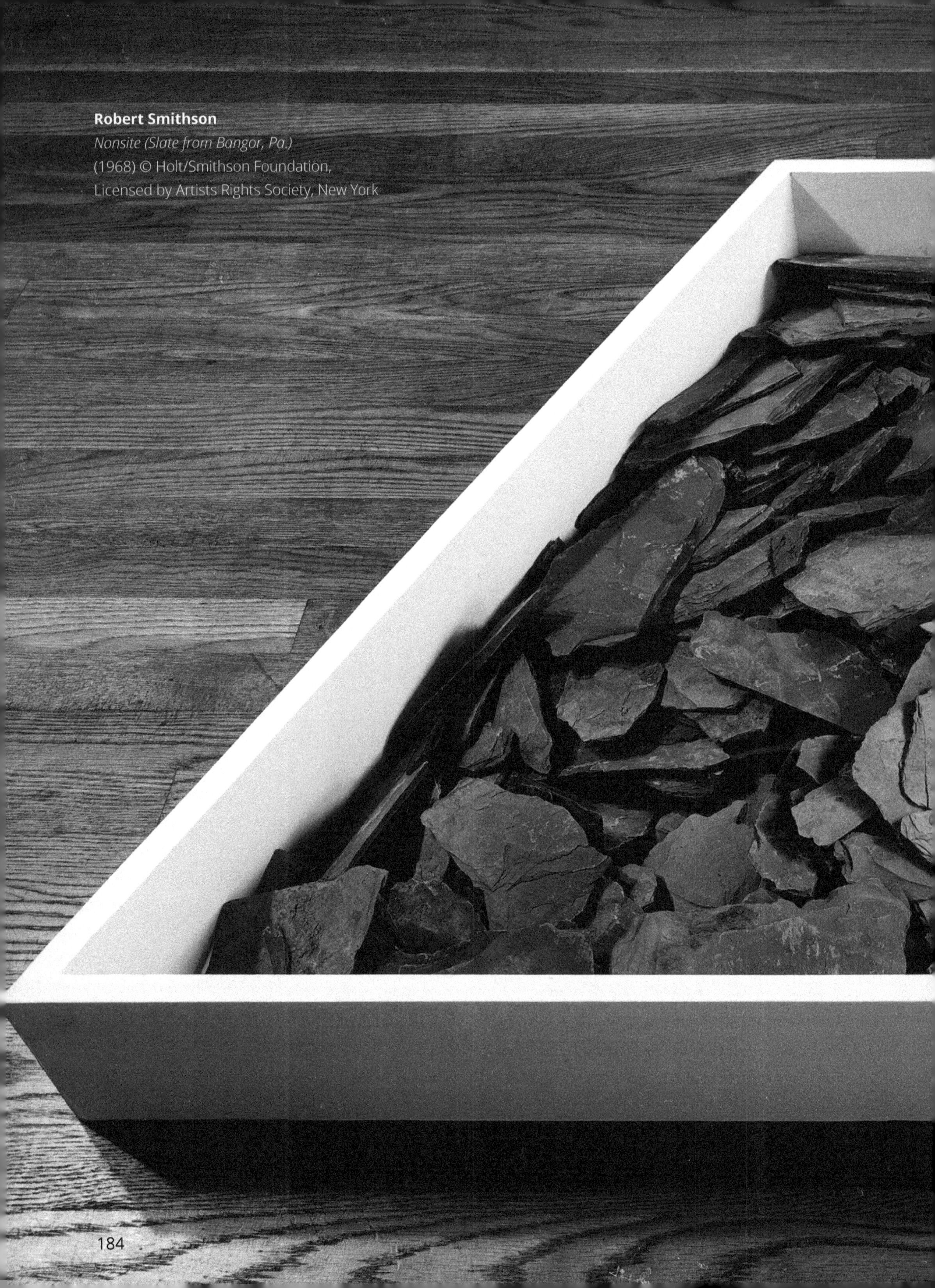

Robert Smithson
Nonsite (Slate from Bangor, Pa.)
(1968) © Holt/Smithson Foundation,
Licensed by Artists Rights Society, New York

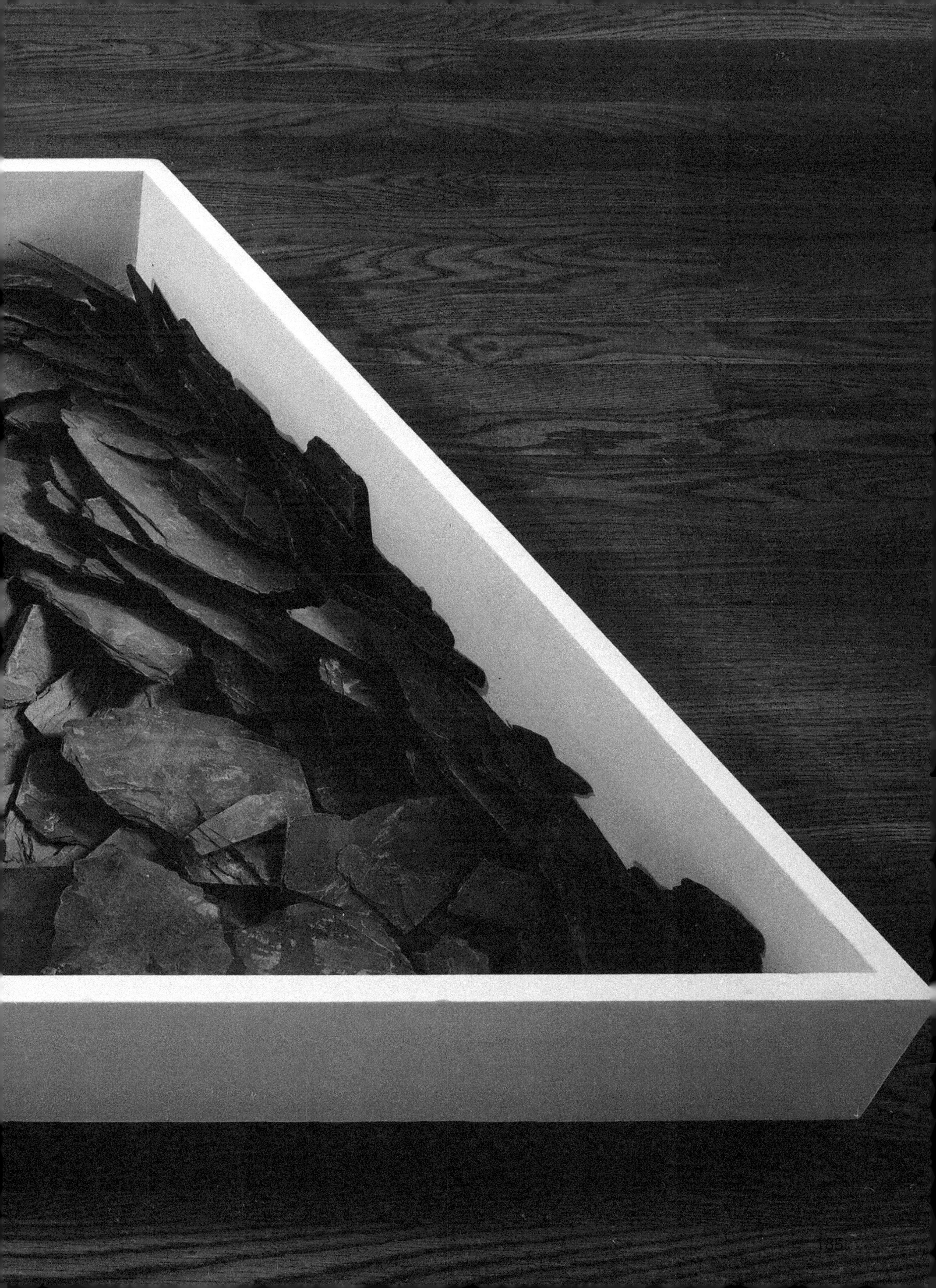

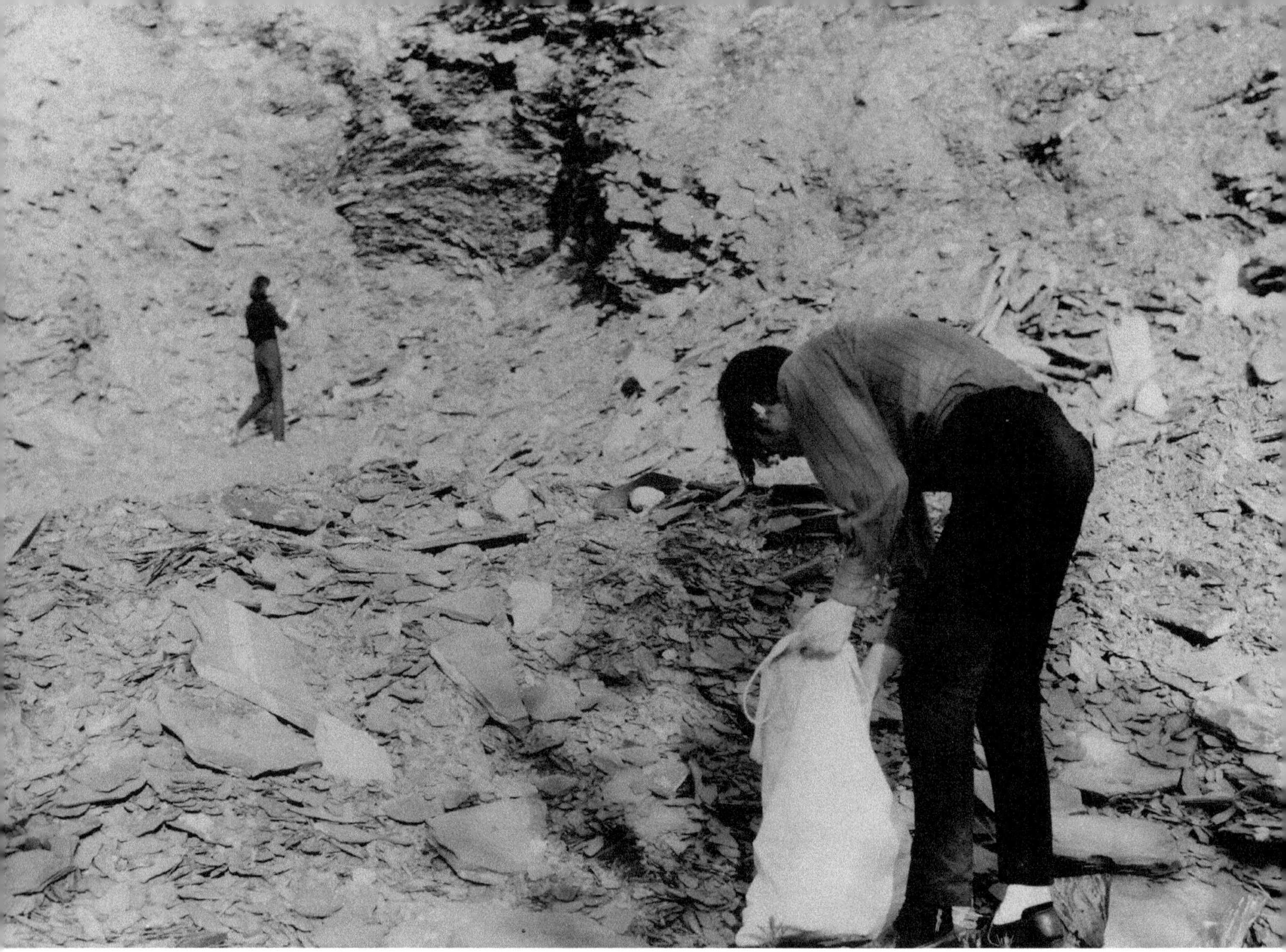

Robert Smithson

Robert Smithson gathering materials for Nonsite (Slate from Bangor, Pa.) with Virginia Dwan, 1968

Photographer yet to be identified © Holt/Smithson Foundation / Licensed by Artists Rights Society, New York

was a critical issue for earth art in the 1960s, and Susan Ballard rightly reasserts the feminist critique that "the signal gesture of land art is one of limiting and framing views, of focusing attention".[40] In *Undermining*, Lucy Lippard is more explicit in naming the logic of land art as colonial, and this critique is amplified by the potential ways that Smithson's work reenacts the myth of the heroic white man mastering the wastelands of the American West.[41] From this perspective, we might also come to question his recurring use of "I" and "My" to describe the process of self-dissolution in the elements, as doing so seemingly reinforces the subject-object relationship his art strives to destabilize.

Yet, I want to consider that the unresolvable dilemma between Smithson's ego-dissolving experience of the earth's convulsive materiality and his mediations of it might productively attune us to the apophatic or negative quality of the quasi-mystical experiences he describes, here understood as an encounter with more-than-human geological and cosmic scales. Though the nature of such experiences is fundamentally ineffable, *accounts* of them must lapse into language. While Smithson's art attunes viewers to its earthly origins, the text, film, and photographs that move within the infinite and centerless sphere of *Spiral Jetty* nevertheless retain their status as anthropomorphic *metaphors* for the site to which they refer.[42] But rather than a failing, the metaphorical movement between these incommensurable poles of mediation and immediacy is the catalytic force of Smithson's art. Metaphor is a

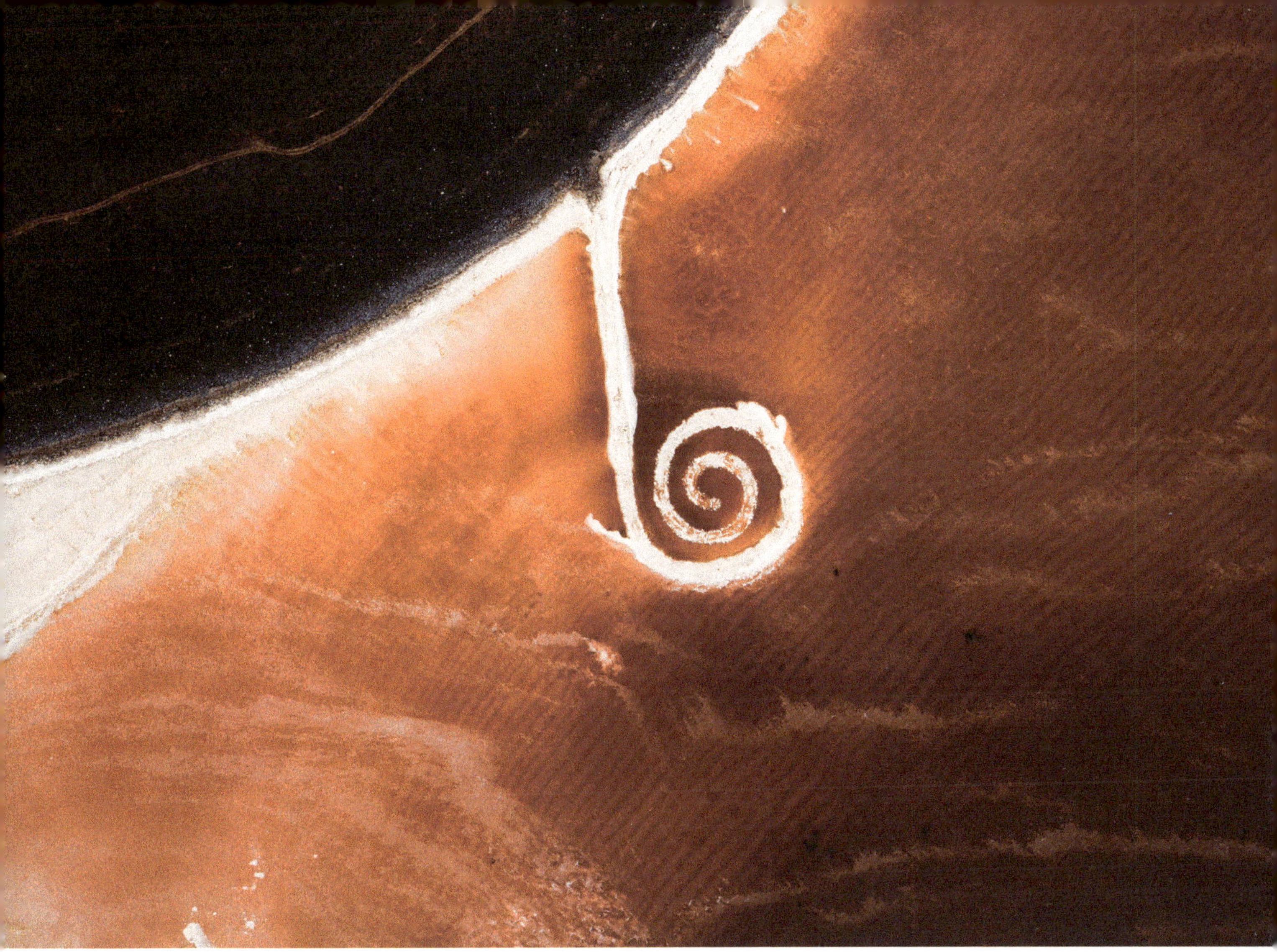

Robert Smithson

Spiral Jetty, 1970. David Maisel, Terminal Mirage 15, 2003, photograph.

Credit: David Maisel © Nancy Holt Robert Smithson Foundation / Licensed by VAGA, New York, NY.

trope that *names what it is not*, and as such reveals the gap between language and the world. By locating the edges of rational knowledge, Smithson art's signals the earthly abyss below it, and awakens a desire for new ways of knowing and being that transcend (or descend) the limits of being human.

At the same time, the mediations themselves are subject to elemental dissolution, and Amanda Boetzkes convincingly argues that "earth art such as Smithson's showed how textual forms could be affected and were ultimately receptive to elementals."[43] Viewed in this way, Smithson's mediations are materially continuous with the sites they manipulate and represent, and thus open a path *into* the outside rather than an enclosure of it. Consider his conception of technology. Rather than an instrument of separation, Smithson reimagined the machines he used to create his work as arrested disruptions in the metamorphic cycles of emergence, refinement, decay, and reabsorption. "The manifestations of technology are at times less 'extensions' of man (Marshall McLuhan's anthropomorphism) than they are aggregates of elements," Smithson suggests. "Even the most advanced tools and machines are made of the raw matter of the earth".[44] Despite the dream of a dematerialized and weightless society, Smithson's insight is equally true in the twenty-first century. Rare-earth lurks beneath our shimmering screens.

The geological forces of the earth flow through the virtual space of

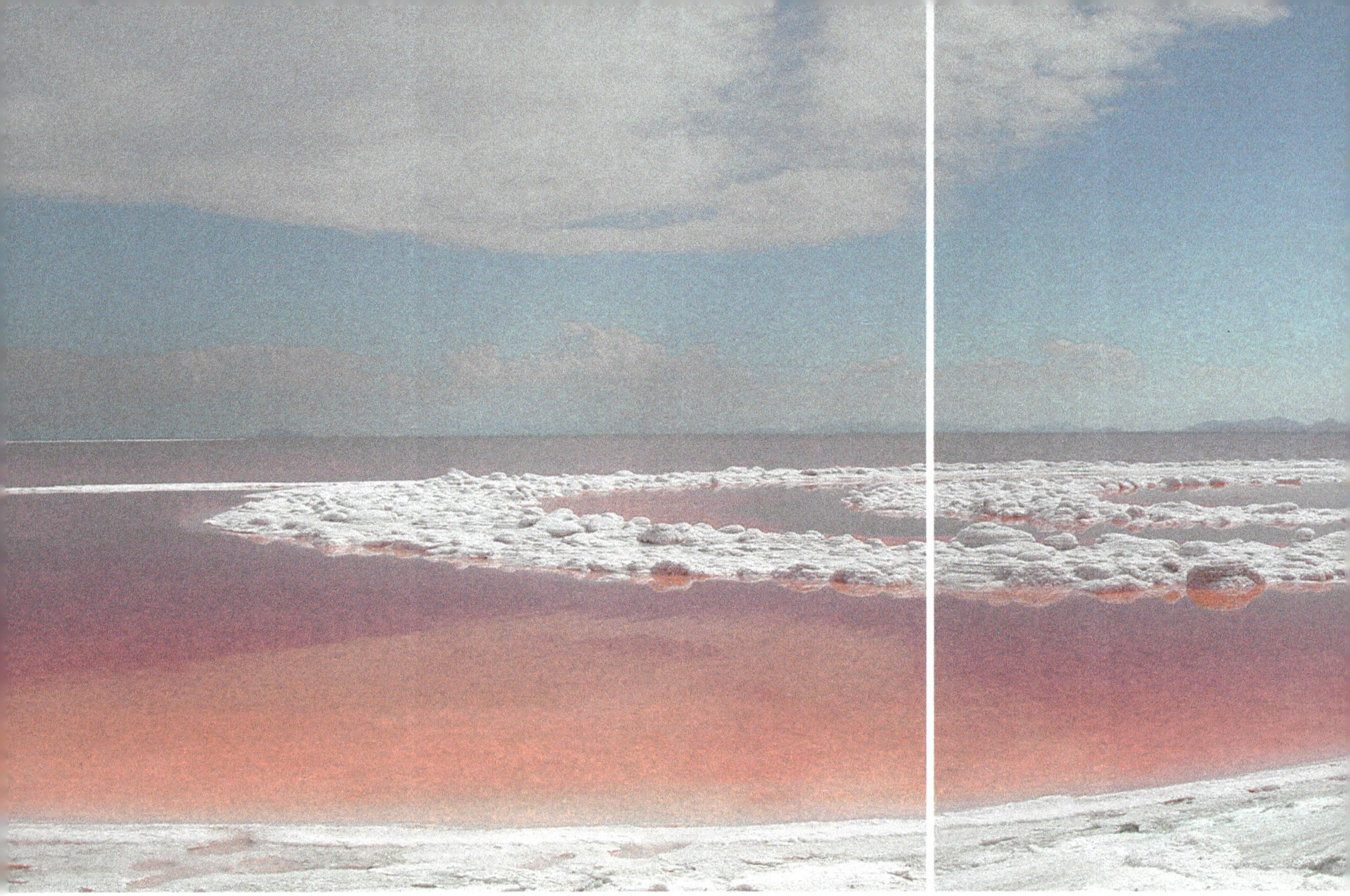

Martin Hogue and Robert Smithson

Above: *Field Recordings: Spiral Jetty,* 2003 Credit: Martin Hogue Copyright: Nancy Holt Robert Smithson Foundation / Licensed by VAGA, New York, NY. Right: Spiral Jetty [still] (1970) 16 mm film, Duration 35 minutes Color, sound © Holt/Smithson Foundation / Licensed by Artists Rights Society, New York. Distributed by Electronic Arts Intermix, New York

Smithson's photographic media as well. Toward the end of the *Spiral Jetty* film, Smithson points toward the entanglement of the celluloid media with the physical site via an image in which the circular reels of the movie camera echo the rotary turns of the earthwork, each spinning the other into existence. Contemplating this elemental connection, Smithson proposes that, "Everything about moviemaking is archaic and crude. One is transported by the medium into the earliest geological eras".[45] How so? Here we should recall the fundamentally indexical nature of photography, which Smithson perceived as a recording of the "diminution of solar energy".[46] Interpreted in this way, a photograph is analogous to the solar materiality of subterranean fossil fuel. Oil and photographs are both indexes of sunlight falling upon the earth. Like the strata of the planet, photographs are fossil records of their own process of becoming, and Smithson's images thus amplify the earthen physicality of *Spiral Jetty* rather than virtually dematerializing it.

While Smithson's account of his oceanic dissolution into the elemental earth of *Spiral Jetty* is likely fictional—I invite readers to take it seriously without having to take it literally— it is a fiction that charts a speculative future that necessarily diverges from the derangement of life on earth in the twenty-first century. Given the current and likely-to-come catastrophes of the Anthropocene, the possibility of being other-than-human—of becoming geological— should be a matter of urgent concern.

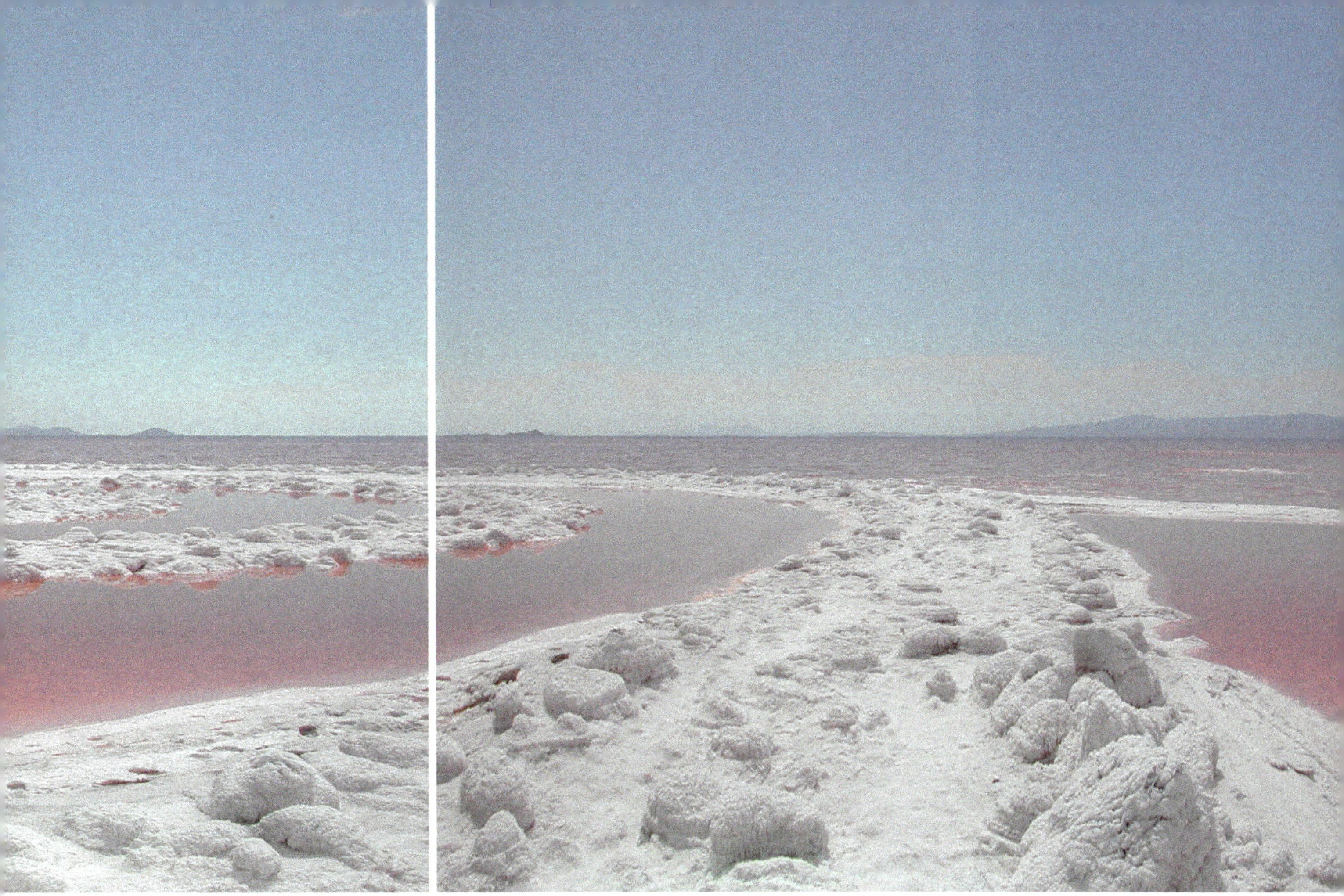

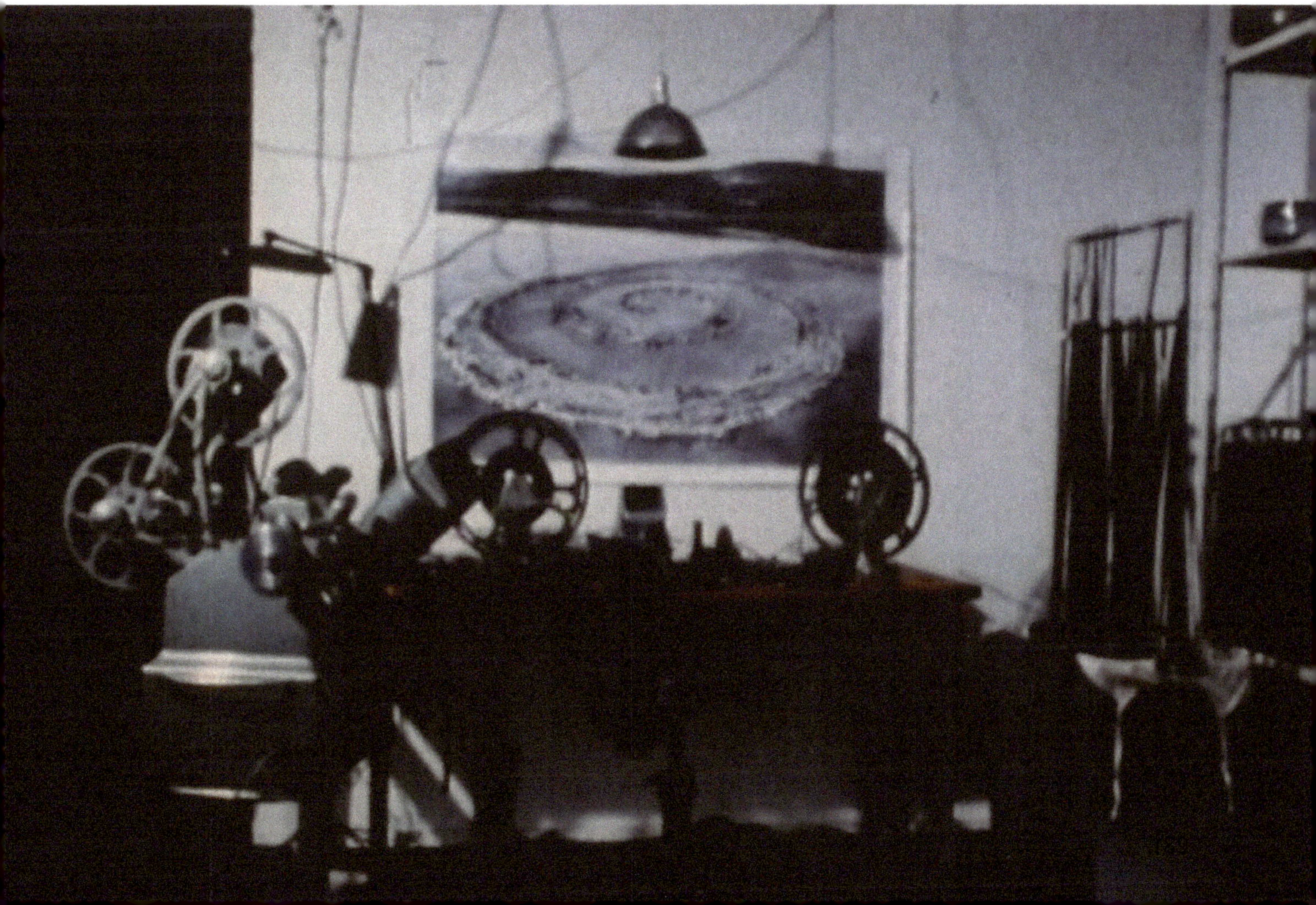

Endnotes

[1] Robert Smithson, "Four Conversations between Dennis Wheeler and Robert Smithson" (1969-1970), in *Robert Smithson: The Collected Writings, ed. Jack Flam* (Berkeley, Los Angeles, London: University of California Press, 1996), 216. Unless otherwise noted, all citations by Smithson are from this collection.
[2] Smithson, "A Sedimentation of the Mind: Earth Projects," 112.
[3] Smithson, "Letter to Martin Freedman" (undated), Robert Smithson and Nancy Holt Papers, 1905-1987, bulk 1952-1987. Archives of American Art, Smithsonian Institution, roll 3834, frame 49.
[4] Gilles Deleuze and Felix Guattari, *What Is Philosophy?*, trans. Hugh Tomlinson and Graham Burchill (London and New York: Verso, 1994), 102.
[5] See Hanjo Berressem's "We Have Never Been Human: Posthumanism Before Posthumanism," unpublished manuscript of Keynote Lecture held at 61st Annual Convention of the GAAS, University Würzburg, Germany, 12 June 2014.
[6] Smithson, "The Spiral Jetty" (1972), 141.
[7] See Jennifer Roberts, "Spiral Jetty/Golden Spike," in *Mirror-Travels: Robert Smithson and History*, 114-128.
[8] For a detailed history of oil exploration and the extraction economy in the Great Salt Lake region, see Hikmet Sidney Loe, *The Spiral Encyclo* (Salt Lake City: The University of Utah Press, 2017), esp. 193-203.
[9] Smithson, "The Spiral Jetty, "146.
[10] See Kathryn Yusoff, *A Billion Black Anthropocenes or None* (Minneapolis: University of Minnesota Press, 2018), 23-64. Other origins are proposed as well, including the ability to control fire, the agricultural revolution, and the Great Acceleration of the twentieth-century.
[11] Bataille, *Oeuvres Complètes*, vol. III, ed. Thadée Klossowski (Paris: Gallamard, 1970), 81.
[12] Reza Negarestani, *Cyclonopedia: Complicity with anonymous materials* (Melbourne: re.press, 2008), 12.
[13] See Raye C. Ringholz, *Uranium Frenzy, Boom and Bust on the Colorado Plateau* (Albuquerque: University of New Mexico Press, 1991).
[14] Smithson, "Incidents of Mirror-Travel in the Yucatan" (1969), 121-122.
[15] Smithson, "The Domain of the Great Bear," 85.
[16] Quentin Meillassoux, *After Finitude*, trans. Ray Brassier (New York: Continuum 2008), 10.
[17] Smithson, "The Spiral Jetty," 152.
[18] Smithson "Talking with Robert Smithson," Interview by Ken Baker, in *Robert Smithson Spiral Jetty*, eds. Lynne Cooke Karen Kelly (New York: Dia Art Foundation, 2005), 160.
[19] Brassier, *Nihil Unbound* (New York: Palgrave MacMillan, 2008), 223.
[20]Smithson, "Four Conversations between Dennis Wheeler and Robert Smithson" (1969-1970), ed. Eva Schmidt, 203; Smithson, "Fragments of an Interview with P.A. [Patsy] Norvell" (1969), 193.
[21] Meillassoux, *After Finitude*, 7. Emphasis added.
[22] Smithson, "The Artist as Site-Seer; or, A Dintorphic Essay," 345.
[23] Smithson, "A Sedimentation of the Mind," 110-111. Emphasis added.
[24]Smithson, "Discussions with Heizer, Oppenheim, Smithson" (1970), 249. Emphasis added.
[25] Ibid., 251.
[26] Georges Bataille and Anette Michelson, "The Ascent of Mount Aetna," *October* vol 36 (Summer 1986): 103.
[27] Smithson, "Strata: A Geophotographic Fiction," 77.
[28] Smithson, "The Spiral Jetty," 146.
[29] On whirlpools, see Ben Woodard, *On an Ungrounded Earth: Towards a New Geophilosophy* (Brooklyn: Punctum Books, 2013), chapter 2.
[30] F.W.J. von Schelling, *First Outline of a System of the Philosophy of Nature*, trans. Keith R. Peterson (Albany: State University of New York Press, 2004), 18.
[31] Walter Benjamin, *The Origin of German Tragic Drama* (London: New Left Books, 1977), 45; Amanda Boetzkes in *The Ethics of Earth Art* (Minneapolis and London: University of Minnesota Press, 2010), 81.
[32]Smithson, "The Spiral Jetty,"145-146; 148.
[33] Ibid., 149.
[34] Ibid., 148.
[35] Astrida Neimanis, *Bodies of Water: Posthuman Feminist Phenomenology* (London: Bloomsbury Academic, 2017), 94.
[36] Smithson, "The Spiral Jetty," 147.
[37]Smithson makes this cosmic aspect clear by his subtle intertextual insertion of Edwin

Hubble's 1958 classic of astronomy *Realm of the Nebulae* into "The Spiral Jetty" film.
[38] Esther Leslie *Liquid Crystals: The Science and Art of a Fluid Form* (London: Reaktion Books, Limited, 2017), 19.
[39] Maurice Blanchot, *Friendship* (Stanford, CA: Stanford University Press, 1997), 240.
[40] Susan Ballard and Liz Linden, "Spiral Jetty, Geoaesthetics, and Art: Writing the Anthropocene," *The Anthropocene Review* vol. 6,1-2 (2019): 148.
[41] Lucy Lippard, *Undermining: A Wild Ride through Land Use, Politics, and Art in the Changing West* (New York: The Free Press, 2014), 88; for a critique of Smithson's "Mesoamerican primitivism," see Jennifer Roberts *Mirror-Travels: Robert Smithson and History*, 110.
[42] Smithson frequently described his non-sites as metaphors. See Smithson, "A Provisional Theory of Non-sites" (1968), 364.
[43] Boetzkes, *The Ethics of Earth Art*, 66.
[44] Smithson, "A Sedimentation of the Mind: Earth Projects," 100.
[45] Smithson, "The Spiral Jetty," 150.
[46] Smithson, "Art through the Camera's Eye" (ca. 1971), 373.

Rory O'Dea is the Assistant Professor of Contemporary Art and Design, and Associate Dean of the School of Art and Design History and Theory at the Parsons School of Design. He received his Ph.D. from the Institute of Fine Arts, and his scholarship explores the relationship between art, fiction, and consciousness as well as the intersections of artistic and scholarly research. He has previously taught at the Yale University School of Art, and also worked as a researcher at the Whitney Museum of American Art, the Morgan Library and Museum, and the Grey Art Gallery at New York University. His forthcoming book *Robert Smithson, Land Art, and Speculative Realities* will be published by Routledge in 2023.

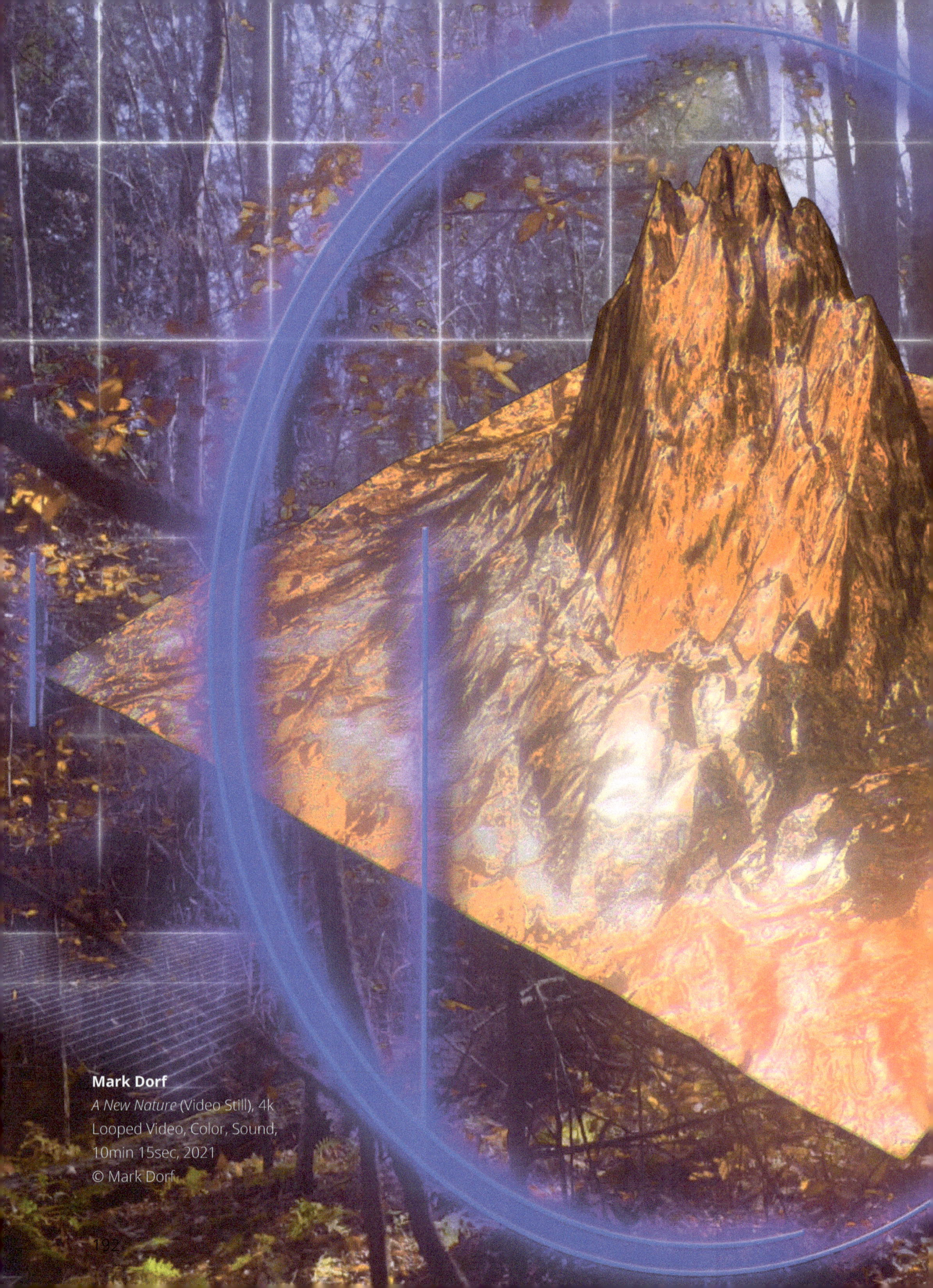

Mark Dorf
A New Nature (Video Still), 4k Looped Video, Color, Sound, 10min 15sec, 2021

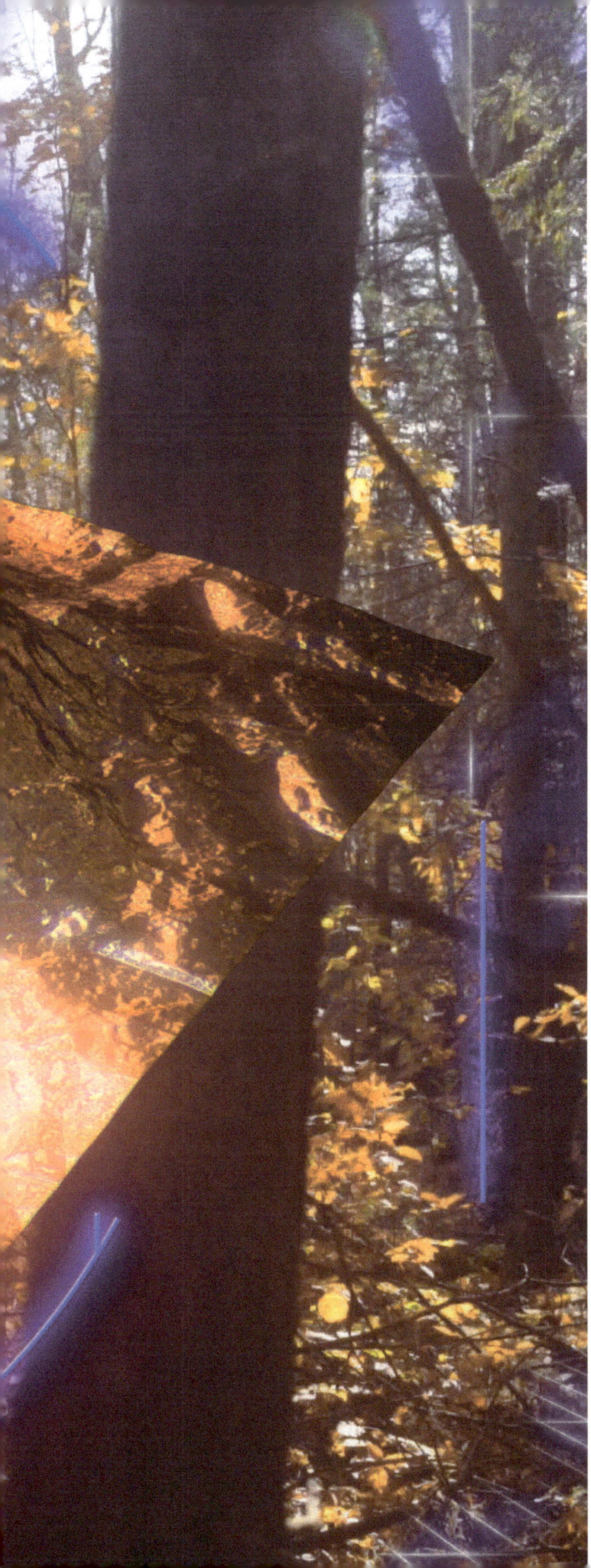

A New Nature

A New Nature depicts the dynamics of our present – a messy, global system in which simulations are entangled with our expectations of real life, and our perception of what constitutes the natural world is mediated, supported, suppressed, amplified, and interrupted by technology.

Integrating gaming and surveillance aesthetics with both animations and footage of the Rocky Mountain region, Mark Dorf collapses the barriers of what's real in a way that echoes our digital consumption of the world. A mass of living tree roots is scanned and imposed over a simulated ocean; a mountain range is represented as a topographical blueprint.

in conversation: **Mark Dorf, Paul CaraDonna, and Giovanni Aloi**

Giovanni Aloi: Mark, Paul-can you tell us about your collaborative approach? How did it start? What brought you to work together?

Mark Dorf: Dr. CaraDonna—Paul—and I began working together at the Rocky Mountain Biological Laboratory, a remote high-elevation biological research station in the Western Colorado Rockies where Paul and his team research every Summer, in 2014, close to about 10 years ago now. We have since worked on a handful of projects together, but perhaps more importantly, we have developed a long-term collaborative relationship and conversation that bleeds into both our respective fields of art and science. The many long and wandering conversations that Paul and I have, both at the lab and over long distances, played a key role in the conceptualization of my last film *A New Nature*. In the end, this work was predominantly shot and produced at the research station and surrounding environment in the Summer of 2021.

I think what makes our relationship unique and so fruitful is that we have avoided, in my experience anyway, what is a common obstacle when an artist and a scientist work together: one is so often in service of the other. The scientist synthesizes something for the artist, or the artist illustrates some biological feature for the scientist. In this situation, there isn't a lot of cross-pollination (no pun intended).

Whereas for Paul and I there is an immense amount of trust at a very base level. We both understand that just being in one another's presence helps to push forward our pursuits and that we learn so much from one another conceptually and ideologically. When you have that openness and trust, [art and science] are bound to seep into both of our works. Art objects or collected data aside, I think creating this kind of space for intellectual crossover is incredibly valuable and important to both of us. The science and the art are more like a symptom of curiosity about the world—we have found that our curiosities can be quite similar, we just go about expressing them in very different ways.

In *A New Nature*, the primary voiceover that you hear throughout the film is Paul—this voiceover was actually a conversation that I decided to record one night in a cabin at the Rocky Mountain Biological Laboratory. Paul and I had been having an ongoing conversation about this idea of a new nature for a couple of weeks. We were really honing in on what "a new nature" meant in our current world, or what it could mean in the face of climate change, or what it means within the context of the post-natural. This two-week ongoing conversation snowballed and became the backbone of the film itself.

Paul CaraDonna: I'll add my perspective from the scientist side of the equation. Our initial collaboration began through a program that I started with another scientist, Dr. Nick Waser, at the Rocky Mountain Biological Laboratory, which we call the "Art-Science Exchange".

The idea of the Art-Science Exchange came out of a conversation with Nick. When we are on a hike, we'll take a rest and do some sort of sketch or drawing or watercolor or whatever to slow down and take it all in. While we were doing this one day, we were commenting on the fact that it's such a totally different perspective on nature, to slow down in this way and draw a picture. And as the conversation went on, we were thinking about how at a biological research station, you have all these scientists viewing and approaching nature in a very particular way, with a very particular set of tools, and through a very particular lens. We realized how slowing down in this way gives us a very different take on the ecosystem that we know and love and have studied for years. And so we were like: "What if we had someone who could come out to the lab and their job is to bring that different perspective and share it with the community [of scientists]." And so we set out to do just that with the Art-Science Exchange.

For a little context, The Rocky Mountain Biological Laboratory is a high-elevation biological research station in western Colorado sitting at about 9,500ft above sea level. It used to be an old mining town in the late 1800s, but since 1928 it has been operating as a biological research station. And so, every summer, it turns

Mark Dorf

Emergent #7,

Carbon Pigment Print, 30in x 24in, 2014

© Mark Dorf

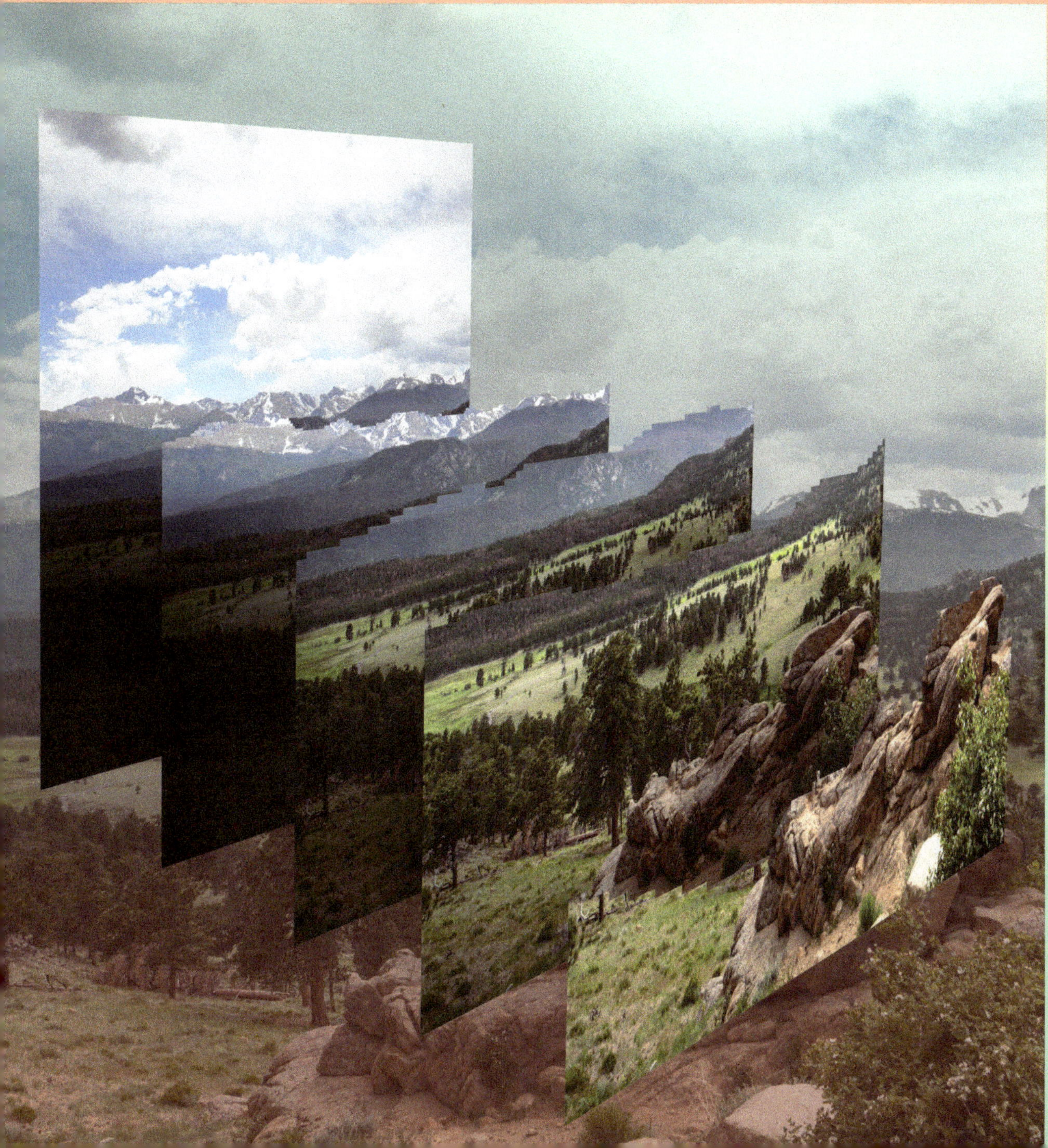

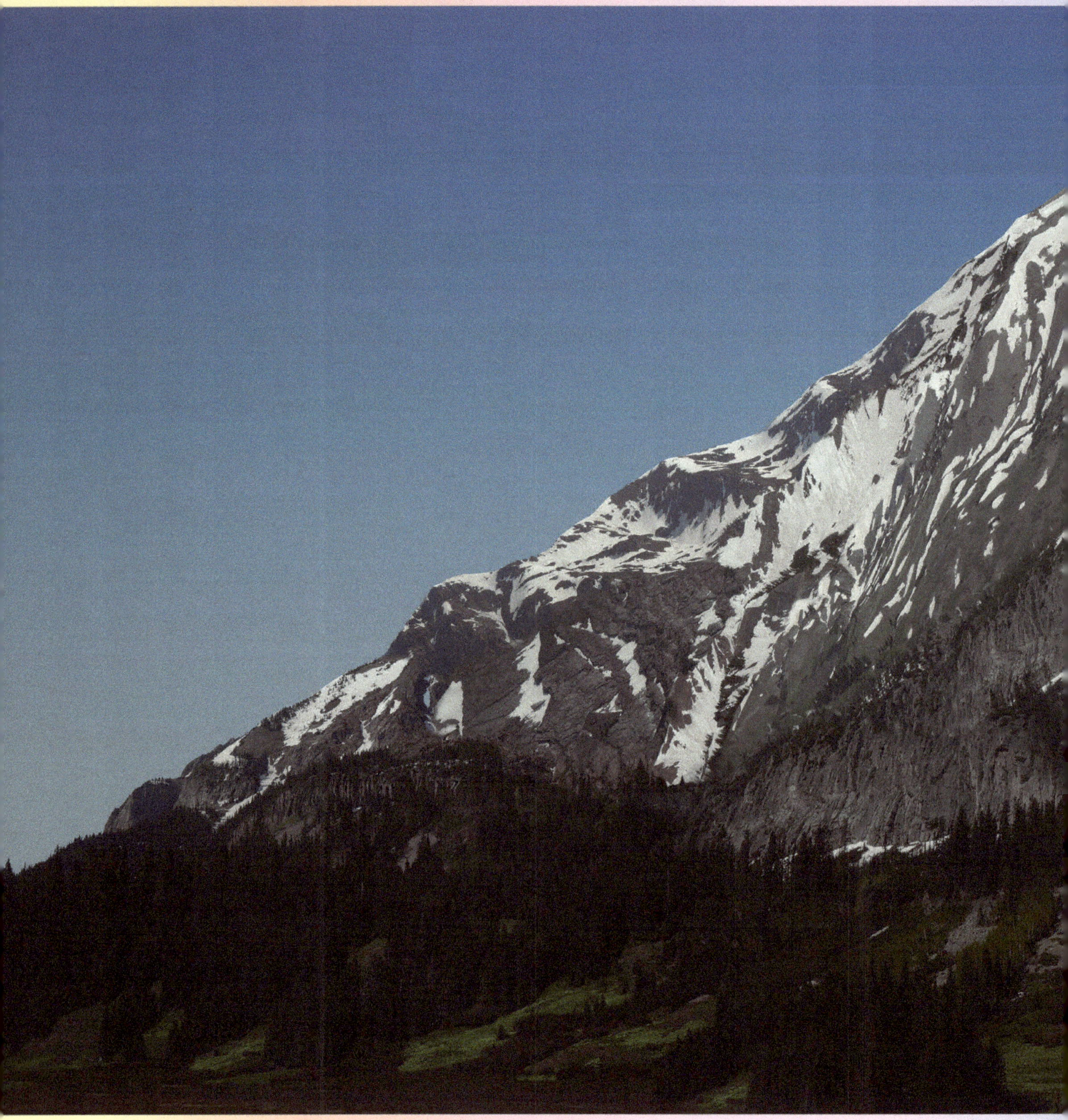

Mark Dorf

Reassemblage #3, Carbon Pigment Print, 40in x 80in, 2014 © Mark Dorf

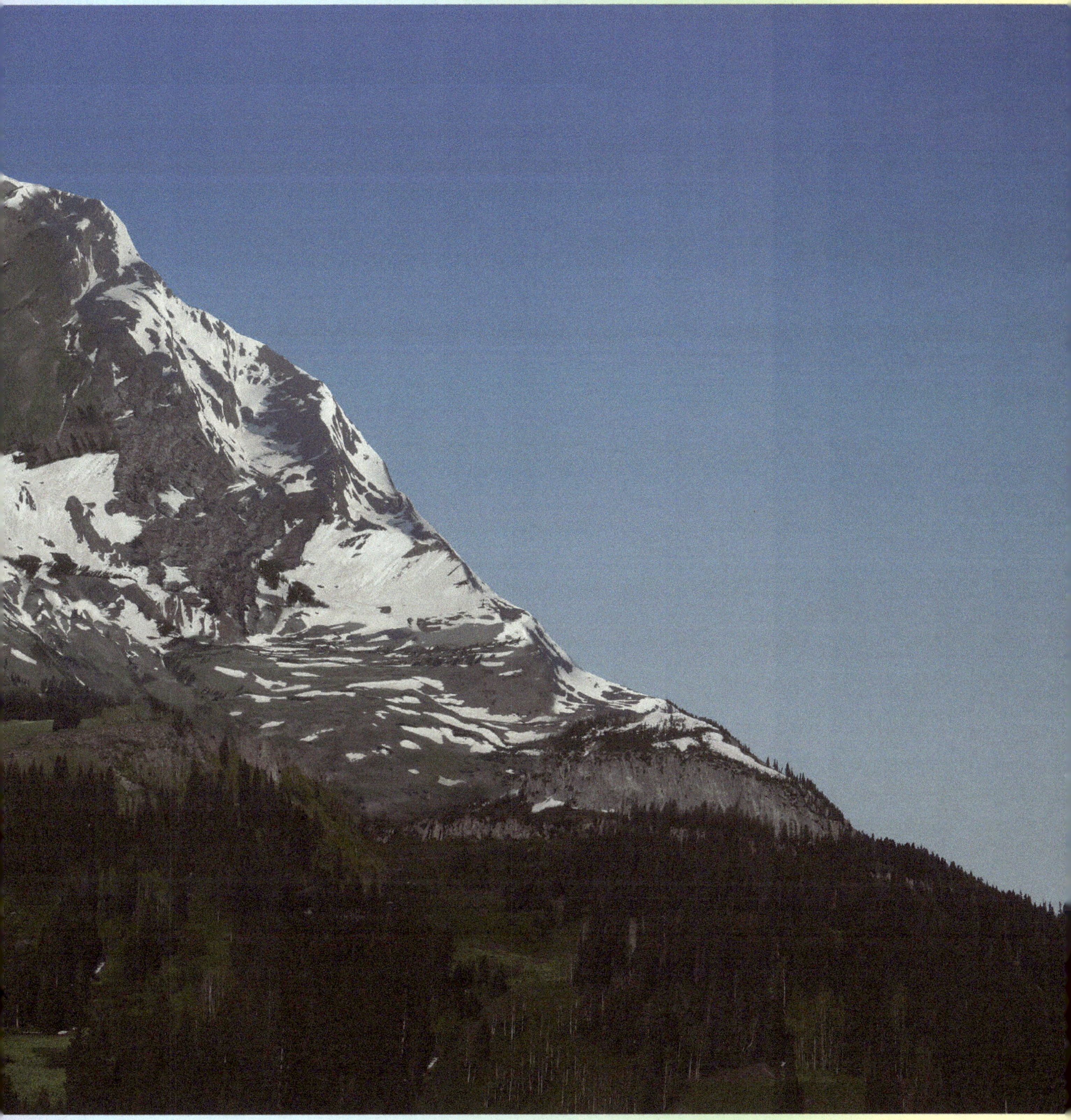

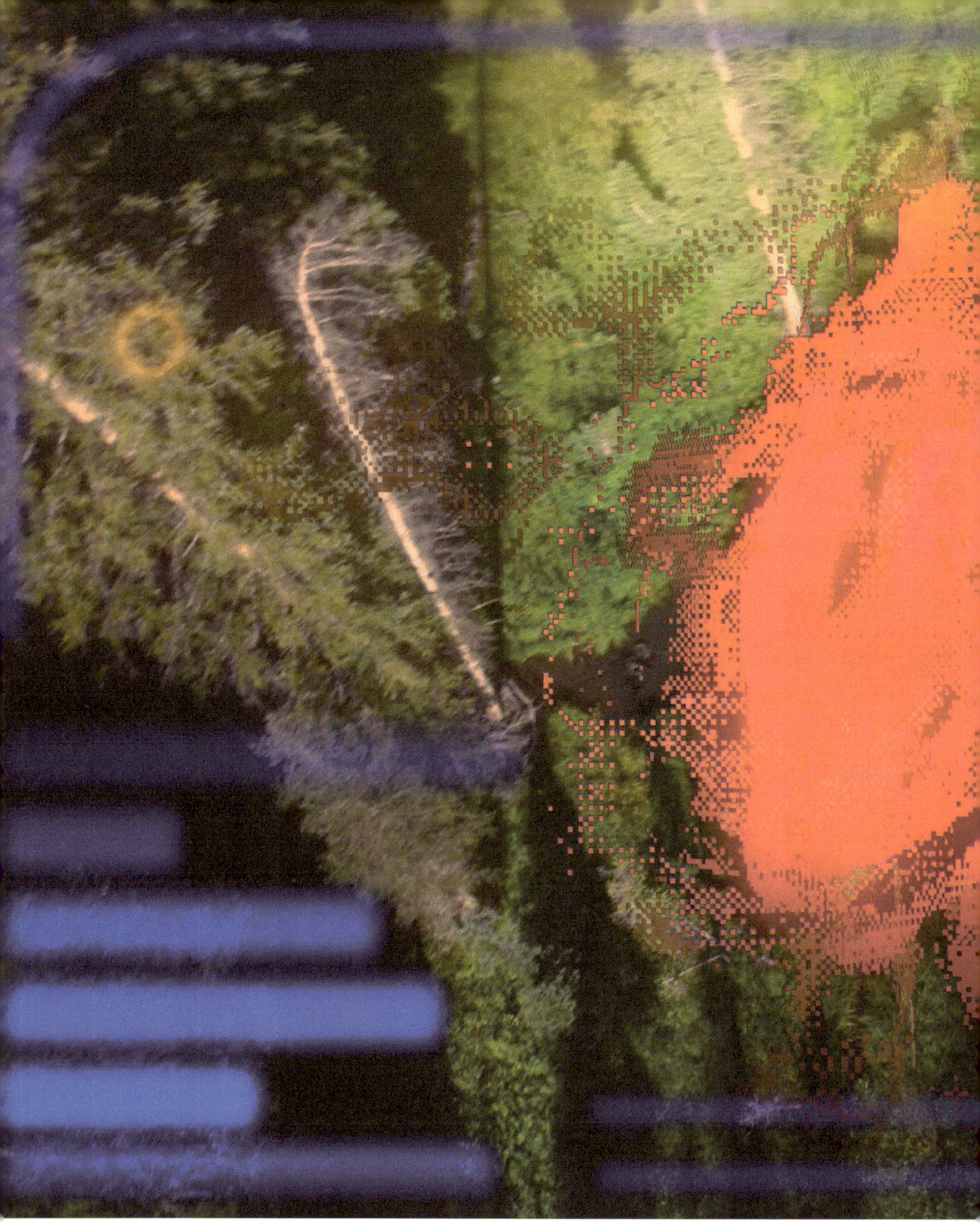

Mark Dorf

A New Nature (Video Still), 4k Looped Video, Color, Sound, 10min 15sec, 2021

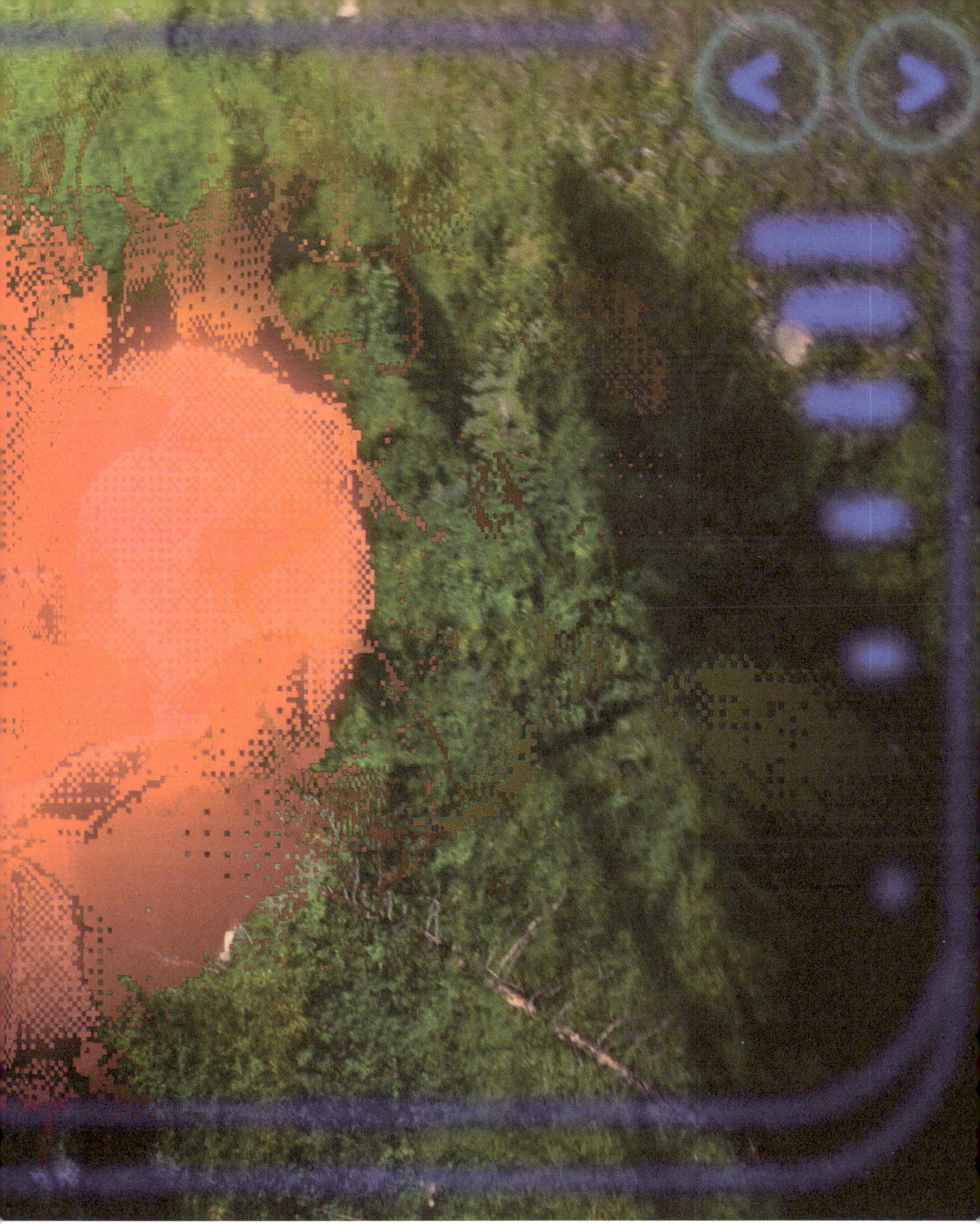

into this lively community of about 180 scientists from all over the world. It is also quite isolated: it is about 8 miles to the nearest little ski town and about 35 miles to the "big city" of Gunnison, Colorado (which has a population of something like 6,000 people). But the great thing about this isolation is that you're isolated up in the mountains with all these scientists who are studying nature—the plants, the animals, the rivers, the geology—and that is really great for building community. I think it is a pretty special thing.

One of the key things that Nick and I envisioned with the Art Science Exchange was creating a venue and context where there could be bidirectional sharing between the sciences and the arts. We wanted ideas to flow both ways—that was really important to our vision. We were also pondering: what might be the product of such bidirectional sharing? Here we are bringing out artists for several weeks to interact with scientists at a remote field station—should they make something to hang on the wall or leave at the lab? And we decided very quickly that we didn't want the Art-Science Exchange to be about the product. We were more interested in the process and what happens when you bring artists together with scientists in this setting. Our only expectation was that the artist comes out to the lab and interacts with scientists, spends time in the field with them, and is part of the community doing their thing as an artist and using their tools as an artist. And the scientific community at the lab was open and supportive of this idea.

So, Mark came out as part of that Art-Science Exchange during the summer of 2014 and he became part of the community very quickly. And just from that, the conversation and our collaboration began. Mark was coming out and helping us with fieldwork, asking questions, looking at scientific figures, taking photos—but we were always having a conversation about nature, the process of science, technology, art—and we were just letting the ideas flow and allowing each other to be influenced by one another without any expectation as to where it was going.

That first summer Mark created his series Emergence. To me, it was obvious from Emergence that the flow of ideas was going both ways. I learned a lot from this work in ways I wasn't expecting. And then over the years, we've just kept our conversation going. When I was able to invite Mark back out to the lab in 2021 it seemed as if there was no time between his first visit. We just sort of blasted off into what felt like a continuous three-week conversation. So, we eventually recorded one of those conversations, and that is where a lot of the voiceovers in A New Nature come from.

For me, I think there are all sorts of things that I've gained intellectually from getting to collaborate with Mark in this capacity. But I also think it is important to note that the collaboration doesn't clearly produce a new scientific paper or my next big grant proposal idea, at least in a hardcore scientific sense. But that's not the point of this collaboration—I'm much more interested in exploring that space between art and science—I think that's the really interesting thing here.

GA: Perhaps not surprisingly, part of this conversation has already cast a focus on "the institution", how our thinking is defined by the restrictions that the institution imposes upon thinking, researching, and outputs. The format and substance of what we are expected to produce are still institutionally defined to the point that any true and meaningful deviation from the canonical norm is seen with suspicion or outright discounted as irrelevant.

This is particularly true of practitioners working at the intersection of art and science since so much of what it produces often does not count as legitimate research in the eyes of the institution. There has been a shift in this context over the past ten years but the change is slow.

I wonder if we can dig a little bit deeper into the idea of multidisciplinary added value - what does art add to scientific discourses? Art, in its collaborations with science, never is just an amplifier of the scientific research. How did you negotiate this difficult aspect in calibrating your collaboration?

MD: Generally, Science tends to have a somewhat clearer image of its use and value. To be overly simplistic: a scientist creates a data set, analyzes it, and publishes a paper or seeks out the application of their findings in a real-world use case—the process is quantified in every way. There is a better collective understanding in the world regarding the "usefulness" or value of science. Art, however, in a general way, has a more nebulous "use"—that being said I'm by no means arguing that art is useless.

Paul and I were just recently chatting about this actually. Science does not create space to think in the same way that art does. Generally, science, however abstract, creates explicit information with the goal being to think about a subject in a concrete way. This effectively narrows the field of view to create a definition. Art on the other hand, so often seeks to create space for questions effectively opening up the field of view even further. That is, art seeks to create space for questioning without the prerequisite of an answer, or alternatively, art seeks to create the potential energy for deviation to gestate. In *A New Nature,* I gesture towards and create space for an idea, but I very consciously provide no answers. I don't think creating answers is necessarily the role of an artist. Nor is it really, I think, the role of a scientist to give an answer per se, but one is clearly more concrete than the other or can be, anyway.

I think that that's a really unique space for Paul and me to share. In my understanding, it's difficult for scientists to be able to enter such a vast space of questioning without the specific intention of coming to a focused conclusive result. We have found that in sharing these different ways of seeing and perceiving the world and allowing them into our respective practices, we have a deeper understanding of the world that we're so curious about rather than a siloed hyper-specific understanding that reflects only our respective community's language and interests.

PC: From my perspective, something that has really stuck with me came up early in the process of working on *A New Nature*. We were chatting about something out in the field, and I asked Mark: "Do you think we should make some explicit statements about climate change, or species extinctions, or something like that?" And Mark replied: "I think I'm less interested in making explicit statements. I'm much more interested in creating a space for someone to explore a set of ideas without an explicit answer." Mark's answer really stuck with me at that moment about *A New Nature*., and about what art can do on its own, and also about what art can do at the intersection of art and science.

His answer also made me think a lot about how we do things in science. A lot of times in the sciences, we're making very explicit statements about things. For example, we illustrate a figure that shows a very particular quantity of an ecosystem, something we've gone out and measured and can measure again, and there is really only so much interpretation of those values and trends in this context. To be clear, there is always some kind of interpretation of what those values and quantities mean, but it is much more direct. We are creating more knowledge for understanding how nature works in a very direct sense—this is a very important part of the scientific endeavor. That's how we can accumulate knowledge—we measure things and quantify things in a very standardized way.

But it's also only one way of knowing, right? I've found that when we arrive at this intersection of art and science, we get to open up new doors with regard to how we think about all the things that we think we understand—at least for me, that is the case. And I think what Mark's work helps to do, at the least in the context of our scientific community at the lab, is to think much more broadly about what we do as scientists and how we approach understanding nature. It causes people to slow down and think about it in a different and interesting way—to think about this place we've spent so much time studying in ways we maybe never have before.

As I mentioned earlier, I don't think this experience, at least in most cases, is going to directly lead to the next prestigious paper in Nature or Science—but again, that's not what we're going after. I think what we're trying to do is to shift our thinking. I think a really interesting goal is to shift perspectives. And indeed, we've had cases where scientists at the lab have had strong reactions to some of Mark's work, where they've been like: "Hey! Wait a second, that's not quite right!" or "That isn't a real mountain! The geology is totally wrong!" or "Isn't that a bit deceptive?" and things like that. And for me, as a scientist, I've been amazed at these reactions by other scientists. It has been totally fascinating because normally my work as a scientist isn't going to generate such a reaction in such a way. The fact that people were responding to the work in strong ways, that it was pushing on people to challenge assumptions they've made about an ecosystem that some of these scientists have been studying for three or four decades seemed really valuable—something was happening here.

And on top of this, we've also had examples where [non-scientists] have seen [*A New Nature*] and shared that the film made them more curious to engage with ideas and concepts about, humans and nature and climate change, for example—things, they were a previously more timid to engage with. And to me, this really felt like a huge breakthrough. That the work could make someone feel like they should engage more with issues like climate change or the Anthropocene—I don't feel like I can do this in science in the same way. Usually, it feels like someone is already on board with the information, or they're against it in some way and refuse to engage with the information. So, in either case, you're not getting a lot of engagement, which is not good. But then with *A New Nature*., it seems it allows for that engagement without bringing a lot of baggage in, it is not yelling at you, and it isn't making direct statements. Mark isn't communicating a specific scientific concept, but he's giving us access to explore some of these more nebulous and challenging ideas about humanity's relationship with nature and what that might look like in the future.

In science, we try to make predictions about what the future might look like, but it's things about the composition of plants under drought conditions, for example, or maybe something about how much variation we might see in an important ecosystem service. We generally are not making predictions about human's relationship with nature and what that might look like in a fuzzier way. And I would argue that we really need that perspective on our own relationships with nature to solve problems of the future. I think that is indeed very utilitarian. I think that's one of the things some of this work helps to do by creating a space to think about these issues.

GA: I could not agree more. One of the questions that I am more interested in about the art and science interface is that of truth, an all-pervasive and not self-naturalizing concept in the history of civilization. The separation of nature/culture which we are only now coming to deconstruct to envision more sustainable futures. A dangerous naturalization of the concept of nature that pervaded the intertwined histories of Western art and philosophy. For instance, there is a repertoire of images, paintings, and photographs that perpetuate the same compositional tropes as well as aesthetic solutions that in a sense repropose a kind of nature that is relentlessly remote, inaccessible, perfected, objectified, and subjugated. There are many famous examples, of course, like John Constable, who perfected the British countryside, at a time in which the Industrial Revolution was devastating the bucolic beauty of the ecological balance of Great Britain. Other very famous works by William Turner, still in that representational camp, capture a picturesque image of nature that's in a sense under human control in one way or another. These paintings "naturally" deploy a repertoire of aesthetic/rhetorical devices, implicit codes, and compositional tropes, that imply human centrality and supremacy over the natural world.

The point of view is one of the most telling and simpler rhetorical devices that the whole artistic genre of landscape painting relies upon. In this painting by Constable, the light, the sunshine bathing the horizon, which invites the viewer to engage in a metaphorical journey from darkness to light–these paintings are imbued with Christian morals–produce an all-pervasive type of highly seductive artificial beauty we have come to call nature.

It is characterized by a sense of calm, an illusion of control. And we know, of course, that nature is rarely if ever like that. This vision of calm control and peace is the result of this fictitious separation between humans and the rest of the non-human world. More recently I came across the work of Davoud Bey, one of the most influential photographers of our time, whose work helped me to better grasp the insidiousness of these aesthetic paradigms and their ability to naturalize. This naturalization process is not race-blind. The point of view that has relentlessly shaped the representation of the Western landscape and with that our very idea of nature, is situated in the whiteness of the straight wealthy, male, landowner who commissioned the paintings. A point of view that we now give for granted and that we unwittingly reproduce when taking holiday snaps, for instance. The aesthetic tropes are etched in our brains.

Dawoud Bey's photographic series *Night Coming Tenderly Black* initiates a decolonizing process that begins with a critical appraisal of the very idea of nature as a Western construct. In my opinion, this series demonstrates how any process of decolonization is implicitly and at once embedded with a reconfiguration of nature.

Bey's photographs visualize the 'Underground Railroad'– a network of safe houses and locations across the Cleveland and Hudson, Ohio landscapes in which fugitive slaves could find shelter on their way towards Lake Erie and the final fifty-mile passage to freedom in Canada. Leaving people entirely out of the picture, Bey makes a plea for empathy and a political statement through images of an often eerie and ambiguous American landscape at twilight. Across the series, images of trees and forests evidence the roles race and white privilege play in defining networked vegetal identities.

Bey's images of forests are strikingly different from those constructed by white photographers or from the landscape paintings made since the 18th century. They are ambiguously quiet and unnervingly enigmatic. They are simultaneously yesterday and today—places of temporary shelter for the fugitive slaves dreading to cross open lands by day and insurmountable barriers or inescapable labyrinths where lives can be lost.

Paintings by John Constable and other artists are aesthetically underpinned by the notion of land ownership and privilege. The paintings are the manifestation of the commercialization of art as an ideological tool of the new mercantile/landowner class. Colonization and capitalism are the matrix of the idea of modern nature in the West.

I'm interested in the way in which you, Mark, and Paul, deploy different aesthetic languages to offset this tradition of the Western landscape as truth, as given, and in the process, you construct something other. Can you want to tell us how that works; How you craft your aesthetic language and what you think it does?

MD: The idea of truth in the context of the landscape has been one that I've been thinking about for a very long time—throughout really all of my work for the last 10 years. In my work, I am not only looking at the concept of nature, or what we call nature in Western culture, through the lens of ecology and science but also through technology and design. Giovanni, you just brought up the history of Western landscape painting and the idea of nature being imaged as remote or sepa-

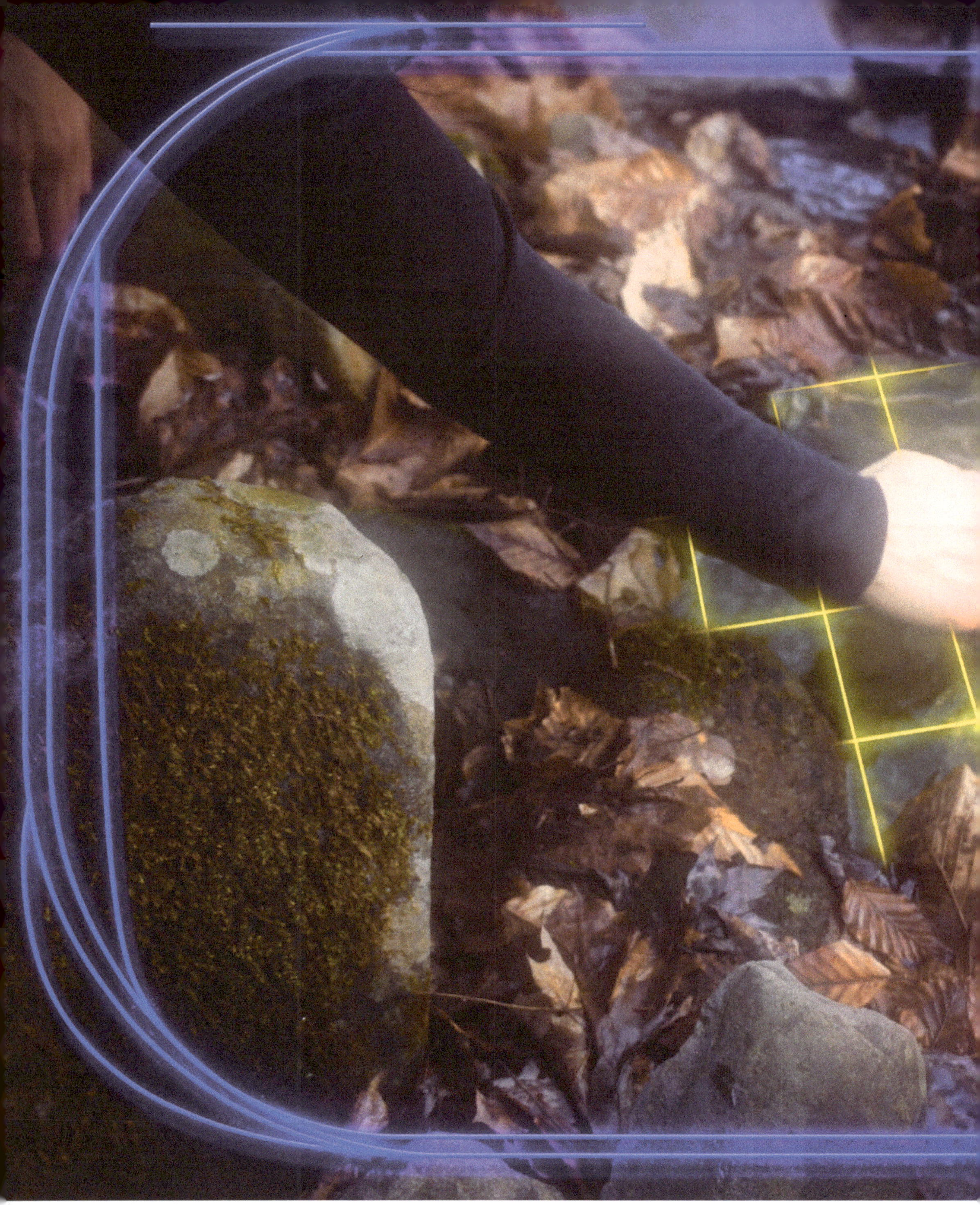

Mark Dorf

A New Nature (Video Still), 4k Looped Video, Color, Sound, 10min 15sec, 2021

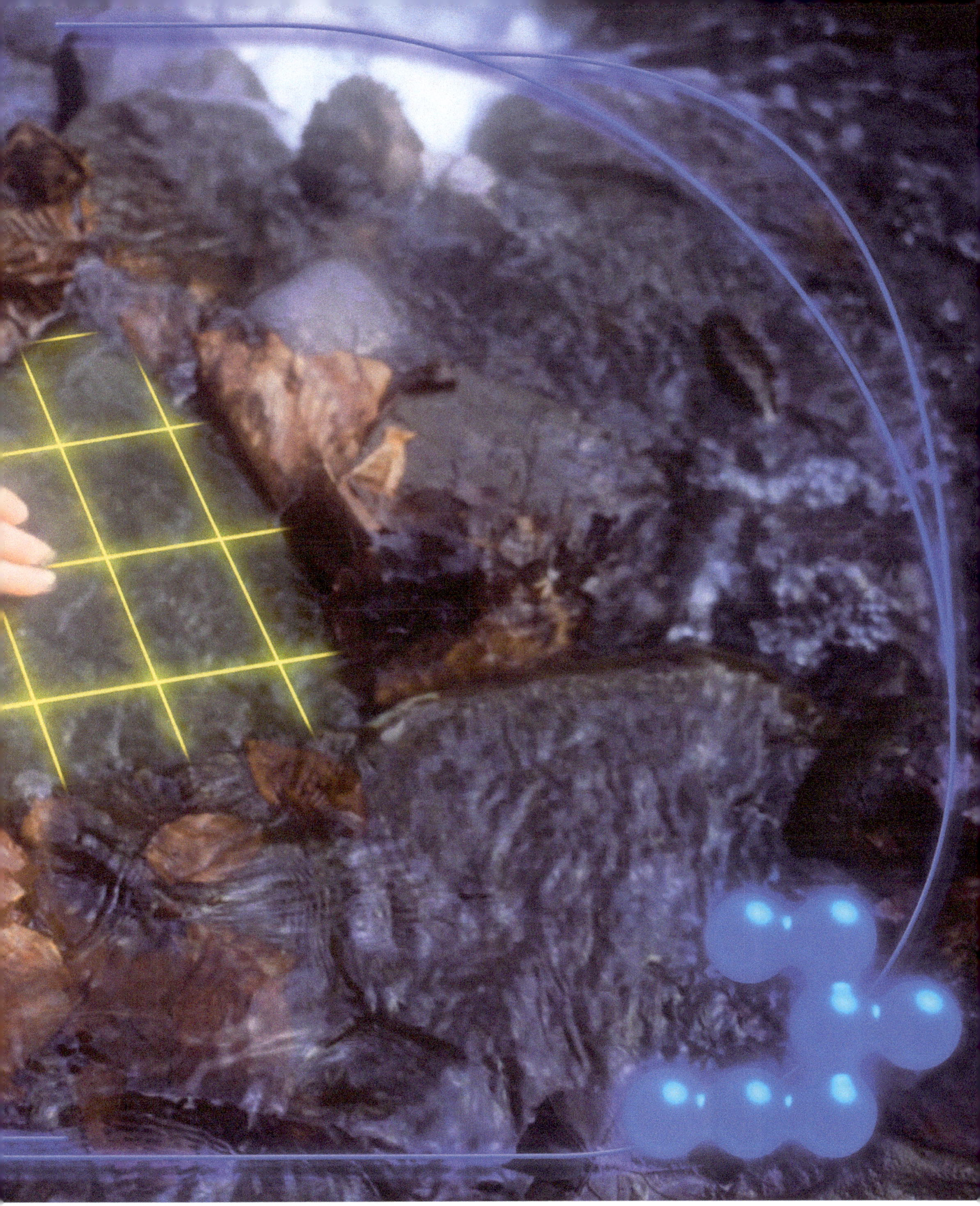

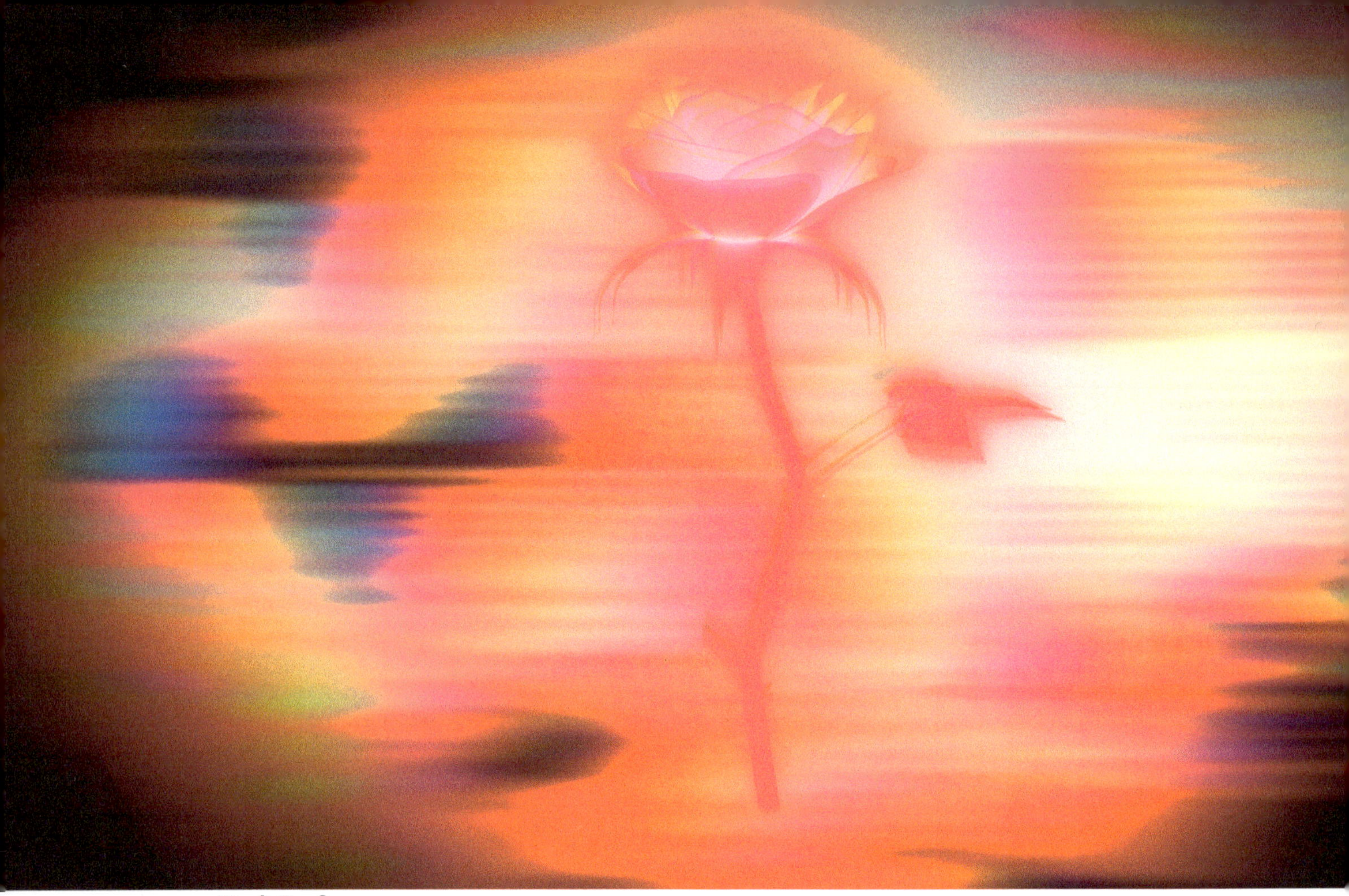

Mark Dorf

A New Nature (Video Still), 4k Looped Video, Color, Sound, 10min 15sec, 2021

rate—something over there, not over here. *A New Nature* has a way of simultaneously creating a version of nature that is far away, referencing the classical notion of Nature, while also bringing it very close through the design elements that are constantly entering and exiting the images. For example, at the beginning of the piece, the viewer finds a 3D chrome form reminiscent of a landscape that is in constant motion surrounded by bright blue formal design elements. These design elements and accompanying sound effects that are experienced throughout the work gesture towards interfaces found in the operating systems and apps of our personal devices.

These experiences are quite close to the user, literally found at the fingertips. When looking at an image of a landscape on a personal device, or when one takes a photo of a landscape with our personal device, you're looking through all these different interfaces. It should be noted that these interfaces, and their designs, are absolutely political in their function: they dictate navigation within the digital sphere. At this moment there is a collapse of space where the user is both far away from the subject—literally in that there is space between the user and the subject being photographed, but also metaphorically in that, the user is likely focused on the image, not the sensory experience that they are imaging—and very close as the subject has been rendered on the screen in their hands. Regardless, the image and subject are experienced in the presence of the operating system and its language of design, the different platforms that this image will be shared on, the different people that it will be shared with, etc. The image is never seen as an image alone, but as an image in the context of all these other visual languages relating to navigable political design—at this moment the platform,

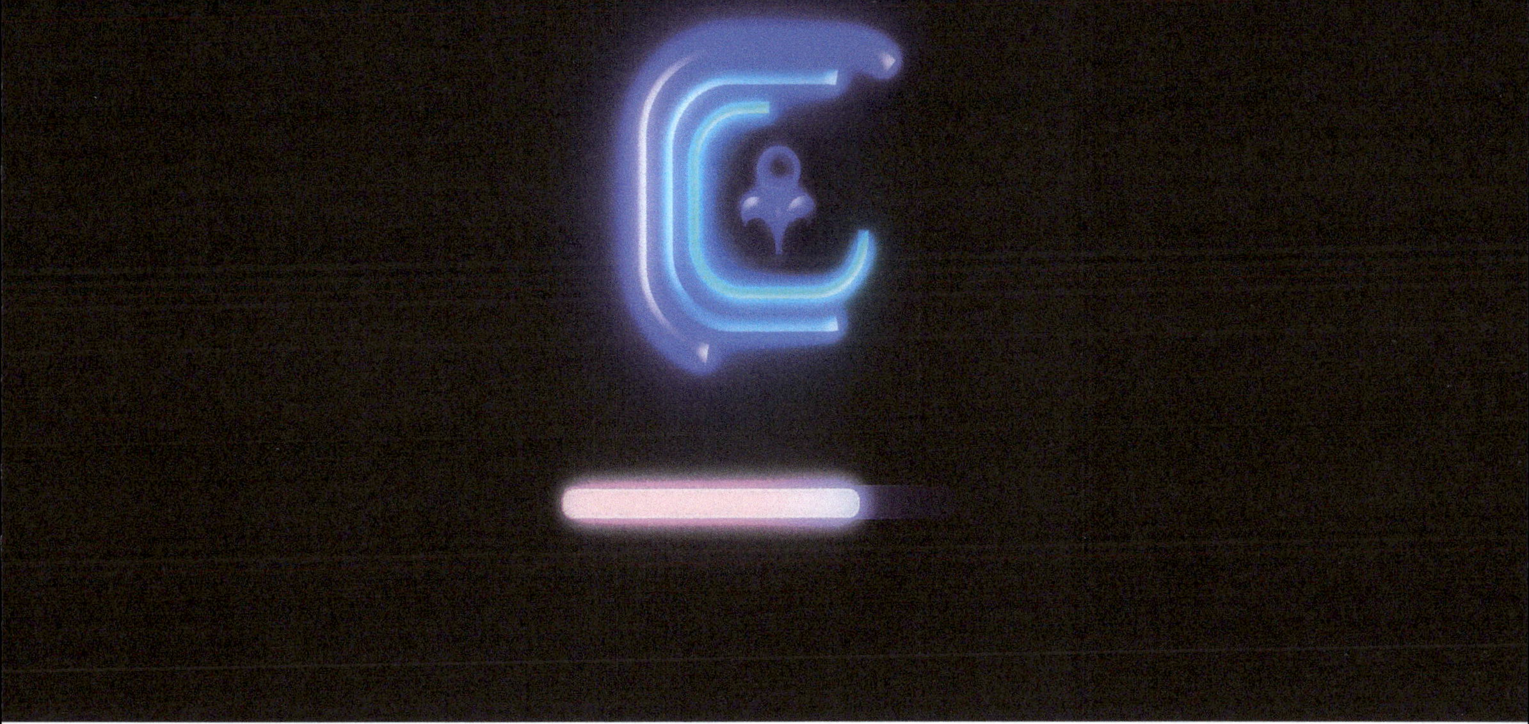

Mark Dorf

A New Nature (Video Still), 4k Looped Video, Color, Sound, 10min 15sec, 2021

surrounding design, and device become part of the image itself. I argue that this is a kind of new pastoral where the device on which you see the image is inseparable from the image itself. The design elements in *A New Nature* begin to draw connections between the politicized history of landscape in Western art and the politicized nature of platforms and their design on how we are able to see, image, and distribute our experiences.

Towards the end of the film, there is a literal deconstruction when the landscape images begin to destabilize. At this point in *A New Nature,* Paul speaks about our relationship with what we call nature, and how the future of nature may not be what we want, but it's something that we should prepare for, suggesting that it might become a sort of grotesque version of itself. Through this visual destabilization and fragmentation, it becomes unclear whether the image and subject are falling apart or whether they are in a state of becoming and transformation. Through this confusion, the images are breaking down the traditional notion of the landscape image. At this moment, the interfaces and formal design elements are no longer present, and at first glance, the viewer finds a sense of relief in that they finally get what they think is a stable landscape image. But upon closer examination, the viewer begins to see that the landscape in front of them is a composite: portions of the landscape are seamlessly assembled, and other portions reveal the hard contours of the collage where the illusion is broken. Collectively a new kind of landscape image is produced that is almost pornographic, where illusion to the highest degree is present leaning into the hyper-saturated fictitious image of nature while also deconstructing that fiction by revealing its seams. The composite however is revealed in such a subtle way that you

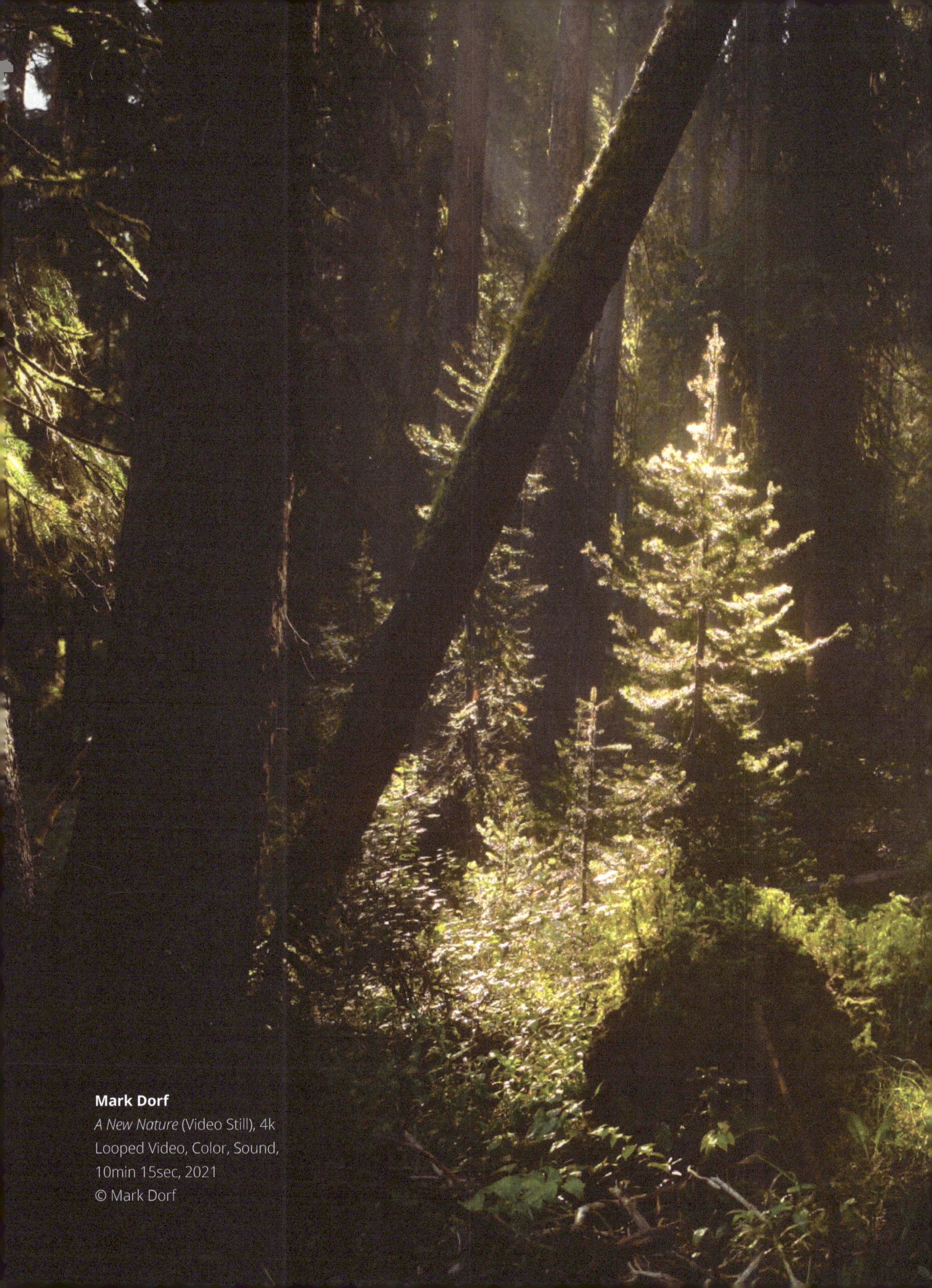

Mark Dorf
A New Nature (Video Still), 4k Looped Video, Color, Sound, 10min 15sec, 2021
© Mark Dorf

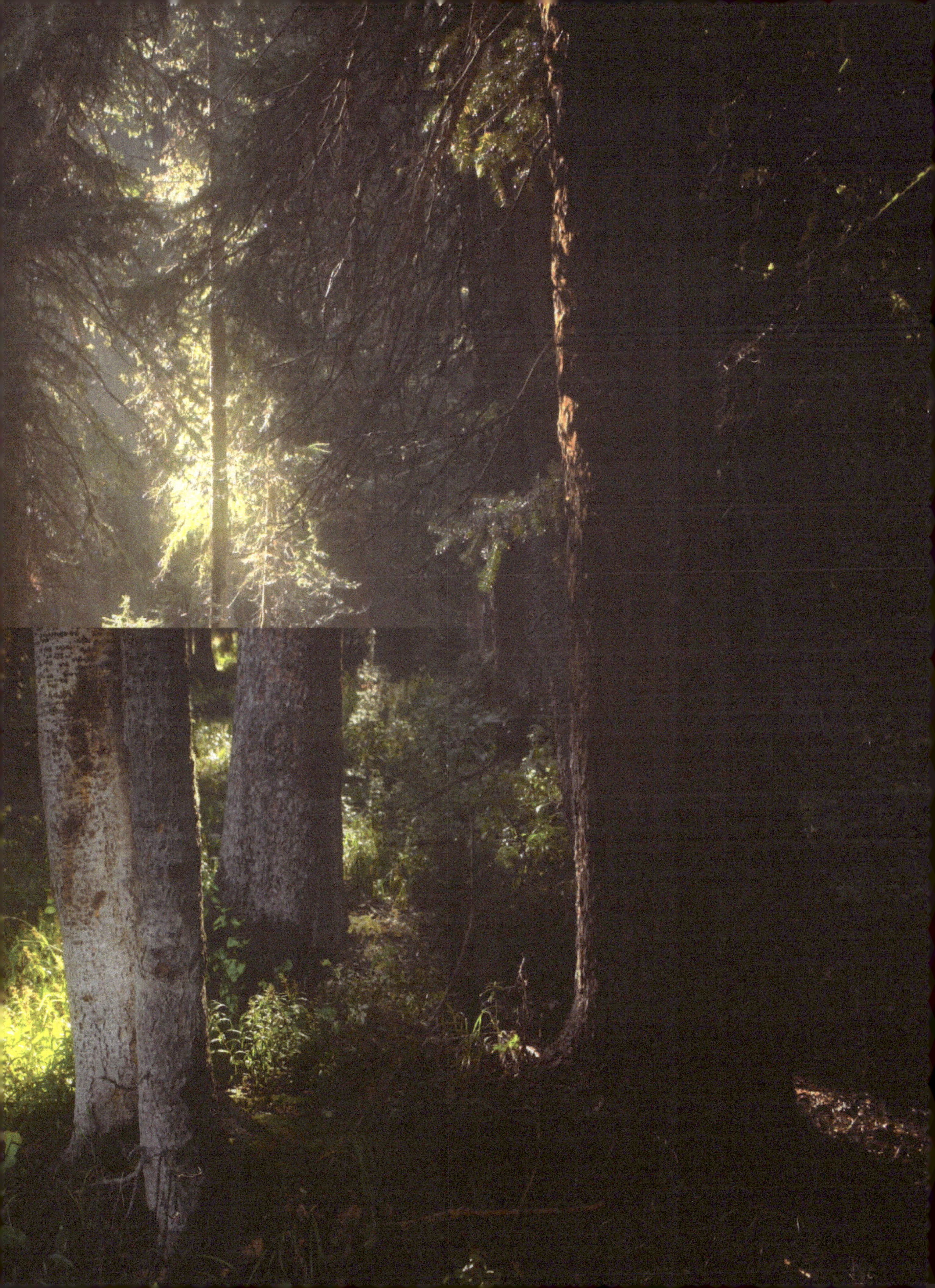

might miss it. The combination of these techniques creates tension between these worlds. It brings them together, reveals their entanglement, but also pulls them apart.

I'm constantly revealing and amplifying this tension between a sensory experience and a reality created by images. In mixing all of these elements together I gesture towards a planetary ecology that includes political systems, design, the internet, the way images move through digital space, and digital images themselves. All these elements coexist and affect one another—it's really not a future that *A New Nature* is trying to depict, a "new nature" points to the present in order to try to create space for us to think about what the future could hold for better and worse.

GA: You put on the map a very important idea: the notion of timelessness which is key to the aesthetic essence of sublime representations of forests especially, or open spaces, in Western art. Another rhetorical device that, we know, separates us from the rest of the natural-it objectifies the landscape as something to conquer.

There is a romantic paradigm that relies upon an aesthetic alignment of timelessness that problematizes notions of commoditization. I am referring specifically to the design elements that you use to summon and foreground the presence of technological interfaces, in the construction of a "new nature". Our conception of nature is always mediated by some kind of technological interface. Painting is also a technological interface. We just don't tend to in common parlance, we don't tend to think about painting as technology, because in our minds technology is grounded in this modernist vision of the machine. That's when technology became industrial. But when you look at the history of technology through time and across cultures, any kind of prosthetic tool that reaches and ties me with the other; the very moment a description or interpretation of the other begins, we engage with technological representation-be it a brush, a chisel, or a pen. And the very moment you begin to describe a landscape in words, it no longer is that landscape. The very moment I use that word to define hillsides and slopes or mountains, I am representing it in a way that simultaneously makes manifest while creating distance. These are the inescapable intricacies of representation.

MD: This connection between representation and technology is directly at the heart of *A New Nature* in so many ways. You speak about how "the very moment you begin to describe a landscape, it no longer is that landscape" - this is precisely what so many of these formal design elements in the video attempt to bring to the forefront. They are a constant reminder that the image itself, the chosen material or technology of representation, is in itself a translation that contains a spectrum of biases brought on by the maker and the tools that were used.

The use of paint as a technology to represent landscape is no freer from these biases than a digital image is. To think that throughout the history of Western landscape painting, because these artists used technology such as oil paint to render an image of what we call nature, the painting is more "truthful" than that of an image produced within the world of digital media, I think can be a bit shortsighted. Because of the added dramatization, compositional adjustments, as well as social and political reasons for making these paintings in the first place, I think it's safer to say that these works were inspired by the ecological world that the artist experienced as opposed to seeing them as some kind of bucolic and pastoral direct reflection.

This extended definition of technology has always been something of great interest to me—technology is something that extends back further than what you called the industrialized form of technology that is more commonly understood today. I like to think about how far you can trace back the influence of these pre-photographic image technologies like painting and drawing to see how they still influence expectations of the world today. I think this is a big portion of how we ended up with what I called earlier, a pornographic version of

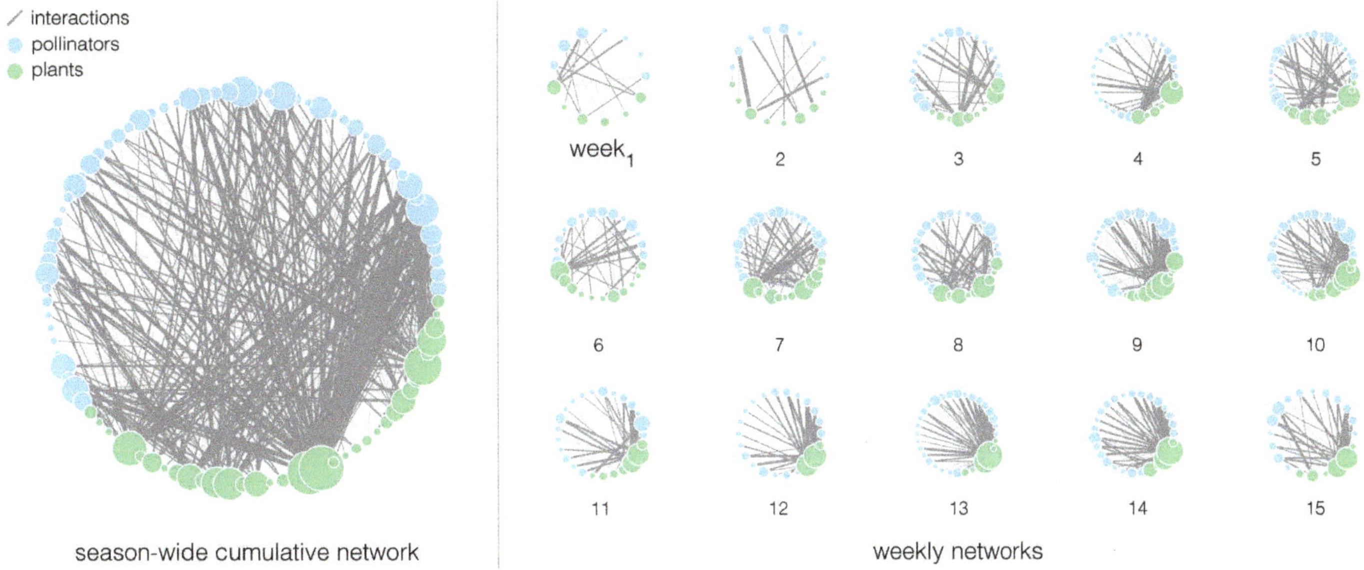

Paul CaraDonna

Temporal flexibility in the structure of plant-pollinator interaction networks.

2020 © Paul CaraDonna

landscape. If you make a search on Google for the Grand Canyon, you'll find images that are neon purple, orange, and blue—images that have run marathons across the internet being downloaded, saturated, compressed, saved, opened, and closed, with each action leaving scars on the image every step of the way. Eventually, you end up with an image that has nearly no basis in reality whatsoever. There is an amount of humor there—a level of absurdity, but their effects on how people expect the world to perform are real. The desire to transform these images in such a way I think stems very much from the history of Western landscape painting. To make perfect the world in front of the maker. These are the kinds of images that I try to both produce and break down in my work.

PC: I'll add to this by referencing some of Mark's past work at the Rocky Mountain Bio Lab—his *Emergence* series from 2014. I found this work to be quite fascinating by the way Mark aimed to emulate the approaches and tools and processes we use in science. What Mark noticed was that as scientists, we go out into nature and we fracture the landscape into pieces as we set up plots and transects where we measure quantities of plants and animals, photosynthetic rates, and other biological processes. In Mark's interpretation of this process, he used his scientific tool—his camera—to capture pieces of the landscape as images. Then he reassembled all these images of the landscape into his own, artificial landscape, but one that has all the things we recognize as a real landscape. What is interesting here, is that this is analogous to how we, as scientists, take all this fractured information and data from the ecosystem and reassemble it to make sense of the ecosystem, which is supposed to represent truth or reality—or at least that's the assumption. We reassemble all sorts of information, data, papers, and ideas, and in this kind of conceptual and theoretical sense, we try and create this depiction

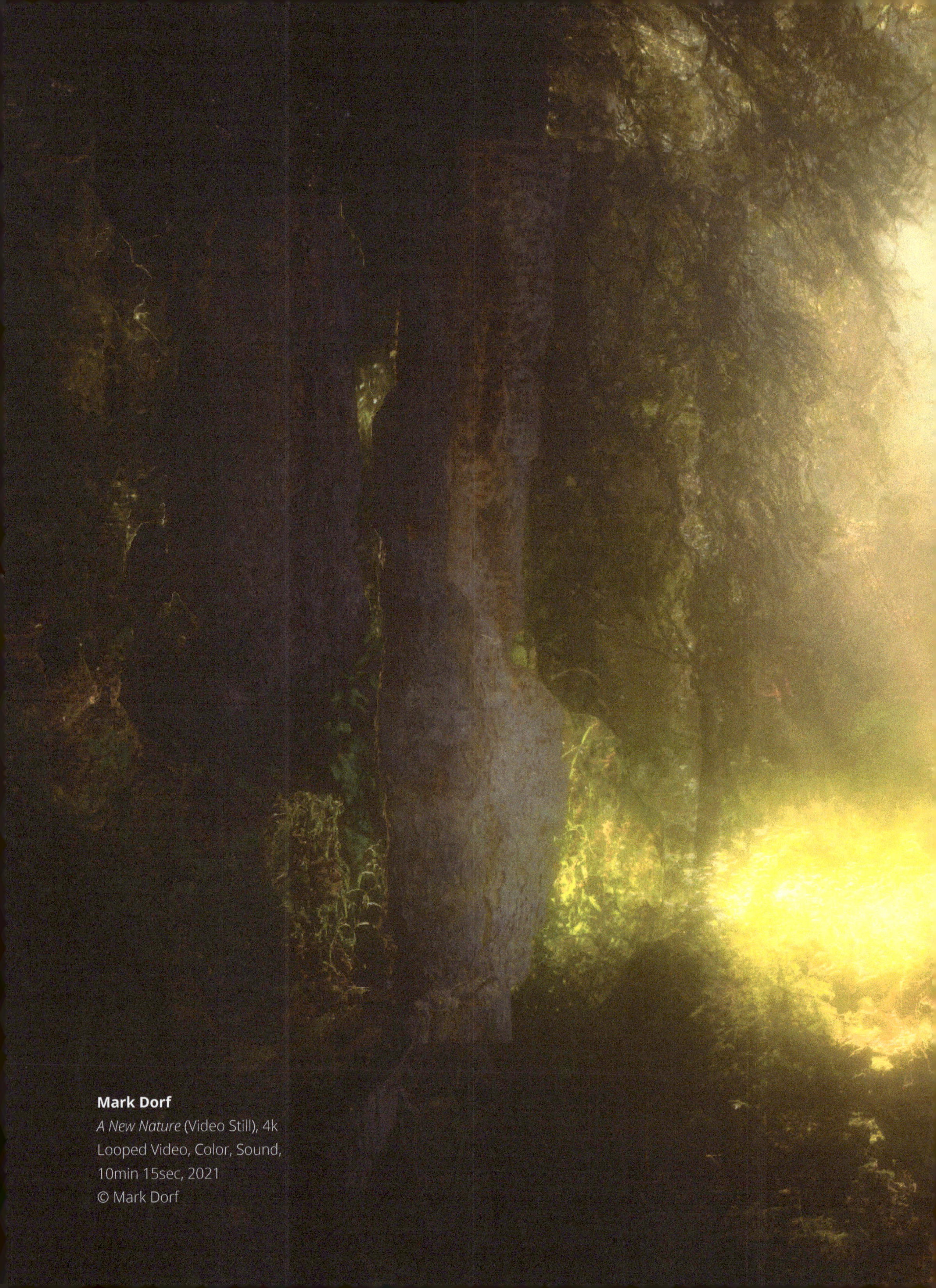

Mark Dorf
A New Nature (Video Still), 4k
Looped Video, Color, Sound,
10min 15sec, 2021
© Mark Dorf

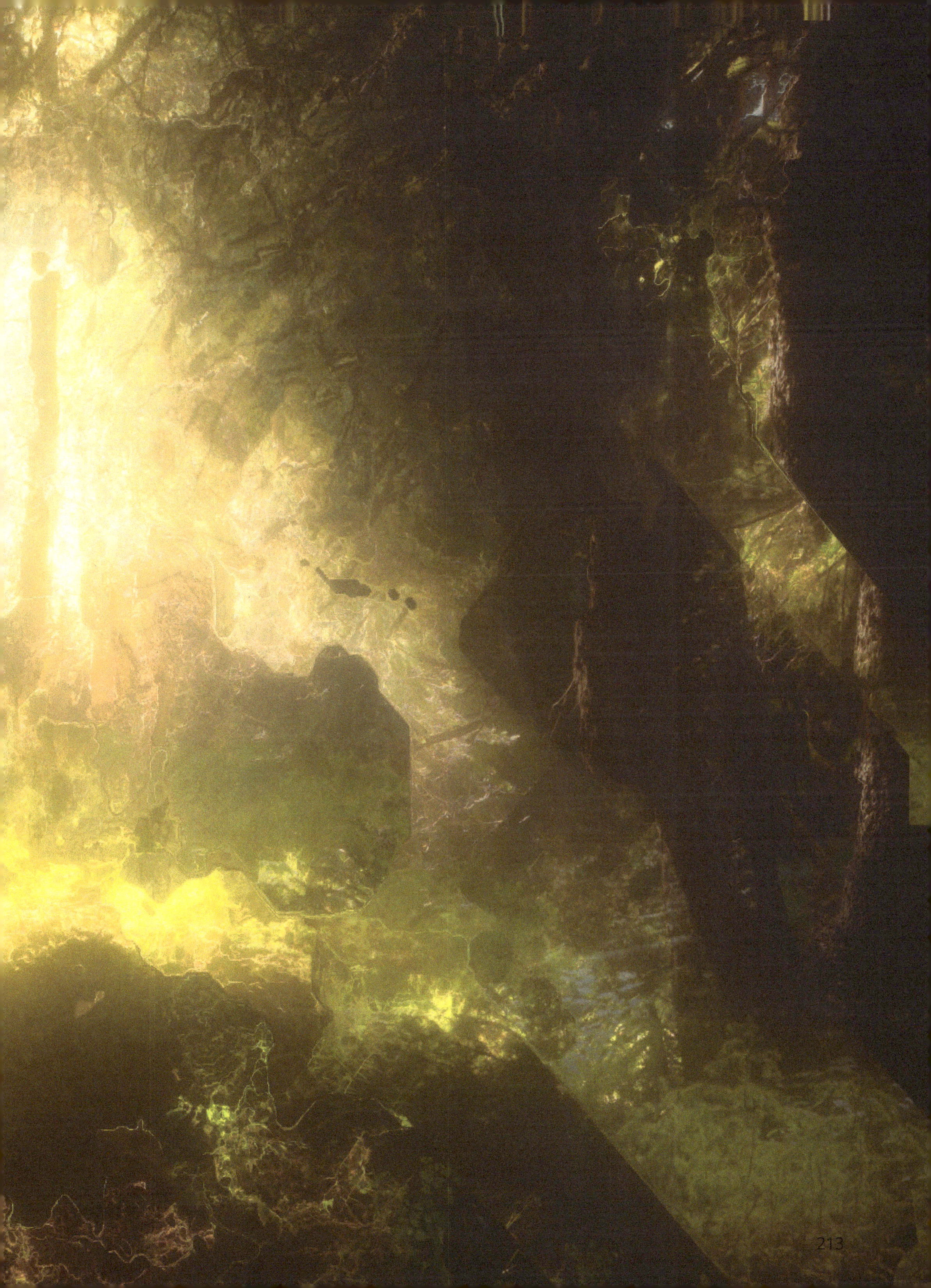

of truth in nature, whether it is expressed as a mathematical theory or a series of hypotheses and evidence that points in a certain direction.

With *Emergence*, Mark was doing the same thing. Take, for example, *Reassemblage #3,* which is an image that most certainly looks like a mountain. In fact, it's basically an idyllic mountain, just like one that a child would draw: It's triangular and it's got snow on the top of it. We've even had some people ask where the photo of this mountain was taken from. But when we showcased this work to scientists at the lab, several in the audience immediately objected to the image, noting with strong reactions that it was not real for many reasons: its geology was nonsensical; there were duplicate pieces of mountains within the image of the mountain; and if you look closely, you can see that many of the trees on the mountain were growing sideways. I found this reaction from other scientists to be rather inspiring and telling. When we are faced with a reflection of our [scientific] process in this way, it really challenges the way that we assemble the world and understand nature with our scientific tools. I think it also reveals how this notion of truth, of what nature is, is quite fluid. It's a construct, and it's very much mediated by the tools that we use to understand it. Sometimes I think that in the sciences, maybe we're not challenged with this kind of thing as much as we should be. For example, although we use all sorts of tools and approaches to make sense of nature, it will always remain as some form of abstraction of nature.

For example, here is a scientific figure from some of my research. What we have here is a series of ecological networks depicting which plants and pollinators are interacting with one another over the growing season in the mountains. Within the context of this work, one point we've made is that as soon as we put things together in this way—here a network diagram—we're automatically abstracting reality. There are plenty of quantitative tools that we can use to analyze these ecological networks so we can better understand their stability and robustness to change—but it's still always some kind of abstraction, no matter how we look at it! I would argue, that as a whole, I wouldn't say that science is particularly comfortable with challenging the assumptions that we make, and how we try and generalize and make sense of the world. I think it's healthy to have work that can push against this. To be clear, by no means am I suggesting that what we do as scientists is wrong. Rather, I just think it is a nice reminder that it is all an abstraction of reality in some way mediated through human cultural constructs. It is just one way of knowing the world we live in.

GA: It's a series of very interesting points, Paul. As a scientist, you navigate a very different territory, and yet one that overlaps with artistic questions. I wonder, too about the speculative dimension of what art does, and the speculative dimension of science. I have, at times, encountered resistance from the sciences in the context of collaborations that entailed the word "speculative". This resistance is particularly surprising given that always speculates at one point or another at least before it finds an epistemic path.

I might be wrong about this. You can correct me, Paul. On the opposite side of the spectrum, art is by nature speculative, at least contemporary art is–speculation is what makes art capable of seeing into the future and connecting principles, ideas, and events in ways that surpass the boundaries of classical taxonomies.

Mark said, "I don't feel the responsibility to provide an answer". Some don't agree with this idea and the discrepancy between the expectations of what science should do and what it does are also difficult to negotiate. I'm interested in this question of truth because I feel that the very idea of truth can eventually hinder our thinking and limit our relationship with the world around us. What I'm interested in is the idea of responsibility. I agree with Mark that contemporary art doesn't have to provide an answer. It would be, it feels wrong for the times in which we live philosophically, and culturally. But people expect science to produce truth. How do we negotiate these tensions in art and science projects?

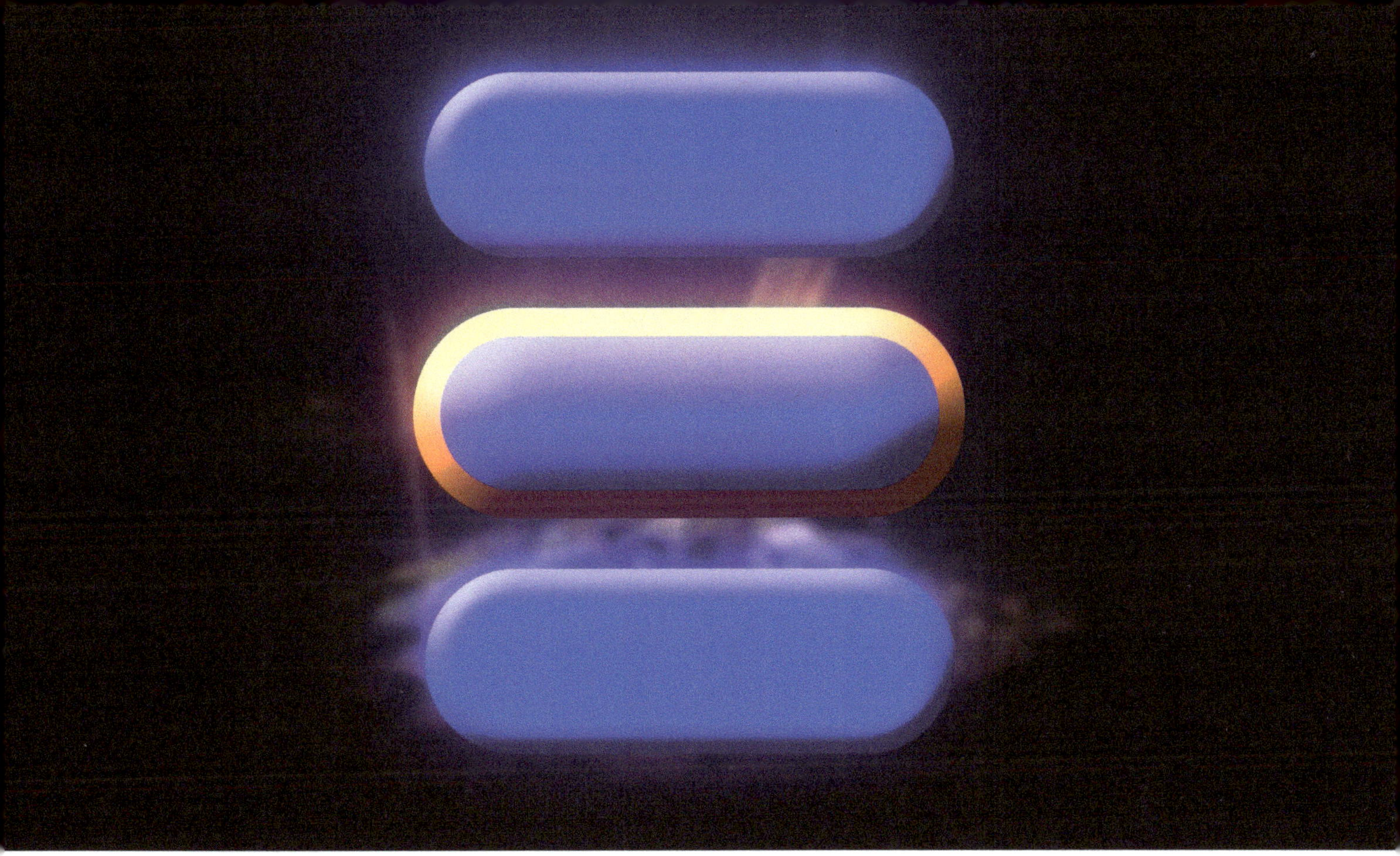

Mark Dorf

A New Nature (Video Still), 4k Looped Video, Color, Sound, 10min 15sec, 2021

PC: I feel like I put on different hats at different times. When I'm writing a scientific paper, there are important formal constraints on how we share and present information. Everything needs to be very clear, explicit, and repeatable. It needs to be framed in the context of the field at that given time. We always have some kind of speculation and interpretation of our results in the discussion part of any scientific paper. But it is a measured amount of speculation. And of course, we have our scientific peer review process, where a reviewer might slap you on the wrist if your speculation and interpretation don't logically follow from your empirical results. But at other times, as the author, you might feel the need to push against the reviewer and make the argument that this is an important point that we need to make. For example, this is where we think the field is heading. We might be wrong, but knowledge is fluid, and we think this is where it is going. And this is our job to continue to figure out where the evidence brings us.

When I'm teaching undergraduate students, I find that there is a common notion that scientific evidence proves that some phenomenon is true. But I always counter that by saying that we don't really prove things in an explicit sense in the sciences because we recognize that our knowledge is fluid and changing in some way. We can never fully capture reality. It is sort of a subtle hint that as scientists, we know that we can't fully capture reality. But I do think that some people convince themselves that what they're learning is a pure reflection of reality. That the evidence that is found is indeed the truth. I disagree with this notion completely. It's just one perspective on reality, and if done well, and in a reproducible way, this perspective can shed light on the mechanisms of how things are working in nature. If the evidence is moving in a particular direction in a consistent manner, we start to have confidence in a prediction for the future. But we'll never really be able to put our finger on the truth.

I'm not always sure that we have these types of discussions in science as much as we should. It's one of the things that I really like about the sort of collaboration and relationship that Mark and I have. I really get to think with someone who, I would argue, is in more of a position to explore that nebulous space. I find that really stimulating because I don't get to do that with my own scientific work all that much. Personally, I don't find any of this at odds with being a scientist. I see it as a different toolkit to address different questions.

With respect to my role as a scientist, I do think it is part of my responsibility to try and figure out how to fix things [in nature]. For example, if we don't understand the problem, then how do we expect to fix it?

For example, how will climate change affect human society in 10 years or 20 years? Are we going to have wild bumble bees pollinating plants in 30 years? Is my daughter going to get to experience these amazing creatures that I have so passionately studied for so many years? I feel it is my responsibility to provide some estimate of the probability that something like this will happen or not, and why.

I also see it as my responsibility as a scientist to help people understand and appreciate the gravity of these problems without needing to understand all of the hardcore scientific details. I think it is really important to help people appreciate the amazing beauty that's out there in nature. That this world that surrounds us is something worth appreciating. And we rely on it to exist! We're part of it! To me, collaborating with Mark allows me to move into this realm in a way that feels a lot harder to do with standard scientific education tools. Nature is not just facts and quantities, there's only a subset of human society across the entire planet that can actually take in that information and make sense of it and do something about it. Even when we have a popular science article written for a general audience, so much of it gets boiled down and lost.

With A New Nature (and Mark's other work), we take a very different approach that hasn't distilled down everything to a few simple factoids or nuggets. I think it really gives the viewer a sense of the vastness of the problems that we're dealing with, but it also provides the viewer with the ability to navigate this vast space, and perhaps even shift their perspective or relationship with nature in some way. I think this is incredibly valuable. I'd like it to be part of my responsibility to help people explore this space.

MD: I like that you brought up the "factual", or quantitative quality in your work, Paul. It feels like you're saying that it's not always useful to think in this concrete manner. Keeping in mind that I am not a scientist, I agree with you. I work towards something similar in my own practice. Personally, I enjoy the essayist flavor of video and contemporary art that is steeped in theory, but that's not really what I'm setting out to do. Rather than quoting theory or quantified facts, in my work, I try to push a sense of emotional knowledge and emotional exploration, albeit informed by theory, towards the environments in which we live. I want to get somebody to feel something through image and sound—whether that is lens-based imagery that is supposedly "factual", I know we've talked about this all afternoon, or a 3D rendered image, or a fully abstract image—it's a unique power of art to speak directly to this emotional response as opposed to the concrete numbers based understanding.

GA: There's an important question here. It's about translation, translation of data, scientific data, translation of discourses that are too specialistic, or that employee jargon that is too cryptic to the public. These collaborations can really help make something tangible and accessible surface. Something audiences can take away and make theirs. This is important If we want to change the course of events, and if we want to effectively motivate people. It seems to me that the conversation has gone far too quickly from not caring about nature to caring about saving the planet without developing a good understanding of plants, animals, ecosystems, and so on. This is certainly what's happened in the arts. Starting roughly with the Renaissance all the way to Romanticism, nature was dismissed as a subcategory in art and culture. The artistic hierarchy reflected Aristotle's scalae naturae and it prioritized anthropocentric subjects like history, mythology, and religion. Nature became a "feminine" subject–a genre lacking moral supremacy. That process of marginalization and erasure came to an end more recently at the beginning of the new millennium with the climate change emergence and the sudden rise in interest in social justice. Finally, climate change is a legitimate topic. But I think that we just rushed to the environment without really understanding the nature problem, how we inherited this concept. Where does it come from? And what we need to do in order to move past it. There has been comparatively little focus on animals and plants per se. And of course, there's been quite an amount of work done in philosophy. In truth, now animals and plants remain subcategories of climate change.

PCD: Something Mark had mentioned just a couple of moments ago was this idea of emotional maturity with our relationship with nature. In science, the tools we use to make sense of nature, truth, and predict the future, however accurate, really have nothing to do with our emotional relationship with nature. This is especially the case, for what Mark referred to as our emotional maturity with nature. Also, Giovanni, you were getting to a similar point too, that perhaps things have moved a bit too fast.

I think it's a really important point to make, and I like to think that our collaboration helps to put us in a better position to consider these kinds of ideas. Where are we with our relationship? What might it look like in the future? And, as we say in *A New Nature*: "We can't break up with nature. This is it. We're stuck with it."

I don't think we spend enough time thinking about this: whether our relationship is one that's emotionally mature. Thinking about this more and grappling with this challenge and creating the space to think about it—is incredibly important.

Mark Dorf is a New York based artist whose practice utilizes photography, video, digital media, and sculpture. Often working directly with ecologists and technologists in the production of his works, Dorf is influenced by human's perceptions of and interactions with what we call "Nature", urbanism, design, and virtual environments. As opposed to seeing these subjects as categorically separate, Dorf reveals their entanglement and integration with one another as an inclusive and lively planetary ecology. Being both self-aware and critical of their own means of production, Dorf's works craft a vision of an ecological future that navigates away from environmental collapse in the Anthropocene and imagine *A New Nature*.

Paul CaraDonna, PhD, is conservation scientist and professor at the Chicago Botanic Garden and Northwestern University. He conducts field-based ecological research at the Rocky Mountain Biological Laboratory in Colorado, USA, each summer. He and his research group focus on the mutualistic interactions between plants and pollinators as a focal system for asking fundamental ecological questions and understanding the consequences of global change. CaraDonna has published more than 30 peer-reviewed publications in scientific journals, and he is the co-founded the Art-Science Exchange, an artist in residence project that seeks to enhance the intellectual collaboration between the arts and the sciences.

Dorion Sagan's thermodynamics of life

Self-described as an artist stuck in the body of a science writer, the writer, theorist, and independent scholar, Dorion Sagan is author or coauthor of twenty-five books translated into fifteen languages, including several with biologist Lynn Margulis on planetary biology and evolution by symbiosis. He has also collaborated with Eric D. Schneider on the thermodynamics of life, and theoretical biologist Josh Mitteldorf on the evolution of aging.

in conversation: **Dorion Sagan and Ken Rinaldo**

Dorion Sagan is a celebrated writer, ecological philosopher, and author or coauthor of twenty-five books, which have been translated into fifteen languages. As an ecological theorist he has been at the forefront of bringing our growing understanding of symbiosis as a major force in evolution into the intellectual mainstream, both within science and the humanities, and rethinking the human body as a "multispecies organism." Sagan has recently continued his lifelong efforts to decenter the human by proposing the concept of Cyanocene in response to the Anthropocene debates (e.g., "Coda: Beautiful Monsters: Terra in the Cyanocene," *Arts of Living on a Damaged Planet*, University of Minnesota, 2017). A serial collaborator on scientific, intellectual, and artistic projects, Sagan's work ethic follows that of evolving life, whose creativity derives largely from symbiotic merger and genetic recombination. With Carl Sagan and Lynn Margulis, his parents, he is coauthor of the entries for both "Life" and "Extraterrestrial Life" in the Encyclopedia Britannica.

The international impact and collaborative character of his work is demonstrated, for example, by the fact that his writing is now regularly used in Japan for college preparation exams. Sagan's close collaborations with multiple scientists from different fields including evolution, ecology, and thermodynamics have helped usher in new, more integral and realistic biological approaches which recognize humanity as a very recent part of a four-billion-year-old biosphere, with important implications for both medicine and the long-term viability of the human species as a planetary life form. His coauthored critiques have helped effect a rapprochement between neo-Darwinism and the biochemistry and microbial ecology of group selection, one bearing fruits for example in the new emphasis among health professionals on the importance of the human microbiome. Sagan has published with university presses (e.g., Yale, Harvard, Oxford, MIT, and University of Chicago), including in anthologies edited by E. O. Wilson and Richard Dawkins in the sciences, and alongside luminaries such as John A. Wheeler, Ursula K. Le Guin, and Jean-Paul Sartre in humanities collections. Increasingly referenced and influential within both academia and popular culture, he is regularly cited by feminist theorists, environmentalists, and drug liberation advocates. Deleuzian political theorist William Connolly of John Hopkins University has described Dorion Sagan's theorization of teleodynamism (explanations of the world that combine natural forces with micro-agency) as "pursu[ing] these theoretical and experimental lines while actively resisting capture by neoliberalism." His work has appeared in *Natural History, Smithsonian, Wired, Cabinet*, and *The New York Times*, among other publications. He is a member of the Lindisfarne Association and the Advisory Network of Psymposia, as well as on the boards of Sputnik Inc and the Pioneer Valley Coral & Natural Science Institute. *Nature* magazine named the book to which he contributed, *Fine Lines: Vladimir Nabokov's Scientific Art* as one of their Top Twenty books of 2016. In 2014 Kevin Kelly, for The Long Now Foundation, listed his book *Biospheres: Metamorphosis of Planet Earth*, a Selected Book for the Manual for Civilization.

Son of astronomer-educator Carl Sagan and renowned American biologist Lynn Margulis, whose complex work he was the first to popularize, Dorion edited and introduced the 2012 collection, *Lynn Margulis: The Life and Legacy of a Scientific Rebel*, an IndieFab Award Winner in ForeWord Reviews' Adult Nonfiction Biography category. He contributed to software developer Bill Atkinson's digital photography book, *Within the Stone*, an American Photo "Best Photo Book of 2004" in the category of "Art and Science." In 2003 he was Humana scholar at Centre College in Danville, Kentucky; in 1986 he won an Educational Press Association of America Excellence in Educational Journalism Award for the article, "The Riddle of Sex," and in 1974 he won Blue Ribbon in the youth contest for sleight of hand in Silent Mora Ring 122, the Boston Chapter of the International Brotherhood of Magicians. He was called an "unmissable modern master" by Stephen Young in *New Scientist*; Nobel laureate Roald Hoffman tagged his book, *Into the Cool: Energy Flow, Thermodynamics, and Life* with Eric D. Schneider "fascinating"; and Melvin Konner, in *The New York Times*, wrote of *Microcosmos*, coauthored with long-time writing partner Lynn Margulis, that "this admiring reader of Lewis Thomas, Carl Sagan and Stephen Jay Gould has seldom, if ever, seen such a luminous prose style in a work of this kind." *What is Life?*, also coauthored with Margulis, was included on a list of "Mind-Altering Masterpieces" by the Utne Reader, and was called "A masterpiece of science writing" by Orion magazine. Sagan has also collaborated on books with British neuroscientist John Skoyles, biosphere system theorist Tyler Volk of New York University (Death/Sex), and theoretical biologist, Josh Mitteldorf (*Cracking the Aging Code*; UK, Australia: *What Good is Death?*). This last book, "the most original popular science book you're likely to read this year," according to Peter D. Kramer, Professor Emeritus of Psychiatry and Human Behavior, Brown University, mounts strong evidence that aging, genetically underlain, tends to prevent fast-growing species from overgrowing their ecosystems. Dorion's current interests include fiction writing, literary criticism, philosophy, and the arts. He is here interviewed exclusively for *Antennae* by bio artist Ken Rinaldo.

Ken Rinaldo: What inspired you to become interested in the origin of life, and how has your understanding of this topic evolved?

Dorion Sagan: I became interested in the origin of life once I thought such a thing was possible. Like anyone else, I was influenced by my parents, and peers. As soon as I finished college (Umass, Amherst, a public school), I was recruited to write books on evolution, with my mother, the great, late-twentieth and early 21st century biologist, Lynn Margulis.

The electron transport energetics of life - which supports many forms of metabolism beyond those of mere animals - seems anticipated in minerals and inorganic chemistry. Life could have originated on Earth, or migrated from space - or, with logic rather than mysticism, it may always have been. When I worked with Eric D. Schneider on the thermodynamics-of-life book, *Into the Cool* (University of Chicago Press, 2006) we explored the possibility of life's origins from inorganic sulfur and iron chemistry, one of many suggestions. But the initial great excitement over the possibility of a local origin came in 1953. This was the year before my astronomically minded future father, and my more cosmopolitan-minded future mother met at the University of Chicago. He was still eighteen, she just fifteen. Carl's future thesis advisor, Harold Urey, a, if not the world expert on cosmic chemistry, guided his graduate student Stanley Miller in a Frankenstein-like experiment: exposing a mock-up of the predicted Earth's early atmosphere - mostly hydrogen-rich gases - to a lightning-like electric discharge. At the time of the presumed origin of life, hydrogen, the lightest element, had yet to escape into space after the birth of the Sun. When gases like water (H_2O), ammonia (NH_3) and methane (CH_4) spontaneously reacted to form amino acids, the key ingredients of proteins, some of the basic materials from which life forms itself and now formed in the lab. Mary Shelley would have been proud.

But did life evolve on Earth? When the brilliant astronomer Fred Hoyle, who coined the term Big Bang but didn't believe in it, wrote the book *The Intelligent Universe*, I was a little surprised that my father gave it a favorable review. I was surprised because Hoyle thought there was no chance that life evolved on Earth. Indeed, he, is credited with discovering the process by which helium becomes carbon inside stars – part of the famous statement that we are "star-stuff," of us carbon-based life forms as touted by Feynman, Sagan and others – said that it was no more likely than a Boeing 747 might be spontaneously assembled by "a tornado sweeping through a junkyard". The comment, latched on to by creationists, ignores the fact that Hoyle by definition wasn't creationist because he considered the cosmos eternal. Hoyle was a fan of panspermia, the idea that Earth life comes from elsewhere in space. Hoyle, who my future father sought in the halls of Caltech in 1956 at 21 when he was meeting people and scouting grad school for his 18-year-old girlfriend, my future mother, thought Mars might have gotten its red surface from from Pedobacterium, an iron oxidizing bacterium; he thought viruses and bacteria from space would be more likely to land when the Sun's magnetic field periodically abates; and in *The Intelligent Universe,* he suggested a kind of eternal battle between life and matter. But I knew that my dad, who kept frozen tanks of hydrogen-rich frozen gases rotating in the lab across from his office – a mockup of the outer solar system where he imagined life might just now be evolving – imagined biogenesis, spontaneous generation of life from nonlife, on Earth or elsewhere.

Thus, when I asked him how he could praise Hoyle's book when panspermia simply jettisoned the problem of life's origins into outer space without answering it, he semi-apologetically shrugged and said without seeming the humor that aging British scientists tended to go a bit dotty in their old age). In retrospect, it seems clear that whatever processes might have happened on Earth to cause biogenesis could also happen have happened elsewhere. Moreover, today we know there are microbes all over the ISS (International Space Station), and there have been many discoveries of extremely hardy extremophiles, prokaryotes suggested to be viable for thousands or even millions of years between phases of active growth. Some may even slowly metabolize on long-distance voyages, for example, in the icy centers of comets.

I now think that the fantastic success of the Miller-Urey experiments, which gave experimental validation of theories by J.B.S. Haldane in the West and Alexander Oparin in Russia, that life could evolve from inanimate matter, biased the fascinating possibility that life could have evolved in situ. And it is crucial to remember that from a history-of-science perspective the deep medieval belief in "spontaneous generation" – that meat could pullulate into maggots, and rags revert to rats – was triumphantly disproved by science. Only with the careful experiments of Spallanzani and Pasteur, using clean glassware, was it realized that life always comes from previous life; it is everywhere, and often invisible. But the 1953 Miller-Urey experiments showed the ease with which some of life's main chemicals can arise. It seems that scientists, like everyone else, did not want to be wrong about being wrong: after disproving the superstitious magic of medieval spontaneous generation, but then showing experimentally that spontaneous generation was indeed quite possible, they were – and are – in no hurry to change their mind again!

KR: Can you explain the second law of thermodynamics in layperson's terms and how it relates to the evolution of complex systems leaving chaos in their wake?

DS: The famous second law of thermodynamics, with its fetishized central term, "entropy", describes a basic and familiar process, but one which is nonetheless crucial to the understanding of complex systems, including ourselves. Entropy is a measure of the spread of energy. At our scale it inevitably tends to increase. In a simple system, for example a room with a burning stick of incense, there are more ways for the smoke to be spread out than not. Similarly, wherever you are sitting now, there is a possibility that all the oxygen atoms in the room will aggregate in a corner and you will asphyxiate; but the chances are so low they can safely be ignored. The association of entropy with "disorder" is, however, misleading. This is because naturally complex systems, including living ones such as ourselves, naturally increase the spread of energy; indeed, that may be their prosaic, metabiological purpose: far from impeding the spread of energy, complex cycling systems at our scale actively aid and abet it. We eat breathe drink metabolize grow reproduce build technologize etc. - all these things not only spread energy through our necessarily open cellular and bodily systems but tend to keep the entropy-producing process going! Far from violating the second law of thermodynamics with their stunning "order," living systems epitomize the process of entropy production - they are active rather than passive entropy producers.

The simplistic identification of entropy with disorder, as the late Frank L. Lambert showed, leads to unnecessary confusions. Almost any collection of atoms above room temperature is almost infinitely disordered, he says, speaking in terms of equilibrium thermodynamics. Equilibrium thermodynamics is classical thermodynamics, a practical science that explored the ways of deriving energy from fuel, and increasing the efficiency of machines.

Complex systems belong to the realm of nonequilibrium thermodynamics. These are systems from that, far from being disordered, are organized, cycling matter internally but also producing wastes, and dispersing energy. Storm systems, autocatalytic chemical reactions, and life are all naturally occurring three-dimensional complex systems. More energy is spread with them than without them and that realization, I"ve argued, is a fourth Copernican revolution: not only are we not at the center of the universe; not only are we not made out of some special stuff; not only are we not the highest life form but part of an evolutionary process; but we also, as living beings, do not violate the second law; far from it, as active entropy producers, we exemplify the very process it describes.

KR: How would you describe NET or non-equilibrium thermodynamics to a layperson?

DS: In thermodynamics "isolated" systems are ones completely protected from all energy and matter exchange across their borders. They are abstract, and ultimately imaginary because all real systems are exposed to gravity, which not only knows no borders, but can create order, producing stars and their new elements from which life itself might arise as geochemistry (or its extraterrestrial equivalent) becomes biochemistry.

Somewhat confusingly, "closed" systems in classical thermodynamics remain open to the exchange of energy, such as heat or electromagnetic radiation, but not materials. NET specifically studies systems that are open and display some sort of evolving organization or ordered. These are not computer programs but actual three-dimensional assemblages, which can be chemical or physical, that have a coherence and a kind of primitive metabolism suggestive of the sort of identity and energy exchange we see in life. Nonequilibrium systems, which in *Into the Cool* we call "the organisms of physics" need not be alive. They do, however, like life, require gradients, differences across a distance, whether of temperature, pressure, or electron potential; they feed on these differences and tend to reduce them, using and spreading energy as they "live," for however long. Convection, such as the hexagonal flow structures called "Bénard cells" first found beneath heated photographic plates, is spontaneous hydrodynamic process that accelerates energy dissipation. So is whirlpool, a continuous whirlpool downstream of Niagara Falls, as well as the biosphere's steady wind and water currents, visible by satellites from space. So are autocatalytic chemical reactions, such as the Belousov-Zhabotinski reaction, which cyclically changes colors to the extent that a priest in an elevator at Georgetown University, seeing one held by a scientist, was prompted to comment: "Are those alive?" to which the scientist replied, "No,

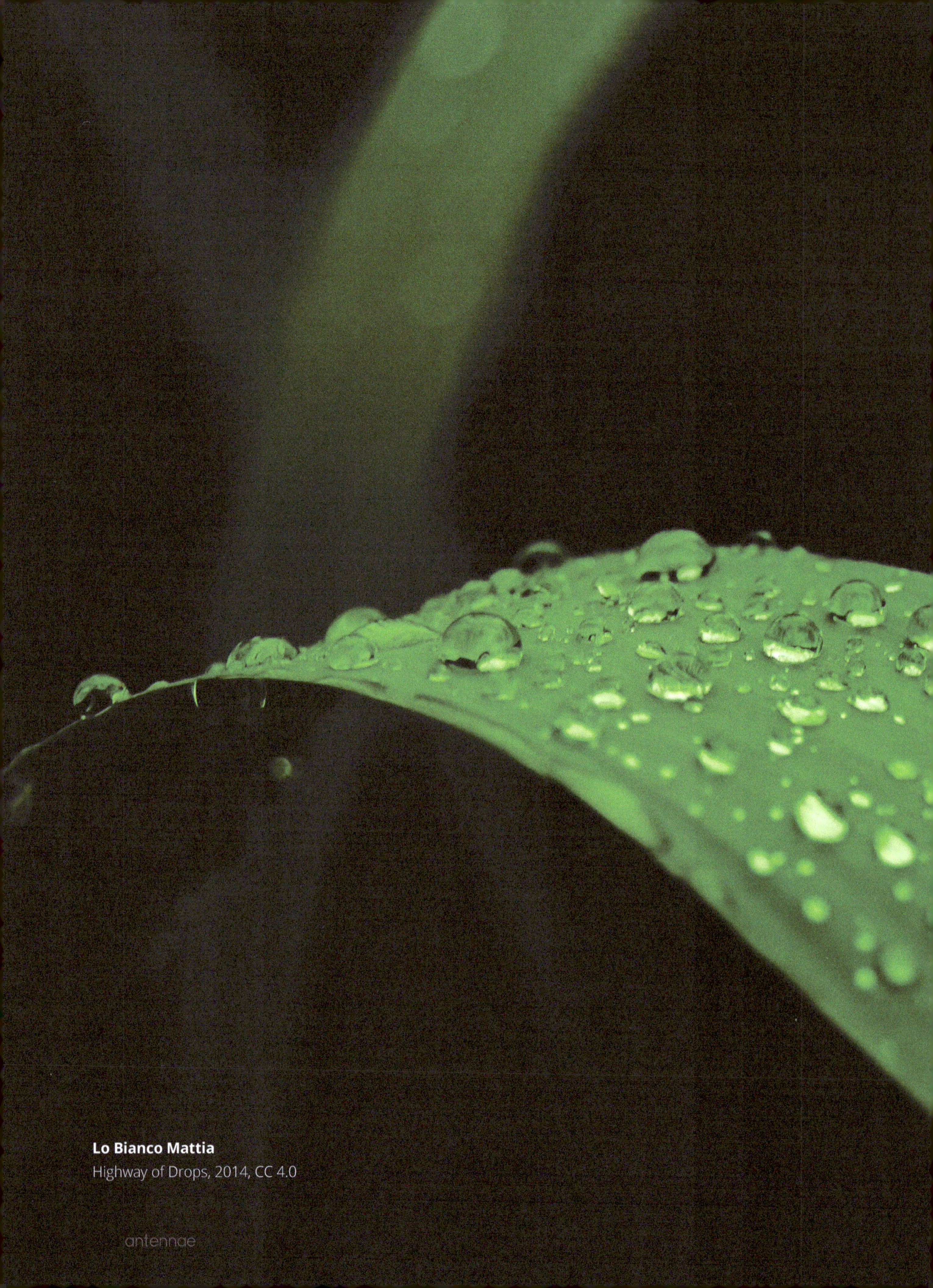

Lo Bianco Mattia
Highway of Drops, 2014, CC 4.0

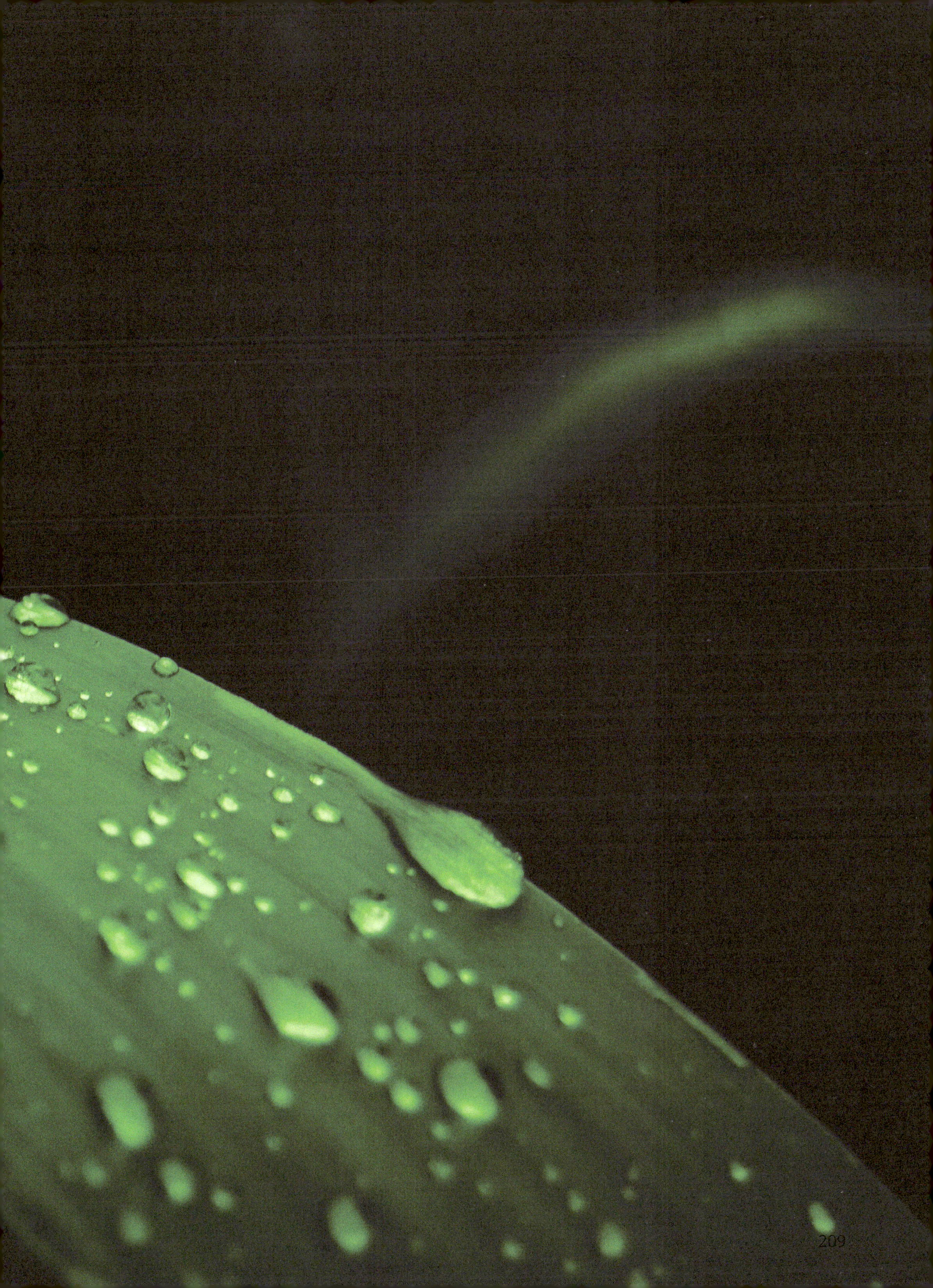

father, they are like you; they metabolize but don't reproduce."

Life itself, from its semipermeable free-living cells, to organisms such as ourselves grown from cells, to the biosphere as a whole, are all metastable, non-equilibrium systems, actively dumping entropy – as solid, liquid, gas or, in the instance of the basically "closed" system, the biosphere, heat – into space. Living systems sense their surroundings and, while they require a source of energy to metabolize, if they use it too fast, or destroy themselves or their ecosystems in doing so, they perish in the aftermath. Indeed, I would diagnose climate warming, insofar as it exists, as literal global thermodynamic dysfunction, insofar as waste heat begins to accumulate too close to life's sensitive surfaces, threatening its dissipative efficacy. NET systems are fascinating. One peculiarity of NET systems is that they have a history and exhibit a sort of physical memory. Taylor vortices, counter-rotating pairs of vortices in fluids that form between counter-rotating metal cylinders, jump to new stable states of fewer numbers of vortex pairs when their rotational energy gradient is lowered. When dictyostelid amoebas run out of food, they secrete cAMP, a signal molecule, and merge to become multinucleate organisms. It is as if they have evolutionarily learned that, under potentially fatal stress, they need to join together to preserve their gradient-reducing form.

NET illuminates' life as not just as an informational system, but, more primarily a metabolic and energetic system involved in steady gradient reduction or entropy production.

KR: You have said, "What we call life is really a form of water, activated and animated not by a divine principle but by the energetic cosmos around it." Can you tell us a bit more?

DS: Well, Arthur C. Clarke pointed out that "our" planet, two-thirds of whose surface is water, would more fairly be called Ocean. Living matter is 70% water; you are seventy percent water. Science (fiction) imagines space as an ocean with planets as islands to be colonized by spaceships as Europeans colonized continents, but space is far more forbidding and planets and moons are not islands; we have not even colonized the oceans. Water is not just a substance but functional: despite the focus on carbon dioxide, water is the most important greenhouse gas: while mists produced by plants heat locally, plant transpiration – the movement of water from roots to leaves and subsequent evaporation – is key to the forming of cooling, light reflecting clouds. Satellite images have revealed Borneo and the Amazon to be as cool in the summer as Siberia in the winter. And an estimated seventy percent of Earth's forests have been cut down by humans in the last two-hundred years. Given that most of the energy gathered by photosynthesis goes not into tree growth and reproduction but into this cooling evapotranspiration, the cardinal "greenhouse" sin committed by humans may not be the production of carbon dioxide, but the destruction of old growth and rainforests. In our religiously macho fantasies of being the highest life form about to conquer the cosmos we are, as they used to say in the thirties, "all wet." In fact, even literally we are not the highest life form: trees are higher.

KR: The Bower bird's creation of a beautiful nest is an example of how sexual selection can drive the evolution of ornamental traits. Females choose males based on the quality of their nest-building and decoration skills, which drives the evolution of more elaborate and complex nests. As art and expression in human cultures, and perhaps the cultures of Bower birds building nests to attract mates, do art and aesthetics play a role in understanding the origins and evolution of life and the natural world more broadly? Can the bower bird's behavior and the evolution of ornamental traits inform our understanding of the role of aesthetics in human culture and society?

DS: Bower birds are apparently so wild about the color sky-blue that males specifically collect this color – including from glass bottles and even blue laundry powder to build their bowers – which supposedly attract females to enter them but then are destroyed in vigorous acts of mating. Darwin's theory of sexual selection – in which he theorized that female choice of males helps shape species – because it is a last vestige, so to speak, of Darwin's forerunners such as Buffon, Lamarck, and Erasmus Darwin (his grandfather) who granted a greater role to the choices of organisms in the evolutionary process. Protist unicells known as foraminifera, important in the locating gas-and-oil deposits, make their shells from various materials. One experiment showed that, when offered, they will choose certain shapes and colors of glass beads over others, in building their shells, or tests. I am persuaded by Samuel Butler, the 19th century novelist and critic of Darwin, who argued that microbes may sense, and have their own "tool-kits," and that the sensations, responses, and habits of nonliving organisms play a role in evolution. From this perspective human aesthetics – who do we associate with? Support? What materials, beings? – would be no exception – not only for us in the near term, but for our descendants, if any. In evolution calcium ions toxic to marine microbes, dumped outside cell membranes, evolved into shells, and later, the bones of multicellular organisms. As active, entropy-producing thermodynamic systems, both in our bodies and our tech, we cannot avoid producing wastes; the aesthetic – which is also the ecological and evolutionary question – is how we integrate them into a four-billion-year living system, which will continue with or without us.

KR: As a young man, my interest in science and ecology began after reading Rachel Carson's *Silent Spring* because it was so poetic; how has your background in magic, poetry, and philosophy influenced your scientific work, and vice versa, and what are some of your favorite examples of art or literature that explore themes related to the origin of life or the natural world? What do you see as the ideal relationship between science and art, and what do you think each field can learn from the other? How do you balance your roles as a science writer, and do you find that one informs the other unexpectedly?

DS: As "an artist stuck in the body of a science writer," I would describe the term science writer, the job description, as Aaronic, referring to Aaron, Moses's brother who was charged, because Moses had trouble speaking. Aaron mediates between the word of God – today Science, if you like, described by a mosaic of scientists – to the masses. Although God's face is not described in the Bible, the typical science writer likes to describe what kind of tie or dress his scientist is wearing, what he or she ordered for lunch.

Such writing embarrasses me; perhaps it is a form of what philosopher Bernard Stiegler would call proletarianization, putting things in their places, a psychosocial flattening to match the economic reductionism of modern life and the media attention it thrives on. True wealth is multiple cultures, and diverse forms of knowledge, including ecological knowledge and aesthetic knowhow. If global warming is literal thermodynamic dysfunction – too much heat produced in the vicinity of the entropy-producing system – then the levelling of the internet, cell phones, and social media may be its sick and sociopathological counterpart, an "artificially intelligent" non-culture, which has forgotten many kinds of depth, and is busy not passing them down to the next generation – part of what Stiegler calls the Entropocene.

Here I think of what the indigenous philosopher and activist Ailton Krenak bluntly wrote, "there are no more scientists." Science has been hijacked by publishing, consensus, information management, academic pressures, vocational emphases, ego, government appropriation, in short, proletarianization: it has been subsumed to money, power, machinic explanation, publicity, governmental machinations. It has lost touch with its heart, the search for knowledge for its own sake, whether we like it or not, and the revelation-like power of a beautiful theory.

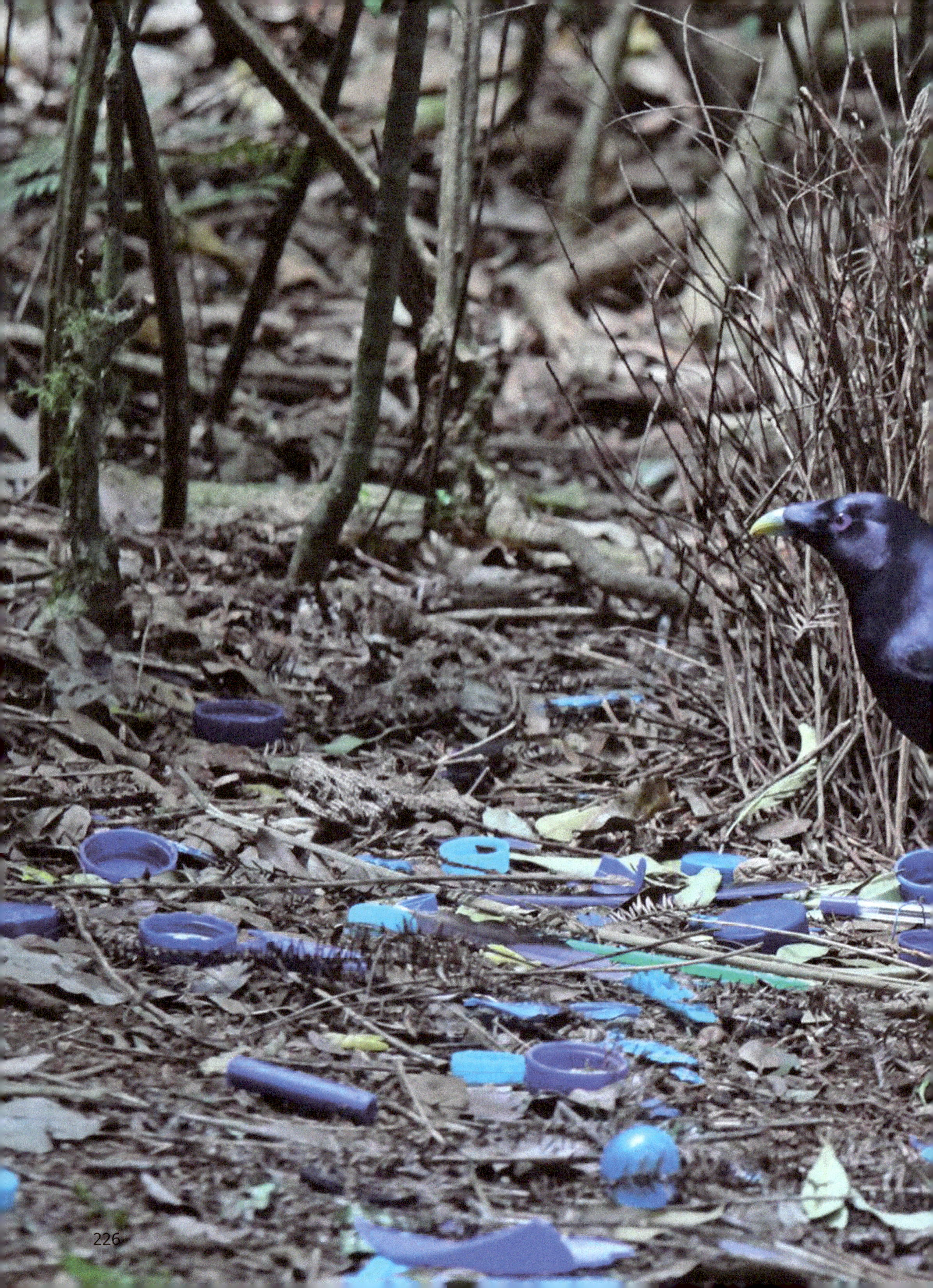

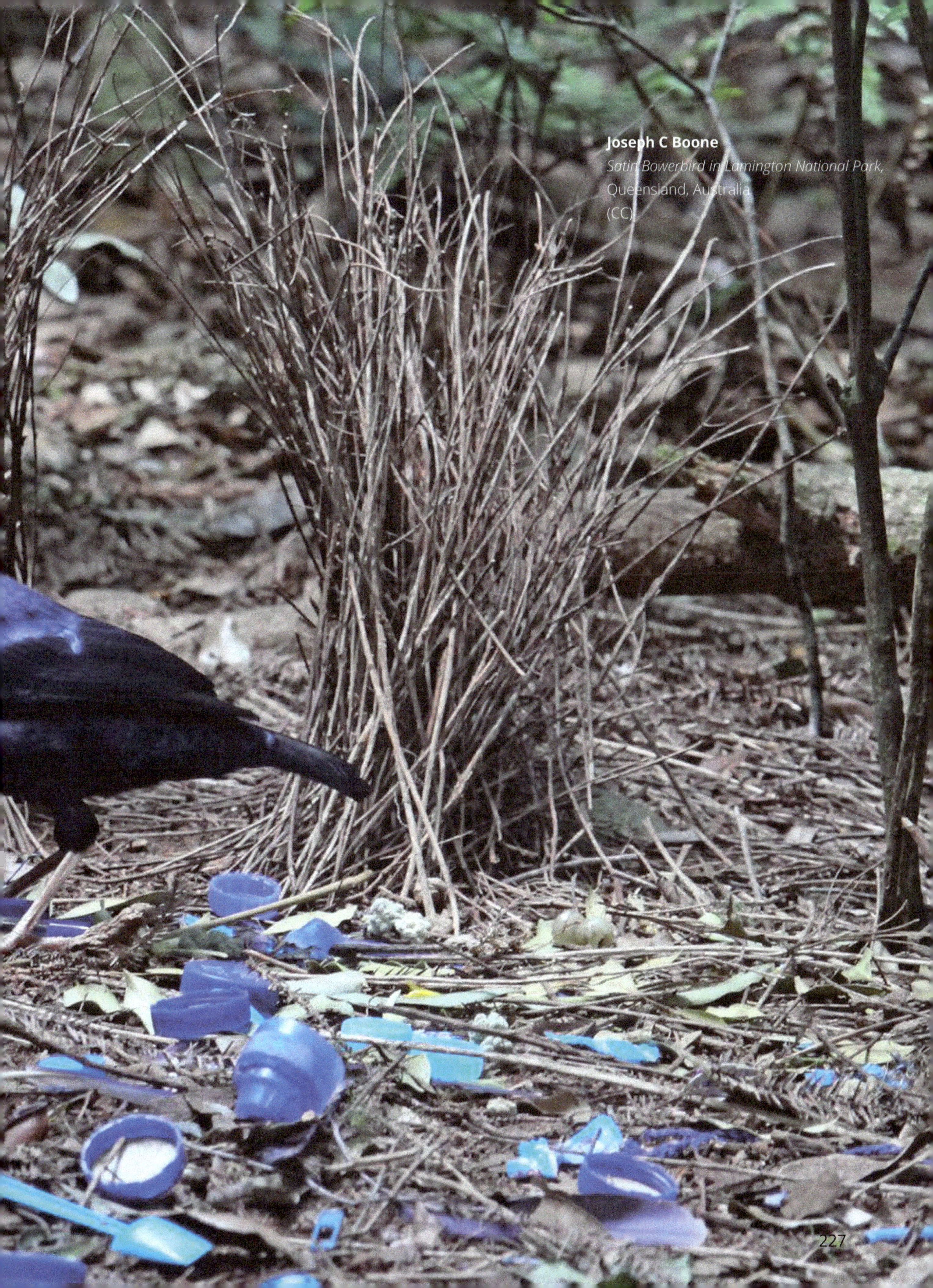

Joseph C Boone
Satin Bowerbird in Lamington National Park,
Queensland, Australia
(CC)

The institutionalization, monetization of science, and its intercalation into a global behemoth of digital sound bites algorithmically trying to sell stuff is a sad spectacle to behold. So is the confusion of knowledge with back-tested supercomputer models. On the other hand, there may be no source so rich for poetry as the subjects explored by science, the need for whose graceful exposition, if anything, increases with the introduction of science writing as a genre. Science, real science, provides material for the flashing heart of the real to show beneath the veil of concepts and words.

KR: The representation of nature artistically, scientifically, and mathematically are all codes of sorts and create factors that impact how and what we believe. It is exciting that Deep mind Alpha fold is using data to predict the 3D structure of proteins, given amino acid sequences, and now reveals the underlying relationships between predicted structures of plants, bacteria, animals, and other organisms and may reveal deep underlying ecological relations. In this process, new and exciting maps, pictorial and relational, will emerge. Do you feel we are experiencing a renaissance with conceptual and artistic flowers emerging from the dark of isolated misunderstandings for an evolution toward an informed "fluid celebration of bio-continuity?" What do you imagine will be the power of this emerging data? Is technology recapitulating phylogeny?

DS: Computers certainly can run algorithms faster, and AlphaZero's beating of IBM's Deep Blue, which beat Kasparov, shows that machine learning faster than humans can keep up can triumph in chess. But computers remain automatons, with no inner sensing (although humans can mistake, a la Turing, computer (and other) operations for sensate being, for organisms with innerness. However, I remain deeply suspicious of computers, or AI, as being capable of innovating anything like a paradigm shift, or new thought style, foundational for epistemologist of science Ludwig Fleck, and his follower, Thomas Kuhn, in producing scientific breakthroughs, important new theories. On the other hand, computer operations, taking the place of human thinking, can aid in military and advertising campaigns, and is already a dangerous handmaiden of capitalism, for example in the data mining of social media, also used for nefarious political purposes. Though protein folding may be an exception, computerization also creates serious problems for science. To take an important example, the IPCC climate models, run on supercomputers, do not even integrate biological feedbacks into their models. Nor do they include the role of water, considered the most important greenhouse gas; and their predictions have been consistently wrong.

Insensate computers may be able to divine the recesses of protein folding, but I'm not sure the Sorcerer's Apprentice-like proliferation of models and digital possibilities will head unimpeded towards your "fluid celebration of bio-continuity." Even the idea of integrating sensors into agroecological enclaves, let alone actual rainforests, seems a possible step in the wrong direction, speaking for life collectively. One can never underestimate the arrogance of humans. Once the world was made in the image of a being like ourselves; now we consider ourselves God, with the powers to create heaven, and life in the form of technology and genes, in our own own hands. But the history of evolution rarely bodes well for those who destroy their ecosystems. An exception is cyanobacteria, whose release of oxygen gas toxified the Earth's whole atmosphere, killing their own and many others, destroying anaerobic ecosystems at the surface, and driving others into the Hades of subterranean life (with some surviving safe inside the bodies of surface organisms, including our own ancestors). But now we live on an oxygen-rich planet, and some of the survivors of the oxygen catastrophe, alphaproteobacteria, drive our own metabolism as mitochondria. Evolution is not always a pretty picture, but it is always based on ecological recycling, the wastes of some becoming the food of others. It always requires multiple forms of metabolism, and is now a deeply multi-species project. We can destroy our ecosystems and ourselves, but seems to me a delusion to think we are a threat to the biosphere as a whole, or that we can create actual life organic intelligence in the form of AI. Nonetheless, over evolutionary time the house can become the body

– the toxic calcium ions extruded upon pain of death by marine unicells, now graces spiral shells we pick up on the sand, provides the infrastructure of our skull and bones, and is involved in the electrochemistry of the nervous system and brain. Some chitons have teeth made of magnetite, ancient bacteria were involved in the deposition of iron from which we make our cars, and magnetotactic bacteria use Earth's magnetic field to swim away from surface oxygen. Life has always been technological, but it's difficult to imagine any species besting humans in technological arrogance. Here again we can sense a threat to the best possible science by the powers of dopamine-triggering media attention, by technology itself, sired by science, increasingly commercialized and politically coopted, science that should be the pursuit of knowledge for its own sake, not for power, prestige, job security or financial gain. Luckily, as Spinoza suggested, scientific seeking provides its own pleasures, and knowing is its own sublime reward. It does not help that one can see the loss of science in the name of science due to the forces of economics in a fateful evolutionary context, one that nonetheless we can hope to avoid. As my mother, and writing partner for three decades, Lynn Margulis, wrote in *Symbiotic Planet* (I ghost wrote the first draft), "The tendency of 'independent' life is to bind together and reemerge in ... new wholeness[s] at ... higher, larger level[s] of organization."

This awesome but disturbing process, in which selves become subordinate or even ghostly semblances of their former selves, seems at play in the continuing malaise of social media, where human "individuals" are morphing from being full-body beings to nodes in ameboid technocapitalist masses. Good science, I think, following the great American ecology G. Evelyn Hutchinson, is like good art, and good theory is like a beautiful work of art. But, as the previously mentioned Samuel Butler – author of *Erewhon, The Way of All Flesh,* and several self-published books on evolution – rightly said, "Scientists are the priests of the modern age, and must be watched very closely."

Sensing biosystems such as our semi-permeable cells have been, and we presently are, come and go in a far-more-than-human, and for billions of years, completely nonhuman, way for billions of years. Destructive and arrogant as we are, we are not running the show. We need to up our game or we are toast. Our latest contraptions show some potential, but all things considered we – "we" because it is not necessarily all of us – may be part of the problem rather than solution. Ecological diversity, genetically supported metabolic multistability, protohuman, nonhuman and more-than-human sensoria and biophenomenology, even knowledge, nonhuman science, immunity and repair protocols, in short, cosmos-worthiness have all already proved more robust than this recent upstart, global technological society, which seems especially fragile now, as it tries – is it really trying? Do any organisms ever? – to become a long-term part of this metastable planetary supra-organism (Gaia).

KR: Might you share one of your poems with our readers?

DS: Sure.

Language Began on the Fifth of May

Come, naïve chameleon
into the enchanted lair of nature squared
spread your feet over my navel
walk on my pencilwritten prose

Become a jewel of galena

Change your clothes

Come to me now
Make the cloacal erasure

You're so famous for, sartorial changeling

Brunette, blonde, or pink:
The difference that makes a difference

Come, naive chameleon
shed your sins
the borderline awaits

You slink between the lines
Mistress of Pigment
Now you must hide
But where?

The tongue too is an eraser.

I have no advice.

(1988)

KR: As enzymes are catalysts of life and drive our metabolisms, activate photosynthesis in living plants, and propel proto-life viruses to replicate, recent research to create synthetic bioluminescence has been successful. In a paper in *Nature,* they describe how a deep learning AI guided by Dr. Baker's team at the University of Washington "hallucinated" over 7,500 promising enzymes to engineer enzymes from scratch, allowing a new enzyme that can now mimic a firefly's ability to give off light. What do you think are the future implications of these developments, and do you imagine humans are responsible enough, to have such power over these sorts of developments? (Beer and cheese aside)

DS: Again, I would suggest that humans have a lack-of-humility problem. Human, from the same Indo-European root, *dghem,* (Earth), supposedly, as humble, humility, and humus, the organic portion of soil.

This planet Earth, better called Water, is alive. From the moon it looks blue, although from Mars it can look just like a light speck, any other planet. From deep in the solar system, it's hard to see at all, although in the Cassini mission, using Saturn as sunglasses, Earth was caught glimmering under a ring, a faint blue, the Moon appearing as a ghostly arc with magnification. And it is not the only one. Saturn's moon Enceladus is a water world, and its geysers apparently feed Saturn's E ring. But life and water have a special relationship. You are 70% water, so are most life forms. Water potentially testifies to the hydrogen richness of the early solar system, which is maintained on Earth by hydrogen-rich life, while the outer solar system has the big planets and moons whose gravity, rather than life's thermodynamic recycling, have kept hydrogen from escaping further into space.

I like this romantic idea because it portrays us a kind of time machine, keeping alive the conditions of the early solar system after it should be gone. Although water is recognized as the most important greenhouse gas, it is too difficult to model, and so is not, including by the supercomputers of the IPCC, who are usually off in their prognostications. Nonetheless, it should not escape our attention that an estimated seventy percent of Earth's forests have been razed in the last two centuries. Although water produces heat near Earth's surface in the form of mist when the pores or stomata of leaves release water vapor and plant compounds that can form the nuclei of rain drops, higher up the evapotranspiration properties of trees produces – as the word rainforest suggests – clouds and rains. Clouds reflect solar rays, cooling the surface. Most of the blame for global warming is on CO_2, which forms still less than a percent of our oxygen-rich atmosphere, but water may be more important.

The ancestors to the plastids, the chloroplasts of plants and green algae, the rhodoplasts of certain kelp, and so on, were once free-living bacteria - cyanobacteria, one of, if not the most successful form of life on Earth. Even today not all photosynthetic bacteria use water to get the hydrogen they need for photosynthesis - some use volcanic hydrogen sulfide, using the hydrogen and excreting little balls of sulfur, others can use elemental hydrogen gas, presumably more common on the early Earth, billions of years ago. Vernadsky called life "animated water." From an NET perspective, the biosphere can be considered an open thermodynamic system in space, transforming the solar gradient between Sun and space, primarily through the advanced, sensitive natural nanotechnics of water-using photosynthesis, into the redox potential of Earth's highly energized, because continuously oxygen-supplied, biosphere.

Real ecosystems are not assembled piece by piece from parts parsed by analytical machines, but by a magnificent panoply of metabolizing microbial wholes, working in myriad ways. Although tinkering with creation - evolution - seems inevitable by capitalism-driven monkey minds, it is ultimately just another form of experimentation, which metabolizing, growing, mingling, changing life has been at for billions of years and of which we ourselves are, even if you're not bowled over by the result, just another example of living bioart. When we consider an estimated thirty million extant species, with over 99.99 percent extinct, and further reckon that gene-trading prokaryotes, which are not technically species we begin to see the startling vanity of the sort of AI project that would safeguard the 3.5 billion year old biosphere with supposedly saving human technical intervention.

Author or coauthor of twenty-five books, translated into fifteen languages, including Danish, Japanese, Turkish, Catalan, and Basque, **Dorion Sagan** has been called an "unmissable modern master" by *New Scientist*; Nobel laureate chemist Roald Hoffman called his cowritten *Into the Cool* "fascinating," and anthropologist Melvin Konner, writing in *The New York Times*, said of his coauthored *Microcosmos* that "this admiring reader of Lewis Thomas, Carl Sagan and Stephen Jay Gould has seldom, if ever, seen such a luminous prose style in a work of this kind." His current projects include poetry and a "metabiography" on his parents' early romance and connected sciences.

Ken Rinaldo is internationally recognized for interactive bioart installations developing hybrid ecologies with animals, algorithms, plants, and bacterial cultures. His practice serves as a platform for hacking biological, and machine symbionts. Inventing and constructing techno interfaces which illuminate and amplify intertwined symbiosis. Rinaldo's installations have been commissioned by festivals, museums and galleries. His work appears in 100s of books and art reviews while traveling to over 35 countries. Rinaldo received an Award of Distinction at Ars Electronica, First prize at Vida 3.0, A United Nations Green Leaf Award, commissions from Nuit Blanche Toronto, Vancouver Olympics, Te Papa Museum NZ, and Kiasma Museum Finland.

Manuela Infante: como convertirse en piedra

Continuing with the speculative exploration begun several years ago, in the works *Realismo* (2016) and *Estado Vegetal* (2017), *Como Convertirse en Piedra* furthers the task of envisioning a non-anthropocentric, non-humanist theater. This is, to counter the modern notion of humanness as the measure of all things. The concept of "the human" has served to sustain and justify significant exploitations and exclusions. Not only towards nonhumans, but also towards humans considered less than human. A non-human theater is a critical endeavor, but also a speculative practice with other forms of organization, other forms of politics, by means of which we try to enact a kind of decolonization of the theatrical practices from human centered and human modeled thinking.

in conversation: **Manuela Infante and Giovanni Aloi**

A play that behaves like a stone: what would that look like? What form would a 'mineral' representation take? What if we try to imitate what is never born, never will grow and never dies?

In *Como Convertisrse en Piedra*, stones, as 'non-living' things, are models for a different kind of resistance. Manuela Infante brings pieces of eroded stories together. The fragments become landscapes and she stacks those landscapes like geological rock layers – using looping and sound landscaping. This creates a 'mineral' representation telling you something about what is written in stones, and what stones have written in us.

In a world where notions of growth, progress and development are central to political and economic rhetoric, stones can shed critical light on how the notion of life – and the living – functions as a form of bio-normatisation: LIFE as a norm leading to oppression and exploitation. *Como Convertisrse en Piedra* zooms in on the similarity between working bodies and geological formations, and their shared history of extraction and depletion. We too are made of stone and can be mined.

Giovanni Aloi: We are going to talk about your performance *Como Convertirse en Piedra*, but I guess that it might make sense to start from *Estado Vegetal,* your 2017 polivocal monolog on plant-being that has now become a cult classic. In my opinion, *Estado Vegetal* put to work the contextual and formal invitations that philosophers Michael Marder and plant neurobiologist Stefano Mancuso mapped during the last decade. But *Estado Vegetal* was always more than a practical application of their theories, it stretched them, and pressure-tested them through an existentialist framework held together by loss and trauma. I think that in many ways, it is the perfect primer for critical plant studies. It encapsulates so many key ideas in ways that transcend the technicalities of theory and propels thinking into the speculative realm through a form of vegetal viscerality that is scene by scene constructed by the play for the play. Has *Estado Vegetal* influenced the making of *Como Convertirse en Piedra*? If so, how?

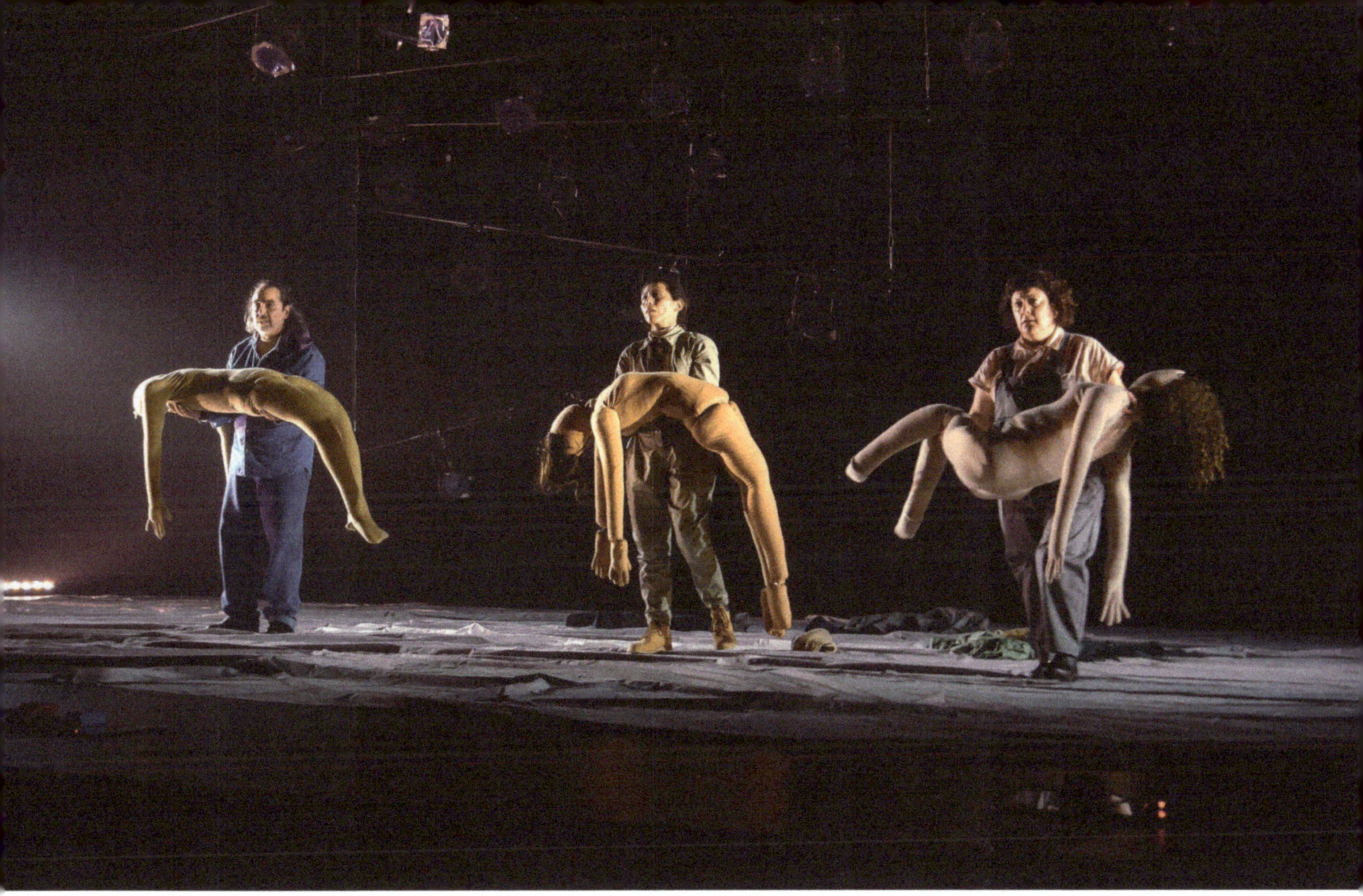

Manuela Infante

Como Convertirse en Piedra, performance, 2021 © Manuela Infante

Manuela Infante: *Estado Vegetal* is not the first piece in which I explored the non-human theatre idea. But it was definitely the one that sort of made it all come together. I always say that *Estado Vegetal* helped to define an ethical approach to my theatre that is also an aesthetic, or a mythology, methodology, and a way of working. It began with the shifting of the question "How is a plant like me?" Instead, I asked, "How am I like a plant?" That shift positioned me in an ethical dimension where I can feel that I can actually work for and about plants without objectifying, extracting, or appropriating. This enabled me to subvert the Aristotelian bio-hierarchy. Things became more complex and difficult but I felt that it was a productive approach so I began to ask myself "How can repeat and expand this process but harder?" That's when I turned to stones and geological strata. In a sense the idea is similar: I try to engage with the being of otherness through every aspect of the performance. *Estado Vegetal* produced an idea of vegetal theatre, so I became interested in what a geological theatre or a stone theatre might unfold. How can I make "non-living theatre" when the very definition of theatre is something that is of the living? This idea was very fascinating to me.

That took me to Japan, to a long residency to explore non-humanity and nature, and how they view nature. I became fascinated with their *karesansui gardens.* Stones are so meaningful in their culture. The whole relationship with Zen, Buddhism, and stones is thousands of years old. That's how the idea came about.

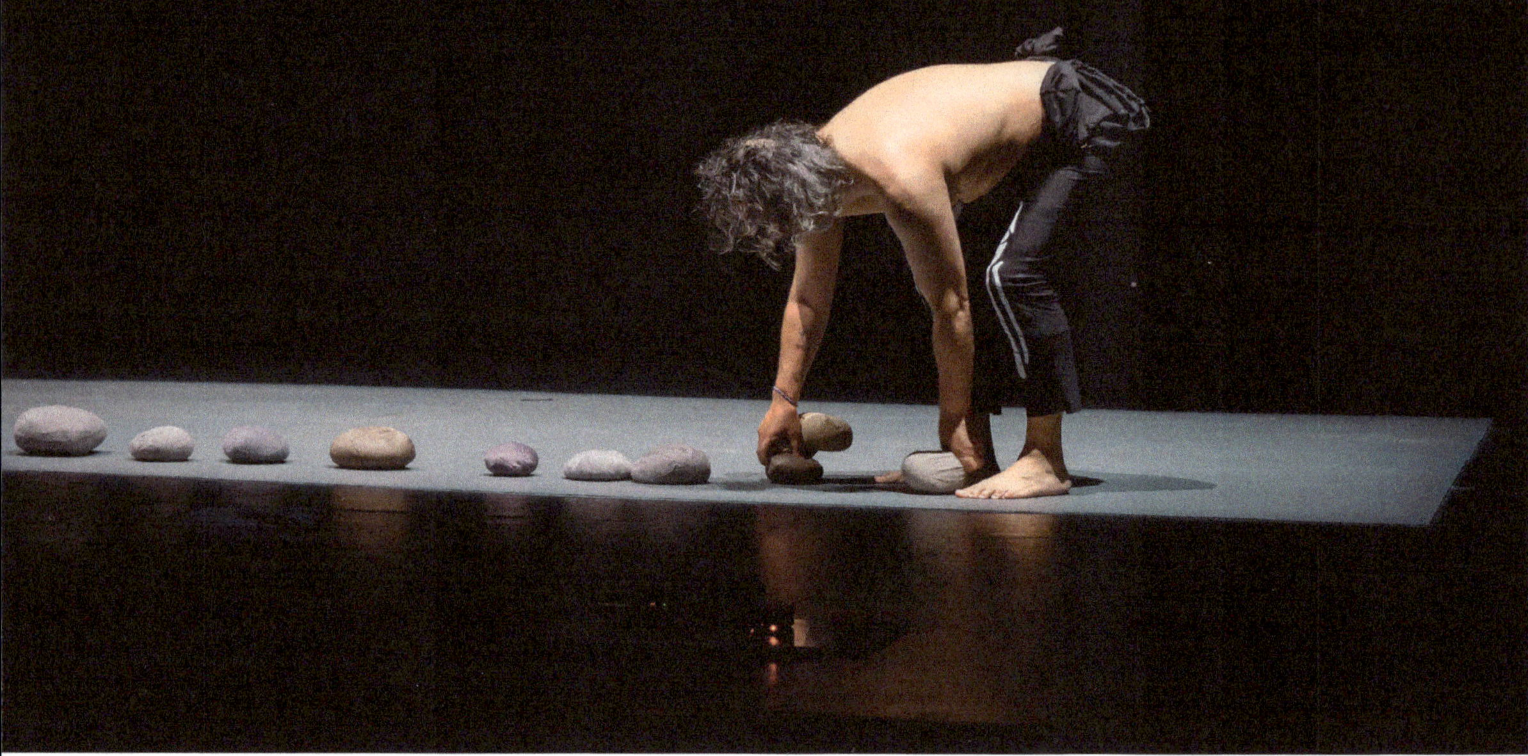

Manuela Infante
Como Convertirse en Piedra, performance, 2021 © Manuela Infante

GA: That's interesting. It brings to mind the hierarchies that you explored in *Estado Vegetal* in the context of empathy and that I also see playing out in *Como Convertirse en Piedra.* It is certainly easier to empathize with a plant than to do so with a stone. But your theater is not afraid of the absurd, it is part of the speculative dimension that you so bravely navigate in your work. Mapping parallels between *Estado Vegetal* and *Como Convertirse en Piedra,* I also found myself captivated by your deconstruction of time in both performances, especially in the context of empathy and how they operate upon it. These both are capacities that we struggle to conceive beyond the strictures of anthropomorphism, so in more than one way they are ripe with possibilities to upturn our thinking on the non-human.

MI: What a fascinating question. It's hard to organize thoughts around something so big. As soon as I went into stones, of course, time became a prominent issue. How could this piece work with geological time, which is completely different and mostly incomprehensible to us? And then something wonderful happened, the looping machine that I experimented with in Estado Vegetal offered me new opportunities to engage with that challenge.

Essentially, the looper piles up time. As one layer is laid upon the next, so is time. When I listen to the result of a looper, it evokes the repetition of geological stratification. It ultimately is what gives the performance its structure. So, each scene is a piling up of layers, but then each act, you could say is a piling up of scenes, and then the whole performance appears to be structured like

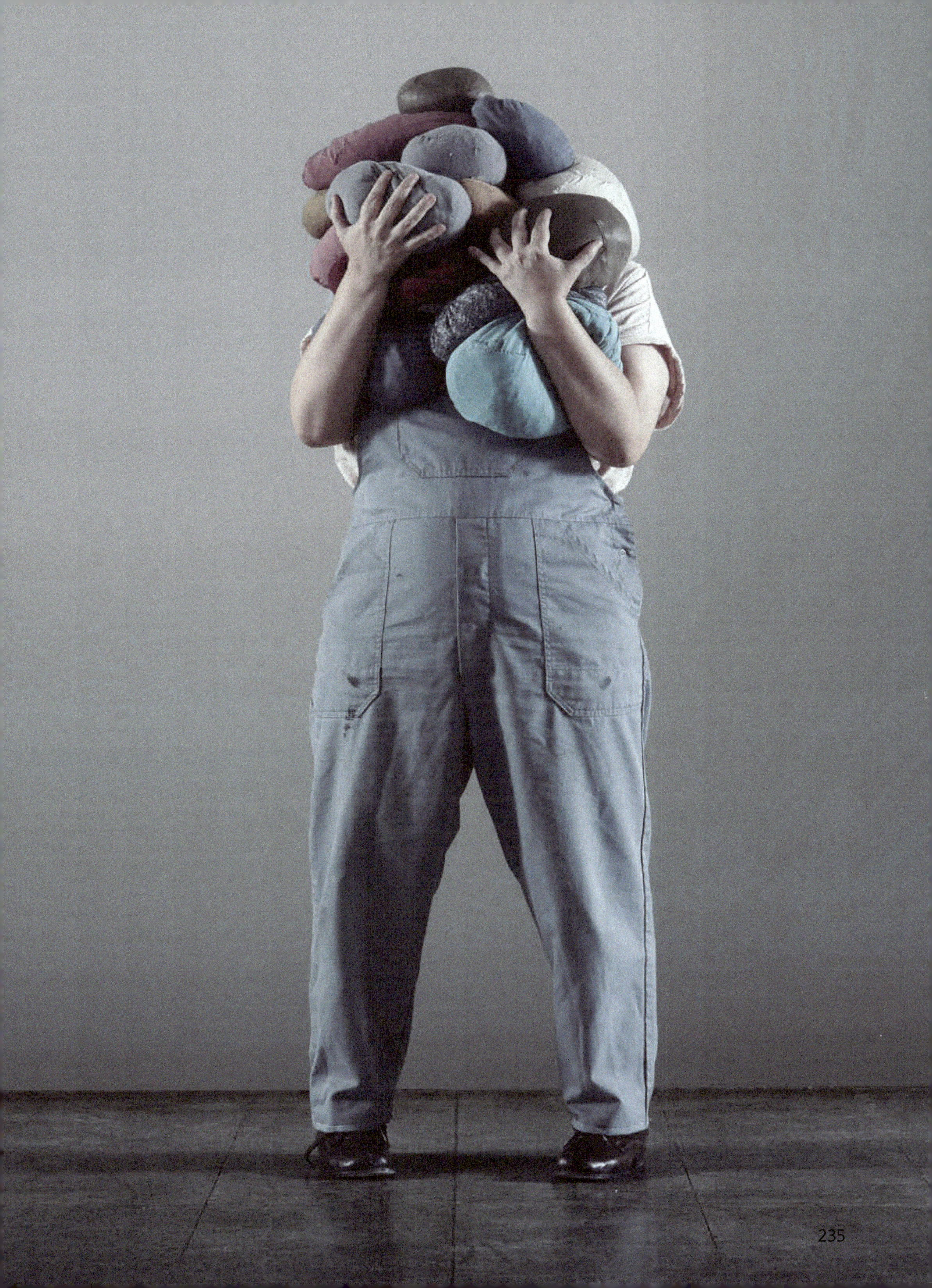

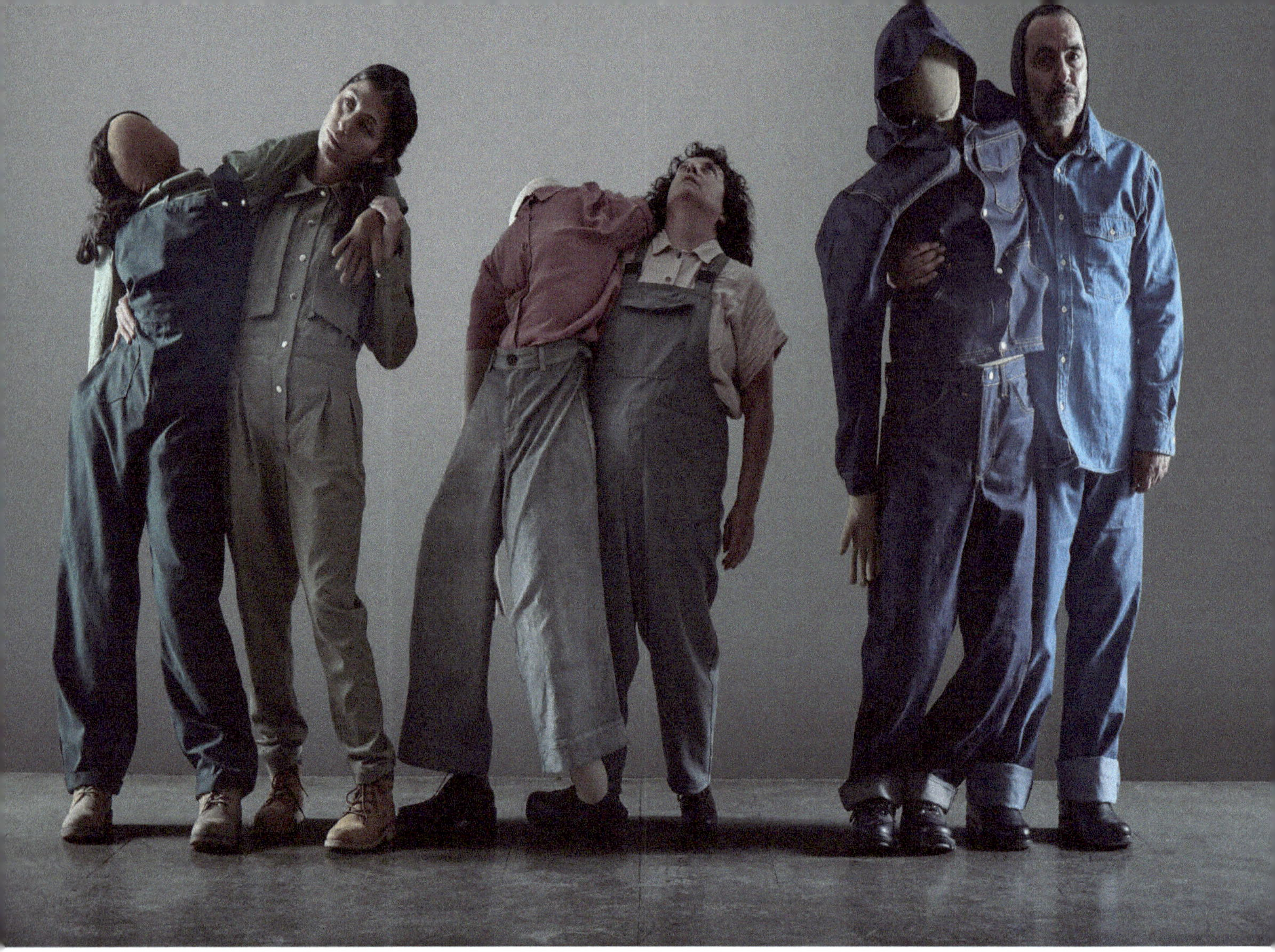

Manuela Infante

Como Convertirse en Piedra, performance, 2021 © Manuela Infante

a sedimented rock. It is a conglomerate of many fragments, different textures, and materials compressed together over time to form a compact mass. That's the model around which the structure of *Como Convertirse en Piedra* is formed—a geological sedimentation. The result is a conglomeration of disparate things like Mars, Japan, mining, and so on...

When I began to think of working with geological time, my first response was to work on something extremely long, like a 24-hour play. But that was just a swift consideration, perhaps too literal, perhaps too obvious. So this is where empathy comes into play—in the crafting of new registers and ethics around which the non-human can be reappraised. Then, through the rehearsals, I challenge myself and the cast to find a way to behave like a stone. It's a methodological practice and an ethical search at once that resolves into a new aesthetic language. To me, these aspects add up to defining empathic registers towards the non-human.

We know that our bones are stone. We know that we're made of the same minerals, etc. But then there's a more existential question underneath that, if you wish, which is "What is the non-living in me?" So I'm a living being and a non-living being at the same time. That's when the idea to duplicate the actors came about. In a way, it is as if they were performing their living bodies.

And as we tried to grapple with this dimension of the performance, we came across the story of these Chilean miners who literally turned to stone. This added a new layer of complexity to the picture. It helped me to geographically and culturally situate the performance in a South — a territory that has historically been exploited.

GA: Yes, this is very interesting. I am actually surprised to hear that the story of the Chilean miners turning green wasn't the starting point for the performance. To me, that point in the plot is where *Estado Vegetal* and *Como Convertirse en Piedra* go in different directions. *Como Convertirse en Piedra*, turns the green vegetaility of *Estado Vegetal*—which brims with agential potential—into a deadly and ominous tale of exploitation. *Como Convertirse en Piedra* becomes much more political than *Estado Vegetal* ever dares to. And I guess that in the context of what it accomplishes with that maneuver one has to wonder what political means in this context.

MI: I think it was a step that I had to take. I was reading all these European authors, and thinking through their ideas, and the whole thing began to unfold. I began to sense a need to counterbalance the universalism of Western philosophy with a more situated dimension. I began to think about the riots in Santiago that took place in 2019—stones were hurled at police, and they became weapons! A very practical and material dimension needed to be represented too.

I worked on a piece on oil not so long ago and the same thing happened. I felt the need to anchor it in a specific context and geographical area. I see the importance of necropolitics playing out in these subjects. There's biopower that needs to be situated as carefully as possible. There are sacrifice zones that cannot and should not be erased or overlooked. This is where the contradictions can be teased out. It's an interesting place to be.

GA: I think that the play also raised an ethical question about what we do in the arts, what we do in writing, what we do as we think through philosophy even. I often think of your work in philosophical terms and how it brings together multiple fragments; how it problematizes. There is something about the way in which you bring together different texts and perspectives, the polyvocal format expands the traditional remit of theatre, but also the traditional remit philosophy at once. The archaeological strata of *Como Convertirse en Piedra* carry a kind of embeddedness that cannot be undone.

And perhaps more importantly, in the background is always the question "Where does this deconstructive approach lead us?", "What is its purpose?". To me, that's where the politics are situated. In that urgency.

This also made me think of your process. The improvisation, the live element. I was wondering about the meditative part, the coincidental part, the improvised part, and the urgency that binds them in the context of the Anthropocene.

Como Convertirse en Piedra is like a manifesto for Anthropocene art, much more than *Estado Vegetal* was. I am specifically referring to the shift towards a sense of tangible vulnerability that is not quite as pronounced in *Estado Vegetal.*

MI: In more than one way, *Como Convertirse en Piedra* is an investigation of the processes with which we mark the land, we mark our bodies, we exploit the land, and we exploit our bodies. But it's not seen from the outside under the pretense of objectivity. It's from within, and I think It's just simply because, as I said all the stories that are there emerged from the question "How are we stones? and not "How have we messed up the stones, and how do we fix them?

GA: Perhaps this is what the "new art of the Anthropocene" entails?

MI: I think that this also is a substantial form of situatedness that I always find myself working within. But I also try to avoid unnecessary apocalyptic thinking. I'd rather think that we are always in the middle. We're not in the end in the sense that "the end" is a construction that entails some kind of resolution. It is anthropocentric. It implies that I know what happened. I know what's happening. I know why it happened.

GA: This is in a sense akin to Donna Haraway's "staying with the trouble"...

MI: Yes, I agree. We cannot create theories of theories. Political theatre always stands at the end of history, telling you how it will all end or how it should have gone. In my practice, the political must be situated to stay in the present tense. We can no longer come up with philosophies that explain everything.

GA: Yes, I agree. This is so interesting. We live in a time where it's impossible to come up with the philosophy of everything. I encounter a lot of resistance to that today and I am not sure why. Speculative Realism and Object Oriented Ontology, for instance, attract substantial unjustified criticism. OOO especially is often accused of obscuring race and gender paradigms even if the very premise of OOO is to look elsewhere or cast a light on a different relational mode. I often wonder what the real issue at stake might be. If one considers the epistemological crises of the past twenty years, it goes without saying that a philosophy of everything could no longer exist because a philosophy of everything implies one perspective.

MI: Yes, and that's why in my performances I accept the idea that darkness is inevitable. If I shed light on something, I will also cast a shadow elsewhere. There's no other way around it.

Country: Chile
Approximate duration: 1 h 30 min (without intermission)
Year of production: 2021
Language: Spanish

Presented in collaboration with the FIT of Cádiz, the Porto International Puppet Festival and the Autumn Festival

Direction and dramaturgy: Manuela Infante
Cast: Marcela Salinas, Aliocha de la Sotta, Rodrigo Pérez
Comprehensive design: Rocío Hernández
Visuals: Pablo Mois
Production: Carmina Infante
Production assistant: María José Duran
Sound design: Manuela Infante
Audiovisual design and sound-light programming: Alex Waghorn
Choreography: Diana Carvajal
Musical collaborations: Valentina Villarroel and Marcos Meza
With music by: Eliane Radigue, Pauline Oliveros, Kali Malone, Senyawa and Beverly Glenn-Copeland
Sound technician: Diego Betancourt and Isabel Zúñiga

Technical sound design: Gonzalo Rodríguez
Theoretical research and playwriting: Camila Valladares
Set design: Set Amorescénico
Props: Gabriel Seisdedos - Taller Madrid
Costume design: Daniela Espinoza

This project was, in part, developed in residence at the Kyoto Experiment Festival and Kyoto Arts Center , Valparaíso Cultural Park and NAVE.

Co-produced by Matucana 100 Cultural Center, Teatro a Mil Foundation, NAVE and Valparaíso Cultural Park.

This project was financed in part by the Chilean Ministry of Culture, Arts and Heritage through FONDART 2020.

Manuela Infante Güell is a Chilean theater director, playwright, scriptwriter and musician. MA in Cultural Analysis at University of Amsterdam. She is well known for offering scenic articulations of contemporary theoretical issues, creating work that stands somewhere between music, theater and literature. Her plays have been published and translated into English, German, Italian and Portugese. Her work has toured important theaters and festivals in North America, South America, Europe and Asia. She has produced work with Festival de Modena (Italy), FIBA (Buenos Aires), KVS (Belgium), TheaterWorks (Singapore), Schauspielhaus Bochum (Germany), Theater Basel (Switzerland), Kyoto Experiment (Japan), Volkstheater Vienna (Austria), Teatre Nacional de Cataluña (Spain), amongst others. Infante is currently producing work with Schauspielhaus Hannover (Germany) and NNT (Holland). In 2015 she was the first woman to be appointed director of The National Festival for Dramaturgy in Chile. In 2019 se was the first Chilean theater maker to be invited to the Venice Biennale 2019 with her plays *Estado Vegetal* and *Realismo*. That same year she won the Stükemarkt First Prize at 2019 Theaterreffen Festival in Berlin. As a musician she has composed, written and produced two albums with her band *Bahía Inútil*, *Stand Scared* (2011) and *Bahía Inútil* (2015). She has also been in charge of the sound design of many of her works. As a scriptwriter Infatne has worked with renowned Chilean film directors such as Francisca Alegria, Marialy Rivas and Sebastian Lelio.

Milton Keynes UK
Ingram Content Group UK Ltd.
UKHW051151180923
428882UK00007B/46

9 781088 257746